THE

Penguin History

of

AMERICAN
LIFE

SHADOWS
AT DAWN

ALSO BY KARL JACOBY

Crimes Against Nature:
Squatters, Poachers, Thieves, and the Hidden
History of American Conservation

SHADOWS
AT DAWN

A Borderlands Massacre

and the Violence of History

KARL JACOBY

THE PENGUIN PRESS

New York

2008

THE PENGUIN PRESS
Published by the Penguin Group
Penguin Group (USA) Inc., 375 Hudson Street, New York, New York 10014, U.S.A. • Penguin Group (Canada),
90 Eglinton Avenue East, Suite 700, Toronto, Ontario, Canada M4P 2Y3 (a division of Pearson Penguin
Canada Inc.) • Penguin Books Ltd, 80 Strand, London WC2R 0RL, England • Penguin Ireland, 25 St. Stephen's
Green, Dublin 2, Ireland (a division of Penguin Books Ltd) • Penguin Books Australia Ltd, 250 Camberwell Road,
Camberwell, Victoria 3124, Australia (a division of Pearson Australia Group Pty Ltd) • Penguin Books India
Pvt Ltd, 11 Community Centre, Panchsheel Park, New Delhi—110 017, India • Penguin Group (NZ), 67 Apollo
Drive, Rosedale, North Shore 0632, New Zealand (a division of Pearson New Zealand Ltd) • Penguin Books
(South Africa) (Pty) Ltd, 24 Sturdee Avenue, Rosebank, Johannesburg 2196, South Africa

Penguin Books Ltd, Registered Offices:
80 Strand, London WC2R 0RL, England

First published in 2008 by The Penguin Press,
a member of Penguin Group (USA) Inc.

Illustration credits appear on page 359.

LIBRARY OF CONGRESS CATALOGING-IN-PUBLICATION DATA

Jacoby, Karl, ———.
Shadows at dawn : a borderlands massacre and the violence of history / Karl Jacoby.
p.   cm.
Includes bibliographical references and index.
ISBN 978-1-59420-193-6
1. Camp Grant Massacre, Ariz., 1871.   2. Apache Indians—Wars.
3. Apache Indians—History—19th century.   4. Massacres—Arizona—Aravaipa Canyon.
5. Indians of North America—Crimes against—Arizona—Aravaipa Canyon.   6. Indians, Treatment
of—Arizona—Aravaipa Canyon.   7. Aravaipa Canyon (Ariz.)—History.   I. Title.
E83.866.J33 2008
973.8'2—dc22   2008028643

Printed in the United States of America

1   3   5   7   9   10   8   6   4   2

Designed by Amanda Dewey
Map illustrations by Jeffrey L. Ward

For Marie and Jason

CONTENTS

In that unbounded moment, I saw millions of delightful and horrible acts; none amazed me so much as the fact that all occupied the same point, without superposition and without transparency. What my eyes saw was *simultaneous*; what I shall write is *successive*, because language is successive.

Jorge Luis Borges, "The Aleph"

FOREWORD

MORE THAN TWO DECADES ago, I began hoping that Karl Jacoby would write *Shadows at Dawn*.

The hope necessarily lacked something in the way of precision. The fact that I had not met Jacoby was one obstacle to specificity, even though—literally without naming names—I had publicly expressed my hope for the appearance of young scholars with his talent and commitment. But when it came to subject matter, my hope came with focus: I ranked the story of the Camp Grant Massacre of 1871 at the top of the category of vitally important but little-known episodes of American history that deserved to have a very good historian to write about them.

Writing an overview of western American history in the mid-1980s, I made my own minuscule contribution to the cause of bringing this episode out of the shadows of memory. The following paragraph appeared at the start of the chapter on the complexities of western race relations in *The Legacy of Conquest*:

> In 1871, an informal army of Arizona civilians descended on a peaceful camp and massacred over one hundred Apaches, mostly women and children. Who were the attackers at Camp Grant? The usual images of Western history would suggest one answer: white men. In fact, the attackers were a combination of Hispanics, Anglo-Americans, and Papago [now referred to as Tohono O'odham] Indians. However different the three groups might have been, they could agree on the matter of Apaches and join in interracial cooperation. Hostility between Apaches

and Papagoes, and between Apaches and Hispanics, had in fact begun long before conflict between Apaches and Anglo-Americans.[1]

In writing *The Legacy of Conquest* two decades ago, I wanted to draw attention to the Camp Grant Massacre because that event acts as a corrective to the habit of mind that has long burdened western American history: the desire to squeeze very complicated events into simple categories. Confronting stories of the West's actual complexity, Americans have worked away diligently, kneading the stories until the complexities of the events they represent have been smoothed, flattened, compressed, and generally made manageable. This popular exercise registers as complete when the tales reach compliance with the platitude "There are two sides to every story."

When it comes to the number of perspectives, interpretations, rationalizations, memories, omissions, and evasions, both intended and inadvertent, that come into play in the history of the encounter between Indian peoples and Euro Americans, "two sides" is an astonishing undercount. Even in the rare cases when two groups stood opposite each other in clearly distinguished ranks on a battleground, the apparent "unity" of either side was honeycombed by differences of motive and goal, struggles of faction and rivalry, and disagreements over tactic and strategy. To invite both Americans and international observers of the United States to reckon with complexity, the Camp Grant Massacre stands as one of the most important and effective examples, case studies, and parables in our inheritance.

And so, after my extremely modest effort at shedding light on this event, I then took up my vigil, waiting for a scholar who would apply to Camp Grant the combination that Jacoby provides here: thorough research, original analysis, compassion, empathy, and a reliable gift for storytelling.

In fact, holding vigils in anticipation of the arrival of a crew of talented young historians had become something of a way of life for me. Two decades ago, responding with inexplicable confidence and cheer to a flood of obituaries and eulogies for the academic field of western American history, I had taken to declaring that the field was actually on the edge of a renaissance, and certainly not fading away. Going on record with such a prediction, I am equipped to testify, causes the pretended prophet to spend her life staying on constant alert for any pieces of evidence that her prophecy might actually carry substance.

One memorable occasion of validation occurred in 2001, when I read a new book called *Crimes Against Nature: Squatters, Poachers, Thieves, and the Hidden History of American Conservation,* by Karl Jacoby. I had not met the author; I had done nothing to help, guide, or encourage him. But when I read *Crimes Against Nature,* I found exactly the realized promise for which I had been scanning the horizon: here was a young and very talented western historian exploring new territory, analyzing his findings in an original and courageous way, and writing in a clear and effective style. In *Crimes Against Nature,* showing how the process of setting aside parks and natural preserves was also a process of suddenly changing the status of local subsistence hunters to that of poachers committing crimes, Jacoby made an entirely persuasive case for the necessity of tying together the history of relationships between human beings and their natural environment with the history of relationships of power and status among human beings themselves. As the publication of *Crimes Against Nature* demonstrated, the renaissance in western American history had been transformed from aspiration and pipe dream to shelves of books that, if anything, suggested I had been too modest in my predictions.

Thus, when Karl Jacoby decided to write a history of the Camp Grant Massacre for the Penguin History of American Life series, the right author and a deserving topic converged. The very nature of this event required him to reckon, from start to finish, with conflicting evidence and clashing interpretation. But I never anticipated that he would take on the challenge so directly, arranging this book into sections that would immerse readers sequentially in the experiences of the four principal groups: the O'odham (or Papago), *los vecinos* (or Mexicans), the Americans, and the Nṉēē (or Apache). In the first part of the book, the four sections track the four routes, through space and through time, traveled by the four groups as they converged at Camp Grant. In the third part, the four sections follow the reactions of the four groups as they live with the legacy of the event and the larger picture of violence that it encapsulated.

Would readers end up dizzy and disoriented with each shift of angle? Would the result of this brave experiment to engage so directly with conflicting points of view be a muddled text and even more muddled readers? Was Jacoby's approach, in other words, going to *work?*

It did. It does.

It works because, with the right guide, even the most tangled labyrinth is rendered navigable. And it works, also, precisely because this story *is* so tangled and labyrinthine: the paths and perspectives intertwine, and no route of approach to Camp Grant is finally separate from the others. As Jacoby observes, "one of the great paradoxes of the [Tohono O'odham's] warfare during this era was that the same violence that produced so many Apache deaths also generated a deep understanding of the [Apaches]." Similarly, in their long and complicated interactions, the Apaches became to the Mexicans "uniquely intimate enemies." And for even the late-arriving Americans, dealings with the Apaches had many dimensions in, as Jacoby puts it, "an uneven pattern of accommodation and violence." These four tracks of experience, in other words, have a degree of compatibility and mutual intelligibility, because the four groups influenced each other, negotiated with each other, and shaped each other's conduct and thinking.

An important feature of Jacoby's exercise in point of view is his use of words from the Spanish, Apache, and Tohono O'odham languages. On various occasions, especially in trying to think of western American history in the context of the worldwide history of colonialism, it has struck me that much of the mental behavior that we sometimes denounce as ethnocentrism and cultural insensitivity actually derives less from our indifference or hostility than from our clumsiness and awkwardness when we leave the comfort of the English language behind. Jacoby's integration of crucial non-English terms into his text pointedly reminds his readers that venturing outside the bounds of the English language exercises and stretches our minds in ways that are essential for getting as close as we can to the act of seeing the world from what would otherwise remain unfamiliar and alien perspectives. By its very nature, this invitation, to travel out of the terrain of familiar words and complacent understanding, produces discomfort. But that discomfort is quite effectively remedied by use of the simple device of a Post-it: place a colorful marker on the first page of this book's glossary, and put that glossary to good and regular use at the first twinge of disorientation from an unfamiliar word.

In sitting down to read *Shadows at Dawn*, you undertake a journey into the deeper reaches of the process that transformed North America from the homelands of many Indian tribes into territory claimed by the United States. If all goes well, when you finish this book, you will look around the places where you live and visit, and you will ask yourself, "What stories, taking place here, bear kinship to Camp Grant in 1871? How did the big process of invasion and conquest manifest itself here?" The outcome—communities living in relative peace in territories that once shook with the most intense forms of human violence and misery—will regain its power to surprise you.

If you know about Camp Grant, you know about the actual complexity and the many dimensions of western race relations; you are set free of efforts to simplify a swirl of encounters, transactions, and conflicts into the familiar pairings of "whites versus Indians," "good guys versus bad guys," "winners versus losers." If you know about Camp Grant, you have faced up to the bitter reality of violence embedded in landscapes that Americans would later come to see as places of natural innocence, separated from the tragedy of history. If you know about Camp Grant, you know that the history of the United States bears an unsettling resemblance to that of areas in Africa, Asia, Latin America, Australia, and New Zealand that underwent the invasion of Europeans into the territories of indigenous people, and you know that American self-knowledge remains dangerously incomplete until that resemblance gets its deserved acknowledgment.

Contrary to what readers might expect, Jacoby ends this book with two sentences that reconcile misery with hope. "What this past asks of us in return," he writes, "is a willingness to recount *all* our stories—our darkest tales as well as our most inspiring ones—and to ponder those stories that violence has silenced forever. For without first recognizing our shared capacity for inhumanity, how can we at last begin to tell stories of our mutual humanity?" It is one of the extraordinary qualities of human experience, in all variations of culture and belief, to track journeys of thought and feeling in which immersion in darkness and despair provides the necessary route to redemption and a return to the light.

A version of that journey begins, ends, and begins again, in Aravaipa Canyon in the memories of the event that took place there on April 30, 1871.

Patricia Nelson Limerick

SHADOWS
AT DAWN

Aravaipa Canyon today.

INTRODUCTION

Arizona Territory, April 30, 1871. The canyon known as Aravaipa lies still in the predawn darkness, the only sounds to be heard in the early-morning calm the song of birds and the lilt of running water as it courses its way toward the nearby San Pedro River. In the desert, water changes everything. Unlike the surrounding mountains, with their dusty reds and browns, their scattered cactuses and creosote bushes, Aravaipa Canyon boasts a profusion of greenery—reeds, cottonwoods, a large sycamore tree. Interspersed among the lush growth along the creek can be found the dwellings of the Nnēē (or, as they are called in English and Spanish, Apache). For the past few months, hundreds of Apache have been camping in Aravaipa, close to a U.S. military base named Camp Grant. Half-domed shelters constructed out of brush and canvas crowd the canyon bottom. The entrance to each gowąh, as the Nnēē term them, faces east toward the soon-to-be-rising sun.

Suddenly, out of the shadows emerges a crowd of newcomers. As they draw near, the intruders, some mounted on horseback, others on foot, whisper to one another in Spanish. A few edge toward the rim of the canyon, where the erosion from periodic floods has carved cliffs some twenty feet high in places. The rest, many clutching clubs made of the dense wood of the local mesquite tree, creep toward the canyon floor.

As the group advances, the Apaches' shelters come into view in the half-light. The intruders begin to sprint upstream along the creek bed, pausing at each gowąh to club to death the adults and seize or kill whatever children they can locate within. For many Nnēē, murdered while they slumber, the attack lasts but an instant. But as the early-morning stillness is broken by hurried footfalls, the crack of club against bone, and the barking of Apache dogs, some Nnēē, awakening, flee in terror. A few succeed in scaling

the steep bluffs lining the canyon or in hiding in the thick brush along the creek bank.
Many others, however, fall victim to the men waiting in the rocks above, who fire down
at them with Sharps and Spencer carbines.

As the sun rises over the jagged peaks to Aravaipa Canyon's eastern end, its light
reveals scores of Nnēē corpses sprawled along the creek. Seeing the camp abandoned, its
once-sleeping inhabitants either dead or dispersed, the attackers set the Apaches' posses-
sions and their empty gowạhs ablaze before withdrawing. A quick count as the raiders
reconnoiter a few miles away reveals that not one of them was killed or injured in the
assault. They succeeded, however, in seizing twenty-nine Apache captives and in killing
perhaps as many as a hundred and forty-four Nnēē, almost all of them sleeping women
and children, in an attack lasting little more than thirty minutes.[1]

T HIS IS A BOOK about what is at once the most familiar and the most overlooked subject in American history. The violence toward Indian peoples that accompanied the colonization of North America has provided the raw material for countless dime novels, Wild West shows, movies, and TV series, not to mention childhood games of "cowboys and Indians." Yet paradoxically it has all too often been considered mere prologue—segregated from the rest of American history as "prehistory" and "ethnohistory"—or collapsed into a single, amorphous story of conflict. As a result, the true magnitude of the violent encounter with the indigenous inhabitants of North America remains unacknowledged even today. So too are its consequences and contingencies unexplored, especially in comparison to the efflorescence of scholarship on ethnic cleansing, genocide, and other manifestations of the age of extremes that it is our fate to inhabit.[2]

In order to contain a topic as potentially vast as this one, which sprawls across much of the American past, the pages that follow focus on a brief but illuminating incident. On April 30, 1871, a combined force of Anglo Americans, Mexican Americans, and Tohono O'odham Indians from southern Arizona descended upon a would-be Apache reservation in Aravaipa Canyon, located some sixty miles northeast of Tucson, killing a large number of women and children. Frequently called the Camp Grant Massacre after the military installation near where it took place, this incident is neither the biggest nor the best known of the flurry of brutal massacres of American Indians that occurred during the closing decades of the nineteenth century. (The dubious honor of leading these categories would probably go to the Bear River Massacre of 1863, in which an estimated 280 Northern Shoshoni died, and the Wounded Knee Massacre of 1890, in which at least 250 Lakota Indians were killed by U.S. Army units armed with rapid-firing Hotchkiss cannons.)[3]

In its day, however, the Camp Grant Massacre commanded unparalleled national attention. Coming at a time when the United States had just inaugurated a self-proclaimed "Peace Policy" toward American Indians, the deaths of scores of Apache women and children at the hands of a civilian raiding party raised troubling questions about the causes and consequences of western violence. The ensuing debate generated a wealth of sources—official reports, newspaper accounts, courtroom testimony, oral histories, and the like—that document with rare detail the perspectives of the various ethnic groups involved in the massacre. As with any violent episode, there is much that remains missing from the historical record, the most telling, of course, being the silenced voices of the Apaches murdered in the attack. But the unprecedented range of materials the incident produced allows one to venture as close as may be possible to the enduring question of what it is that brings "ordinary" people to commit extraordinary acts of violence against one another.[4]

Reckoning with this violence involves facing some of the more difficult aspects not only of the American past but of the historical enterprise itself. Unlike almost any other object of historical study, violence simultaneously destroys and creates history. The physical annihilation of another human produces a profound absence that distorts the historical record for all time. One of the most immediate manifestations of violence is thus a terrifying silence that no testimony of the past can fathom in its entirety. As Primo Levi once commented, "The destruction brought to an end, the job completed, was not told by anyone . . . no one ever returned to describe his own death."[5]

Even when not pursued to this extreme, violence ruptures history in other ways. The psychological horror and physical pain inherent to violence can, in the words of the literary critic Elaine Scarry, lead to a "shattering of language," as lived experience comes to exceed the limits of human description. Intimidation can render storytellers mute or confine their narratives to the margins of society. The denial of materials can inhibit the creation of the records so essential to the historical enterprise.[6]

And yet as one of the most elemental of human experiences, violence also spawns a vast outpouring of explanations, accusations, and justifications from its survivors and perpetrators alike. Violence may begin as a contest over resources, but it often ends as a contest over meaning, as the participants struggle to articulate what has happened to them—and what they have, in turn, done to others. This impulse is perhaps most immediately apparent in literate societies with their monuments, museums, books, and other visible forms of recordkeeping. It operates, however, in oral societies as well. Indeed, far from being condemned to an existence as a "people without history," such groups possess numerous sophisticated ways of narrating the past. "You can't understand the world without telling a story," the scholar Gerald Vizenor has observed in relation to Native American oral traditions. "There isn't any center to the world but a story."[7]

To many at the time (and since), the Camp Grant Massacre fit easily within a preexisting genre of tales about the winning of the American West. As much mythic as real, these stories were defined by their irrepressible violence and their familiar cast of characters: blue-coated army regulars, Anglo-American and Mexican cowboys, American Indians. Of this latter group, the Apache who featured so prominently in events in Aravaipa Canyon occupy a particularly fabled place. Not only have they come to serve as the stock villains in many a classic western movie (*Fort Apache*, *Stagecoach*, *Arizona*); the 1886 surrender to the U.S. military of the Apache leader Geronimo—for most Americans, one of only a handful of recognizable Native American figures—features in many accounts of the American West as the official end of the nation's "Indian wars."

This frontier narrative, however, is only one way of representing the past. Even though the Camp Grant Massacre was intended as an act of silencing, the rich array of documents that the attack generated had the ironic and unintended consequence of illuminating—as perhaps no other event from the period can—the distinct ways that each of the borderlands' varied ethnic groups relates to the past. In order to recapture the unique character of these ties as well as the shattering effects of violence on history itself, I elected in *Shadows at Dawn* not to meld the stories each group told about the massacre into a single, unified account. Instead, the book's chapters trace four different narratives, each one foregrounding the experiences of one of the four communities—Anglo Americans, Mexican Americans, Tohono O'odham Indians, and Apache Indians—involved in the brutal events of April 30, 1871.

Because of the passage of time, the transformation of oral stories, many of them initially delivered in Apache, Tohono O'odham, or Spanish into written English, and the inevitable gaps in sources, the narratives in this book remain what all histories are—imaginative re-creations of the lost world of the past. Nonetheless, in fashioning these re-creations, I tried to remain sensitive not only to questions of historical evidence (in which the perspective of an outsider, alert to evasions, elisions, and distortions in each story, can at times be as much a help as a hindrance) but also to the narrative conventions of each of the four groups involved. *How* the stories were told—the language, time scale, sense of space, and manner of recordkeeping employed—was often as important as *what* they told, for such elements were an integral part of establishing the ethical universe that made an event like the Camp Grant Massacre possible.[8]

With one notable exception, the narratives follow the order of each group's arrival in the borderlands. The first account traces the experience of the O'odham, whom archaeology and oral tradition alike link back to some of the region's earliest settlements. The second account details Spanish and then Mexican experiences in the region, and attests to the remarkable scope and longevity of the Hispanic presence in the Americas. Not until the third account does the narrative shift to the group usually considered the central subject matter of American history, Anglo Americans—an arrangement designed to underscore how much the "American West" was constructed on the foundations of other, far older societies. The final account endeavors to revise all that has come before by recovering the perspective of the Western Apache.

The title of this volume is designed to evoke the underlying challenges that violence poses to all those who attempt to understand it and its legacies. The phrase "Shadows at Dawn" is intended to call to mind the instant when the approaching party first emerged at Aravaipa Canyon in the dim early-morning light of April 30, 1871—the pregnant, unformed moment just before the attack when different choices might have been made and a different reality emerged. Many groups in the borderlands timed their raids to take place at dawn, and so the uncertain light of a new day was the time when one had to be most alert to whether the shifting shades along the horizon were a genuine threat or just a trick of the imagination. The title alludes, too, to the murky, often elusive nature of historical truth—that shadowy world of fragmentary evidence and missing perspectives that historians must confront if they want to make sense of the past—and to the long shadows that the past casts into the present. Indeed, if violence has all too often constituted the raw material out of which history is constructed, the historian's task of representing physical force presents dilemmas of its own. Far from serving as a purely impartial record, history is regularly invoked to justify new forms of domination and terror. History is thus seldom about past violence alone, but violence in the present and future as well.

The word "borderlands" appears in the subtitle for similarly deliberate reasons. In part, this term speaks to the physical space in which the Camp Grant Massacre took place: that vast and contested region where the peripheries of Mexico and the United States intersect. But it also points toward the conceptual terrain that this book seeks to excavate: the borderlands between history and storytelling, which, much like the U.S.-Mexico border itself, has not always been as clearly demarcated as some might expect. As we shall see, it is a place that casts in sharp relief the challenges historians confront in trying to understand the thoughts and actions of those who came before.[9]

Although the Camp Grant Massacre receives little mention in most histories of the United States, my goal in the pages that follow is not simply to persuade readers that they need to add one more event to the canon of American history. Rather, I hope that encountering this incident will lead readers toward a deeper revisioning of the American past. The seeming inevitability of the western story—Manifest Destiny, U.S. national expansion, Indian loss of land and independence—has long desensitized us to both the region's violence and its other ways of being. Once we begin to think of the West not only as the "West"—the trans-Mississippian portion of the United States—but as an extension of the Mexican north and as the homeland of a complex array of Indian communities, we allow far different narratives about this space to emerge. Fresh historical actors seize center stage. Conventional figures find themselves cast in an unfamiliar light—not only presidents and generals but even Geronimo, who, as a member of a band distinct from the Western

Apaches dwelling near Tucson and Aravaipa, serves as little more than a bit player in the stories below.[10]

The four-part format of this book is not without risks. Some may feel that it sidesteps the historian's responsibility to create a single, authoritative narrative of the past. Others may decry it as suggesting an inappropriate moral equivalence between the perpetrators and the victims of mass murder. The intent of this arrangement, however, is not to evade issues of historical interpretation but rather to highlight them. The proposition at the heart of *Shadows at Dawn* is that the most honest way to engage with the issues of ethical responsibility that an incident such as the Camp Grant Massacre presents is by spotlighting the fraught relationship between storytelling and historical evaluation. While such an arrangement demands more of the historian, who must now portray the competing perspectives of several different groups, it demands more of readers as well. Instead of being borne along on the current of a single narrative, they are now being asked to grapple with an array of different interpretations. In short, they are being invited to become active participants in that most common of human endeavors: finding meaning in our elusive past.

A NOTE ON TERMINOLOGY

IN CONTRAST WITH English and Spanish, the O'odham and Western Apache languages have only recently made the transition to written form. As a result, the spellings employed for these two languages can differ considerably, all the more so when one takes into account the varied dialects that exist in both. Nevertheless, other than a few minor changes for consistency, I avoided tinkering with the spellings in direct quotations so as not to risk changing the dialect or possibly even the meaning of the speaker. Whenever I employed Apache terms in the pages that follow, I attempted to follow the system developed by Willem de Reuse with the assistance of Philip Goode in *A Practical Grammar of the San Carlos Apache Language*. In writing O'odham, I endeavored to use the official orthography of the Tohono O'odham Nation, developed by Albert Alvarez and Kenneth Hale. I am grateful to the linguists Willem de Reuse and Colleen Fitzgerald for their considerable assistance in guiding me through the challenges of meshing Native American languages and historical research.[1]

Those readers who find the inclusion of non-English words in the text disconcerting are encouraged to consult the glossary that starts on page 285. In a few cases, the O'odham and Apache terms in this book represent educated guesses—retranslations of words that were poorly transcribed by English- and Spanish-language recordkeepers. In such instances, these terms, along with their possible proper spellings, are indicated in the glossary by the presence of question marks.

Because race and ethnicity, like languages, are unstable human creations, the labels attached to the varied human communities in the borderlands remain subject to debate—so much so, in fact, that it has become almost obligatory in histories of the region to include an explanatory comment on when the author employs such nomenclature as "Chicano," "Mexican," "Anglo," or "white." I have approached this dilemma by using the terms most commonly employed by whichever group is the focus of a particular section. Members of the same community will therefore appear as, for example, Apaches, 'O:b, or Nnēē at different points in the text, although readers will note passages where, to avoid undue repetition, I resort to more generic terms. Particular care should be taken to avoid confusion in the sections focusing on the O'odham and the Nnēē, as the in-group term for each of these communities is perhaps best translated into English as "the People." In a telling illustration of the subjectivity of ethnic labels, however, the O'odham's "People" is not at all the same as the Nnēē's. Readers will also find that the term "American" in these pages is often confined to peoples of European descent, even though present-day Apaches, O'odham, Chicanos, and others are, of course, Americans as well. This conflation of "white" with "American" is no small part of the history that follows.

PART ONE

VIOLENCE

THE O'ODHAM

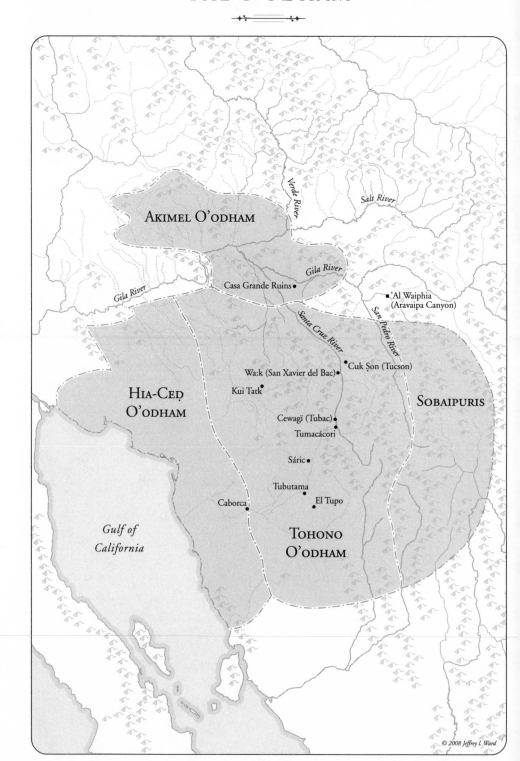

Akimel O'odham

Verde River

Salt River

Gila River

Casa Grande Ruins

Gila River

'Al Waiphia
(Aravaipa Canyon)

Santa Cruz River

San Pedro River

Hia-Ceḍ
O'odham

Wa:k (San Xavier del Bac)

Cuk Ṣon (Tucson)

Kui Tatk

Sobaipuris

Cewagĭ (Tubac)

Tumacácori

Sáric

Tubutama

Caborca

El Tupo

Gulf of
California

Tohono
O'odham

© 2008 Jeffrey L. Ward

THE O'ODHAM

T O THEIR MEXICAN AND ANGLO NEIGHBORS, they were the Pima and Papago Indians. To the Apache bands living to the north and east of them, they were the Sáíkiné ("Sand House People") or Kełtʼah izláhé ("Rope Under Their Feet People," for the sandals they wore). But among themselves, they were simply the O'odham, the People. For as long as the People could remember, they had made their homes amid the arid plains and river valleys of the Sonora Desert. Over the years, the People had learned not only how to survive but how to thrive in what to outsiders could appear a forbidding homeland—a territory surrounded by steep mountains, where the few streams that existed often disappeared for miles at a stretch, and where the rainfall in some places averaged as little as four inches a year.[1]

Just as the desert itself varied from place to place—with arroyos that were barren much of the year but brought flash floods in the rainy season, to high peaks where, amid the cooler breezes, one could find mule deer or bighorn sheep grazing on bunchgrass—so too did the People.[2] By the nineteenth century, the O'odham recognized several broad groupings within the People, each evoking the ecological variations of their homeland. Along rivers such as the Gila, there dwelled the Akimel O'odham, the "River People," who built permanent villages and supported themselves through irrigated agriculture, cultivating fields of corn, cotton, beans, and squash. In the dunes near the Gulf of California lived the Hia-Ced O'odham, the "Sand People." Here it was too dry to farm, so the people followed a hunter-gatherer lifestyle, migrating from spot to spot in accordance with the seasonal fluctuations of plants and animals.

Between these two groups, in the heart of the Sonora Desert, lived the Tohono O'odham, the "Desert People." The Tohono O'odham followed a lifestyle that mixed small farms, typically located in the floodplains that sprang up during the summer rains (and therefore termed *aki-ciñ*, or "arroyo mouth," farming), with the gathering of wild foodstuffs from the desert during the winter.[3]

While terms such as "River People" and "Desert People" hint at the intimate scale of the O'odham's world, modern English nonetheless strains to convey how the People thought about themselves during much of their early history. The present-day notion of a tribe, for example, fits poorly. Although loose webs of kinship and trade connected the Akimel O'odham, the Hia-Ced O'odham, and the Tohono O'odham to one another, the People did not possess a unified political structure. For the greater part of the year, most of the People lived in small groups organized by extended family, dispersing themselves widely over the landscape so as not to overburden the desert's fragile ecology and limited water supplies. Periodically, villages would gather together for trade, festivals, or other events. Groups from the Tohono O'odham might exchange venison, wild plants, or sea salt for some of the agricultural surplus of the Akimel O'odham or help with the River People's harvest in turn for a share of the crop. At other times, villages would collect for intercommunity footraces and events such as the *Nawait-'I'idag* ("Wine Drinking Ceremony") that marked the ripening of the saguaro fruit and ensured the continuation of the all-important summer rains.[4]

Because of the relative isolation their way of life fostered, the People spoke a variety of dialects, and confrontations were not unknown between rival villages. Above all, O'odham society rooted itself in the tangible, everyday structures of family and village. Marriage partners were typically selected from neighboring O'odham villages, with the woman customarily joining her husband's family. If a community grew too large for its local ecosystem, it might split into "mother" and "daughter" villages, which retained close ceremonial and social ties. Forced to assign a modern-day label to such social arrangements, one might describe the early People not so much a tribe as an ethnic group: a constellation of communities sharing a loose sense of themselves as related and surrounded by others who were not, for one reason or another, like themselves—people who were not, in short, "the People."[5]

No one knows how long the People have lived in the area that they now call their home. Outsiders have tended to locate the beginning of the People's

The People: Tohono O'odham village, photographed in the late nineteenth century.

history in the sixteenth and seventeenth centuries, when the first Europeans passed through O'odham settlements, producing the scattered documents that have provided the basis for almost all written histories of the region. Despite the obvious changes that such contacts brought to the O'odham, however, it is nonetheless a conceit of others to see the arrival of the Spanish as the defining moment of the People's history.[6]

On the surface, O'odham life, with its yearly cycle of harvesting, planting, traveling, and hunting, each tied to specific lunar months, might appear timeless. The "Saguaro Ripe Moon," when the cactus's fruit became edible, was invariably followed by the "Dry Grass Moon," when the rains ended, and then shortly afterwards by the "Lean Moon," when rabbit, deer, and other game had little fat. Yet the People's history had been evolving along its own trajectory long before European contact. Asked in later years to relate their history, the O'odham often responded in ways that emphasized a different, deeper past. Some of the most frequently told stories by the O'odham stretched back centuries before the Spanish appearance to tell of I'itoi ("Elder Brother"), the O'odham cultural hero. Recited in the winter months and differing slightly from community to community, these tales described how a god named Earth Shaman created the earth, sun, moon, I'itoi, and other beings. I'itoi, however, caused a flood that destroyed Earth Shaman's work, leading the ancestors of the People to retreat inside the earth.[7]

After surviving the flood by taking refuge inside a giant pot, I'itoi emerged to rule the world. His efforts to teach humans how to farm by withholding the rain, however, led some inhabitants to seek the help of Vulture, a powerful magician who dwelled near the Salt and Gila rivers. Vulture slew Elder Brother by creating an intense heat that dried up all of I'itoi's water holes. After a period of time, I'itoi returned to life. Still weak, he hid inside the earth, where he encountered the ancestors of the People. Together, I'itoi and the People returned to the earth's surface. Singing special songs to protect themselves, they attacked the villages of Elder Brother's enemies, defeating them all, even Vulture.[8]

Although outsiders often relegate such tales to the status of "myth," with all the implications of doubtful veracity that that term connotes, many of these stories echo the archaeological evidence in the region, particularly the apparent surge in warfare between communities that accompanied the collapse of several large irrigated villages around 1400, a time of unprecedented environmental change in the region when droughts and sudden, destructive floods seem to have become more common. To the O'odham, the former inhabitants of these ruined villages, the vestiges of which still dotted their homeland, were the Huhugam ("Vanishing People") and the O'odham their descendants.[9]

These stories of ancient battles, abandoned settlements, and migration to new homes refute the notion that prior to European arrival, Indians such as the O'odham inhabited a static "prehistory." Rather, the People viewed themselves as the heirs to a unique sequence of historical events, one that rendered outsiders like the Spanish latecomers and temporary distractions from the more fundamental forces governing O'odham existence.

Yet as much as the People may have envisioned themselves as the center of their world and of its history, they could not dismiss European intrusions altogether. The first impact of European arrival was the most devastating yet also the most mysterious. Having lived apart from the peoples of Africa, Asia, and Europe for thousands of years, the indigenous inhabitants of the Americas proved exceptionally vulnerable to the diseases residing within the bodies of Spanish

"Casa Grande": one of the dramatic abandoned settlements of those the O'odham called the Huhugam ("Vanishing People").

invaders. Following the first Spanish landfalls in the Caribbean and Mesoamerica, viral and bacterial infections swept through native populations, often racing far ahead of their European hosts along well-established Indian trade routes. Given the vast distances involved, it is unknown whether the initial outbreaks of typhus, smallpox, measles, and other diseases that racked central Mexico in the 1520s and '30s spread all the way to the People's homeland. But whatever respite the O'odham enjoyed from this epidemiological disaster was at best temporary. By the early to mid-1600s, the diffusion of the Spanish northwards unleashed smallpox, malaria, dysentery, and other maladies among the People, killing large numbers.[10] Although continued exposure would bring less horrific outcomes over time, the early death rate among a previously unexposed population like the O'odham from a disease like measles or smallpox could be staggering, reaching fifty to seventy-five percent. Combined assaults from such illnesses may have contributed to the collapse of entire villages or encouraged some bands of the People to scatter across the desert in an attempt to flee infection.[11]

The same indigenous trade networks that facilitated the spread of diseases also brought other signs of change into the O'odham homeland. When missionaries made their initial forays into O'odham settlements in the late 1600s, they noted to their surprise that "although never in that village or in the others of this vicinity . . . had there entered another white face or Spaniard," bands of the People were already cultivating flax, watermelons, and wheat—all crops of Old World origin—and in some cases even using iron tools of European manufacture.[12]

The initial arrival of these diseases and trade items among the O'odham remains unrecorded in written or oral accounts, and so the meanings the People first assigned to them are now lost to time. Nevertheless, as a result of Spanish colonialism's reverberations, the first friars to arrive in the People's homeland in the 1680s were not, as they often imagined themselves, the discoverers of a new and previously untouched native land. They were instead early witnesses to a new world in the process of being born. It was a world where slave raids and previously unknown diseases, plants, and tools had already left deep imprints. So had the flow of ideas. Missionaries reported being greeted with arches, crosses, and other artifacts that suggest a familiarity with certain European symbols, and some of the People seem to have quickly picked up Castilian or to have had some preexisting knowledge of it. If the missionaries who came to live among the O'odham in the seventeenth century were strangers, not everything about them was, it seems, strange.[13]

Despite popular perceptions of Europeans inserting themselves into native societies in the Americas through military conquest alone, the actual process of colonization often revolved around a much more ambiguous set of encounters. Seldom absent altogether, violence lurked in the background in these interactions as the participants struggled in quite quotidian ways over how to deal with the others in their midst. Such negotiations loomed particularly large, when, as with the People, the native community occupied the very outer edge of empire, where the strength of colonial institutions was at its most attenuated. No immediate conflict, for instance, resulted from the first Jesuit settlements among the People. Instead, the fathers found themselves greeted by O'odham delegations inviting the priests to visit their villages and baptize their children.[14]

To understand such behavior, it helps to recognize that for a people still reeling from the impact of foreign diseases, the strange new arrivals, with their talk of floods and access to supernatural powers, may have seemed like a variation of a familiar figure among the O'odham, the *ma:kai*, or healer. Present-day members of the People differentiate between "staying" sicknesses—specific to those O'odham who violate certain ceremonies or offend a powerful animal or object—and "wandering" sicknesses that travel from one community to the other. This distinction may have arisen during the colonial period, when the People noticed previously unknown epidemics "wandering" from one indigenous population to the next. The newly arriving *mamakai* (healers) may have seemed to offer a remedy to such illnesses, hence the O'odham's desire to have the black-robed strangers treat the most vulnerable members of their community—their children—in the hope of protecting them from the terrifying diseases assaulting them. While this reception was initially advantageous to the priests, who found rival O'odham villages jockeying for their attention, it also set the stage for possible disillusionment later on. It was not unusual for the People to abandon a healer whose practices did not seem efficacious or to accuse a *ma:kai* of inflicting sickness maliciously—both of which happened to the priests as previously unknown illnesses spread despite the new *mamakai*'s preaching.[15]

The O'odham exhibited a similar wary attitude toward the material benefits the missionaries offered. Rather than having to trade with neighboring native groups for a trickle of secondhand European goods, the People now received ample distributions of metal tools, chickpeas, barley, pomegranates, lentils, and other crops, plus an item that had rarely made its way before to O'odham villages: livestock. On their excursions into the People's homeland, the priests were accompanied by vast herds of cattle, horses, goats, and sheep, and they bestowed some two thousand cattle alone to the People in their initial years in the region.[16]

To the O'odham, whose desert ecosystem possessed a limited growing season and few large mammals, the missionaries' unusual plants and animals presented unprecedented sources of food, hides, and transportation. Yet the People could not help noticing that these same goods also unleashed unwelcome changes. Indeed, one O'odham community offered a litany of reasons for being "disconsolate" at the priests' arrival. The fathers had distributed new crops, the People reported, but the priests "required so much labor and sowing for their churches that no opportunity was left the Indians to sow for themselves." Similarly, the introduction of livestock had upset their homeland's delicate ecology: the Spanish "pastured so many cattle that the watering places were drying up." The people also gave evidence of being keenly aware of the limitations of the new *mamakai*'s healing powers. The missionaries, they charged, "killed the people with the holy oils" (a possible reference to deaths

Old World grain, New World people: Tohono O'odham woman at the turn of the century winnowing wheat, a crop that had become one of the People's agricultural staples. Photograph by Edward S. Curtis.

from illnesses that occurred to those O'odham who received baptism) and "deceived the Indians with false promises and words."[17]

Faced with these powerful yet unnerving newcomers, the O'odham improvised a number of responses. Some bands sought out the priests in an effort to gain access to their spiritual and material resources, while others retreated farther into the desert, beyond the reach of Spanish institutions. Still others included the missions as a temporary stop on their yearly migratory cycle or resorted to them only at times of duress. "Ordinarily they come as skeletons made by hunger," griped one missionary, who explained that to attract the People to his church, he "was accustomed after mass on different Sundays to open the pantry and to distribute the provisions free to all who came."[18]

PERHAPS THE MOST SUCCESSFUL initial accommodation between the People and the Spanish could be found in the alliance they forged against the Apache, a group that the O'odham called simply *'O:b*, or "Enemy." The extent to which the People's hostilities with the Apache predated Spanish arrival is hard to determine. It is possible that O'odham contact with the southwardly migrating *'O:b* increased during the fifteenth century, and in the face of escalating friction between the groups, the People welcomed the arrival of European aid against a growing Apache threat. Or it may be that the Spanish, by disrupting relations between the Apache and Pueblo farmers to the east, and introducing livestock into O'odham communities, inadvertently set the stage for an unprecedented wave of Apache raids on the People's tempting new herds.[19]

For their part, the Akimel O'odham linked conflict with the *'O:b* to the origins of death itself, which I'itoi and Earth Shaman created to prevent the People from becoming too numerous.

> They [I'itoi and Earth Shaman] made a plan. They caused a quarrel between an Apache child and an [Akimel O'odham] child, and the Apache child cried and came to its mother. She was angry and whipped the [Akimel O'odham] child. Then the [Akimel O'odham] mother fought the Apache mother, and the [Akimel O'odham] father came to help her, and the Apache father came and fought also. So there was a fight between the Apaches and the [Akimel O'odham], and Earth [Shaman] taught the Apaches to live on the north side of the Gila Valley. Earth [Shaman] sang:

> *"On the tops of the mountains you shall live.*
> *You shall live on the roots and plants on the mountains."* [20]

The first documented confrontation between the O'odham and the Apache occurred seven years after the Spanish arrival in the People's homeland in 1694, when the People accepted the newcomers' invitation to join a retaliatory attack against Apache stock raiders. Within a few years, ceremonies celebrating successful campaigns against the *'O:b* were a regular feature of O'odham settlements. In the village of Quiburi along the San Pedro River, observers noted that "[h]anging from a high pole in the center [of the village] were 13 scalps, bows, arrows and other spoils taken from the many Apache enemies they had slain." At the town of Jiaspi, commentators found "scalps of six Apache enemies, who they [the People] had killed recently, and two young [Apache] prisoners."[21]

Although the People accepted war as an unavoidable fact of life, they also treated it as an activity that released dangerous forces and therefore needed to be contained within a tightly prescribed sphere. Ideally, several days of ritual preceded a *gidahim* (war campaign). The leaders of a band who wished to undertake an attack would make a speech invoking the early battles waged by I'itoi, which served as an invitation to neighboring villages of O'odham to join in the upcoming campaign. Bundles of tally sticks might be distributed among nearby bands as well. Usually, there were ten sticks in a bundle, and the people would break one stick each day to keep track of the time remaining until the war party departed.[22]

In the days before an attack, the men who volunteered to participate would prepare their sandals and other supplies, practice their skills with club and bow, and engage in various rituals—such as appealing to the owl spirits who could seek out the Enemy's hiding places—designed to curry favor with the supernatural power required to ensure victory. When the "sticks were all knocked down" in the bundles distributed among the various bands, the war party would rendezvous in a previously selected spot. Although in a few cases confrontations between the People and their enemies took the form of orchestrated duels between champions from each side, the most common form of assault was the surprise attack. Traveling by night, the O'odham would attempt to "make a house" for their opponents, surrounding a campsite on all sides under the cover of darkness and attacking at first light.[23]

To the People, the bodies and belongings of the *'O:b* were suffused with dangerous powers. The impact of touching the Enemy was so profound that upon killing or otherwise coming into contact with one, a now-weakened O'odham was expected to withdraw immediately from the field of combat, taking but a single trophy—a scalp, a weapon, or a piece of clothing—tied to a long pole to keep it at a safe remove from the rest of the party. Those who slew an Enemy might also paint their face black—a color that warned others not to approach them and that, because it summoned up images of drunkenness and dizziness, embodied for the People the disorienting passions released in warfare. As the ritual oration from one Tohono O'odham village put it:

> *My desire was the black madness of war.*
> *I ground it to powder and herewith painted my face.*
>
> *My desire was the black dizziness of war.*
> *I tore it to shreds and herewith tied my hair in a war knot.*[24]

Before they could rejoin the rest of the People, all those who had touched the Enemy for the first time had to undergo a ritual to dissipate the threatening forces this contact had unleashed. The killer remained secluded outside his home village for a number of days, during which time he cleansed himself through fasting and bathing. In the meantime, the rest of the community performed a number of dances around the pole on which the trophies were suspended. These culminated in a ceremony in which the killer was welcomed back into the village and his trophy returned to him. Now that the People's dances had purified and domesticated it, the trophy was "like a relative." Its power could be added to the killer's and harnessed for the People's healing and fertility rituals.[25]

Power was thus central to the O'odham conceptualization of the violence between themselves and the *'O:b*. The conflicts between the two groups were often interpreted as having little to do with material resources but rather as revealing the spiritual strength of those involved. As one of the People's narratives about Older Brother put it:

He [I'itoi] put power between the Apaches and the [O'odham], so that when the Apaches were victorious they acquired the power; and when the [O'odham] won, in their turn they acquired power. Elder Brother said, "I did not think this enmity would come between these tribes but since it has happened, it has happened. Let it be so."[26]

We do not know exactly when the People's *gidahim* ceremonies arose. Although it was not until the nineteenth century that visitors regularly provided complete descriptions of O'odham purification rituals, even the earliest Spanish accounts mention practices, such as post-raid dances and the placing of Apache trophies on a pole, consistent with the People's cleansing ceremonies. To the O'odham, the central risk in failing to observe such rites was to bring illness to oneself or one's family members, while their successful completion allowed one to gain healing powers. It may therefore be that these rituals solidified during the late 1600s as warfare with the *'O:b* and European-introduced diseases became increasingly prominent in O'odham communities, causing the People to search for ways to understand—and control—these novel and seemingly tandem threats.[27]

"The black madness of war": examples of the shield and war club used by the Akimel O'odham in the latter half of the nineteenth century.

The elaborate customs surrounding O'odham warfare ensured that the People's campaigns were short and little concerned with plunder. Indeed, the perils of touching an item that had once belonged to the *'O:b* were such that after a successful attack, all of an Enemy's goods—houses, clothing, and supplies—were burned. The only exceptions to this rule were the Enemy's women and children, who might be seized for what became a thriving trade in captives with the Spanish. Even so, these prisoners were required to leave all their clothing and possessions behind, which were then burned along with everything else.[28]

Despite such restrictions, the People proved effective warriors. From childhood, boys among the O'odham trained with the People's primary weapons: the bow and arrow, the shield, and the club. The latter two could be a fearsome combination in the hands of a skilled practitioner. Experienced combatants among the People would use their hide-covered shield to deflect oncoming arrows while rushing toward their opponent. After closing the distance, they crushed the Enemy's skull with a heavy club made of mesquite or ironwood.[29]

E VEN GIVEN their shared antipathy to the *'O:b*, the tentative alliance tak- ing shape between the O'odham and the Spanish could not bridge all the early tensions between the two groups. In 1695, just one year after the first joint action against the Apache, some of the People dwelling at a mission called Tubutama killed three *'O:bad*—Christianized Opata Indians from the south—that the priests had placed in charge of the village's livestock. They then moved on to several other missions, where they destroyed Spanish goods and murdered a priest.

While the presence of *'O:bad* outsiders may have played a role in the out- break—O'odham from Tubutama later complained that the Opata "caused them to be whipped every day" and "told the padres everything the Indians did"—the People focused much of their outrage on the Spaniards' spiritual practices. After killing the Opatas at Tubutama, the O'odham "distributed the padre's vestments, finery, and clothing, which all tore to pieces." In the adjoining village of Caborca, the People left in their wake "the image of an angel pierced with an arrow; another arrow pierced the heart of the [statue of the] Saint." As it was far from uncommon for the People to kill their religious leaders when they believed them to be spreading disease or otherwise conspir- ing against the community, such actions may represent a rejection of particu- lar black-robed *mamakai* rather than an assault on Spanish colonialism itself.[30]

Such an interpretation would seem to be borne out by the peace parley that took place between the People and the Spanish shortly afterwards at a site called El Tupo. Many bands of O'odham had had nothing to do with the attack on the Opatas or the priest. Viewing themselves as uninvolved in the conflict or seeing the killers' actions as appropriate in light of the *mamakai*'s misdeeds, they readily identified the incident's participants. Once the Spanish commenced to behead the suspects, however, the assembled O'odham, most of whom had come to the meeting unarmed, "with crucifixes in their hands," tried to flee this unexpected brutality. In the ensuing chaos, Spanish troops and auxiliaries killed almost fifty People. Reported one O'odham, "she saw them [the Spanish and their allies] kill the people who had gone with her, but she did not know why." These deaths precipitated a far larger conflict as the People retaliated against the missions in their midst, burning buildings, "profaning the holy ornaments," and slaughtering livestock "only to cause harm, for the carcasses were intact and none of the meat was taken."[31]

As the Spanish, rallying, brought in more troops, most of the People melted away into the desert. With the Spanish unable to locate the People— although they did manage to burn some O'odham fields and kill the few individuals unlucky enough to fall into their grasp—and the People unwilling to risk direct conflict, the result was a stalemate. This impasse was ultimately resolved through another round of negotiation (this time, fortunately, with no untoward beheadings). The Spanish promised to cease their actions if the People once again accepted friars in their communities and delivered up the men whose attacks at Tubutama and Caborca had sparked the outbreak. Claiming that they were "tired of seeing the killing, suffering hunger and thirst, and fleeing to the hills and mountains with their children and wives," and doubtless bewildered by what must have seemed like a random pattern of hostilities, representatives from the O'odham acceded to the proposed arrangement, pleading only to be allowed "to prepare their fields to plant corn and beans."[32]

Although short-lived, this conflict nonetheless demonstrated the unstable foundations on which Spanish colonialism rested in the People's homeland. For all their heightened access to crops and livestock, the O'odham found their numbers shrinking from introduced diseases and heightened warfare with the Apache, and their village life disrupted by strange *mamakai* who interfered with the People's ceremonies and traditional leaders. Little surprise if under such pressures the People and the Spanish came to view each other across a chasm of distrust and misunderstanding. "[T]he Indians," in the words of one priest, "are secretive towards the missionaries."[33]

Perhaps nowhere was this mutual incomprehension more manifest than in the confused assortment of names that the Spanish used for the People. The newcomers had at first assigned most of the O'odham to the Pima tribe, based on the similarities between their language and that of Indians farther south in Mexico. As was so often the case during colonial encounters, this new tribal name corresponded not to the term that the People used to describe themselves, but seems instead to have arisen via miscommunication, potentially being derived from the O'odham word *pi ha'icu* ("nothing").[34]

Despite their desire to lump all the People into a single tribe, the Spanish could not help recognizing the diversity of O'odham communities. The newcomers attempted to resolve this puzzle through two measures. The first was to create an ever more fine-grained taxonomy of names in the hope of capturing the O'odhams' "true" tribal organization. Spanish colonial commentators invented tribes of "pima aytos," "Pimahitos," and "Papabotas" (this last term the result of another possible misunderstanding, this time of the word *babawi oodham*, or "bean eater"). Even with such efforts, the Spanish struggled to discern the tidy tribal arrangements that they believed must exist. One eighteenth-century missionary was reduced to speaking of "those Pima Indians called 'Papagos,'" while a military officer, after referring to distinct "Pima, Soba and Sobaipuri Indians," contended that all of these groups, despite their different names, constituted "one tribe" since they spoke the same language "with the exception of some verbs and nouns."[35]

If one Spanish response was to try to find tribes where none existed, another was to endeavor to make these imagined organizations more legible. During their initial forays into the O'odham homeland, missionaries and military officials distributed elaborate staffs of office in hopes of creating an identifiable set of leaders through whom they could govern. With the establishment of missions, leadership positions among the People were formalized into a number of offices, ranging from the *gobernador* (governor) who "[o]nce or twice daily . . . must report everything of a political as well as a military nature to the missionary," through the *fiscal* (church official), whose job it was "to see that the Indians attend Holy Mass and prayer on Sundays and Feast days," down to the *topil* (bailiff) "who will administer the prescribed lashes to an offender with lusty power."[36]

Although the Spanish believed that having a clear tribal hierarchy would make the People easier to govern, these offices in fact provided new avenues for O'odham resistance. As one missionary discovered much to his displeasure, once he taught O'odham officials to read, he no longer controlled the flow of information through the community: "no book was secure from them, and suspicion moved them to open letters and betray the contents to their compatriots." The People's new leaders also became skilled in manipulating their resident priests. "Very frequently when they [the O'odham] were contemplating a nocturnal dance and revelry they used all kinds of lies and subterfuges to get the father away from the village, so that he would not hinder them," complained a missionary. "They might trump up a story about a sick person whose circumstances were so perilous that the father would have to hear confession, all to get him to leave the village."[37]

At times, resistance took more overt forms. In November 1751, many of the People rose up in a rebellion against the Spanish. Unlike the spontaneous uprising of 1695, this event had been planned across several communities. And ironically its leaders were the very same individuals the Spanish had selected to serve as rulers among the People. The apparent ringleader of the rebellion was an O'odham with the partially Hispanized name of Luis Oacpicagigua ("Brain Splicer"). Reflecting some of the changes from almost eighty years of Spanish colonialism, Oacpicagigua spoke fluent Spanish and had led more than four hundred O'odham auxiliaries during Spanish campaigns against the Apaches to the north and the Seri Indians to the south. In gratitude, the Spanish governor appointed Oacpicagigua in 1750 to the newly created post of captain-general of all the O'odham.[38]

Oacpicagigua may have seen this new position as allowing him the opportunity to right earlier wrongs against the People. One of his followers recalled that on their way back from the campaign against the *Şe:l* (Seri), Oacpicagigua stopped to contemplate El Tupo, the site of the 1695 massacre of the O'odham. Or it may be that he was offended by the refusal of local missionaries to acknowledge his new status. In either case, the ensuing confrontation revealed the People's desire to transform the novel posts the Spanish had created for them into true positions of power. It took little effort, after all, for Oacpicagigua to imagine how as captain-general he might govern the O'odham directly, without deferring to the Spanish at all. "Brother, I am possessed with this evil of serving in this charge that was conferred upon me by the Father Visitor and confirmed by the Lord Governor in the name of the King," Oacpicagigua reportedly told his followers during a meeting in November of 1751, at which they plotted to expel the Spanish and their supporters from the O'odham homeland. "It is better that we should live with our liberty."[39]

Word of the planned rebellion was passed via runners to other settlements. Although in a few communities sympathetic individuals among the People warned the Spanish of the upcoming insurrection, the O'odham achieved near-total surprise in many villages. In his home community of Sáric, Oacpicagigua, using the subterfuge of an impending Apache attack, ushered eleven Spanish women and children into his home. Oacpicagigua and his compatriots then barred the door and set the house on fire, killing all those trapped inside. Using similar tactics, in the first days of the rebellion the People succeeded in dispatching over one hundred Spaniards and their sympathizers. The survivors fled south, leaving the People's homeland free of outsiders for the first time in half a century.[40]

The same Spanish governor who had elevated Oacpicagigua to a position of authority now found himself forced to lead a campaign against his former protégé. After a single encounter between the People and Spanish military forces, however, the O'odham, as was their custom, dispersed. Oacpicagigua, whose son Cipriano had died in the confrontation, surrendered soon afterwards in the O'odham village of Cewagï ("Cloud," recorded by the Spanish as Tubac) on the condition that the most abusive foreign missionaries be withdrawn from the People's communities. There would be smaller incidents of unrest, perhaps inspired by Oacpicagigua (who would die in a Spanish prison in 1756) for several years following. But most of the O'odham appear to have concluded that they were unable to displace the Spanish through force alone. Still, they may have been consoled by the fact that their uprising did force the Spanish to moderate some of the harsher aspects of their rule. Although friars trickled back to O'odham communities, following the 1751 rebellion and Spain's 1767 expulsion of the Jesuits—the primary evangelists among the People—never again would missionaries play so prominent a role in the O'odham life.[41]

I N THE AFTERMATH of Oacpicagigua's revolt, a new institution—the military—gradually eclipsed the mission as the primary arena for Spanish-O'odham interactions. In 1782, the Crown, instead of relying as before on informal alliances with the People, created its first permanent company of Piman auxiliaries. Five years later, this eighty-man unit relocated to Tubac, where the Spanish had erected a fort to prevent further uprisings among the O'odham like the one led by Luis Oacpicagigua. Over time, however, the post concentrated more and more on confronting the Apache. The O'odham auxiliaries' main duty became assisting soldiers from nearby Tucson—like Tubac, founded on the site of one of the People's villages (Cuk Ṣon, or "Black Base")—in their campaigns against the '*O:b*.[42]

This growing warfare would remake the social geography of the People's world. By the mid-1700s, many O'odham began to retreat into the remote western portions of their desert homeland or to collect themselves into larger villages so as to better protect themselves from Enemy attacks. "They [the O'odham] are reluctant to settle," explained one priest in 1773, "because they say that in the missions the Apaches kill them but that in their own lands that Apaches do not fall upon them as often."[43]

Particularly hard hit were the People dwelling along the San Pedro River, whose towns, located on the far eastern periphery of the O'odham homeland, were most exposed to the incursions of the '*O:b*. When missionaries first visited their villages in the 1690s, the inhabitants, whom the Spanish termed "Pima Sobaipuris," or simply "Sobaipuris," had numbered over two thousand people and had dwelled in seven to fourteen large towns, one of the largest being Ojío, located at the confluence of the San Pedro River and Aravaipa Canyon.[44] By 1762, the surviving descendants of these villagers agreed to abandon what one observer termed "their pleasant and fertile valley" and resettle in San Xavier del Bac (from the O'odham word *Wa:k*, or "Standing Water") and other less vulnerable communities to the west—a move that ended the People's long-standing presence along the San Pedro River.[45]

The first half of the nineteenth century brought further geographic shifts. After a decade of rebellion, in 1821 the new nation of Mexico supplanted the centuries-old Spanish empire. Then in 1848 and again in 1854, this young republic surrendered significant portions of the O'odham homeland to an expanding United States. Still, as the People's world was incorporated into one nation-state and then another, the meanings of these changes remained indistinct. In part, the People, with their autonomous, family- and village-based lifestyle, found it difficult to conceive of institutions that organized millions of people into a single political entity or of rulers who never appeared among their subjects. "The Indians recognize the King of Spain as their over-lord," noted one missionary. "However, they have no better understanding of him than that he is a great captain or alcalde because they have seen no other overlords." But more important, what was for a newly created Mexico and

"Standing Water": Although Spanish missionaries first arrived at the Tohono O'odham village of Wa:k in 1692, construction of San Xavier del Bac mission (shown here in the 1870s) did not begin until 1783.

United States the outermost margin of their national territories remained for the O'odham the center of their world, an indigenous space where the People retained considerable sway over daily events.[46]

Our understanding of the People's history in this period is enriched by a remarkable set of artifacts known as "calendar sticks." Made from the rib of a saguaro cactus, these sticks, in the words of Akimel O'odham elder Anna Moore Shaw, were carved with "[d]istinctive marks, each designed to remind the calendar stick keeper of important happenings." Events were recorded in a year-by-year fashion (reckoned, in O'odham style, from one summer to the next, when the rainy season and the accompanying planting cycle took place). "When the analyst was asked about an event," remembered Shaw, "he would slowly run his fingers over the carved stick, and with a faraway look he would tell the record of a certain year." Most every O'odham village had its own calendar stick keeper, usually a man who had distinguished himself when still a young boy as an astute recollector of the People's history.[47]

In contrast with the stories about I'itoi, which connected the People to events centuries old, calendar sticks tended to be a far more immediate chronicle, typically only recording incidents that had occurred within the keeper's lifetime. Whether the keeping of such sticks first arose as a response to European forms of writing or represents a long-standing O'odham custom is uncertain. The oldest sticks now known only document events going back to the early 1800s. What this absence tells us about the origins of the calendar stick custom, however, is unclear: in the twentieth century the People typically destroyed the sticks upon their caretaker's death. Presumably, this practice held in earlier times as well.[48]

What the calendar sticks do reveal is the vast difference between the People's perceptions of the past and those of their American and Mexican neighbors. Consider two of the earliest surviving entries, both of which date to 1839. The first comes from an Akimel O'odham community (here denoted as Pimas in accordance with the label that most outsiders, following Spanish colonial precedent, assigned to them in the nineteenth century), the second from a Tohono O'odham village (here, again in keeping with Spanish colonial custom, termed Papago).

Late in the spring a party of Pimas went to Tucson to buy clothing and other needed supplies. On their return they were ambushed and barely escaped massacre. The Apaches had concealed themselves on either side of the trail, and when the attack was suddenly made the Pimas were at first panic-stricken, but recovered sufficiently to repel their assailants, with the loss, however, of two men killed and a boy captured. This youth is said to have been a very handsome fellow, skillful in the use of bow and arrow. Fearing a renewal of the conflict, the Pimas hastened home.

A few months later they obtained their revenge upon a party of Apaches who came to the villages to steal horses. The enemy were seen and chased across the river. On the way they were met by a party of Pimas, returning from a council, who called out to the approaching horsemen to ask who they were; on receiving no answer they shot one of them. An Apache called "Slender Leg" was pushed off his mule and two Pimas jumped off their horses and tried to hold him, but he was

"With a faraway look he would tell the record of a certain year": Joseph Head (right), an Akimel O'odham calendar stick keeper, in the early 1900s.

too strong for them and they had to tie him. He was taken to the well-swept plaza of the village . . . where the people gathered and danced and sang around him. Two widows of men killed in an ambuscade earlier in the season walked four times around the outside of the circle of dancers, and then passed inside as an avenue was opened for them. They carried long clubs of mesquite, with which they beat the captive into insensibility.[49]

This was the year when "the world went wrong." There was fighting in Mexico and the calendar keeper was so impressed and frightened that he began the stick. During the hottest part of the summer a Papago named Take-a-Horse killed an Enemy.[50]

Although the early anthropologists who transcribed the People's calendar sticks dismissed many records as "village gossip rather than history," the sticks should more accurately be considered exemplars of a specific historical genre: the annals or year-by-year chronicle. It is true that to an outsider accustomed to thinking about history as the doings of nation-states, the People's annals can appear disorientingly particularistic—a collection of small and obscure stories rather than one grand narrative about a single leader. Incidents follow one another in an order that, while chronological, offers no clear causation and suggests no fixed moral. Instead, the stick's caretaker recounted each episode, in the words of one observer of the ceremonial telling, "with no hint of glorification . . . or blame for the enemy."[51]

Nonetheless, even expressed in this manner, history expressed certain judgments. Most obviously, it offered what might be termed a "People-centric" vision of history, in which the frame of reference rarely extended beyond the teller's home community. Outsiders and their doings might make brief appearances— the "fighting in Mexico" that the Tohono O'odham recordkeeper mentioned, for example, refers to confrontations between different political factions over the governorship of Sonora in the 1830s, in which the participants attempted to enlist the People—but only to the extent that their actions touched upon the teller's home village. In addition, certain conditions were treated as historical givens. As the two entries above suggest, for example, by the early nineteenth century, the O'odham took the hostility of the Apache for granted—as well as their right to kill the '*O:b* whenever and wherever they encountered them.[52]

Euro-American historians sometimes speak of the difference between the "little history" of households and families and the "big history" of empires and nations. But for the People, whose basic units of social organization were the family and village, such distinctions mattered little. To the O'odham, their "little history" *was* their "big history"—and vice versa. This perspective emerged with particular clarity during the period from 1846 to 1849, when Mexico and the United States waged their war over the People's homeland. Despite the seeming import of this event for the O'odham, the surviving calendar sticks give a very different portrait of the era.[53]

1845–48: Three peaceful years.[54]

1846–47: The Apaches came one moonlight night to steal horses. Leaving their own mounts tied in the brush, they crept toward the houses near which were the Pima ponies. They were discovered and pursued to the river, where all were killed in a running fight.[55]

1848–49: A disease killed many of the children. The people from Burnt Seeds and Saddle Hanging [villages] had gone to Sonora to harvest beans for the Mexicans. There, they fought with the Enemy and some People and some Enemies were killed.[56]

In a similar manner, the calendar sticks include no mention of Mexico's sale of most of the People's territory south of the Gila River to the United States in the early 1850s.

1852–53: A few people from Mesquite Root [the site of a large Apache raid the previous year] had been away from the village and had not been killed. Those people could not go back to live where so many had died; so they camped at Grassy Well. They were very frightened. That winter they held the prayerstick festival, which should be held every four years, to keep the world going right, for so Elder Brother told us.[57]

1853–54: The Apaches came to steal horses and brought a live vulture with them. They were discovered and several killed.[58]

1855–56: [The village of] Skââkolk was approached one evening by seven Apaches, who were discovered and surrounded. Six escaped in the darkness, but one was tracked into the arrow bushes, where he dropped his bow. He was soon found to have secreted himself in a hole washed deep in the sand. The Pimas could not see or reach him, so they shook live coals down upon the fugitive, which caused him to yell and suddenly leap out among them. The apparition so startled everyone that no move was made to detain him. As he was passing through their line some asked those around them, "Can we catch him?" but he was such a giant and the peculiar manner of his appearance among them so unnerved for a moment the courage of the men whose deepest instinct was to crush out the life of the Apache, that he made his escape.[59]

"Distinctive marks ... were carved upon its surface": portion of a Tohono O'odham calendar stick.

It would be a mistake, however, to assume based on such accounts that the People remained unaware of the larger changes going on around them. The U.S. Army officers who mapped the new border between Mexico and the United States in the 1850s reported several encounters with the O'odham in which the People expressed concern at the surveyors' presence. During a trip to secure provisions from the Akimel O'odham villages, one soldier noted the River People's "rich fields of wheat ripening for the harvest." "As I sat upon a rock, admiring the scene before me," added the officer, "an old grey-headed Pimo [*sic*] took great pleasure in pointing out the extent of their domains. They were anxious to know if their rights and titles to lands would be respected by our government, upon learning that their country had become part of the United States." So anxious, in fact, that a delegation from the Tohono O'odham and Akimel O'odham visited the head of the U.S. survey at his camp in Nowa:l (Nogales) shortly afterwards "to consult as to the effect upon them and their interests of the treaty with Mexico."[60]

The officer's response—that "by the terms of the treaty, all the rights that they possessed under Mexico are guarantied [*sic*] to them by the United States"—proved simultaneously prophetic and mistaken. Initially, the doings of the *Milga:n*, as the People came to call the newcomers (after their term for themselves, "American"), brought few noticeable changes, which may explain why the O'odham decided that their meetings with the surveyors did not merit being recorded on any of their surviving calendar sticks. Even though most of the People's homeland officially became part of the United States in 1854, the *Milga:n* were slow to settle their new possession. As the chief surveyor admitted during his meeting with the O'odham in 1855, he did not expect representatives of the new government to appear for another "five or ten months," possibly longer. In the meantime, the officer urged the People to "obey the Mexican authorities" and, above all, defend the territory "against the savage Apaches."[61]

Still, U.S. annexation planted the seeds of what would grow to be substantial changes for the People. The new boundary mapped by the joint commission of Americans and Mexicans bisected O'odham territory, leaving one-third of the People's lands within Mexico. Given the porous border of the mid-nineteenth century, this shift had little immediate impact on the People. But it nevertheless laid the groundwork for dramatic transformations to come.[62]

As American administration gradually took shape in the late 1850s, it continued many Mexican practices toward the O'odham. The office of *gobernador* for each of the People's villages, itself a carryover from Spanish colonial practice, remained a cornerstone of Indian policy, albeit with each *gobernador* now termed a "captain." The U.S. government also retained the O'odhams' role as military auxiliaries against the Apache. Many of the first appearances of the *Milga:n* in the People's records thus relate to joint actions between the O'odham and the newcomers. In 1856–57, one community's calendar stick noted that "[t]he Pimas . . . joined the white soldiers in a campaign against the Apaches." The following year, another village's calendar stick recorded that "[t]he Whites and the People together started taming the Enemy."[63]

Much as they had done with the Spanish, the O'odham endeavored to take what was useful from these newcomers while still preserving their autonomy. The People readily accepted the iron tools, cotton cloth, tobacco, beads, American flags, and military uniforms that U.S. authorities, anxious to curry O'odham support, distributed to them. Likewise, the O'odham welcomed the livestock and other rewards that American civilians and officials, following Spanish and Mexican custom, offered them after successful raids against the Apache.[64]

Nonetheless, the O'odham envisioned clear limits to this evolving relationship. One calendar stick recorded a telling encounter between the People and the *Milga:n* in 1856–57:

> The White men said the government would help them and civilize them and from now on they were to live by laws. . . . The chiefs agreed but they said: "The White people must not bother us." An old man made a speech and told the Whites: Every stick and stone on this land

belongs to us. Everything that grows on it is our food—cholla, prickly
pear, giant cactus, Spanish bayonet, mesquite beans, amaranth, all the
roots and greens. The waters is ours, the mountains. . . . These mountains, I say, are mine and the Whites shall not disturb them.[65]

D URING THE INITIAL YEARS of American annexation, the O'odham
managed not only to preserve this hoped-for self-sufficiency but even
to enjoy a minor economic boom. Rising *Milga:n* immigration into the region
provided the River People with a growing market for agricultural goods. The
Akimel O'odham responded by bringing more and more of their lands along
the Gila into production, becoming the territory's preeminent farmers. As one
Milga:n admitted, it was the River People, far more than the local Mexicans
or Anglos, who were "in fact, the laboring population of that Territory. They
produce supplies both for the army and for the miners." In 1860, the Akimel
O'odham sold some 400,000 pounds of wheat to the newly arrived Overland
Mail Company. The following year, they sold an almost equal amount of wheat
to the U.S. Army, along with quantities of corn, beans, and dried pumpkins. By
1862, the People's annual sales had climbed to more than one million pounds
of wheat and 250,000 pounds of corn, along with lesser amounts of "cotton,
sugar, melons, beans, and other small crops." This surging agricultural market, in the words of one observer, left the River People "in a very prosperous
condition . . . nearly all had money, in amounts varying from fifteen to twenty-
five dollars. . . . They also have fine stock in cattle and horses."[66]

Lacking the predictable water supply that the Akimel O'odham enjoyed,
other groups of the People could not expand their agriculture in as dramatic a
fashion. Nonetheless, they found new opportunities in American annexation
as well. With the Akimel O'odham increasing their farm production, many
of the Tohono O'odham found themselves in greater demand during harvest
time, when they journeyed north to aid the River People in exchange for a
portion of the crop. After Americans opened several mining companies, the
Tohono O'odham incorporated these establishments into their seasonal migratory cycle, too. Some Tohono O'odham pursued temporary employment in the
mines in exchange for food or wages. Others sold the salt that they had long
collected along the shores of the Sea of Cortez to the new U.S. mining com-

"The laboring population of that territory": the enormous woven baskets that the Akimel O'odham used for storing surplus agricultural produce.

panies, which came to use thousands of pounds of People-gathered sea salt in their smelting operations. Still others bartered milk, pottery, firewood, hay, and *bahidaj-sitol*, the sweet syrup the O'odham produced from the fruit of the saguaro cactus, in Cewagï (Tubac), Cuk Ṣon (Tucson), and elsewhere.[67]

From the perspective of the *Milga:n*, such events would soon be overshadowed by a bloody civil war that represented a pivotal turning point in their young nation's history. This war did not escape the notice of the O'odham, for the River People's villages, as the most important agricultural sites in the region, emerged as key targets in the struggle between Union and Confederate forces. In 1861–62, according to the People's calendar sticks, a leading Anglo trader among them "was captured by the 'soldiers from the east'"; that same year, "[t]he soldiers from the west fought the soldiers from the east at Picacho and were defeated." (To the People, the Confederates, since they came from Texas, were "soldiers from the east," while Union forces, which arrived via California, were "soldiers from the west.") But from the O'odham point of view, the Civil War years were memorable for a far different set of stories.[68]

1863–64: Some of the People were behind Turkey Neck Mountain (near San Xavier), roasting mescal. There they met the Enemy and had a big fight. Two Enemies and one of the People were killed. The People burned their slain warrior as must always be done with anyone touched by the Enemy, and then they burned all the mescal, saving only enough to eat until they got to the Rotten Ground. There they picked more and roasted it and took it home.[69]

1864: The sickness "Black Vomit" again occurred among the Indians who went to the lowlands. It was either a milder form or the Indians fled sooner, for only a few died.[70]

With most troops busy farther east, the Civil War years witnessed a heightened reliance by Confederate and Union officials alike on using the O'odham to fight the Apache. In 1862, Arizona's Confederate commander urged "the chiefs of the Papagos and Pima Indians to help me clean out the Apache Indians." When Union forces reclaimed the territory a few months later, they too regarded the People "good spies and auxiliaries"—so much so, in fact, that they distributed some one hundred percussion muskets and several thousand rounds of ammunition to the Akimel O'odham.[71]

Although the *Milga:n* lauded the O'odham as "a barrier between the frontier settlements and the wild tribes," they discovered much about the People's style of warfare to be "a source of annoyance." The divergent approaches of these two erstwhile allies were cast in sharp relief in a series of incidents that took place at the close of the Civil War at a recently reestablished U.S. Army base at the intersection of the San Pedro River and 'Al Waiphia ("Little Springs," or Aravaipa Canyon). An officer at the fort noted that when a handful of Apache Indians were spotted nearby waving a white banner—the symbol for peace—it was only with "the greatest difficulty" that the People could be restrained from attacking the approaching negotiators. A few hours later, a report that O'odham scouts had spied another party of *'O:b* prompted the assembled People to rush the Apaches, "knocking their brains out with the stock of the carbine." This preference among the O'odham for using their firearms as clubs puzzled the *Milga:n*. "They [the People] are well acquainted with the use of all our fire-arms," observed one, "but . . . they do not generally discharge their pieces on contact with the Apache, but rely on close quarters, their war clubs, or the stocks of the musket or carbine."[72]

Following these Apache deaths, the majority of the auxiliaries at 'Al Waiphia then withdrew from further campaigning. "[A]lthough they had started on the understanding of a month's scout," complained their commanding officer, "after this small affair at the camp but four out of, say fifty, would go on." On other occasions, army officers found to their displeasure that if the People's war leaders decided that the signs for a successful campaign were not auspicious, the O'odham would return home without setting out after the Apache at all, "and neither threats nor entreaties could prevail upon them to proceed further."[73]

To the People, of course, such practices were perfectly logical. Killing from afar, be it with bow and arrow or with a firearm, did not bring one into direct physical contact with the Enemy and therefore did not permit one to go through the purification ritual that allowed one to claim the power of a dead Apache and to ascend to the status of *siakam*—"Enemy Killer." Moreover, given that war was a measure of power, it made little sense to undertake an expedition that did not promise success. If anything, it was the practices of the *Milga:n* on such subjects that struck the People as odd. One calendar stick from this era described an American's scalping of an Apache using a borrowed O'odham knife. "Then he asked whose knife it was and wanted to give it back but no Indian would take it because it had touched an Enemy, so he threw it on the ground." Added the recordkeeper, "He could have kept the knife if he had wished to be purified with it, but no White man does that."[74]

Given the awkward fit between the People's customs and U.S. Army tactics, most officers suggested that rather than a "regular enlistment" alongside American soldiers, the People be offered "a reward, money, food, or clothing, for every scalp of any Apache brought." O'odham were still incorporated upon occasion into *Milga:n* expeditions, but most of the time they were encouraged to range on their own, killing the Apache wherever and whenever they encountered them. Bands of the People bringing various Apache body parts or captured Apache children to American settlements were soon a familiar scene in the territory. "100 Pima Indians came here this morning on their way to Sonora," noted a resident of Cuk Ṣon (Tucson). "They brought a lot of Apaches' ears, drew some rations and started on their journey." A settler in Cewagï (Tubac) observed "[s]everal Pima Indians . . . here with captured

Apache children for sale. The Pimas had a fight last week with some Pinals, killed eleven of them and brought in four children prisoners. They sell readily at from $45 to $100."[75]

This trade in trophies and captives extended far beyond the end of the Civil War. Indeed, the People's calendar sticks made no note of the end of hostilities between the "soldiers from the east" and the "soldiers from the west" in 1865, focusing instead on what had become a bitter struggle with the 'O:b:

1864–65: In a raid in this year two Apaches were killed and their ears cut off and nailed on a stick.

1864–65: The Pimas and Maricopas went on a campaign against the Apaches and met a band that had probably ambushed some American soldiers, for they had arms and other army property. The allies rushed the camp of the enemy and captured all that had been taken from the soldiers. When they returned with their spoils to the villages some whites accused them of having killed the soldiers. They told how they obtained the things, but the whites would not believe them. "That is why I do not think the white man is good enough to trust us," said Owl Ear. When several guides took the whites to the battle ground they were satisfied when they saw the dead Apaches there.[76]

1865–66: Another war party attacked an Apache camp, described as the one at which the children were playing and piling up gourds, and killed several of the enemy.[77]

1866–67: A party of Pimas accompanied the soldiers to the Verde region and there they killed a number of Apaches, among whom was a man with a very long foot.[78]

The *Milga:n* likewise exhibited few changes in the years after 1865. Despite the end of hostilities between "east" and "west," they continued to reward the O'odham for attacking the Apache. In 1870, for example, territorial newspapers celebrated an encounter in which 110 mounted Akimel O'odham overtook a band of Apaches, killing thirteen. The People proceeded to the closest

U.S. Army base where in exchange for "the trophies of their victory" the fort's commander rewarded the O'odham with provisions.[79]

One of the great ironies of the People's warfare during this era was that the same violence that produced so many Apache deaths also generated a deep understanding of the 'O:b. "[B]ecause there was such close fighting between Apaches and Papagos," recalled a Tohono O'odham named Ramón Anita, "most of the Papagos knew the Apaches personally, and had [nick]names for them." Indeed, the stories that the O'odham told about the 'O:b often depicted the targets of their raids in poignant detail.[80]

The men all separated and each one waited outside one Apache wickiup, till the signal to attack. My father was outside a wickiup where there were several women roasting something and he listened to their strange voices and wondered if they were saying, "The Desert People are here." Finally the signal came: the call of a roadrunner. Our men attacked, whooping. The women ran out of the houses and the men stood at the doors waiting to club them. My father took hold of an old woman but she was strong and wrestled with him. He called to the others, "Help! The old enemy woman is killing me!" So others came and they broke in the old woman's skull. A few other men killed but the rest of the women got away. Our men burned the houses and the booty and went home.[81]

The people from Dried-and-Burnt and from Saddle Hanging [villages] went on the warpath. They found Enemy tracks at Ash Tree Standing; then they found peelings of cactus fruit, still wet and then, on a little hill, they found Enemy moccasins and wicker water bottles. The Enemy always carried two pairs of moccasins, one for cold weather and one for warm. It was warm in the Desert country, so they had left their cold weather moccasins and their water bottles while they were lying in wait for the passing wagons of the White man. The People thought the Enemy would come back and so they camped, waiting, and they sent two scouts to look for them. The scouts saw the Enemy in an arroyo, laughing and talking over a little fire. They came back and told the others and they decided to encircle the Enemy and club them to death.

The Enemy put out their fire and went to sleep. Now there was one medicine man among the Enemy who had said to them: "Let us not go on, there is something evil in the wind." But a rival medicine man said: "It is a lie. Go on unless you are afraid." So they went on. But that night the first medicine man said to a friend of his: "Do not sleep. There is danger." All the others went to sleep but the medicine man kept throwing pebbles at his friend to keep him awake. At last, he crawled over to the friend and said: "Something is going to happen. There is a sound like wind coming toward us. The sleepers are groaning. It is a bad sign. Let us two escape."

So the two went under a palo verde tree and stood there. It was dark and they could hear the People coming. The People were making a circle but it was not joined; so the two Enemies ran through the gap and escaped.[82]

Although O'odham women seldom participated in raids against the 'O:b, their rare seizure as captives—and even rarer escapes back to their people—allowed a few to serve as conduits for especially intimate portrayals of the Apache. The aunt of the Tohono O'odham Matilda Romero provided one such portrait, although family members recalled that it took several years for her to be willing to speak about her experiences. The aunt had been captured along with her daughter and several other women and children in a surprise assault on her village of Kui Tatk ("Mesquite Root") in the mid-nineteenth century. After a forced march over several days in which some of the People died and several O'odham women killed their children or resisted their captors so strenuously that they were executed, the aunt was separated from her daughter and placed with an 'O:b family, who forced her to help them prepare mescal cactus. During her captivity, remembered her niece, "[s]he used to cry a lot."

One of the younger Apache girls would cry with her. They would cry together every evening. This girl felt sorry for her. . . . The [Apache] men would go hunting and the women would be left by themselves gathering the mescal and carrying it in a *kiho* [basket] to the pits. The oldest lady took the best mescal and put them out on a rock and then she gave her her own pair of *tewas* [*cew ṣu:ṣk*, "long shoes"?] She made motions like "Go and I won't tell."

Taking advantage of the *'O:b* woman's apparent generosity, Romero's aunt managed to sneak away to the Akimel O'odham villages. After recuperating among the River People, she rejoined the surviving members of her family in their desert home.[83]

While this tale might seem to hint at the recognition of some sort of shared suffering between O'odham and *'O:b* women amid the widespread violence between their two groups, its denouement suggested a different lesson altogether. The aunt's daughter was recovered four months later during one of the People's raids, along with another young Tohono O'odham woman. This other woman, having spent a great deal of time with the Apaches, had learned their language and habits, and used to accompany the People on their attacks against the *'O:b* to help scout and translate. All other links between herself and the Apache she erased. The woman "had a baby by an Apache and killed it," explained Romero's niece. "People do not keep things that come from the Apaches."[84]

N OT LONG AFTER Romero's aunt made her traumatic escape, a "pale white Mexican" known to the People as Elías approached some of the Tohono O'odham about participating in an attack against the *'O:b* in 'Al Waiphia (Aravaipa Canyon). This was scarcely a surprising request. Elías, who lived along the road between the Tohono O'odham settlement of Standing Water (San Xavier del Bac) and Black Base (Tucson), owned one of the largest cattle herds in the region, much of which he pastured in the vicinity of Wa:k because of the extra security that the People offered. On many occasions, People from Wa:k had assisted Elías and his brothers in their efforts to recover livestock taken in Apache raids.

After discussing his query among themselves, the People decided to join the proposed expedition. As usual during a *gidahim*, the war leaders sent bundles of sticks to nearby villages, inviting them to share in the attack. "[Standing Water] sent messengers to call Coyote Sitting and Mulberry Well," noted one calendar stick. "They said: 'Don't stop for food or for weapons. The women at [Standing Water] will be grinding corn for you and the pale whites will give you guns.' So all came, some with bows and some without but, at [Black Base], the Mexicans gave them guns."[85]

Close to one hundred Tohono O'odham from Wa:k and its daughter villages joined in the war campaign, making the People—as was often the case in nineteenth-century raids against the Apache—the largest contingent in the group. "Some Mexicans came too," according to the People's chroniclers, "and they led the way." Traveling by night in keeping with O'odham practice, the party made its way to 'Al Waiphia. It was a location that may have held particular significance for some of the raiders. A number of O'odham from Wa:k—the community from which most of the attackers were drawn—still spoke of themselves as descendants of the Sobaipuris who had dwelled near 'Al Waiphia before being displaced by Apache raids in the 1760s.[86]

The party reached the *'O:b* campsite in Aravaipa Canyon early on the morning of April 30, 1871. In typical O'odham fashion, the group "made a house" for the Apache, surrounding their shelters on several sides. Then, "before dawn," observed the calendar stick from Standing Water with characteristic terseness, "the Mexicans and the People encircled the village and killed those who were asleep."[87]

LOS VECINOS

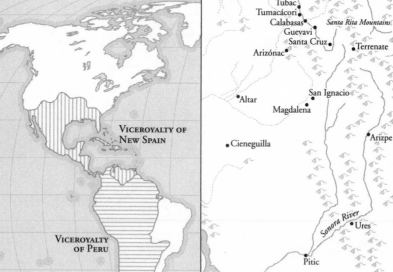
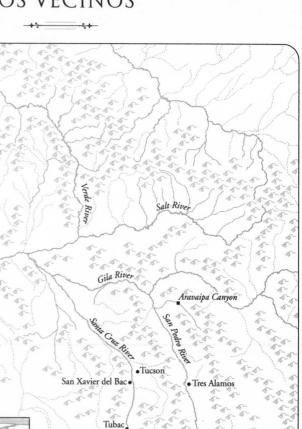

Pimería Alta

Verde River

Salt River

Gila River

Gila River

Aravaipa Canyon

San Pedro River

Santa Cruz River

Tucson

San Xavier del Bac

Tres Alamos

Tubac
Tumacácori
Calabasas
Guevavi
Santa Cruz
Arizónac

Santa Rita Mountains

Terrenate

Fronteras

Altar

San Ignacio

Magdalena

Bavispe

Cieneguilla

Arizpe

VICEROYALTY OF
NEW SPAIN

VICEROYALTY
OF PERU

Sonora River

Ures

Pitic

© 2008 Jeffrey L. Ward

LOS VECINOS

WHEN KING FELIPE IV of Spain contemplated his realm in the 1690s, his mind's eye took in much of the known world. Spain at the close of the seventeenth century ruled over a global empire, one that embraced the Philippine and Mariana islands in the Pacific, scattered holdings in Europe (Sicily, Sardinia, and Luxemburg as well as most of the Iberian peninsula), and vast portions of North and South America. In the New World alone, the Spanish realm stretched from Buenos Aires on South America's Río de la Plata thousands of miles north to the most recent lands to be brought under the Crown's dominion, Pimería Alta (upper Pima land). Befitting its location on the outermost fringe of empire, Pimería Alta was bordered on most imperial maps by the blank spaces that denoted the limits of Spanish sovereignty and knowledge alike.[1]

As a "Christian king" responsible for his subjects' religious and material well-being, Felipe sat atop a vast bureaucracy. From all corners of the empire, reports on matters both spiritual and secular flowed to Madrid for consideration by the king and the Council of the Indies, the body charged with overseeing Spain's possessions in the Americas. These missives rendered the creation of written histories fundamental to Spanish colonialism and a key element of the fantasy of the imperial archive: the dream that all relevant knowledge about the empire could be collected and systematized, and that this control of data would lead inevitably to the control of territory and of peoples.[2]

By the time that the line of Spanish settlement reached Pimería Alta in the 1680s, over a century and a half had transpired since Spain's colony of

Nueva España first came into being with Hernando Cortez's conquest of the Aztec empire in central México. Although the desire to claim the riches of "another México" had propelled *conquistadores* to the fringes of Pimería Alta as early as the sixteenth century, a more permanent Spanish presence awaited the development of a different model of colonization, focused on the conversion of Indian peoples via the mission.[3] Through enticements of food and other goods, Catholic priests were to expose Indians to a sedentary lifestyle and the array of practices—from Christianity to agriculture to dress to the Castilian language—that to the Spanish mind constituted civilization. Over time, as the Indians adopted European cultural forms, the expectation was that the mission could be converted into a community parish, and its residents into taxpaying subjects of the Spanish Crown. To emphasize the imagined benevolence of this approach, in 1573 King Felipe II issued the Comprehensive Orders for New Discoveries, which forbade the word "conquest" to describe Spain's activities in the Americas in favor of the term "pacifications."[4]

Accordingly, as Jesuit priests planted the first missions in Pimería Alta in the late 1680s, their Italian-born leader, Eusebio Kino, presented his activities to the Crown as the divinely sanctioned conversion of a grateful Indian populace. The threat of Spanish violence, however, remained close at hand. At the same time that Padre Kino was making his first ventures into Pimería Alta, the Crown also founded the region's first military installations: the *presidios* (forts) of Janos in 1691 and Fronteras in 1692. When the O'odham arose in what the Spanish termed the Pima Revolt of 1695, killing several Opata Indians along with a priest, it was a *compañía volante* (flying column) from Fronteras that, in the words of one Spanish officer, "punish[ed] [the Pima] in a manner worthy of their wickedness," killing close to fifty during a peace parley Kino arranged at a site that the Spanish came to call Ciénega de la Matanza (Slaughter Marsh).[5]

Spanish policymakers would wrestle for decades with the underlying dilemmas that the "evil" of native opposition to the Crown presented. After all, indiscriminate brutality against Indian peoples—what Spanish officials termed *la guerra de fuego y sangre* ("war of fire and blood")—undermined the vision of peaceful pacification through superior, Christian civilization that undergirded the mission program. In keeping with this concern, when the Crown undertook a reorganization of what it had come to call the Provincias

Internas del Norte in 1729, it placed clear limits on the use of force against Indians. The Spanish military was not to attack Indians along the northern frontier until all efforts at peaceful persuasion had been exhausted, and officers were to accept all Indian requests for peace, provided they could reach a written agreement with the tribes involved.[6]

Such cumbersome rules were complicated by other changes in the region. In 1736, Spanish prospectors found a rich outcropping of silver ore in a location along the upper reaches of the Santa Cruz River. The site, which came to be known as the Real de Arizónac—a term apparently derived from the O'odham phrase 'Al ṣonag, or "Place of the Small Spring"—attracted a surge of migrants from central México into Pimería Alta, for whom Arizónac symbolized the promise of quick wealth.[7]

These newcomers presented a mix of benefits and challenges to colonial rule. In a reflection of the ethnic hybridity that had developed in Nueva España, the new arrivals hailed from a variety of backgrounds—"various *castas, mestizos, coyotes, mulatos,* and a few Spanish," in the words of one missionary.[8] Although they were often derided by priests and Crown officials alike as rootless "vagabonds," the acculturation of such peoples to Spanish society and their relative loyalty to the Crown led to their gradual acceptance along the northern edges of New Spain as *gente de razón* (people of reason)—a status that elevated them above the local Indians, who remained *gente sin razón* (people without reason). "[T]here is hardly a true Spaniard in Sonora," observed the Jesuit missionary Ignaz Pfefferkorn at midcentury. "Practically all those who wish to be considered Spaniards are people of mixed blood." The influx of such "Spanish" peoples into the Real de Arizónac helped increase the colonial population and invigorate the local economy.[9]

Economic growth, however, also invited violence. Almost as soon as they arrived in the region in the late 1600s, the Spanish had complained about the "destruction, thefts, killings, and . . . ambushes" by the Indians inhabiting the "rugged sierras" beyond the Crown's fragile sphere of control. The threats posed by these raiders, whom the Spanish, apparently corrupting the term *'a paču* used by New Mexico's Zuni Indians, came to call Apaches, only grew with the spread of mines and ranches following the discoveries at Arizónac.[10]

Before long, a once sporadic pattern of Apache raids had grown into a fearsome phenomenon. To many Spanish, it seemed that it was themselves, rather than the Indians, who were being subjected to *la guerra de fuego y san-gre*. "Previously they [the Apaches] attacked only two or three times a year always at full moon," lamented the Jesuit missionary Juan Nentvig in 1764. "Now they attack at any time and in larger numbers."[11] The Franciscan priest Bartholomé Ximeno attributed the surge in hostilities against Spanish settle-ments to the Sobaipuris' abandonment of their villages along the San Pedro River in 1762: "Until recent times there was not such a danger of . . . the fury of the Apaches as there is now, because a tribe called the Sobaipuris . . . served as an impediment to their passage to farther lands." To such commentators, it was impossible "to assure the progress of the new Christianity" of Pimería Alta unless the Apache were stopped.[12]

Over the years, the Spanish experimented with a variety of tactics against *"los crueles bárbaros apaches"* (the cruel Apache barbarians). The first was a famil-iar strategy from past Spanish conquests: enlisting one indigenous group to fight the other. In the aftermath of the 1695 Pima Revolt, the Spanish insisted these Indians attack the Apache to demonstrate their loyalty to the Crown. As Kino's frequent companion, Lieutenant Juan Mateo Manje, put it, "if they [the Pima] were loyal friends of the Spaniards, they would . . . make a campaign against the avowed murderers throughout the province." This standard—in which the Spanish judged Pima loyalty according to their willingness to kill Apaches—held in later years as well, with the commander general of the Inte-rior Provinces, Teodoro de Croix, observing in the 1770s that "[t]he Pimas Altos gave proofs of their fidelity in two campaigns which they made against the Seri and Apache."[13]

Another tactic the Spanish hoped might stem the tide of Apache raid-ing was extending the presidio system. A number of new forts were added at strategic locales in the mid-eighteenth century: Terrenate and Pitic in 1741, Tubac and Altar in 1752, and Buenavista in 1765.[14] In 1772, the Crown under-took a reform of its northern frontier that would remain in place until the end of Spain's North American empire. The centerpiece of this new approach was a uniform cordon of presidios across the entire 1,500-mile-long northern edge of Nueva España. By creating an impenetrable barrier between the Apache and themselves, the Spanish hoped to wage a "defensive war" that had "as its object the prevention of entry of the enemy into the interior of the provinces."[15]

Yet neither of these solutions—the employment of Indian auxiliaries and the creation of a chain of presidios—halted Apache attacks, while both posed new problems for Spanish colonial rule. Many Pimas interpreted Spain's reliance on them to fight groups such as the Apache as a sign of the Crown's military weakness, persuading the O'odham leader Luis Oacpicagigua—"the traitor Luis" to early Spanish chroniclers—that his effort to expel the Spanish from Pimería Alta in 1751 would meet limited resistance. The presidio system not only proved expensive to maintain; mobile Apache raiders found it easy to bypass the fixed forts and raid deep into Sonora. What was supposed to be an impenetrable wall turned out, in fact, to be a scattering of disconnected outposts.[16]

The years after the 1772 reforms thus witnessed, if anything, an expansion in conflicts with the Apache. "Sonora [is] submerged in Apache hostilities," reported a frustrated de Croix in 1781. The following year, a force of Apaches that Spanish witnesses placed at six hundred launched an unprecedented assault on Tucson—established in 1776 as Sonora's northernmost presidio—temporarily occupying several houses within the fort's adobe walls. In a second raid a few months later, Apaches ran off all the fort's livestock. Setting off in pursuit, troops managed to recover some of the animals and to kill several Apaches. "The soldiers cut off seven of their heads, as is our custom," related the presidio's commander, Pedro Allande y Saavedra. These gory trophies Allande added to the "[l]ines of countless Apache heads [that] have crowned the palisade" surrounding Tucson.[17]

Those Apaches who escaped being transformed into disembodied heads atop a presidio wall were often incorporated into the Spaniards' thriving captive trade. This fate was most commonly reserved for Apache infants seized during the Crown's military campaigns ("[a]s a general point," instructed one commander, quarter was only to "be given to children who are not older than seven years") and for the women and youths ransomed from the Pima and other indigenous allies.[18] So regular did this trade with the Pima become that much of it took place at, in the words of one Tucson resident, a yearly "festival" especially for this purpose, attended by many of the *vecinos* (residents) of the nearby presidios of Tucson, Santa Cruz, and San Ignacio. Observed Friar Diego Bringas in 1796:

As a result of the frequent campaigns they carry out against Apaches, the Gileño Pimas take their captives, both women and children, to the

pueblo of Tucson. There they turn them over to the Indians and inhabitants at low prices. These captives are then taught the catechism and
serve to increase the population of the pueblo.

Since the justification for holding such prisoners was to Christianize and civilize them—and also, in Bringas's view, to prevent, in the name of "religion
and humanity," the loss of the souls of the Apache women, who would otherwise be killed by their Pima captors—the prevailing term for these captives
was *criado*, from the Spanish verb *criar*, to raise. These captives, in the words
of one observer, "form[ed] Sonora's servant class." Unlike servants, however,
criados could be sold from one settler to another, and they were often expected
to render lifetime service to their new families.[19]

Although frowned upon by the Crown, the Sonoran trade in *criados* was
extensive. In December of 1753 alone, the priest Ignacio Xavier Keller of
Guevavi mission baptized twenty-eight Indian children presented to him
by Spanish settlers. One of these, a young *"apachito"* whom Keller christened
Xavier, was purchased by Captain Don Juan Tomás de Beldarrain, captain of
the new presidio of Tubac. During the next few years, Beldarrain would add
three more Indian captives to his household as servants for his wife and growing family. The 1798 census of the Sonoran town of Arizpe recorded a similarly large number of captives among the upper reaches of colonial society. Of
the fifty-two Apache children and young adults in the community, almost all
were servants in households the census takers identified as "Spanish."[20]

Criados and their offspring were incorporated into Sonoran society through
the unique category of *nixoras*, a term that indicated a detribalized Indian.
Over time, many *nixoras* blended into the larger Spanish community, adding a
new layer of complexity to a welter of ethnic classifications already struggling
to convey the realities of Sonora's shifting demographics.[21]

If the *criado* program imparted Spanish "civilization" to individual
Apaches, it also incited fresh waves of violence. Not only did *criados'* value as
trade goods provide the Pima and Papagoes with an extra incentive to attack
the Apache; the holding of their people as captives caused the Apaches to seize
prisoners of their own whom they could then use to ransom their captured
kin. Whenever Apaches learned of family members seized by Spanish soldiers,
explained Padre Pfefferkorn,

they [the Apache] assemble their Christian prisoners, Spanish or Indian, go with them to the nearest Spanish garrison and establish themselves peaceably not far off. . . . After the Indians have made known their arrival to the Spanish captain and have offered to exchange prisoners, all Apaches who are in Spanish custody are assembled with the exception of children, who are intended for instruction in Christianity and for baptism. Then the exchange is made by mutual agreement.[22]

I N 1786, recognizing that the Crown could claim few lasting victories against the Apache despite almost a century of bitter warfare, the recently appointed viceroy for the northern frontier, Bernardo de Gálvez, adopted a pacification plan based in part on Spanish imperial policies in North Africa. Arguing that "[p]eace is founded, as everything else, on private interests," Gálvez—whose own experience with the Apache included being wounded while leading an attack on them along the Gila River in 1771—proposed that the Crown bestow weekly rations of grain, meat, *piloncillo* (brown sugar), tobacco, and other goods to Apaches who settled peaceably near Spanish presidios. In exchange, these Apaches would be expected to serve as auxiliaries against hostile Indian groups. While this program did not portend the complete subjugation of the Apache that most Spanish officials longed for—"[i]n the voluntary or forced submission of the Apaches, or in their total extermination," opined the viceroy, "lies the happiness of the Provincias Internas"—it did promise to reduce the violence of recent years to a more tolerable level: "[A] bad peace with all the tribes which ask for it would be more fruitful than the gains of a successful war."[23]

The Apaches who accepted such arrangements and settled near the presidios along Spain's northern frontier came to be known as *apaches de paz* (peace Apaches) and their camps *establecimientos de paz* (peace establishments). But Gálvez's program was not one of total pacifism. Patrols from the presidios—now guided by *apaches de paz*—continued to set out on campaigns against those bands that, through their failure to settle in *establecimientos de paz*, were now categorized as hostile. "War must be waged without intermission in all of the provinces . . . against the Apaches who have declared it," insisted the viceroy. The objective of such attacks was either to destroy these bands or to drive them to the far side of the presidio barrier that constituted Nueva España's northern limit. Captured Apaches were to be exiled from the region. At first, captives were marched in chains to México City. But after a number escaped and, in the face of incredible odds, made the perilous 1,500-mile journey back to their homelands, the Crown adopted the policy of shipping all Apache captives across the Caribbean to the sugar plantations of Cuba.[24]

Gálvez's reforms witnessed the settlement of large numbers of Apaches in *establecimientos de paz*. By 1793, royal censuses revealed 1,995 Apaches living at various settlements in the far north, a number that increased over time, as new bands entered into agreements with Spanish villages. To some, the military-run *establecimientos de paz* with their regular gifts of grain, meat, cigarettes, and *piloncillo* represented a sad departure from the lofty goals of the missions. Rather than civilizing the Indians as the Jesuits and Franciscans had done, the military, it seemed, encouraged a degrading idleness. "Drunkenness, tobacco, and cards were the gods of the *apaches de paz*," lamented Ignacio Zuñiga of Tucson in 1835. Yet even Zuñiga had to acknowledge that the new policy had brought tranquillity to much of Sonora. The region from Janos to Tucson—in Zuñiga's words, "a bloody theater of war for a hundred years"—soon had more than "fifty *rancherías de paz*," and the countryside began once again to be filled with "*ranchos* and *haciendas* that offered the beautiful vision of peace and abundance." No longer exposed to constant Apache raids, Sonora's population rose, and *Sonorenses* accumulated enormous livestock holdings. By 1804, Tucson boasted some 1,000 inhabitants and a herd of 3,500 cattle, 2,500 sheep, and 1,200 horses grazing outside its presidio walls.[25]

To Zuñiga and others in Sonora, the *establecimientos de paz* era, which stretched from the early 1790s to the early 1830s, would soon come to be remembered as their province's golden age—an epoch marked by the founding of new towns and the reopening of mines and ranches that had been abandoned for over half a century. Whether this arrangement might have endured even longer remains an open question. Perhaps the benefits to *vecinos* and Apache alike would have been sufficient to overcome whatever obstacles might have arisen. Or perhaps the growth of Spanish herds and settlements, which impinged on many of the resources upon which Apache bands still relied, would have incited fresh conflicts at some future moment.[26]

In either case, this new dynamic never had a chance to play itself out. In

the opening years of the new century, some of the varied inhabitants of Nueva
España came to imagine a new identity for themselves, not as subjects of a
distant monarch but as *mexicanos*, citizens of an independent nation-state. The
ensuing rebellion engulfed Nueva España for more than a decade, prompting
Spanish commanders to withdraw troops from the far northern presidios—
among the best equipped in the colony—and to redirect funds from the *establecimientos de paz* to battling the insurgency.[27]

These changes ensured that upon gaining its independence in 1821, México
inherited little more than a hollowed-out version of Spain's northern defenses.
The republic nonetheless endeavored to continue the policies of its colonial
predecessors. The central government's first effort at constituting a military
policy for the far north—a set of regulations released in 1826—preserved the
main features of Spain's presidio system, and in 1834 México reissued Spain's
1772 regulations for the northern frontier verbatim, down to the royal signa-
ture, "*YO EL REY.*"[28]

The new nation's financial difficulties, however, left the already weakened
northern presidios chronically short of soldiers and supplies. By the late 1820s,
the once-generous rations issued to the *apaches de paz* had withered to little
more than a handful of corn or wheat, and in 1832 the governments of Sonora
and Chihuahua stopped distributing even these modest supplies. Mexican officials briefly entertained plans to turn the *apaches de paz* into "useful citizens"
by giving them individually owned plots of land. But with no such support
forthcoming, a large number of *apaches de paz* decided to leave the presidios
where, in some cases, they had been living for a generation. Many soon turned
to raiding to obtain the goods that *mexicanos* had once distributed to them.[29]

With the frontierwide administrative program that Spain had created for
the north in shambles, there emerged in its place a far more localistic arrangement distinguished by what observers at the time labeled "partial treaties of
peace." These tended to be agreements between specific Mexican communities and particular Apache bands in which each side pledged not to attack
the other, sometimes supplemented by the distribution of rations or gifts
to the Apaches involved. Such pacts proved to be of varying endurance. In
Tucson, a significant number of Apaches—now termed *apaches mansos* (tame
Apaches)—remained throughout the Mexican period, with a July 1835 census
revealing 486 *apaches mansos* dwelling in the town, a total not much less than

the village's *vecino* population. In many cases, however, the dominant feature of such truces was short-term expediency. When a group of *vecinos* clashed with some Apaches outside of the presidio of Janos in 1848, for example, the two sides soon opted for a less violent, albeit temporary, solution: "[B]y mutual consent [they both] fell back: a treaty was immediately entered into by the alcalde of Janos, on the part of the inhabitants thereof, and the Apache chief, for *six months.*"[30]

Such partial peace agreements did not so much reduce violence as displace it. Having made peace with an Apache band, it was not uncommon for a Mexican village to undertake a thriving trade with their new associates in goods seized from other settlements. "[W]hat was stolen from one Mexican found ready sale to another," noted an observer, "the plunder from Sonora finding its way into the hands of the settlers of Chihuahua, or . . . selling without trouble to the Mexicans living along the Rio Grande." In 1840, a large pack train left the New Mexican capital laden with whiskey, arms, and other goods to trade with Apaches for booty seized in raids on the neighboring provinces of Sonora and Chihuahua. "This traffic was not only tolerated but openly encouraged by the civil authorities," commented one onlooker. "[T]he highest public functionaries were interested in its success—the governor himself not excepted."[31]

"Partial peace" arrangements thus sowed the seeds of new conflicts. As certain pueblos acquired reputations as places where the Apache could "receive supplies of arms, ammunition, &c., for stolen mules," *vecinos* from other communities launched harsh counter-raids against them. In the 1840s and '50s, Sonoran militiamen, outraged that Chihuahuan border towns such as Janos, Corralitos, El Barranco, and Casa Grandes were trading with their resident *apaches mansos* for livestock and other goods stolen from Sonora, repeatedly invaded these villages. Their surprise raids inflicted devastating losses on Chihuahua's *apaches mansos.* In 1844, Sonoran troops destroyed three Apache encampments outside Janos, killing over eighty Apaches, including several children, whom they disposed of by "beating them against rocks." Seven years later, Sonoran soldiers occupied Janos itself for five days, during which time they slew twenty-one of the town's Apaches and captured some sixty women and children—many of whom they found only after searching the houses of Janos's residents, with whom the Apaches had taken refuge.[32]

To Mexican authorities, the troubles of their northern frontier were not only "sorrowful" for the border provinces but also "transcendent for the rest of the Republic." México's early sense of nationhood would be shaped by its fragile and frequently violated territorial integrity, of which the northern border was the leading exemplar. As a result, the woes of the *"frontera de la república"* filled pages upon pages of the annual reports from México's Office of War and Navy.[33]

The new nation found its northern border vulnerable not only to the raids of Apaches but also to an expansionist United States. México, as its secretary of state, Manuel María de Sandoval, put it, was "menaced . . . by two grave dangers: the invasions of adventurers and the depredations of barbarous tribes." Even worse, it seemed to many *mexicanos* that Americans and Apaches had merged into a single menace. As early as the 1820s, American traders had begun to enter illegally into northern México, offering arms, ammunition, and alcohol to the Apache in exchange for livestock and other goods stolen from Mexican pueblos. *Los americanos* precipitated, in the eyes of Sonorans, a rise in the frequency and lethality of Apache attacks.[34] Francisco Javier Vázques, the priest at Cieneguilla, told of encountering raiders "outfitted and armed with rifles that we know are supplied by the Anglos who have definitely been seen among the Apaches." Other *Sonorenses* detected a still more active alliance. On more than one occasion, military forces at Tucson discovered Indian trails in which, alongside Apache moccasin prints, there appeared the distinctive tracks of "new American shoes . . . readily distinguished . . . by their larger size and heels." To *Tucsonenses*, such prints proved that a combined raiding party of Apaches and Americans had passed through the presidio's outskirts.[35]

As much as México's government acknowledged its "sacred obligation . . . to protect its citizens from the hostilities of barbarians and to support them against the insults of one's neighbors," it lacked the resources to do so. In many of the republic's early years, in fact, its proposed military budget exceeded the nation's entire annual revenue. The central government experimented with transferring units of the National Guard to the northern frontier and transforming the former Spanish presidios into "military colonies." But in the absence of additional funds or manpower, none of these policies had much effect on the "cruel war devouring our border," and officials came to wax nostalgic for the Spanish presidial system.[36]

Yet even as México revisited Spanish colonial history in search of a model

Apache policy, memories of the *establecimientos de paz* proved remarkably perishable. Mexican officials instead distilled from the Spanish experience a different interpretation of the past altogether: the Apaches as irreconcilable opponents of settled society. "They [the Apaches] belong to that indigenous race that did not receive even one of those weak rays of light that existed in the continent before the conquest introduced European civilization," opined Secretary of State José María Tornel in 1844. "These tribes maintained with the Spanish a war of three hundred years duration, forever marked by deeds of horror and cruelty." Such a history, in which the Apache remained antithetical to "civilization," justified the harshest of tactics against them, with officials calling for the deployment of "the most serious and efficient means to exterminate these nomadic tribes."[37]

In the absence of a strong central government, however, implementing this or any other Apache policy increasingly fell to *Norteños* (Northern Mexicans). Sonora responded by expanding its militia system, which came to include all able-bodied men other than those able to pay a small fine to avoid service.[38] Building on this militarization of border life, in 1832, representatives from several pueblos on Sonora's far northern frontier, including Magdalena, San Xavier del Bac, Tumacácori, and Tucson, joined with the Pima leader Francisco Carros to form their own military organization, La Sección Patriótica (The Patriotic Section). Headed by Joaquín Vicente Elías, the scion of a prominent local family, La Sección Patriótica was designed to wage more aggressive campaigns against the Apache than the underfunded regular troops. In early June 1832, with close to two hundred volunteers, including thirty or so Pimas, Elías led an expedition from Tucson to Aravaipa, where the party surprised some of the former *apaches de paz* from Tucson and Santa Cruz who had settled in the canyon. In a four-hour fight, the Patriotic Section managed to kill over seventy Apaches and take thirteen children captive, while suffering only one casualty.[39]

Elías's triumph, soon memorialized in a *bando* (a government broadside designed to be read aloud in the region's scattered villages) entitled *"Triunfo sobre los apaches"* ("Triumph over the Apaches"), ignited a controversy along the northern frontier. No one questioned the ethics of killing a large number of onetime *apaches mansos* cornered in Aravaipa Canyon, distributing their children as *criados*, or executing adult captives. But there were concerns voiced about the wisdom of Elías's actions, which were seen in some border settlements as "exciting their [the Apaches'] revengeful temperament" and inevitably leading to Apache counter-raids. Custagio Martínez, San Ignacio's justice of the peace, pleaded with Sonora's governor for rifles and ammunition for his town's inhabitants, claiming "already we have them [the Apaches] in our homes."[40]

Given its limited success against the Apache, however, the Sonoran government soon turned to harsher tactics as well. In 1834, the state legislature issued its own appeal for volunteers and officially condoned the practice of allowing those who engaged in raids against *los apaches* to keep whatever goods they seized from them. The following year, in the name of "justice, humanity, and the inherent interest of self preservation," legislators passed a declaration of war against "the barbarian Apache" that imposed a further mix of obligations and incentives on all male *Sonorenses*. According to the decree, each district in the state was ordered to maintain a supply of weapons to be used against the Apache; those *vecinos* who were too poor to make contributions to these depots were also required to serve a fifteen-day stint in the military each month. In addition, as the Apaches were now considered "outside the law," the decree instituted what would become a common reward in Sonora and Chihuahua for much of the rest of the century: a cash bounty on all Apache scalps.[41]

This decree added a new volatility to the era's "partial peace" arrangements. Some of the Mexican towns and American traders who had in the past negotiated truces with local Apache bands now turned on their erstwhile allies, killing and scalping them during trading parleys in order to receive the new bounties. Across *la frontera*, hostilities with the Apache spiraled upwards. By 1841, Juan Nepomuceno Almonte, the Mexican minister of war and navy, could speak of the existence of a continual "state of war" along México's northern border in spite of all the "measures taken for the persecution and extermination of the barbarians."[42]

A S IF THE ESCALATING HOSTILITIES with the Apaches were not enough, for many years the beleaguered inhabitants of *la frontera* had foreseen that the tensions between their republic and the expansive nation to their north might well end in war. "In light of current events in Texas," opined

Rafael Elías González, Sonora's provisional governor, in 1837, "the United States of America has already as much as declared a state of war between our two nations." Yet when U.S. annexation of the rebel province of Texas resulted in war in 1846, the position of Sonora in the unfolding conflict was marked by deep ambivalence. Outraged that the central government had allowed the presidio system to collapse, the Sonoran government initially declined to contribute to the war effort. In December of 1846, for example, troops at Tucson offered no opposition to the American forces that passed through the presidio on their way to California. Sonorans justified such behavior by explaining that they needed to conserve their limited resources to fight the province's more pressing war with "the Apache barbarians." [43]

Given how much Americans and Apaches already overlapped in the minds of most *Sonorenses* as alien intruders, however, this proved to be the proverbial distinction without a difference. Only a few months after the uncontested passage of American forces through Tucson, Luis Redondo, then vice governor of Sonora, issued a number of *bandos* that merged the U.S. and Apache threats into a single, unified invasion. "[T]he enemy Apache, joined together with a considerable number of North Americans, have already penetrated to the outskirts of the presidio of Fronteras," declared Redondo, who called upon all Sonorans to expel the attackers and, by so doing, "be recorded in the annals of history." [44]

Other than the American column that passed through Tucson in 1846 and a U.S. Navy blockade of the port of Guaymas from 1847 to 1848, however, the war between México and the United States took place hundreds of miles to the south in central México. Not so the conflict with the Apache. By 1848 the raids sweeping across northern Sonora had become so intense that the inhabitants of Tubac, Fronteras, and Tumacácori abandoned their homes and relocated to the Tucson and Santa Cruz presidios, where slightly larger populations offered marginally more safety. This surrender of territory in the face of a northern invader was paralleled across the republic as a whole later that same year. With U.S. troops having seized its capital, México was forced to surrender some 500,000 square miles—almost half of its national domain—to end the hostilities. This event prompted an anguished outpouring of historical studies from elite *mexicanos* seeking to understand their nation's humiliation. As Antonio García Cubas remarked in 1847, "[O]ur history is written simply by saying that Mexico and the United States are neighbors. At least France and England are separated by the Channel; between our nation and our neighbor there exists no other border than a simple mathematical line. . . . God help the Republic!"[45]

For Sonorans, the Treaty of Guadalupe Hidalgo that concluded the war was notable principally for moving the international boundary south to the Gila River, sacrificing the upper portion of what in the colonial period had been the province of Sinaloa and Sonora. In actual terms, however, the loss of territory was less noticeable: the areas surrendered were all lands that, because of their proximity to the Apache, had long since slipped out of Sonoran control. Nevertheless, transforming the Gila into an international boundary had the unwelcome result of placing most of the region's Apache bands on the U.S. side of the border. This state of affairs complicated the already difficult process of controlling Apache raiding, transforming it overnight from a national into an international problem. Mexican negotiators had tried to address this eventuality by insisting in Article XI of the Treaty of Guadalupe Hidalgo that the United States restrain the Indians inhabiting its territory from raiding into northern México and that citizens of the United States be forbidden from purchasing goods stolen in México. Given the attractions that the trade in Mexican plunder held for *americanos* and Apaches alike, however, this provision turned out to be little more than an empty promise.[46]

If the Treaty of Guadalupe Hidalgo ended hostilities between México and the United States, it had much the opposite effect on the conflict between México and the Apaches. Raids on Sonora continued, and, if anything, the Apaches appeared bolder, knowing that they would be secure from Mexican retaliation once they made their way back across the border. In one single raid in January of 1849, according to Sonoran officials, the Apaches struck as far south as Ures, killing eighty-six persons. The following year, reported the Sonoran writer José Velasco, "more than ever the ferocity of these savages spread over the unfortunate Sonora." The Apaches burned haciendas, ran off livestock, attacked caravans bound for California, and carried women and children into captivity. When Mexican troops under Colonel Carasco undertook a retaliatory raid, the Apaches simply "withdrew to the other side of the dividing line."[47]

As Apaches ventured deeper and deeper into Sonora's fertile heartland, the flight of *vecinos* from outlying farms and mines continued apace, until much of the state was, from the Mexican perspective, *tierra de nadie* (no-man's-land). "What better testament [to Apache raids] than these deserted fields, sprinkled with blood?" lamented Velasco. "What better witnesses than these abandoned haciendas, ranches, and towns?" Tucson's once vast herds dwindled, until Teodoro Ramírez, the town's leading storekeeper, could report that sheep-herding had been abandoned altogether "because of the danger of the Apache enemy."[48]

Those settlements that remained adopted elaborate fortifications. Juan Téllez, whose family settled in Tucson in the early 1800s, recalled not only the twelve-foot-high adobe wall that encircled the village but also the consid-erable defenses that *Tucsonenses* constructed for their livestock: "[a]round the corral on the outside was a ditch deep enough that the cattle would not jump it should the fence be torn down. All of this was to make it as hard as pos-sible for the Indians to get the cattle." Some *vecinos* even went so far as to lock their animals inside their houses. Still, such measures only seemed to invite more intrusive Apache attacks. "There is so little stock left now in Sonora," noted one observer, "that the Indians are obliged to come to the very corrals in the towns to steal animals." Indeed, on more than one occasion, Apache raid-ers slipped surreptitiously into the walled town of Fronteras, which Mexican forces had reoccupied in 1850.[49]

What rendered such attacks all the more disquieting for Sonorans was the sense that the Apache had become a uniquely intimate enemy. Many Apache, after all, had lived amid the Mexicans of northern Sonora for decades during the *establecimientos de paz* era or inhabited Mexican villages for extensive peri-ods of time during various "partial peace" agreements.

Others could even be considered Mexican. A significant portion of the vari-ous bands raiding northern Sonora was composed of Mexican captives and their descendants, who had been adopted into Apache society. The seeming willingness of such individuals to attack their onetime relatives and neigh-bors may explain why the epithet that *vecinos* most frequently directed toward the Apaches at this time was "barbarians"—nomads who embodied the very opposite of the Catholicism and settled, agricultural life of *mexicano* civiliza-tion. Sonorans came to believe that the reason that *los apaches* could strike their villages so unexpectedly was because of the Indians' unnervingly detailed knowledge of *vecino* life. "At night some Apaches who spoke Spanish used to call out that the flood gates were open," recalled Carmen Reuteria Lucero of Tucson, "and when [the] farmers went out [the] Apache would kill them."[50]

The conflict with the Apache also shaped Sonoran folklore. Newcomers to the region found themselves subjected to "strange and terrible tales . . . of the daring forays made by the fierce and warlike Apaches of the mountains on the . . . inhabitants of the northern portion of Sonora." At local *bailes* (dances) the centerpiece was often a "peculiarly touching song in which men and women joined—whose burden was Indian atrocities and lamentation for the Mexican border people."[51]

Sonorans experienced a tandem geographic and demographic decline during the 1840s and '50s. Some of this population loss could be attributed to *vecinos* killed or captured in Apache raids, but most resulted from migration to other, more promising locales. When gold was discovered in California in 1848, scores of Sonorans—five to ten thousand according to various estimates—joined the rush to the former Mexican province of Alta California, hoping for wealth as well as relief from Apache attacks. Thanks to their proximity to California as well as their prior mining experience, Sonoran men and women quickly established themselves as prominent fixtures of the early rush—so much so, in fact, that one of the towns they settled came to be called Sonora after the new arrivals' home province.[52]

Sonoran success, however, stirred Anglo resentment. *Mexicano* forty-niners soon found themselves subjected to a variety of forms of harassment, ranging from vigilante attacks to the 1850 foreign miners' tax, which levied a monthly twenty-dollar fee on all non–U.S. citizens. Mexican disgust at this discrimination found voice in the stories that arose around a figure named Joaquín Murrieta. According to Mexican storytellers, Murrieta was a Sonoran who, together with his brother, Jesús Carrillo Murrieta, and wife, Rosa Felíz de Murrieta, went to California in 1849. Instead of finding peace and prosperity, however, Murrieta and his family were subjected to a series of outrages, culminating in the rape of his wife, the murder of his brother, and Joaquín's whipping at the hands of jealous American miners. In revenge, Murrieta robbed and killed *americanos* across California.

For Anglos, Murrieta came to represent the archetypical Mexican bandit, blamed for most any untoward happening in California during the Gold

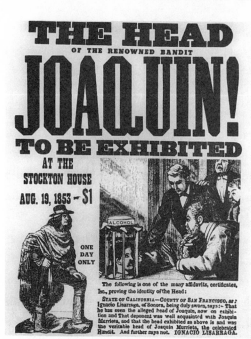

Rush. A posse ambushed a man they claimed was Murrieta in 1853, cutting off his head and the hand of one of his compatriots to exhibit throughout California as proof of their deaths. But for Sonorans, Murrieta served as a Robin Hood–type figure, restoring—in the symbolic world of folklore at least, for there is some doubt as to whether Joaquín ever really existed—Mexican honor in the face of American prejudice.[53]

It was against this background of Apache attacks and *americano* abuse that the border between Sonora and the United States moved yet again. As much as the on-again, off-again president of México, Antonio López de Santa Anna, had tried to forestall American demands for further territorial concessions, his need for funds to prop up his tottering government combined with the threat of another American invasion led him in 1853 to accept a proposal from the U.S. negotiator James Gadsden to sell a portion of his republic's northern territories. The *americanos* extended five options, including the purchase of all Sonora and Baja California. But Santa Anna, alert to the potentially explosive repercussions of any deal (indeed, he insisted that any treaty be negotiated in secret), opted for the most minimal, surrendering 30,000 square miles along the Gila River known as the La Mesilla Valley. This decision moved the border just below the town of Tubac, which a garrison of Mexican troops had reoccupied in 1852.[54]

Because the United States' failure to prevent Apache raids into northern México had proven a constant irritant to relations between the two countries, American negotiators also managed to secure their release from this commitment in exchange for the treaty's promised payment of ten million dollars to Santa Anna's cash-strapped government. Well aware that this agreement would leave several hundred of their citizens on the U.S. side of the redrawn border, Mexican officials insisted, as in the earlier Treaty of Guadalupe Hidalgo, that any new agreement grant these individuals "the enjoyment of all the rights of citizens of the United States," including religious freedom and the property they had possessed under Mexican law.[55]

If the tensions surrounding national expansion would soon trigger a civil war in the United States, the pressures of national contraction had a similar effect in México. The furor that greeted what *mexicanos* called the Treaty of La Mesilla crystallized outrage over the autocratic character of Santa Anna's rule, eventually leading to a civil war that consumed México from 1854 to 1861.[56]

Sonorans were spared the opening acts of this war, but resentment at the Treaty of La Mesilla was nonetheless widespread. Observers commented that passing Sonorans regularly defaced the monuments that U.S. and Mexican surveyors had erected to mark the new border between their two countries to manifest their dissatisfaction with the new treaty. "Very little of it [the border monument] now remains save an unshapely pile of stones," noted one. "Wandering bands of Sonoranians [*sic*], in their hatred of everything American, had doubtless mutilated it as an expression of national antipathy. These people say they never consented to the sale of any portion of Sonora, and still regard Arizona as legitimately part of their territory."[57]

For the six hundred or so residents of Tucson—the largest Mexican settlement affected by the new treaty—the coming of *americano* rule forced a decision between home and homeland. Did they feel a greater allegiance to the place where they and in many cases their parents and grandparents before them had spent much of their lives—the *patria chica* (small fatherland) of their home community? Or did they see themselves first and foremost as citizens of

México, in which case they might choose to remain within the bounds of their newly diminished native country by resettling elsewhere in Sonora?[58]

No doubt many residents felt the tug of both poles. José Velasco captured Sonorans' simultaneous affection for México and resentment at the central government's inability to protect them from Anglo and Apache attacks.

> Shall we not some time merit being considered an integral part of this great nation to which we belong? Is it possible that in the 19th century, in which man comes closer to the perfection of his inalienable rights under the auspices of the best of governments, that we continue to be treated with the abandonment and indifference that exists here? What fatal destiny has condemned us to suffer so much? Shall we in the end be the prey of barbarians, the disappearing Sonoran race?

ULTIMATELY, most *Tucsonenses* decided to stay. When Joaquín Comadurán withdrew his troops from the town in 1856 to a new post across the border in Imuris, Sonora, he was joined by only a handful of *Tucsonenses*, including the shopkeeper Ramírez, who, as a fluent speaker of the Piman language, was a frequent translator for the Mexican military.[59]

Despite the new flag flying over the plaza and the soldiers in unfamiliar uniforms roaming Tucson's streets, the shift in sovereignty brought but minimal changes at first. The newly created border was not surveyed for several years, and even once it was mapped, it remained little more than a series of stone monuments that exercised little control over the circulation of peoples and goods in the region. Even ardent nationalists such as Ramírez regularly journeyed back and forth across the border to visit familiars in Tucson and to check on their property in town.[60]

Local folklore contains numerous stories that emphasize the fluid, unmonitored character of this early border, perhaps none more revealing than the tale of a Mexican who discovered that the new border survey had bisected his lands, leaving part of them in México and part of them in the United States. "The [new border] line was marked at intervals by 'monuments' which were simply piles of stone," recalled a resident. "The Mexican naturally wanted all of his land in his own country but as he could not pick up that part of it which

BOUNDARY MONUMENT.

"Piles of stones": marker indicating the new United States–México border.

the line indicated was in the U.S. and move it over to Mexico, he did the next best thing by moving the line so that it ran along the northern boundary of his land. This was not a difficult thing to do. All that was necessary was to move the piles of stones from one place to another." [61]

This tale of a Mexican single-handedly moving the new international boundary encapsulated the odd contradiction of inhabiting a region where the border was simultaneously freighted with great symbolism yet physically insubstantial. Even though the Treaty of La Mesilla had detached northern Sonora politically from the rest of the Mexican republic, powerful social, cultural, and economic ties connected the two territories, blurring the boundaries between Arizona and Sonora, México and the United States. For many years following the Treaty of La Mesilla, for example, immigration into the region was more Mexican than American, as *Sonorenses* fleeing civil war and Apache raids sought refuge across the newly created border in the United States. Other new arrivals were not so new at all, having crossed the border years before. Several Sonorans who had settled in California during the early years of the

Gold Rush abandoned what had become an increasingly hostile state for Mexicans and, in a homecoming of sorts, established themselves in Arizona.[62]

Such migratory patterns meant that *americanos* were an overwhelming minority in the region throughout the nineteenth century. Of the 622 inhabitants of Tucson in 1860, for example, only 173 were Anglo or European. The other 449—seventy-two percent of the town's residents—were either from México, one of its former territories, or, in a few rare cases, elsewhere in Latin America. In Tubac, the demographic preponderance was even more pronounced. Of the 163 people living in the village in 1860, only twenty-five—fifteen percent—were of Anglo or European origin.[63]

This *vecino* demographic preponderance was paralleled across countless other facets of daily life in the territory. New arrivals noted that despite the change in sovereignty, "the Spanish language is more often spoken than the English." This state of affairs could be attributed not merely to the prevailing population, but also to the legacy of almost two centuries of Spanish colonialism and Mexican nationhood, which had rendered the Spanish language, as one American put it, "the universal medium of communication"—the single tongue the disparate inhabitants of the borderlands could rely upon when conducting trade or other negotiations among themselves. When *americano* newcomers and Indians whose ancestors had lived in the region for generations encountered one another in the mid-nineteenth century, they communicated in Spanish, despite the fact that it was not the first language for either group.[64]

Alongside the endurance of the Spanish language was the survival of many Mexican ways of organizing space and time. Well into the American period, Tucson continued to be oriented around a series of public squares that dated to the Spanish colonial era. La Plaza de las Armas, an open space that had been a central meeting place in the original walled presidio, remained in use through the early years of American rule. Likewise, with members of the Catholic clergy settling in Tucson for the first time since the Spanish era, the plaza abutting the church became an increasingly important site for public events, both planned and spontaneous. When a young *vecina*, Mercedes Días, was successfully redeemed from the Apaches in 1860, her return to Tucson became the occasion for a mass popular celebration in the plaza adjoining the church: "The church bells were rung, the populace assembled in the Plaza and the

little girl . . . passed from one to another to receive their embraces, congratu-
lations and welcome." [65]

Such plazas functioned not only as the physical center of Tucson, but as its
social and cultural centers as well. Perhaps at no time was this more apparent
than when the plaza served as the space where *Tucsonenses* celebrated the various
festivals that marked the passage of the Catholic calendar. On May 15, *vecinos*
took part in the Fiesta de San Isidro, the patron saint of farmers, asking him
to bless their crops. In late June came San Juan's Day, heralded by "a horseback
procession composed of both sexes of the Mexican population, . . . carnival
sports, and a grand baile or dance in the evening." On August 28, the residents enjoyed the high point of their year: the Fiesta de San Agustín, Tucson's
patron saint. During these celebrations, which often lasted a week or more,
members of the congregation marched around the plaza, led by a statue of the
saint "decorated in fine style with flowers," carried by four specially selected
townspeople, "together with the cross & lighted candles." [66]

Such festivals fulfilled worldly as well as spiritual needs. Since they gathered most of the local community together, Tucson's fiestas offered important
opportunities to trade as well as to partake in religious ritual. As a result,
they drew large numbers of Indians and Anglos, despite the sometimes tenuous connection of both groups to the Catholic faith. By the 1870s, it was not
uncommon for a thousand or more people to crowd into the plaza at the peak
of the Festival of San Agustín, passing time by gawking at the visitors from
outside of town, the stands with their fluttering flags of the United States
and México flying side by side, and the unusual foods being offered for sale:
"watermelons, pomegranates (grenadas) & peaches . . . [pies] made of jerked
beef & red pepper." [67]

Much of the trade carried out at such festivals continued to flow along the
same north-south axis that it had followed for more than a century. "[I]mmense
red wagons pulled by twelve-mule teams, and the still more numerous . . . ox
carts" would bring to Tucson imported luxuries from the Mexican port of Guaymas as well as "wheat, barley, corn, fruits, salt, coarse sugar, tobacco, cigars and
other products" from the rich farmlands along the Sonora River near Hermosillo.
More than a decade after the Treaty of La Mesilla, newcomers were struck by
how much Tucson remained a satellite of the Sonoran economy. Merchants often
set their prices in Mexican pesos rather than dollars, and Tucson's newspapers

American place, Mexican space: Tucson's Plaza de las Armas as it appeared in the 1880s.

featured stories well into the 1870s heralding the arrival of oranges, sugarcane, and other goods from Sonora, requests for "Sonora SEED WHEAT," and ads boasting "highest market prices paid for Arizona and Sonora produce."[68]

If the new international border did little to change these long-standing trade patterns, it nonetheless altered some of their meanings. The duties that the United States and México alike levied on goods such as alcohol and tobacco created an opening for those who knew how to slip "through the mountain passes" between the two nations, avoiding the newly erected customhouses on both sides of the new border. For many years, it was an open secret that "Tucson reaped a harvest from smuggling both ways, in buying and selling, which enriched the merchants who controlled that trade."[69]

To a considerable extent, these merchants, whether smugglers or legitimate businessmen—a distinction none too sharply drawn in the early years of the American occupation—remained *mexicanos*. "The contraband trade," observed the *Weekly Arizonan* in 1871, "is carried on by all nationalities, but chiefly by the Mexicans." Not only were *vecinos* far more likely, as longtime residents of the region, to have the intimate understanding of the local geography necessary

*The richest man in Tucson?:
Leopoldo Carrillo (center)
with sons Leopoldo Jr. (left)
and Luis (right).*

for successful freighting (including the knowledge of how to cross the border
surreptitiously if they so desired), they also possessed preexisting connections,
many based on family ties, with merchants in Guaymas, Hermosillo, and
other Mexican commercial hubs.[70]

The centrality of this trade with Sonora created a class of *vecino* entrepre-
neurs who remained crucial to the region's economy well after the assumption of American rule. The Tucson census of 1870 reveals that in addition
to the considerable portion of the Mexican population that made its living
through such transportation-based occupations as wagon master, teamster,
and wheelwright, there was a sizable cluster of *vecino* merchants and storekeep-
ers in town. These ranged from such relatively modest figures as Sacramento
Varela, a forty-year-old storeowner from Sonora worth $1,750, to community
leaders like Leopoldo Carrillo. Born in Moctezuma, Sonora, Carrillo settled in
Tucson in 1859, where he rapidly became a prominent freighter and landlord.
In 1870, he appeared in the census as a thirty-four-year-old retail merchant;
his $75,000 in property made him one of the wealthiest men in Tucson, Anglo
or Mexican, at the time.[71]

Tucson's merchant elite: Estevan Ochoa and his wife, Altagracia.

So well established were merchants such as Carrillo that those American newcomers who became involved in commerce typically opted to do so in partnership with Mexicans rather than attempt to compete with them. In the late 1850s, Estevan Ochoa, who had previously participated in the Santa Fé trade from his native province of Chihuahua, formed an enduring association with Pickney Randolph Tully, an *americano* who, like Ochoa, had recently moved to Tucson. Their joint firm of Tully & Ochoa freighted goods from Guaymas and Missouri to stores throughout Arizona, soon becoming the predominant mercantile house in the territory. By 1880, Tully & Ochoa, which had branched out into ore processing, sheep ranching, and blanket weaving, was the largest taxpayer in southern Arizona, with hundreds of employees and a capitalization of $100,000.[72]

Such *vecino-americano* partnerships also became a notable feature of a more intimate realm: the family. Unlike the members of the relatively gender-balanced Mexican community, the first Americans who made their way to Tucson in the years after 1853 were almost all male. The 1860 census records the presence of only eight Anglo-American women over the age of seventeen in the pueblo. In contrast, this same census tallied 122 men born in the eastern United States (two of them African American), thirty-one from various parts of Europe, three from Canada, and one from the East Indies. Even in 1870, at which point the population of Tucson had multiplied almost fivefold to 3,224 from just 622 a decade before, of the 1,304 women of marriageable age residing in the town, only twenty-two were not of Mexican descent—and of these, five were recently arrived nuns from Ireland and France.[73]

Given this unequal gender ratio, marriage between American men and Mexican women became an unavoidable fact of life in Tucson and Tubac. Unlike many other parts of the borderlands, where such couplings appear to have been an upper-class phenomenon, prompted by *americano* desires to marry into influential landholding families, in Arizona, where an entrenched class of large landholders was not a prominent feature of Mexican society, such unions cut across a variety of classes. Examples of *mexicanas* married to American partners thus ranged from the likes of Petra Santa Cruz, married to Hiram Stevens, a merchant worth $110,000 according to the 1870 census; to María, whose husband, James Lee, earned a comfortable living as the owner of a grain mill; to seventeen-year-old Ufemia from Sinaloa, married to George Tinker, a propertyless cook from New York; and Fermina, whose spouse, William Bailey, according to the census, was likewise without any real assets.[74]

If there was any consistency to intermarriage, it was that it typically featured a Mexican woman married to a much older American man. Among the thirty-five intermarriages in Tucson that appear in the 1870 federal census, the husbands were regularly a decade or so older than their wives. Sometimes, as in the case of Manuela, a seventeen-year-old from Sonora, married to Michael McKenna, a thirty-four-year-old clerk from Rhode Island, or Brijilda, a sixteen-year-old *Sonorensa* wed to D. C. Glasscock, a fifty-two-year-old physician from Virginia, the age difference was even more dramatic.[75]

For the women in such relationships, wedding an American man, for all its linguistic or cultural stresses, offered the opportunity to literally domesticate these new arrivals. Marriage linked Americans to specific *vecino* families, channeling whatever knowledge or capital the *americanos* possessed to one's immediate relatives. In addition, for *mexicanas*, the arrival of an enlarged pool of potential partners enabled them to strike a more advantageous bargain in the marriage market than they might have done otherwise, allowing them to

wed partners who were wealthier or socially better connected. The orphaned
Tucson native Atanacia Santa Cruz, for example, resolved what might have
been a difficult situation when, shortly before she turned fourteen in 1863, she
married the Welsh-born merchant Samuel Hughes, a well-to-do newcomer
twenty-one years her senior.[76]

On a more subtle level, *mexicanas* may have welcomed such unions because
they inhibited certain American critiques of *vecino* culture. Although Sonorans
in the 1850s occasionally used the term *blancos* (whites) to describe themselves,
this sense of whiteness derived in large part from Latin American notions of
race, in which one's racial category was as much a matter of social performance
as biology or skin color, and from Sonorans' position on México's outer frontier,
as *gente de razón* juxtaposed against an often hostile *gente sin razón*. Incoming
americanos, however, tended to think of race purely in terms of blood and other
physical phenomena, and so tended to emphasize what they perceived to be
Sonorans' mixed racial heritage.[77]

These competing definitions left early Arizona's *vecinos* in an uncertain position. Mexicans were listed as white on all the initial federal censuses and voted in the territory's first elections with little interference. But
at many moments they occupied what was at best a liminal racial category
between black and white—a status perhaps best suggested by the common
Anglo epithet of "greaser," with its connotations of indeterminate color. Marriage thus offered a vehicle for *mexicanas* to erode the divisions that some Americans sought to erect between themselves and the region's *vecinos*. The notion of
Mexican peoples as somehow "other" became harder to sustain, after all, if the
line between "Mexican" and "American" revealed itself to be capable of being
bridged within a single family—especially with the birth of children, whom
their Anglo fathers invariably expected to be received with the full privileges
of whiteness.

Yet if intermarriage fostered new connections, it also sowed ugly tensions as
americanos and *mexicanos* contended for the region's limited number of females.
"The Mexican women are far superior to the men and almost universally amiable and have pretty forms," related one *americano*. "Their kindliness of disposition greatly contrasts with the sour and suspicious glances of their treacherous
men." Mexican men for their part could not help noticing *americano* efforts to

Vecinas y extranjeros: *Petra* (left) *and Atanacia Santa Cruz* (right) *with their husbands, Hiram Stevens and Samuel Hughes.*

claim the fertility of Mexican women as if it were just another of the region's natural resources.[78]

The resentments this state of affairs encouraged could be volatile, especially when combined with the frictions generated by the American employment of Mexican men at wages well below those of their *americano* counterparts. In February of 1860, an American-run business, the Sonora Exploring and Mining Company, located outside of Tubac, witnessed the explosiveness of *americano*-ruled Arizona firsthand. To celebrate its new mill building, the company sponsored a *baile* to which it welcomed "large numbers" of the "gay señoritas of our vicinity." But when "several peons, partially intoxicated, undertook to engage in the dance," the American supervisors had the men "unceremoniously ejected." In revenge, one of the excluded Mexicans stabbed the first "white man" he saw, a German named Henry Alfeng, before fleeing across the border into Sonora.[79]

While the retreating worker left no statement behind to explain his actions, his behavior speaks volumes as to the strange new world that American annexation had created for *vecinos*. The United States had reordered the landscape by imposing a new international border. Yet this new boundary opened up new opportunities to the region's Mexicans who could, if they so desired, reinvent themselves as smugglers; it also provided a refuge for those, such as Alfeng's assailant, who sought to distance themselves from the American legal system. The shift in sovereignty had brought a foreign political order and foreign capital to the area. Yet Spanish remained the predominant language, and trade continued to flow south through Guaymas and Hermosillo, following the same paths that the escaping murderer no doubt used on his way out of Tubac. *Americanos* subjected many Mexicans, such as the fleeing mineworker, to the daily indignities of unequal wages and called into question their masculinity and racial status. And yet the newcomers also regularly married Mexican women and avidly sought to enter into business partnerships with elite *vecinos*. As the onetime colonists of Pimería Alta faced the reality of their colonization by their American neighbors, they had ample cause to ponder such developments—and to wonder what their place in the fracturing social geography of their former homeland might become.

A PARTIAL RESOLUTION to the dilemmas confronting the region's *vecinos* soon presented itself from an unexpected source. Initially, the treaties of Guadalupe Hidalgo and La Mesilla had projected most conflicts with the Apache south of the border onto Sonora. But once Americans transformed themselves from the occasional interlopers of the 1820s and '30s into the sovereign power of the 1850s and '60s, tensions between the new arrivals and their former Apache trade partners escalated. With what *Sonorenses* had not so long before considered a single, unified American-Apache threat eroding about them, a number of *vecinos* seized upon a valuable new role for themselves: military allies to their onetime *americano* rivals.

As newcomers to the region, incoming U.S. Army officers quickly realized that "a guide acquainted with the country" was essential to any expedition against the Apache. From the very first U.S. military venture against the Apache—an 1857 campaign along the Gila—the army thus experimented with enlisting local Mexicans as "Guides and Spies" to catch their elusive prey, turning combinations of Mexican expertise and American military force into a defining feature of early Indian campaigns in U.S.-ruled Arizona.[80]

This budding military alliance offered *vecinos* multiple benefits. Perhaps most important, the connection of soldiering with citizenship reinforced *vecino* claims to full membership in American civil society. But in addition, participation on Indian campaigns countered the emasculating imagery that Anglo newcomers had projected onto *vecinos* by demonstrating the qualities—bravery, physical toughness, sacrifice for the well-being of the community—that *mexicanos* and *americanos* alike recognized as lying at the core of manliness.[81]

Military service, however, soon raised thorny new questions of nationalism for *vecinos*—both because of the competing pull between México and the United States and because of the growing antagonism between North and South. As their new homeland spiraled into civil war and Arizona's Anglo community ruptured along sectional lines, most *vecinos* attempted to dodge the vexing issue of national allegiance altogether. "[T]he Mexicans," observed John Baylor, a lieutenant colonel in the Confederate forces during his army's short-lived occupation of Arizona, "are much divided on the subject . . . of taking part in the war at all." Some *vecinos* were doubtless more invested in the politics surrounding the French invasion of México in 1862 than in the affairs of a nation that they had only recently come to inhabit. Others may have been reticent to adopt a position that might cast their already tenuous citizenship into further doubt.[82]

For *vecinos*, the other defining feature of the Civil War was the redeployment of the few U.S. Army forces in the region to the eastern seaboard, a situation that left Arizona's residents to face the Apache on their own. "[T]he Indians were robbing and stealing everything they could," recalled the Tucson rancher Juan Elías. "It was just a sort of civil war between us and the Indians." In this "sort of civil war," many *vecinos* proved willing to fight on either the Union or Confederate side, so long as their opponents remained constant: the Apache. In 1862, Baylor complimented the "many native-born citizens of Arizona and New Mexico" who assisted the southern forces in their campaigns against the Apache. The next year, Baylor's Union counterpart offered almost identical praise for the support that *vecinos* had lent his forces: "Many of them have been conspicuous for their courage, and all have shown a settled determination to assist the military in their efforts."[83]

Following the Union reoccupation of Arizona in 1862, the federal government institutionalized this civilian assistance by raising several companies of local troops, all of whom were assured that "they would be ordered against no enemy except the Apache." This was the first time the military had attempted to enlist *vecinos* as soldiers rather than scouts, and officers were overwhelmed by the enthusiastic response. One recruiter reported to his superiors that he had exceeded his enrollment quota by "a surplus of nearly fifty men." Ultimately, of the five militia units that the territory raised, three—Companies A, E, and F of the Arizona Volunteers—were "composed entirely of native born Arizonians (Mexicans)."[84]

Over the next few years, Companies A, E, and F would win a distinguished reputation for their actions against the Apaches. In February 1866, Manuel Gallegos, a onetime army captain in Sonora who was now the lieutenant of Company E, led a patrol that located a band of Apaches camped in some caves. Gallegos and his men surrounded the site during the night in an approach so silent that not even the Apaches' dogs detected their presence. As soon as daybreak offered enough light to see, the volunteers attacked. Within minutes, "[a]ll of the caves that were accessible were filled with dead and wounded [Apaches]." As evidence of their success, Gallegos's unit brought back to their camp thirteen Apache scalps, along with two women and ten children. A little over a month later, Gallegos's compatriot Primitivo Cervantes of Company A led an expedition that likewise encircled an Apache *ranchería* and surprised it at first light. In a "general and desperate" fight lasting twenty-five minutes, Cervantes and his men killed twenty-two Apaches and seized two prisoners.[85]

Gallegos's and Cervantes's expeditions were among the most successful Apache attacks in Arizona since American annexation. As news of the incidents made its way into the territory's newspapers, Gallegos, Cervantes, and their men found themselves lionized for "know[ing] how to hunt the Apache." Richard McCormick, the territory's acting governor, rewarded Gallego and the other men of Company E with extra rations of tobacco along with a letter lauding them "for the severe blow you have dealt to our common and

*"A sort of Civil War between us and
the Indians": Tucson rancher and
Indian fighter, Juan Elías.*

barbarous foe." "[T]hese native volunteers, . . . who are at home in the country," concluded McCormick, "are the men to hunt the Apache."[86]

Vecinos' official role as troops ended in 1867, when the War Department
declined to renew the authorization that had created the Arizona Volunteers.
But Mexicans continued to serve on campaigns against the Apache in a variety
of ad hoc ways that blended *vecino* and American practices. The ambiguous
character of these expeditions, in which *vecinos* were sometimes the primary
instigators and on other occasions facilitated Anglo attacks, is encapsulated in
the careers of the brothers Juan Elías and Jesús María Elías.

The Elíases were members of a family that had long enjoyed a position of
prominence in northern Sonora, much of it derived through military service
against the Apache. The family traced its lineage to a Spaniard named Francisco Elías González de Zayas, who immigrated to Sonora in the 1720s. Not long
after his arrival, Elías González accepted a commission in the Spanish army,
serving first at the Janos presidio and then as the commander of the Terrante

presidio until his retirement in 1770. Many of his male descendants continued this tradition of military service, with members of the Elías family appearing as soldiers and officers at the Tucson, Tubac, and Santa Cruz presidios during the Spanish and Mexican periods (and even, as the career of Joaquín Vicente Elías demonstrates, as leader of the short-lived Sección Patriótica). After Mexican independence, several members of the family used their positions to secure extensive land grants on former mission lands outside Tubac, where they ran cattle herds that reportedly numbered into the thousands.[87]

Juan and Jesús María Elías had both been born in Tubac in the opening decades of the nineteenth century. By the time of American annexation, however, they had relocated to Tucson, where their father, a former soldier in the town's presidio, was serving as the village's *alcalde* (mayor). During his youth, Juan worked for his father until he reached the age of eighteen in 1856, at which point he began to farm on his own, "[p]lanting corn, beans, wheat and barley" and raising cattle, following the path pursued by his older brother Jesús María, eleven years his senior and a prominent rancher who would represent Tucson in Arizona's first Legislative Assembly.[88]

Juan's and Jesús's childhoods coincided with the collapse of the *establecimientos de paz*. Confrontations between *vecinos* and Apaches thus constituted some of their earliest memories. As Jesús put it, "they [the Apache] had been fighting [my] father and robbing his cattle and killing my people ever since I can remember." For his part, Juan's "first recollection" was the day he learned that a large band of Apaches had ambushed twenty soldiers and citizens from Tucson in some nearby mountains, killing all the *Tucsonenses* after they ran out of ammunition. In 1850 and again in 1851, Juan would witness such conflicts firsthand when the Apache attacked Tucson itself, slaying several of its residents and driving away much of its livestock. In 1853, Apache violence would again touch Juan and Jesús's family: the boys' uncle, José M. Orosco, would be slain while attempting to defend a ranch in Calabasas from a raid led by what those in Tucson insisted was a combined party of Apaches and *americanos*.[89]

Juan's own difficulties with *los apaches* commenced once he began ranching in the late 1850s. By 1858, he owned about two hundred cattle, which he kept in an area known as Silver Lake about two miles south of Tucson.

Because of the risk of Apache raids, he employed several men to watch over the animals and took the additional precaution of corralling his livestock at night. One afternoon, as he was riding out to check on his cattle, he encountered one of his herders walking toward Tucson to report that a band of Apaches had taken most of Elías's animals, except the forty or so calves penned in the corral.

Juan raced back to Tucson to gather help. Although he was only twenty years old, there were, he noted, many "old and practical men" with experience "following Indians" in the village. With their assistance, he and nine other *vecinos* tracked the retreating Apache raiders all night out beyond the San Pedro River. Eventually, running short of supplies and far from any other settlements, Elías's party called off their pursuit. "[We] never got sight of them: just saw their fires and saw the fresh meat where they had been eating it. We ate some of the meat that they left because we had no food with us."[90]

It was after this raid, in which he lost a majority of his livestock, that Juan killed his first Indian. In February 1859, Juan joined the pursuit of some Apaches who ran off the cattle of the *vecino* Guillermo Estillas. "I started with some eight or ten men," he recalled, "and followed them [the Apache] and killed two of them." Juan did not elaborate on what meanings the taking of these men's lives might have possessed in nineteenth-century Tucson, but it was clearly a pivotal event for him, as he later identified 1859 as the date when he started "fighting the Indians." The sense of empowerment and personal honor that this act of violence represented may explain why, a few months later, Elías shot an *americano* named Samuel Wise in the stomach after the two quarreled over the ownership of a cow near San Xavier del Bac. Elías was apparently never charged with any crime in the incident. If so, the shooting's uneventful resolution must have reinforced the perception on his part that *americanos* and Apaches alike only respected one's person and property when compelled to do so through the fear of forceful retribution.[91]

Whatever reputation Juan may have begun to enjoy as a man unafraid to inflict violence on his opponents, it did little to slow the pace of Apache depredations. Throughout the 1860s, Indian incursions repeatedly struck Elías's herds. The next attack came in December of 1860, when, together with several of his family members, Juan was planting wheat on one of his father's fields along the Santa Cruz River with several yoke of oxen. Around sunset, he instructed his younger brother Tomás to drive the animals to a nearby hill to graze. The following morning, when Tomás went out to collect the animals, he could not find them. Scouting the vicinity, Juan cut the tracks of an Apache raiding party. Gathering together several of his brothers and other *vecinos*, Juan pursued the Indians, who had taken six yoke of his cattle, all the way "to the edge of the Gila River," before he abandoned the chase. Afterwards, with no oxen of his own left, Juan "had to hire oxen to finish planting my crop."[92]

As the Civil War removed what little military protection had existed in the territory, the tempo of Apache raids quickened. In November 1861, Juan's brother Ramón was killed while on an expedition to recapture some cattle from the Indians. It fell to Juan and Jesús, both of whom had been out of Tucson at the time, to recover their brother's corpse. When they finally located Ramón's remains in the Tortolita (Turtle Dove) Mountains north of Tucson, they discovered that the Apache had crushed Ramón's hands with rocks, which the brothers interpreted as "a sign that he was a brave enemy."[93]

A little over a year later, in three raids spread across February, March, and April of 1863, Apaches absconded with almost 325 of Juan's remaining cattle, which he had purchased not long before from a rancho in California in an attempt to restock his herds. In the inevitable pursuit following the last of these raids, Elías's party caught up at nightfall with six mounted Apaches near the San Pedro River. These Indians had remained behind to slow their pursuers, hoping to enable the others in their band to drive the livestock north toward Aravaipa Canyon. "We attacked those Indians that night," recalled Juan. In the course of the ensuing skirmish, however, Elías's brother Cornelio was mortally wounded when an Apache shot him in the head.[94]

Perhaps because of Cornelio's death or perhaps because of the growing frequency of Apache attacks, shortly after this incident Juan and his brother Jesús managed to orchestrate an unusually large retaliatory strike on the Apache. The group was composed not simply of the usual *vecino* volunteers along with some Anglos and Papagos, but contained twenty-five soldiers of the recently returned U.S. Army under the command of Captain T. T. Tidball. Juan's brother Jesús helped guide the party, which over the course of five days surreptitiously made its way toward Aravaipa Canyon. Traveling at night, hiding during the daylight hours, and never lighting a fire or breaking silence, the attackers surprised the Apache band living in Aravaipa Canyon at daybreak, killing sixty or so and taking another ten captive. So unexpected was the attack that the party suffered only one casualty, an American civilian. The raiders seized sixty-six head of cattle from the Apache, some bearing Juan's distinctive ear notch. But few of these animals made it back to Juan's possession. As Jesús Nuñez, one of the *vecinos* on the expedition, remembered, some were butchered to provide food for the hungry raiders, while the rest "were distributed around amongst all the volunteers who started out."[95]

As this sharing of recaptured livestock in keeping with Mexican custom illustrates, the expedition to the Aravaipa Canyon folded the U.S. Army into a *vecino* pattern of vengeance as much as it enlisted Mexican civilians in support of a military campaign against the Apache. These overlapping agendas generated more than a little confusion among its participants as to who was the raid's true leader. Juan remembered that "[t]he expedition was under the command of my brother, Jesús M. Elías," while the brothers' niece, Amelia Elías (Cornelio's daughter), later offered what was doubtless the prevailing *vecino* perception of the Elías family: "All of my uncles were Indian fighters but my uncle, Jesús María Elías, was the boss of all the wars." Military records, however, indicate that the army placed Captain Tidball in charge of the expedition. "Jesus Maria Elias will have charge of the Mexicans," Tidball's commanding officer instructed him. "All will be strictly under your orders."

The point of such discrepancies is not that the Elías family later claimed a larger role for Jesús than the documentary record supports. Memory can be malleable—but so too can written records fail to capture lived reality. As a relative newcomer to the region, Tidball must have relied on the expertise of Jesús Elías, both to rally *vecino* volunteers (of which there were thirty-two, more than the army's contribution of twenty-five troops) and to reach the distant Aravaipa Canyon undetected by the Apache. Little surprise, then, if in the eyes of many participants, Jesús was more the group's leader than the officer the U.S. Army placed in command of the raid.[96]

The attack in Aravaipa Canyon represented one of the more dramatic victories over the Apache in the 1860s, both in terms of the number of Indians slain and the surreptitious incursion deep into Apache territory. Indeed,

"The boss of all the wars":
Jesús María Elías.

for the region's newspapers, it was "the greatest threshing [the Apache] ever received." Like Gallegos and Cervantes a few years later, Juan and Jesús reaped tangible benefits from their violence against the Apache. In 1864, the territory's governor appointed Juan to Tucson's first town council, one of only a handful of political posts in Arizona occupied by a *vecino*. A few years later, Jesús achieved political success of his own, being voted once again to represent Tucson in Arizona's Legislative Assembly. At much the same time, he secured a position with the U.S. Army as a guide, cementing his reputation as one of the most skilled Indian-fighters in the territory.[97]

Jesús's service as a guide underscores the peculiarly intimate character of the conflict between Arizona's *vecinos* and Apaches. What made a scout like Jesús useful to Americans, after all, was his ability to translate even the faintest traces left by the Apache. "There is no Yaqui or no Papago, or any other Indian, that uses the same class of moccasin, or that can make the style or class of moccasin that an Apache does," noted Jesús, explaining how he distinguished Apache footprints from those of other inhabitants of the borderlands. "They make a very narrow long slim moccasin, and draw it up here at the toe to a very fine point, and then they have a toe-piece that turns up. . . . [T]hey put on sort of what we would call a half-sole—not a full sole either, but a piece." Jesús could also read the larger messages that tracks offered a skilled observer: time of creation, speed of travel, the maker's intentions. "By their manner of procedure and the manner of their trail and everything[,] I could tell even if they were bare-footed if they were Apaches or not."[98]

In addition to his tracking ability, Elías possessed a knowledge of Apache culture far beyond that of most *americanos*. Over years of contact with Apache peoples, Jesús had come to comprehend a great deal of their language and something of their band structure. "If an [Apache] Indian is to speak to me in Indian I can understand and can judge more or less what tribe of Indian he is. . . . [T]he [Apache] language is the same but the manner of pronouncing it is different—the dialect is different." Some of this information Jesús had acquired as a participant in *vecino* raids against the Apache and as a guide for the army. But much of it may have come from a source closer to home.[99]

Throughout much of the 1850s and '60s, Jesús's household included an Apache *criado* named José, captured as a child during one of the Elíases' attacks on the Indians. José, who took the Elías surname as his own, lived with the Elíases for five or six years until he was a teenager. According to family lore, José passed away unexpectedly of a fever contracted when he and Jesús were out cutting lumber in the Santa Rita Mountains near Tubac and was buried where he died. But other *vecinos* maintained that José had, in fact, escaped back to his people, and indeed an Apache band led by a man bearing the name José María Elías would trouble Mexicans on both sides of the border well into the 1880s.[100]

Whatever records once documented José's interactions with Jesús are now lost to time. Based on accounts of other Apache captives held by *mexicano* families, however, we know that such individuals provided an unusually personal window onto Apache culture, often instructing their captors in whatever language and customs they remembered. So even though Mexicans, like the Spanish before them, justified taking Indian children as captives as part of their mission to Christianize and civilize "barbarous savages," it may have been, in fact, José who instructed Jesús, teaching him his people's words and practices. One cannot help but wonder how Jesús negotiated the emotions involved in incorporating an Apache into his family while at the same time using the information he gleaned from José to lead further attacks against his new kinsman's relatives and former band members. How did the "boss of all the wars" respond to José's death or his flight back to the Apaches after so many years in Jesús's household?[101]

The unusually intimate conflict between Arizona's Apaches and *vecinos* also exhibited itself in a series of incidents that Juan and Jesús experienced in 1867. At the time, Jesús was employed by the U.S. Army as a guide at Camp Grant, a military installation located at the intersection of the San Pedro River and Aravaipa Canyon. Hoping to tap the rich agricultural land along the San Pedro River that had long lain fallow because of Apache attacks, the Elías brothers began with the help of several hired hands to plant barley and other crops at a site three miles south of the fort. They were soon joined by an elderly Apache man, who, having been captured by the army some time before, was being held at Camp Grant but wanted to move to the Elíases' plot and "plant a little corn and pumpkins." In late May, after living with them for a short while, the Apache joined three of the Elíases' hands for a trip into Tucson.

What happened next is subject to dispute. On their way to Tucson, the travelers were ambushed at the Cañada del Oro (Gold Gorge) by a band of Apaches; the three *vecinos* were slain while the Apache man escaped unharmed back to the Elíases' farm. Seeing that the Apache man seemed "scared and excited," the brothers suspected that he had been in surreptitious contact with other Apache bands, and Jesús escorted him to Camp Grant.

That same night, the Elíases' San Pedro farm experienced an unusual Apache raid. Jesús had the habit of sleeping outside on a wooden cot during the warm summer months. Spying the bed in its accustomed spot, an Apache crept close under the cover of darkness and fired a single shot into the cot's sleeping inhabitant. Jesús, given the danger that his scouting skills posed for the Apache, was doubtless the attack's target, but he was still at Camp Grant. Instead, the shot struck his brother Juan, who had borrowed the bed for the evening, on his lower neck and upper shoulder. Had his assailant been better armed, Juan's injury likely would have been fatal. But the Apache had fired a shotgun loaded with a makeshift ammunition made out of seeds from the mescal plant. Juan recovered, although he spent several weeks in the hospital at Camp Grant, picking the seeds out of his wounds, and carried a scar from the attack for the rest of his life.[102]

While Juan was in the hospital, the Apaches, perhaps having learned that their effort to kill Jesús had been unsuccessful, struck the Elías farm again. This time, Jesús, who was cutting brush at the edge of one of his fields, managed to secrete himself in the undergrowth once he realized what was taking place. From his hiding place, he caught a clear enough glimpse of the raiders to recognize that they were members of the bands led by the Apache chiefs "Eskimizen" and "Capitán Chiquito." "I know them, and I know even to what band they belonged," he recalled. "They belonged to Eskimizen's band—the Pinal mountains, and the Sierra Mescal—[Capitán] Chiquito." Although the Apache narrowly missed killing Jesús on this raid, they ran off almost all of the brothers' horses and killed one of the ranch's workers. "[H]e had formerly been a captive," remembered Juan. "[H]is name was Francisco."[103]

Even though it unfolded in the shadow of a recently constructed U.S. military installation, this conflict was not that dissimilar from those that had long taken place between *vecinos* and Apaches in the borderlands. Not only had the participants on both sides become familiar enough to recognize one another; a number of them had made journeys across the boundaries separating the two groups. In describing Francisco, the man who died at his farm, as a former captive, it is unclear whether Juan meant that Francisco was a Mexican who had been captured by the Apache and later returned to *vecino* society or whether Francisco was, like José, an Apache adopted as a young boy into a *vecino* household. In either case, it spoke volumes about the complex relationship between *vecinos* and Apaches that the only person to be killed in the Apache attack on the Elíases' farm was an individual who had spent a portion of his life living among the Apache as a member of one of their bands.

Ironically, the same close interactions with Apaches that made *vecino* scouts such as Jesús useful to incoming *americanos* also rendered them objects of suspicion. Throughout the 1860s and '70s, *americanos* voiced concerns about the unduly porous boundary between their *vecino* neighbors and the Apache. In 1862, the commander of the Union forces reoccupying the territory ordered his officers not to make news of a planned expedition against the Apache public, "so the Indians, through the Mexicans, may not know of your plans." A few years later, the *Arizona Miner* accused local Mexicans of "bandy[ing] words with the Apaches."[104]

Although such concerns were magnified by American anxieties over the biological links that Mexicans, as peoples possessing what *americanos* considered a mixed racial heritage, shared with the region's Indians, they were more than mere fantasies. At several times in the 1860s, the military chanced upon groups of *vecinos* who, in keeping with their policy of "partial peace," were illicitly trading *"rifles, powder, camps, blankets, hats,* etc." to local Apache bands. Such traders even went so far as to "fully inform the Apaches in reference to the movements of troops in the Territory," enabling them to evade army patrols.[105]

F ROM JUAN'S AND JESÚS'S PERSPECTIVE, the close of the Civil War brought but little change to the pattern of Indian hostilities. Thus, when a band of Apaches swooped down on Juan's herds outside of San Xavier del Bac on April 12, 1871, running off some fifty cattle, the brothers responded much as they had in the past. Tomás, the Elíases' youngest brother, discovered the loss of the animals near daybreak. After sending word to Juan in Tucson, he promptly set out with another *mexicano* to trail the fleeing raiders. His brothers soon joined him, along with several *vecinos* and an *americano* named William Zeckendorf. The party pursued the Apaches for over forty miles as the raiders drove the cattle north. The trails "were very bad," Juan recalled, and to prevent any animals that lagged behind from falling into the hands of their pursuers, the Apache shot or lanced them, until scores of dead animals lined the path.[106]

Despite such distractions, the Elías party slowly closed on the raiders. "They [the Apaches] were traveling very rapidly; we could see them. . . . It was about sundown when we overtook them. We had been riding all day and they were getting down towards the San Pedro River." In the ensuing fight, the pursuers managed to kill one of the Apaches and seize their horses, along with five or so of the remaining cattle from Juan's herd. One of the *vecinos* in the party, Jesús María Mangia, scalped the fallen Indian and presented the grisly trophy to Zeckendorf, the lone *americano* in their midst.[107]

The party's reprisal against the Apache might have ended at this point. After all, compared to many of the other pursuits of the Apache in which Juan and his brothers had participated, this one could be considered among the more successful. Rather than the pursuers having to abandon their mission because of a lack of supplies, an uncertain trail, or injury to one of their party, the *vecinos* managed not only to recapture some of their livestock, but also to take a number of the Apaches' animals and enact a measure of vengeance by slaying one of the raiders and lifting his scalp.

Yet this particular incident instead precipitated a far larger and more aggressive attack on the Apache. Although the Indian the pursuers killed "said nothing, but merely screamed," according to Rais Mendoza, one of the *vecinos* on the chase, some in the party became convinced that they recognized him because of a missing front tooth as a member of Eskimizen's and Capitán Chiquito's band, the same group that had carried out the attack on Jésus's and Juan's farm in 1867. Ordinarily, such knowledge would have been of only limited utility, since locating the offending Apaches in the region's rugged mountains could be a next-to-impossible task, even for an experienced tracker like Jesús. At the moment, however, it was common knowledge that both chiefs and their followers were gathered in Aravaipa Canyon, where they were drawing rations from the U.S. Army as part of a truce agreement worked out with Camp Grant's commanding officer some months previous.[108]

In much the same way that *vecinos* had not always seen themselves as parties to the arrangements worked out between particular Mexican towns or provinces and the Apache during the era of "partial peace," the Elíases and many of the other *vecinos* living in Tucson and San Xavier del Bac apparently exhibited little sense of being governed by the negotiations between the U.S. Army and the Apache at Camp Grant. Over the next two weeks, the Elías brothers collected thirty or so *vecinos* for an attack on the Apaches camped in Aravaipa. In many respects, the raid differed little from the one that Jesús had helped guide to the very same canyon to such acclaim in 1863. The U.S. Army would not, of course, be participating in the mission, but a large number of Papagoes agreed to take part, as did a handful of *americanos*.

Members of this latter group had already been meeting for several weeks in an effort to organize some sort of civilian campaign against the Indians. But according to an *americano* participant in the attack, for all the Americans' professed desire to exterminate local Apaches, no concrete plan of action emerged until Jesús Elías proposed a mission against the bands camped in Aravaipa Canyon. Although it may be that Tucson's *americanos* were retroactively trying to attach the blame for what would become a controversial undertaking onto the village's *vecinos*, it is also true that Juan and Jesús were far more accustomed to organizing raids against the Apache than almost any American in the territory; they may have also sought revenge against Eskimizen and Capitán Chiquito for Juan's near-fatal shooting in 1867.[109]

What appears most noteworthy about the intended raid, in short, is how much it fell within the established pattern of *vecino* attacks upon the Apache. In this respect, the Camp Grant Massacre bears many of the hallmarks of what scholars have identified in modern-day episodes of ethnic conflict. Far from being spontaneous and unplanned, such outbreaks of violence often tend to follow a recognizable, almost ritualized script—to demonstrate, in the words of Donald Horowitz, a leading student of such incidents, a sort of "lucid madness" rather than a "blind fury."[110]

After slipping out of Tucson on the chosen date—April 28—in small groups to avoid alerting the U.S. Army forces stationed near town to their plans, the attackers gathered on the Pantano (Marsh) Wash near Tanque Verde (Green Tank), where Juan and several other *vecinos* had ranches. Once assembled, the attackers held a brief discussion in Spanish, the one language common to members of all three ethnic groups involved, and reportedly voted Jesús the group's overall leader. Over the next two days, as he had done so often before on other raids, Jesús guided the party toward the Apache, selecting the little-used Cabadilla Pass so that they could approach their target unseen. Shortly before daybreak on April 29, the attackers hid themselves near the San Pedro River, only moving out once darkness could obscure the dust that such a sizable party would raise. Despite some momentary confusion when the attackers realized that they needed to cover thirty miles to reach Camp Grant, not the sixteen Jesús had initially expected, they pressed on through the night, nearing Aravaipa Canyon shortly before dawn.[111]

As the first glimmers of sunlight began to spread their glow over the nearby mountains, the party descended upon the Apache shelters along the banks of Aravaipa Creek. In a lifetime of violence against the Apache, the next few minutes would constitute the single most devastating attack in which Jesús or Juan ever participated.

THE AMERICANS

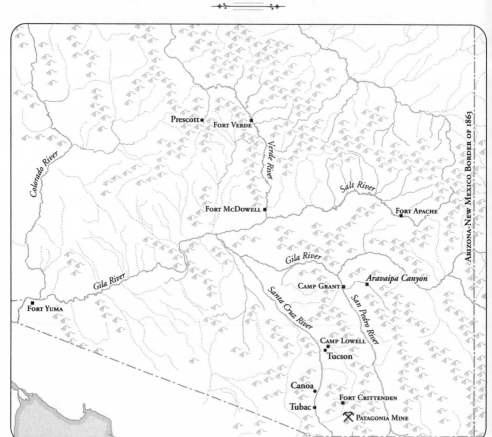

© 2008 Jeffrey L. Ward

THE AMERICANS

IF HISTORY CONFINED ITSELF neatly to national borders, the American version of our story would not begin until April 25, 1854. On this date, the U.S. Senate ratified what it termed the Gadsden Treaty, transferring some 30,000 square miles of Sonora to the United States in what turned out to be the last adjustment of the United States' continental boundaries after a half century of breathless expansion. Selecting a single moment in this way, however, lends a misleading precision to a far longer and messier set of interactions between those who called themselves "Americans" and the other inhabitants of the borderlands. Much as the U.S.-Mexico border never completely separated the communities on either side of the boundary, the "Mexican" and "American" eras in the Southwest do not divide neatly at some moment in time, but rather bleed into one another, mutually constructing the borderlands of the nineteenth century—and beyond.[1]

Almost as soon as their nation came into being in the late 1700s, Americans had begun to cast an appraising eye on what were then the northern reaches of the Spanish empire. The region seemed to many in the United States to be characterized by the paradox of backward peoples living amid tremendous natural wealth. "New-Mexico and California," stated an 1801 textbook for American schoolchildren, were "very valuable . . . there is a good pearl fishery on the coast; gold mines are found in the interior country, and large plains of salt lying in a solid mass." Yet the "Spanish settlements are weak, and the people jealous and suspicious. They do not care to publish the natural advantages of their country, lest other nations should be induced to visit it."[2]

For all the region's rich resources, Americans were at first reluctant to contemplate incorporating it into their new nation. Many feared that the United States' fragile experiment in republicanism was too delicate to stretch over the vast distances that such an acquisition would require. By mid-nineteenth century, though, these concerns had receded, replaced by the belief that it was the United States' mission to extend its virtues to all of North America. These ideas—soon known by the shorthand label of "Manifest Destiny" after the avid expansionist John L. O'Sullivan editorialized about the nation's "manifest destiny to overspread the continent allotted by Providence"—acquired the force of fact in 1845, when the United States annexed the rebel Mexican province of Texas, triggering a war between the United States and its southern neighbor. By 1848, the United States had added almost half of Mexico's territory to its national domain.[3]

If these events illustrate the ways in which Americans imagined a place for themselves in northern Mexico long before such a reality existed, the day-to-day experiences of Americans and Mexicans in the region reveal an even more complex set of interactions. As much as they liked to see themselves as the bearers of "civilization," most of the earliest Americans to pass through northern Mexico did so, admitted one, as "interlopers, and smugglers" who had little respect for Mexican trade and immigration law. These illegal immigrants kept to Mexico's outer periphery, where they established illicit trading partnerships with the local Apache communities.[4]

War between Mexico and the United States temporarily propelled additional Americans into northern Sonora. In 1846, U.S. troops under Lieutenant Colonel Philip St. George Cooke briefly occupied Tucson during their march to San Diego. After replenishing his column with wheat from Tucson's public granary and trading for "Flour, Meal, Tobacco, Quinces" with the local population, Cooke departed, allowing the town to be reoccupied by Mexican troops, who much to the Americans' surprise had abandoned the fort rather than contest their approach. In his wake, Cooke left behind a letter in Spanish addressed to the governor of Sonora, emphasizing the benefits that closer ties between Sonora and the United States might bring in controlling the "murderous, cowardly Indians" plaguing the province.[5]

Although the 1848 Treaty of Guadalupe Hidalgo left Tucson within the boundaries of a diminished Mexican republic, the discovery of gold in California that same year brought a another stream of Americans to the village. For these argonauts, Tucson and the nearby Pima settlements emerged as important trading posts on a grueling transcontinental journey. Despite a few unhappy moments, as when a passing group of Americans stole food from villagers at Cieneguilla and staged a mock hanging of the local priest, interactions between American travelers and northern Sonorans during this time were often cordial. As K. Beeching, a New Yorker who reached Tucson in September of 1849, observed, "Tucson is similar to other Mexican towns[—]all mud buildings[—]the inhabitants appear to be noted for their hospitality, and have a great respect for Americans."[6]

Tucson might have remained as it was in the 1840s—an isolated northern Mexican village—had international politics not intervened yet again. The territory separating Mexico and the United States had been so inaccurately mapped that the chart used to negotiate the Treaty of Guadalupe Hidalgo—J. Disturnell's "Map of the United Mexican States"—spawned considerable confusion when surveyors tried to locate the newly agreed-upon borderline. U.S. president Franklin Pierce seized upon this lack of clarity as a pretext to wring further territorial concessions from Mexico. Although some Americans derided the ensuing "Gadsden Purchase" as "a dreary district" where "the land [was] bare, sandy, parched and sterile," the new acquisition met with the approval of such ardent southerners as then secretary of war Jefferson Davis, for it contained enough land to allow construction of a railroad linking the southern states with the Pacific Ocean. The cession also pleased those Americans who desired a forbidding desert, rather than an easily crossed river like the Gila, as a more "natural" border between their nation and Mexico.[7]

For all the importance that U.S. authorities placed on the creation of a new, more secure boundary, it took over two years for a joint task force of American and Mexican surveyors to erect a series of stone monuments "tracing and marking [the border] . . . on the face of the earth." Even then, as the chief American surveyor of the post-Gadsden border, William Emory, observed, the control that the creation of a border implied was largely illusory. The international boundary "passe[d] through the very heart of the warlike savages who have devastated Sonora and Chihuahua," leading Emory to predict that "many of the monuments will be removed by the Indians." As insubstantial as the border markers were, the notion that there should be a clear physical separation between the United States and Mexico remained essential in Emory's mind—even if this separation had to be preserved in cartographic representations rather than on the ground itself. As Emory concluded in his official report, "it is fortunate that two nations, which differ so much in laws, religion, customs, and physical wants, should be separated by lines."[8]

Yet here again the U.S.-Mexico borderlands suggest some of the ways in which the logic of nation-building did not coincide with the region's realities. All nation-states may be, as the political scientist Benedict Anderson once famously observed, "imagined communities." But at the border the degree of imagination necessary to bring the nation into being emerged with singular clarity. Even the completion of a border survey delineating the geographic limits of the United States did not necessarily herald the arrival of American sovereignty on the ground. Because of delays in dispatching American forces to this remote new corner of the United States, Mexican troops remained in Tucson to provide security to local residents until March of 1856—almost two years after the village had technically become American soil—when they were replaced by a unit of U.S. Dragoons.[9]

Having brought an American flag with them, the dragoons' first act was to hoist it over Tucson's adobe walls on a crude flagstaff of spliced-together mesquite poles. Such rituals, the new arrivals hoped, sent a tangible message that Tucson and its environs were now forever part of the United States. Figuring out how this new territory fit within the nation in other respects, however, proved far more difficult. Initially, the Gadsden Purchase was folded into the Territory of New Mexico, which promptly redrew its maps to add the Gadsden Purchase to its Dona Aña County. Santa Fe, the capital of this new, expanded territory, however, was hundreds of miles away. As a result, the New Mexican government exercised little tangible control over the region, leading at least one observer to call the Tucson area "a paradise of devils" because of its lack of civil authority.[10]

American residents of the Gadsden Purchase soon agitated for a separate territory, which they hoped to call Arizona after the legendary silver mines of the Spanish Real de Arizónac. This proposed arrangement did not come into being, however, until 1863, when the Civil War finally resolved the explosive tensions over national expansion that the seizure of Mexican land posed for the United States.[11]

"A paradise of devils": Tucson's Gem Saloon in the early 1870s.

For many early American arrivals into the region, the sight of an American "flag floating in the plaza" of Tucson and other newly acquired villages
sent a comforting sign "of soldiers and security." Yet such gestures papered
over a stark reality: Americans were, in fact, but recent arrivals to a territory
where the vast majority of the residents had lived most of their lives pledging
allegiance to another government. Moreover, U.S. sovereignty rested not on
a claim of popular enthusiasm for joining the Republic, as in Texas, or even
on the right of conquest, as was the case in much of the rest of the American
Southwest, but rather on a far more peculiar notion: purchase.[12]

Since a real estate deal seemed but thin justification for the United States'
claims to sovereignty, many Americans turned to history to defend their
newfound control over the region. Comparing the recent pasts of Mexico
and the United States provided all the proof most Americans required as to
why the Gadsden Purchase was more logically ruled by the United States
than by Mexico. Unlike the westward-expanding United States, Mexico had

TUCSON.

"Soldiers and security": the American flag flying over one of Tucson's central plazas.

withered in the face of Indian conflict. Even though, as Emory put it, Sonora had been "peopled by a Christian race, countrymen of the immortal Cortez," the Apaches—"a savage and uncivilized tribe"—were causing the states of the Mexican north to lose "population, commerce and manufactures, at a rate, which, if not soon arrested, must leave them uninhabited."[13]

The lesson to be drawn from such observations was as clear as it was simple. Since Mexico could neither protect its citizens nor spread "civilization," it should relinquish these lands to a nation that could fulfill such tasks. This interpretation transformed the long-standing Hispanic occupancy of the region from a defense of Mexican sovereignty into a critique. Instead of suggesting an enduring right to the land, this history weakened Mexico's claim by proving its deficiencies as a colonizer. Americans comforted themselves with the notion that they came to Sonora not as conquerors or as the beneficiaries of an unlikely real estate deal, but rather as liberators, charged with freeing the inhabitants from a defective Mexican state and a dangerous Indian foe.

If history was integral to how Americans justified their newfound control of northern Sonora, the denial of history was critical to how they perceived the region's complex ethnic relations. Most Americans tended to read the conditions that they encountered in the 1850s not as manifestations of a particular moment in time but as permanent features of the landscape. Unaware of the intimate connections between the River People and the Desert People, of the changes brought by European crops and diseases, or of the revolts of 1695 and 1751, for example, Americans divided the O'odham into distinct Pima and Papago tribes, both of whom they defined as placid peoples welcoming of European colonization. "The most interesting fact in the history of these people [the Pima]," contended the travel writer J. Ross Browne, "is, that as far back as the records extend they lived, as they do to this day. . . . [T]he Pimos [*sic*] have always manifested a friendly disposition towards the whites, and seem much devoted to the peaceful pursuits of agriculture and stock-raising."[14]

This same sense of timelessness pervaded American explanations of the region's ethnic conflicts. From the American vantage point, violence between the Papago, Mexicans, and Apaches had little to do with scarce resources or cultural conceptions of power and vengeance—and everything to do with unalterable traits of these communities. "The Pimos [*sic*] and Apaches," asserted the Arizona mining entrepeneur Sylvester Mowry, "wage hereditary and fierce war."[15]

To many Americans, it was the United States' supposed ability to quell these ancient animosities that justified their sovereignty over the borderlands in the first place. The replacement of the "savagery" of the Apache with a "civilized" landscape of farms and mines, however, was frequently undermined by contemporary events. The initial encounters between Americans and Apaches, after all, had more often been marked by mutual accommodation than irreconcilable differences. Benjamin Wilson, whose trips to the Gila River in the 1820s and '30s made him one of the first Americans to come into contact with Apaches within the future Arizona Territory, observed that the Apaches were "extremely kind and friendly to the Americans," whom they welcomed as valuable new trading partners. A subsequent party of Americans likewise reported receiving a "friendly" reception from "large numbers of Apaches" along the Gila River from whom they bought "mules . . . taken from Sonora, Mexico."[16]

Although difficult to quantify because of its surreptitious nature, this Anglo-Apache trade in Mexican plunder was a persistent feature of the early borderlands, engaged in not only by trappers like Wilson but even by U.S. officials such as Stephen Kearny and John Parke, who bartered with Apaches for livestock while surveying the area in the early 1850s. Even some of the spectacular massacres of the Apache during the Mexican era—in which notorious Anglo "scalp hunters" such as James Kirker and James Johnson, enticed by the bounties offered by the Sonoran and Chihuahua governments, ambushed large numbers of Apaches—speak to this fugitive landscape of Anglo-Apache exchange. The usual pattern for bounty killers was to meet with a band of Apaches and then, at a prearranged signal, suddenly attack their unsuspecting trading partners. But such strategies only worked, of course, if the Apache were already accustomed to exchanging goods with Americans on a regular basis.[17]

The shadowy world of Anglo-Apache exchange imprinted itself both on the treaties that the United States and Mexico negotiated in 1848 and 1853, with their articles outlawing such trade, and on the land itself. Early visitors to the Gadsden Purchase remarked upon the "well-beaten Apache trails from Arizona to Sonora" that ran through the region, eloquent testimonies to routes "long followed in raids upon the Mexican ranches and stock." "Our road was crossed by a half dozen or more recently made trails of stock: horses, mules and cattle, driven by the Gila Apaches from the Sonorian settlements," commented John Reid during a visit to the region in the late 1850s. "We often saw the tracks, and occasionally the fires of these marauders, but they avoided us."[18]

The Americans' and Apaches' shared position as outsiders to Mexican society facilitated their initial accommodation. As this situation shifted after 1853— as Americans came to the area as permanent settlers rather than temporary traders—new tensions soon arose between the two. Preliminary efforts at negotiating these pressures took place on an individual, informal level. With settlers often arriving in the region well before federal administrators, Apaches and Americans arranged unofficial "calico treaties" between themselves, so named for the gifts that accompanied such agreements. Upon opening a mine in the then-abandoned town of Tubac in 1854, for instance, Charles Poston struck a representative treaty with one Apache band. In exchange for the Apaches' tolerating Poston's operation in their midst, Poston offered modest presents and promised not to interfere with the Apaches' raids into Mexico.[19]

Despite their lack of governmental sanction, these "calico treaties" facilitated a relatively tranquil transition to American rule during the initial years of the Gadsden Purchase. Throughout the 1850s, Poston explained, the Apaches did not give his operations in Tubac "any trouble; but on the contrary, passed within sight of our herds, going hundreds of miles into Mexico on their forays rather than break their treaty with the Americans." Poston even employed several Apaches as stock herders and laborers at his mine. Thompson Turner, who, like Poston, settled in Tubac, similarly commented on the lack of any Apache attack on Americans "[d]uring the seven years which have elapsed since the cession of the Gadsden Purchase by Mexico." The travel writer Samuel Cozzens concluded that "in '58, '59, and '60, the Apaches were generally regarded as being at peace with the white man"—so much so, in fact, that Cozzens spent several days as the guest of the Apache chief Cochise.[20]

A further reason private treaties were so prevalent in the early years of the Gadsden Purchase was that federal Indian policy during the 1850s was in a state of flux. For much of the early nineteenth century, the United States had favored a policy of removal, in which native peoples were expelled from the eastern United States to lands across the Mississippi. The nation's rapid expansion across North America, however, called this policy into question, for there was no longer a line of settlement beyond which the United States could locate Indian peoples. "[N]ow the white population overleaps the reservations and homes of the Indians, and is beginning to inhabit the valleys and the mountains beyond," observed George Manypenny, the commissioner of Indian affairs at the time of the Gadsden Treaty. "[H]ence removal must cease, and the policy [be] abandoned."[21]

The handful of federal officials charged with overseeing affairs in the Gadsden Purchase experimented with a variety of approaches to dealing with the Indians in the region. One of the earliest efforts came in 1857, when Colonel B. L. E. Bonneville, the acting commander of the Department of New Mexico, attempted to use military force to overawe the Apache. He directed three U.S. Army columns, along with a "spy company" of Mexicans and Pueblo Indian scouts, to converge near the Gila River and to remain in the field until the Apaches in the region were never "heard of again as a distinct people." For the next month and a half, the soldiers fruitlessly searched the rugged mountains bordering the Gila—"a most elevated and tumbled-up region" in Bonneville's opinion and "perfectly worthless." Rather than confronting this large, well-armed force, the Apaches instead fled, burning the underbrush as they went to deprive the soldiers of forage, a tactic that successfully caused many army mounts to starve.[22]

Finally, after almost seven weeks in the field, the column surprised an Apache rancheria, killing twenty-four of the inhabitants and taking twenty-six women and children prisoner. According to John DuBois, a lieutenant on the campaign, the lone male captive, "by Col. Bonneville's desire, or express command, was taken out with his hands tied & shot like a dog by a Pueblo Indian—not thirty yards from camp." DuBois expressed disgust at this "brutish & cowardly" execution, as well as a subsequent order from Bonneville that the lieutenant and several of his men conceal weapons under their uniforms and seize the Apache leaders if they came to parley under a flag of truce. "I could not avoid asking myself," DuBois wondered, "why we had killed these poor harmless savages. It is not pretended that they ever did any harm to us . . . , robbing only from the Mexicans of Sonora." Negotiations with the Apache collapsed, however, and a few weeks later, running short of supplies and horses, the army abandoned the campaign, having fallen far short of Bonneville's goal of destroying the Apache.[23]

Unable to control the region through military force alone, officials adopted a policy not all that dissimilar from the "calico treaties" of their civilian counterparts. In the late 1850s, for instance, the military, along with an agent from the federal Office of Indian Affairs, negotiated a treaty with the band of Apaches dwelling in Aravaipa Canyon. In exchange for a promise from the Indians "not to molest Americans in their persons or property," the U.S. government pledged to distribute grain, beef, blankets, and other supplies to the band on a yearly basis. The agreement was as notable for what it did not mention as for what it included. Much like the "calico treaties," it made no effort to limit Apache mobility by confining the band to a reservation. It also turned a blind eye toward Apache raids into Sonora. Indeed, as soon as the treaty was finalized, "quite a number of citizens," having accompanied the government officials to the negotiations, took advantage of the amiable conditions arising in the agreement's wake to trade with the Apaches, who possessed "a large supply of animals" seized across the border in Mexico.[24]

This continued American enthusiasm for trafficking in Apache plunder underscores one of the central fault lines running through the U.S. occupation of the borderlands. As difficult as the United States found it to police the border between itself and Mexico, it discovered that the boundary between "civilization" and "savagery" was even more uncertain. That some Anglos actively traded with the Apaches, exchanging alcohol or ammunition for goods taken on raids into Sonora, showed how supposedly civilized Americans could abet Indian destruction. Likewise, the military's inability to discipline a few, scattered bands of Apaches, as demonstrated by Bonneville's ineffective campaign of 1857, called into question how advanced Americans truly were, while the brutal tactics that Bonneville tolerated during his campaign—executing a bound prisoner and plotting to seize captives during a peace parley—revealed how fragile the veneer of American civilization might be. These developments deeply troubled many at the time. As one early settler in Arizona expressed with alarm after witnessing the enthusiasm with which his compatriots attacked an Apache camp, "savage civilized men are the most monstrous of all monsters."[25]

Such concerns presented Americans with the classic dilemma of all colonial encounters: How should those who imagine themselves representatives of civilization act in the face of what they saw to be another's savagery? Was it permissible to meet savagery with savagery, on the assumption that primitive peoples understood no other way of being? Or did the embrace of brutal measures, no matter the character of one's opponents or the worthiness of one's goals, undermine the claim to moral superiority that was so fundamental to justifying the occupation of another's land in the first place? Americans might take their own "civilization" for granted, as well as the "savagery" of their Apache opponent. Nonetheless, they often differed on their answers to such questions. As a result, relations between the Apache and Americans would be shaped not only by the tensions between both groups but also by those dividing the American population itself.

DESPITE THE TENTATIVE ACCOMMODATION that prevailed in the early years of the Gadsden Purchase, by 1861 the relationship between Americans and Apaches had descended into a violent vortex of raids and counter-raids. Commentators at the time disagreed as to whether this conflict was an inevitable outgrowth of the collision between "civilization" and "savagery" or could be traced to unfortunate—and ultimately avoidable—misunderstandings between Americans and Apaches. Those in the first camp insisted, as did John Denton Hall, an engineer who settled in northern Sonora

in the early 1850s, on what they saw as fixed laws of nature: "the white and
Indian race cannot exist together. The inferior must succumb." Supporters of
this perspective pointed to what they saw to be an intractable Apache habit
of treating their "calico treaties" as temporary expedients rather than as bind-
ing agreements. "[N]ot only the Pinals, but the Coyoteros and Mescaleros
have time after time violated their treaties," contended the *Weekly Arizonian*
in 1859. "They have improved the period of ostensible peace in . . . spying
out the ground for future plundering expeditions, as everybody who knew the
false and treacherous character of the Apaches expected they would do."[26]

The opacity of Apache society exacerbated the Americans' sense of betrayal.
To newly arriving settlers, differentiating the Apache from other Indian peoples was difficult enough, let alone fathoming the fluid Apache band structure. Under such circumstances, "Apache" often became a catchall term for
any group of Indians believed hostile. "Excepting the Pimas and Maricopas,"
recalled one army officer, "the Indians were all called Apaches." While other
Americans recognized a greater diversity in the territory's Indian peoples, they
nonetheless perceived the Apache to be assembled into an arrangement not
altogether dissimilar from their own. "[A] Tonto Indian is an Apache Indian
on the same recognized principle that an Ohioan is also a citizen of the United
States," explained one settler unhelpfully in the 1860s.[27]

A measure of the uncertainty that prevailed among Americans at the time
can be found in the widely varying descriptions of Apache tribal structure
that appeared in the *Annual Report of the Office of Indian Affairs*. Some years the
office spoke confidently of a unified "Apache nation"; at other times, it made
a distinction between "Apaches" and "Southern Apaches"; and on other occasions, it offered a shifting taxonomy of bands. Only occasionally did officials
let slip their utter confusion. "[A]lthough we find officers and citizens who
speak in great confidence of their knowledge of this tribe and that tribe of
the Apaches," the office reported in 1868, "when their statements are sifted
down we often find them mere speculations." As a result, it was often difficult for Americans to discern exactly which band they were entering into
peace arrangements with as well as which group was conducting the raids that
outraged settlers labeled treaty violations. If one considered all Apaches to be
members of a single nation, as many Americans at the time did, there seemed
to be little other explanation for the tendency of some tribe members to make

"Building a state in Apache land": Charles Poston, early Arizona settler, treaty maker, and historian.

treaties while others simultaneously stole livestock or robbed travelers than the natural duplicity of "Johnny Apache."[28]

Nonetheless, some of the best-known stories settlers told about the rising violence of the early 1860s suggested that it was the misunderstandings of outsiders, rather than any inherent conflict between Americans and Apaches, that triggered the slide into hostility. Poston, who as one of the first settlers in the Gadsden Purchase also imagined himself one of its first historians, emphasized in his memoirs, *Building a State in Apache Land*, the role that two incidents played in undermining the relative tranquillity of the "calico treaty" era.

The first episode took place in late 1860, when a group of Mexicans crossed the border in pursuit of an Apache band that had seized several hundred horses and mules from their ranches in Mexico. The Sonorans stopped at Tubac in an effort to enlist the help of Poston and his workers, offering them per Mexican custom half of whatever livestock their combined force could reclaim from the Apaches. Poston, however, "remembering our treaty with the Apaches, and how faithfully they had kept it, . . . declined." The Sonorans then called upon some recently arrived Anglo lumbermen working at nearby Canoa and made them the same offer. Unfamiliar with Poston's treaty, the lumbermen agreed to help ambush the unsuspecting Apaches. A few weeks later, the Apaches retaliated, surprising the lumbermen in their camp, killing them all and tossing three headfirst into the camp's well. Although Poston reported no general outbreak of hostilities between his camp and the local Apaches after this event, a company of U.S. Dragoons pursued the band into the mountains and a new sense of wariness hung over the region.[29]

It was not until several months later, in Poston's view, that a second, "much more disastrous" incident sparked war between the two groups. A rancher named John Ward was living along the Sonoita Creek with a Mexican woman named Jesusa Martínez and her son, rumored to have been fathered during the woman's captivity among the Apache. One day in January of 1861, Poston reported, Ward beat his stepson, causing him to run away to the Apache band he had lived with earlier. What might have been just another borderlands family quarrel became something much larger, however, when Ward complained to the U.S. Army that the Apaches had stolen his stepson. A unit of soldiers, under Lieutenant George N. Bascom, who had arrived from Kentucky only three months before, was dispatched to try to rescue Ward's stepson, who Ward believed to be residing with the Apache band led by Cochise, the same man who had been Cozzens's host a short time earlier.

Up until this time, Cochise's band had abided by its informal agreements with local Anglos. A military patrol that had visited the band's territory only a few months before reported large groups of Apache "men, women, and children . . . living apparently on the most friendly terms" with the employees of the Overland Mail Company, which operated two stations amid the Apaches. "[A]t all the stations of the Mail Company," observed Colonel Bonneville, the patrol's leader, "I found the horses were turned out to graze without herders or a guard." Travelers were so confident of the peace arrangements that Bonneville encountered several who ventured, alone and unarmed, deep into Apache territory.[30]

Thus, when Bascom, flying a white flag, asked for a parley, Cochise and his family readily met with him. To Bascom's demands for the return of Ward's stepson, Cochise replied that the boy was not with his followers, but he would try to locate him among the neighboring Apache bands. Bascom, not understanding that Cochise exercised no formal control over other Apache groups, attempted to seize the Apaches to guarantee the return of Ward's stepson.

Although Cochise escaped capture, reportedly by cutting his way out of the tent in which his parley with Bascom took place, the lieutenant's soldiers took his wife, nephew, and several of his children hostage, along with a number of Apache men. Cochise retaliated by seizing an employee of the Overland Mail along with several luckless members of a passing wagon train.

When Bascom declined Cochise's subsequent efforts to exchange these prisoners for his family members, Cochise and his followers killed and muti-lated their four captives. Bascom in turn ordered the six Apache men he had seized hanged from a large oak tree overlooking Apache Pass. The result of this "foolish" misunderstanding, in Poston's telling, was Cochise's determination to wreak "a terrible vengeance" for what he considered to be the deceit of the Americans. His band began to attack Americans wherever and whenever they found them, leading to open warfare between the two groups.[31]

A LTHOUGH AMERICANS MAY never have regarded the "calico treaties" of the initial years of the Gadsden Purchase as anything more than tem-porary expedients, the accelerating violence of the early 1860s caused many settlers to embrace a far harsher set of responses to the territory's "saucy and insolent" Apaches. Instead of negotiating treaties that promised gifts and unfettered movement, the federal government, numerous Anglos maintained, should adopt a much more constrained option: force the Apaches onto reserva-tions, where they were to be treated as prisoners. As Thompson Turner put it, "Place the Indians on reservations North of the Rio Gila, establish military posts along their limits, and shoot every Indian found off the reservations."[32]

Whatever peace this policy might bring to Arizona, it was to be created not through mutual compromise as in the earlier "calico treaties" but rather via the dictate of Americans—a peace that offered no place for the Apaches in the territory other than prison camps from which "escape [wa]s impossible." That peace should take place on American terms was, for many Anglos, a reflec-tion of the only proper relationship that could exist between representatives of civilized society such as themselves and "savages" such as the Apache. "This is our country;—not [the Apaches']. American blood and treasure secured it from Mexico," editorialized the *Weekly Arizona Miner*. "[T]he American people cannot now do otherwise than help us to fight the great battle of civilization;

LITTLE SAMMY AND HIS INDIAN PROTÉGÉ.

MRS. COLUMBIA. "What is all this trouble about?"
SAMMY. "Boo-hoo! I got all his playthings, an' I kicked him into the corner, an' I was a-goin' to chuck him out er the winder, when he up an' slapped me. An', ma, wouldn't you please Exterminate him?"

"Wouldn't you please exterminate him?": cartoon from Harper's Weekly.

to overthrow the barbarians and teach them that white supremacy, even in Arizona, is decreed of God."[33]

If the proposed reservation system did not take effect, many Americans were willing to entertain an even more extreme option. "Extermination is our only hope, and the sooner the better," declared a writer for the *Arizona Miner*. "There is only one way to wage war against the Apaches," maintained Sylvester Mowry. "A steady, persistent campaign must be made, following them to their haunts—hunting them to the 'fastnesses of the mountains.' They must be surrounded, starved into coming in, surprised or inveigled—by white flags, or any other method, human or divine—and then put to death."[34]

The ultimate responsibility for these proposed atrocities, asserted such advocates of mass murder, rested not with them but with the Apaches. "The Indians really have possession of this Territory," asserted one American. "It is feared that the Hualapais, the Yavapais, and the different tribes of Apaches, with some straggling Navajoes, have combined for the purpose of exterminating the whites." Such an impulse was seen as the manifestation of an ancient Apache hostility for those more civilized than themselves. The ruins of ancient irrigated Indian villages that dotted the Gila and Salt river valleys, referred to by the O'odham as the homes of the Huhugam, suggested to Americans that the Apaches "have been waging for ages . . . unceasing war against the cultivator of the soil." Having exterminated the Indian peoples who had created these earlier settlements, the Apaches were now attempting to do the same to the territory's "Anglo-Saxon" newcomers.[35]

This projection of the desire for extermination onto the Apache, in combination with the unraveling federal presence in the region, turned Arizona Territory, in the words of one observer, into a vast "theater of desolation." Americans had long congratulated themselves on the stability of their political system in contrast with other New World republics such as Mexico. In the 1860s, however, the intertwined issues of slavery and national expansion engulfed the United States in a civil war far bloodier than anything its neighbors to the south had yet endured. Even though it was the acquisition of new western territories that had sparked the conflict, Arizona's distance from the war's main theaters rendered it of little strategic value. In 1861, having already lost many officers to the Confederate forces, the U.S. Army abandoned the two posts then existing in the territory, Fort Buchanan outside Tucson and Fort Breckenridge at the junction of Aravaipa Canyon and the San Pedro River, burning them along with whatever supplies they could not carry with them as they withdrew toward Kansas.[36]

The Civil War in Arizona would witness the invasion of Confederate forces under Lieutenant Colonel John Baylor of Texas, a counter-campaign led by the California Column of General James A. Carleton in 1862, and a fracturing of the American population along sectional lines. Depending on the forces occupying the territory, those deemed disloyal might find their property confiscated and themselves jailed or expelled. "Even the few Americans left in the country were not at peace among themselves," recalled Poston. "[T]he chances were that if you met on the road it was to draw arms, and declare whether you were for the North or the South." Union and Confederate authorities also engaged in shadowy plots along the border to curry the favor of the governments of

Sonora, Chihuahua, and other northern Mexican states: in light of Mexico's own civil war, both sides imagined that these provinces could be enticed into an expanded United or Confederate States of America.[37]

Above all, though, in Arizona the Civil War became a conflict not of North against South but rather of Anglos and their Pima, Papago, and Mexican allies against Apache peoples. Much of the combat was prosecuted by civilian groups, sometimes working in concert with whatever Union or Confederate forces happened to be in power and sometimes launching their own campaigns as "citizen volunteers." During the short-lived Confederate occupation of Arizona, for example, a number of American miners from Pinos Altos formed a group they called the "Minute Men." Although they sent an appeal to Baylor for weapons and ammunition, they remained much more intent on attacking the Apache than on the hostilities between North and South. Elsewhere in the territory, another group, calling itself the "Arizona Guards," adopted as its mission the "protection of the settlements against the Indians."[38]

Detailed portraits of these civilian campaigns come to us from the recollections of two new arrivals to Arizona in the early 1860s. The first of these chroniclers, the Connecticut-born Joseph Pratt Allyn, journeyed to Arizona in 1863 when President Lincoln nominated him to serve as one of the territory's first federal judges. Immediately upon his arrival, Allyn noted the harsh measures of Arizona's white population toward the Apaches. "[A] war of extermination has in fact already begun," he conceded in a letter home. "Indians are shot wherever seen." Residents seemingly possessed few scruples about how they went about killing Indians. A number of Anglos told Allyn how they had recently invited a group of Apaches to a parley. As the Indians were enjoying the food their hosts provided, the Americans each fired on a preselected member of the band, killing some thirty Apaches.[39]

In late 1863, Allyn witnessed several organizational meetings for civilian campaigns against the Apaches, at which settlers not only volunteered their own services as "Indian hunters" but also contributed toward a bounty "for Indian scalps." Such undertakings, according to Allyn, were remarkably popular. "[P]ersons were constantly coming in who wished to join the party, one and all believing and talking of nothing but killing Indians," he noted. "It is difficult to convey . . . an adequate idea of the intensity of this feeling." Allyn's recently appointed colleague, Governor John Goodwin, a New Englander who had attended Dartmouth College (a school founded to educate Indian youth), encouraged the assembled throng a few days later through a speech that, in Allyn's words, "took all by storm" through its powerful advocation of "the extermination of the Indians."[40]

Daniel Ellis Conner of Kentucky, who arrived in Arizona at around the same time as Allyn, not only observed such meetings but also participated in several resulting campaigns. Like Allyn, Conner noted that by the 1860s, the majority of settlers in the territory had adopted a policy of killing all Apaches they encountered: "[I]t was the rigid rule all over the country to shoot these savages upon sight." In the minds of many Arizonians, the elusive character of the Apache justified such actions. As one settler put it, "We have a horror of them [the Apache] that you feel for a ghost. We never see them, but when on the road are always looking over our shoulders in anticipation. When they strike, all we see is the flash of the rifle resting with secure aim over a pile of stones." Since Americans seldom possessed the skills to detect such raiders, they responded by attacking whatever Indians they did encounter, on the assumption that such "savages" were likely to be involved in past or future assaults on Americans. Such logic transformed the shooting of Indians on sight into a telling example of what the historian Philip J. Deloria has termed the notion of "defensive conquest": that Americans were forced into aggression as a result of Indian violence.[41]

If the stated goal of the campaigns in which Conner participated was to eliminate potentially hostile Apaches, the unstated goal was to call the Indians' very humanity into question. On a patrol designed to "chastise [the Indians] into peace," Conner watched a fellow citizen brave "a storm of bullets" to reach a recently killed Indian, whom he scalped and "robbed . . . of some trinkets." The scalp was brought back to Prescott, where it ended up spending several years nailed to the door of the town's newspaper, the *Arizona Miner.* On another occasion, after several Anglo miners ambushed a party of Indians, one of the participants cut the heads off five of the Apaches slain in the encounter and used their brains to tan a deerhide—behavior that unnerved some Anglo onlookers and brought peals of laughter from others.[42]

A similar blending of Apache killing and spectacle was engaged in by King Woolsey, an Arizona rancher who would receive a "resolution of thanks" from the territory's Legislative Assembly in 1865 for leading several scouts of

APACHE HANGING.

"A conspicuous mark": memento of a passing American patrol.

"civilian volunteers" against the Apache, including the one Allyn recorded in which the raiders slew thirty or so Apaches during a parley. In 1861, Woolsey killed the leader of an Apache band with a shotgun blast. "[D]etermined to make a conspicuous mark of the dead chief," he dragged the man's body to a nearby mesquite tree and hung the corpse by the neck. The body dangled in this spot for several years for all to see. "One of the feet and both hands had been cut off or torn away by the coyotes," reported a visitor. "The head was thrown back, and the eye-sockets glared in the sun." [43]

Despite the U.S. Army's claims to more professional detachment in its exercise of violence, its soldiers often mirrored the behavior of their civilian counterparts. When a patrol from Camp Grant under Lieutenant Charles Veil captured an Apache whom they recognized as previously having visited their post, the soldiers summarily hanged the Indian from the nearest tree. "Three or four years afterwards," reported Veil, "I passed that same point and the Indian was still hanging there, a perfect 'mummy.'" During the same scout, Veil and his troops surprised an Apache rancheria. One of the cornered Apaches attempted to surrender, but Veil, noting "we weren't taking prisoners of that kind," commanded his soldiers to shoot the defenseless man instead. [44]

The shared code of violence between civilians and the military emerged even more clearly when Conner and his compatriots met with the Apache leader "Mangus" (so called because of his Spanish name, Mangas Coloradas) under a flag of truce. During their parley, Conner's party seized Mangus, whom they then turned over to a U.S. Army unit. That evening, Conner saw the soldiers guarding Mangus heat their bayonets in a campfire and apply the red-hot blades to the chief's legs and feet. When Mangus told the sentinels in Spanish that he was "no child to be playing with," the soldiers shot and killed him on the excuse that he was trying to escape. One of the guards, borrowing a knife from the unit's cook, then scalped Mangus. A few days later, soldiers dug up his body and mutilated it further, decapitating the Apache leader and boiling his head. An army surgeon sent the chief's skull to the renowned phrenologist Orson Fowler, who displayed Mangus's cranium for its extraordinary powers of "Cunning" and "Destruction." [45]

Yet for all the atrocities it recorded, Conner's memoir also suggests the limits to the American embrace of extermination. On one occasion, Conner and a friend stumbled across a sick Indian. The man was evidently starving, for he was painfully thin, with only a small supply of "maggoty" venison. Conner's companion urged shooting the Indian, contending that if he recovered he would kill American settlers. Conner, however, declined to shoot a harmless individual. After "quite an argument" between Conner and his companion, during which their potential victim was forced to "await . . . the result of the pow-wow, of which he seemed to understand the purport," Conner motioned for the man to leave. Although Conner's friend urged him to "keep our part on the Indian's life a secret if we didn't want the community to call us dupes and fools," Conner felt no such compunction, for which he was rewarded with the "bitter complaints" of many settlers. [46]

The moral dilemma this particular incident posed—killing an Indian who posed no physical threat—took on an even greater immediacy during expeditions against the Apaches. In such campaigns, parties of Americans, typically led by a Pima, Papago, or Mexican scout, tried to surprise the Apache in their rancherias, ideally striking just before daybreak when the Indians were least prepared. Such a strategy inevitably meant that the attackers not only encountered potential raiders—healthy young Apache men—but women, children, and the elderly. For some Americans, such distinctions mattered little: they killed all the Indians they could, often justifying the dispatching of women with the claim that they were especially ruthless in torturing prisoners. The civilian scout leader Woolsey, for example, was blunt in his embrace of such tactics. "As there has been a great deal said about my killing women and children," he wrote to the territory's military authorities, "I will state to you that we killed in this Scout 22 Bucks 5 women & 3 children. We would have killed more women but [did not] owing to having attacked in the day time when the women were at work gathering Mescal. It sir is next to impossible to prevent killing squaws in jumping a rancheria even were we disposed to save them. For my part I am frank to say that I fight on the broad platform of *extermination*." [47]

Conner's experiences, however, highlight the ambivalence a segment of the American population possessed about killing all Apaches, especially noncombatants such as the very aged or the very young. For Conner, "the worst case of brutality" that he witnessed in 1864 was the shooting and scalping of "an old gray-headed squaw" by a fellow member of an expedition against the Apache. Revulsion at the man's behavior was widespread enough that he was summarily subjected to a "drumhead court martial," although it is unclear from Conner's account whether it was the killing of the elderly woman or her mutilation that proved most objectionable to him and his compatriots. The party excused the scalper after it was found he had been previously treated for insanity. But, Conner reported, the man was "never afterward permitted to take part in the raids after the Indians." [48]

The exercise of violence against Indian children was even more fraught. At several points, parties in which Conner participated treated infants almost as if they were innocent of the quarrels of the adult world. When one of their raids stumbled across a rancheria from which most adult Apaches had fled, abandoning three babies, Conner and his compatriots left the infants behind in the hope that their relatives, presumably hiding nearby, would soon reclaim them. Similar practices were followed by at least some U.S. Army units: as one soldier reported after an attack, "most of the papooses we left to be picked up by their friends." On those occasions when children were seized, they were often treated more like orphans than prisoners of war: when a scouting party Conner participated in found an Apache child wounded by an Anglo rifle shot, the group brought the child back to Prescott and "placed it in charge of the kindly wife of an immigrant." [49]

Nevertheless, violence against children was not unknown—in fact, it was unavoidable, given the American penchant for attacking camps of sleeping

Apache families. On one raid, for example, some of Conner's companions fired upon an escaping Indian. Closer examination revealed that their target had been a woman with an infant on her back and that the attackers' shot had not only killed the woman but broken the baby's leg. "[T]he men," Conner reported, decided that the appropriate response was to "kill it [the injured child] to put it out of its misery." While considered distasteful, this death excited little controversy among the participants, presumably since the initial wounding of the child was not considered intentional. Nor did anyone comment on the fact that a leg wound was not necessarily a fatal injury.[50]

In contrast, the conscious targeting of children generated far more unease, as revealed in a series of incidents involving a settler known as "Sugarfoot Jack." In the course of yet another campaign against the Apache, a band of American civilians, having found a rancheria, proceeded to burn the wickiups and other supplies to prevent any surviving Apaches from reclaiming them. In his search of the camp, Sugarfoot Jack happened upon an Apache infant, whom he tossed into one of the fires and watched burn alive. Revolted at Sugarfoot's behavior, several other Americans attempted to reclaim "the little, black, crisped body" from the flames. But "the skin peeling off every time it was touched made the 'boys' sick," and they left the dead child in the still-smoldering ashes. Meanwhile, Sugarfoot Jack located yet another Apache infant. Soon he could be seen to "dance it upon his knee and tickle it under the chin and handle the babe in the manner of a playful mother." When he tired of this game, Sugarfoot drew his pistol, a heavy dragoon revolver. Placing his weapon against the child's head, he pulled the trigger, "bespatter[ing] his clothes and face with infant brains."[51]

Sugarfoot's callous treatment of these Apache infants, in Conner's words, "threw the apple of discord into our ranks." At last noting the repugnance that his behavior had occasioned among some of his compatriots, Sugarfoot prudently retreated into the brush, leaving the rest of the party to debate the appropriate way to wage war against the Apache. Some Americans "thought that it was no harm to kill an Indian of any age, size, or sex," nor did they much care how such killing was done. Others declared that "they could not nor would not support such brutality" and refused to participate in any campaign that countenanced a policy of intentionally targeting Indian women and children.

The two sides proved so incapable of reconciling their differences that eventually the party split. Of the original group of one hundred or so, seventeen (of which Conner was one) quit the campaign. An ex-soldier with similar qualms about the campaigners' goal of exterminating all the Indians they encountered joined the dissidents a few days later. The man apparently felt strongly enough about absenting himself from the expedition that he was willing to travel for several days alone across a terrain filled with Apaches seeking revenge for the Anglo raiders in their midst.[52]

As such behavior indicates, there remained some Americans at midcentury who expressed limited enthusiasm for extermination. A few even sought to reestablish the previous "calico treaty" system of mutual accommodation. In 1869, after years of brutal conflict between Anglos and Apaches, army officers continued to complain about the presence of "unprincipled white traders" among the Apache. That same year, a U.S. Army patrol, detailed to "exterminate . . . [a] whole village" of hostile Apaches, discovered, much to their surprise, "a Mr. Cooley and Mr. Dodd," both miners, living in a camp of bloodthirsty "savages." A few months later, Tucson newspapers reported on "Dr. J.C. Handy" who, because of his success in treating illnesses among the Apache and his ability to "speak their language quite fluently," traveled, unmolested, in Apache territory.[53]

More common was the belief that Indians, much like native peoples in Australia, Tasmania, the Pacific islands, and elsewhere, were fated to disappear and should therefore be permitted to disappear quietly on their own. "To exterminate the aborigines of the forest and the mountains is a policy that no enlightened citizen or statesman will propose or advocate," contended E. A. Graves, an Indian agent in New Mexico at the time of the Gadsden Purchase. Despite his opposition to purposeful annihilation, Graves believed that Native Americans were "destined to a speedy and final extinction . . . [this fact] seems to admit of no doubt, and is equally beyond the control or management of any human agency. All that can be expected from an enlightened and Christian government, such as ours is, is to . . . smooth the pass-way of their final exit from the stage of human existence." Such a position distanced Americans from any direct responsibility for the disappearance of Indian peoples, while at the same time accepting a certain obligation to ease the final moments of North America's doomed indigenous population—a policy that might perhaps best be dubbed extinction with honor.[54]

Americans' belief in the imminent extinction of Indian peoples nonetheless created an opening for tactics intended to hasten this disappearance. One may have been willing to wait for the inevitable extinction of a harmless Indian people, but in the case of a group like the Apache—"the most treacherous, blood-thirsty, implacable fiends that roam anywhere on the face of the earth"—actively pursuing extermination appeared to some Americans less like mass murder than a humane act, designed to speed the arrival of peace. "[W]e maintain that Arizonans are not called upon to regard as 'atrocious' any measure however extreme," asserted the *Weekly Arizonan* in defense of its position to "make no truce, and show no mercy to adult [Apache] males."[55]

While at least a few Americans believed that the only path to peace was to annihilate every last member of groups like the Apache, others appeared willing to contemplate extermination as a tactic rather than a final solution. Once the Indians ceased to resist American domination and confined themselves to a clearly defined spot, the need for physical destruction would cease. "So long as an Indian has life and power he is dangerous, and this is peculiarly true of the fiendish Apache," editorialized the *Weekly Arizona Miner* in 1864. "There can be no hope of peace or prosperity in Arizona until he is exterminated or forced to accept a reservation." The Apaches were free to decide whether or not to accept this latter option. If they did not, it was not the fault of Americans, asserted the *Miner*, that they were obliged to "drive him to death."[56]

The unsettled and unsettling question of how active a role Americans should take in extinction manifested itself most clearly during the short-lived Confederate occupancy of Arizona Territory. Marching west from Texas, Lieutenant Colonel John Baylor and his men occupied Arizona in the summer of 1861. As military governor of the new Confederate Territory of Arizona, Baylor set about organizing a campaign to "clean out the Apache Indians." In March of 1862, he ordered his subordinates to entice the Apaches into treaty negotiations, kill all the adults, and enslave the children. "[U]se all means to persuade the Apaches or any tribe to come in for the purpose of making peace, and when you get them together kill all the grown Indians and take the children prisoners and sell them to defray the expense of killing the Indians. Buy whisky and such other goods as may be necessary."[57]

Baylor's willingness to contemplate extermination in such a duplicitous manner disgusted Jefferson Davis, who, as secretary of war, had been instrumental in arranging the Gadsden Purchase less than a decade before. Now president of the Confederacy, Davis denounced Baylor's plan when a copy of it reached his desk as "an infamous crime" and demanded an investigation into the colonel's behavior. Although Baylor offered as an excuse the rumor (quickly disproved) that the Congress of the Confederate States had passed a law "declaring extermination to all hostile Indians," the centerpiece of his defense was that for an opponent such as the Apache—prone to "barbarities almost beyond conception"—the only remedy was the "extermination of the grown Indians and making slaves of the children."

Such a solution seemed eminently moral to Baylor. Southern slaveowners had long condoned the "peculiar institution" as a method for civilizing the savage peoples of Africa. Given the Apaches' similarly barbarous character, Baylor was puzzled why the "extension of that system to the youth of the Indian race [was] a measure deserving of rebuke." Yet as willing as he was to lead the Confederacy into a prolonged, bloody war to ensure African Americans' enslavement, Jefferson Davis balked at exterminating Apache adults. He ordered the Confederate secretary of war, G. W. Randolph, to remove Baylor from command and revoke his authority to raise troops.[58]

The Union army, which reoccupied Arizona in 1862, adopted a policy toward the Apache that, on its face, seemed less harsh than Baylor's; it certainly excited less debate among Union officials. In practice, however, it too laid the groundwork for dramatic violence against the Apaches. Upon his arrival in the territory, Carleton, the commander of the U.S. forces, declared that the Apaches "should not be fired upon or molested until they committed toward us some act of hostility. They were to be the aggressors so far as this column was concerned." Even though this arrangement held for several months, its proffered leniency, in the mind of Carleton and his aides, justified adopting the severest of measures should the Union's goodwill be abused. As First Lieutenant Ben C. Cutler of the California Column advised a subordinate in early 1862, "If the Tontos are hostile he is to shoot or hang every one he sees." When in Carleton's view an Apache band violated the truce with Union forces a few months later, the colonel called for devastating reprisals on the Indians "for their treachery and their crimes": "There is to be no council held with the Indians nor any talks. The men are to be slain whenever and wherever they can be found."[59]

Unlike Baylor, Carleton did not envision engaging in deceptive parleys or killing Apache women and enslaving their children. But to many observers, the ultimate difference was slight: the disappearance of the Apache from the territory seemed as likely under Union as under Confederate rule. Carleton's cavalrymen soon adopted a marching song that went as follows:

We'll whip the Apache
We'll exterminate the race
Of thieves and assassins
Who the human form disgrace

Concluded James McNulty, a surgeon with the California Column: "[the Apaches'] race is nearly run. Extinction is only a question of time."[60]

In a telling juxtaposition, it so happened that Carleton's campaigns against the Apache in Arizona coincided with the United States' effort to codify its rules of war. The ongoing Civil War, arguably the first example of industrialized, total war in human existence, had fostered the need among Union leaders for clear guidelines for their campaigns in the Confederate heartland, where they confronted for the first time large civilian populations and widespread guerrilla resistance. For advice, Union officials turned to a former Prussian soldier turned law professor named Francis Lieber. The resulting "Lieber Code," approved by President Lincoln on April 24, 1863, as General Order No. 100, established policies for dealing with prisoners and for distinguishing between civilians and combatants. Lieber's rules, however, only applied to certain kinds of opponents. His code drew a sharp distinction between "barbaric" and "civilized" military practices, with the implication that the Apaches' behavior released the United States from following the same moral standards that applied to the southern secessionists. Thus, although the United States was engaged in two conflicts at the same time in the 1860s—one against the Confederacy, another against Indian peoples in the West—it saw fit to practice quite different forms of "total war" in these two campaigns.[61]

Despite the army's willingness to contemplate far more violent measures against Indians than Confederates, some settlers in Arizona believed that the military's reliance on any rules at all left it too restrained in its approach to Apache warfare. "In the field engaged with civilized foes familiar with tactics, an infantry officer is valuable," contended Turner. But "for Indian fighting" one needed to adopt the more severe methods of "veteran frontiersmen":

> The "army" having withdrawn from the field, we may expect little safety to life or property if the citizens themselves do not do something to spread terror among the savages, and teach them that what depredations they commit will be returned with ten-fold force upon their own heads.

Such calls to action reflected settlers' belief that there was only one form of communication that Indians ultimately understood: brute violence. "His [the Indian's] reason," opined one American, "can only be reached by physical power or force." [62]

Unsurprisingly under these conditions, while the end of the Civil War in 1865 brought peace to North and South, it had much the opposite effect on the conflict between the Americans and the Apache. Not only could the Anglo forces that had once been arrayed against one another now unite against the Apache; such campaigns emerged as a convenient way for Arizona's authorities to reconcile the deep sectional animosities still lingering in the territory. If there was one subject that partisans of North and South alike agreed upon, it was the desirability of eliminating the territory's Apache threat. Attacks on Indians thus expanded markedly in the latter half of the decade. In 1865, with most of its resources still directed toward its confrontation with the Confederacy, the U.S. Army killed only twenty-nine Apaches in Arizona. In 1866, by contrast, soldiers killed 154 Apaches in the territory and seized fifty-seven prisoners. This pace continued in following years. In 1867, regulars killed 172 Indians and captured forty-three, and in 1868 the U.S. Army killed 129 and took forty-nine captives. [63]

The territory's settlers kept no such meticulous records of the carnage caused by civilian campaigns during these years, but anecdotal evidence suggests a similar wave of violence against Arizona's Indians. Alonzo Davis, a soldier who had come to Arizona as part of the California Column during the Civil War, recalled that soon after the war was over, some of his neighbors laced several bags of sugar with strychnine and then left them where they were sure to be found by local Indians. "One package was put into a greasy sugar sack and accidentally (?) left by the big rock where we cooked our supper. The other was put upon an Indian trail running out to Rock Springs." Davis confessed that "[t]his incident may seem harsh to people who know nothing of conditions on the old frontier, but it was the only way we could get hold of those natives who never would stand and fight."[64]

The resort by Davis and others to strychnine—a poison commonly used on wild animals—demonstrates the depths to which the dehumanization of the Apache had sunk by the close of the Civil War. Among many settlers, the Apache had come to be perceived as little more than, in the words of one, "a biped brute who is as easily killed as a wolf." Indeed, the wolf, the target of avid extermination campaigns throughout the nineteenth century, was the leading point of comparison in settler descriptions of the Apache. "In character they [the Apache] resemble the prairie wolf,—sneaking, cowardly, and revengeful," wrote Cozzens.[65]

This portrait of the Apache as more animal than human gained additional potency from American outrage at the Apaches' torture and mutilation of those they killed. The Apache, wrote one army officer, "has all the ferocity of the most savage wild beast. . . . The outrages perpetrated by Apaches upon the bodies of their living and dead victims would be utterly incredible if they were not strictly authenticated." Newspapers abounded with terrifying stories of what happened to those unfortunate enough to fall prey to the Apache. "Children are placed on spears and roasted over a slow fire. . . . Men are hanged by the feet and a slow fire kindled at the head." "Old Eskiminzin says he buried an American alive in the ground once and let the ants eat his head off." One American told of finding an acquaintance transformed into little more than a collection of "scraps." "We went and found his body and that of another man, literally cut to pieces. Their moustaches were picked with the lip and all, as it had been trimmed off the teeth. Their arms and fingers were cut off and they were really disjoined all over. . . . They were otherwise mutilated in a manner too shocking to relate."[66]

Americans interpreted such horrors as a source of perverse pleasure for the Apache and therefore proof of their subhuman character. "The quality of mercy is unknown among the Apaches," stated John Cremony of the U.S. Boundary Survey. "They frequently take birds and animals alive, but invariably give them to their children to torture. A warrior is seized with delight

A GRAVE ON THE SANTA CRUZ ROAD.

"Killed by Indians": grave of an American murdered by Apaches.

when his son exhibits superior skill in this way." Given their imagined treatment by the Apache, many Americans in Arizona advocated suicide rather than falling into the hands of such "monsters." Upon his posting to Arizona, one U.S. Army officer presented his wife with a loaded pistol and instructed her to kill herself and their infant son should they ever be in danger of being taken into captivity. "Don't let them get the baby, for they will carry you both off and—well, you know the squaws are much more cruel than the bucks. *Don't let them get either of you alive."* [67]

DESPITE THE POST–CIVIL WAR YEARS' explosion of violence, this period also witnessed significant changes in federal Indian policy. Following the Civil War, many onetime abolitionists, Lucretia Mott, Henry Ward Beecher, and Samuel Tappan among them, perceiving the grand mission of ending slavery as having come to a close, turned their attention to what they considered the United States' other great ill: its treatment of Indian peoples. "[N]ext to the crime of slavery the foulest blot on the escutcheon of the Government of the United States is its treatment of the so-called 'Wards of the Nation,'" wrote Richard Dodge, a former Union officer active in the Indian reform movement. "The crimes against the Negro were open to, and seen by, all the world. The crimes against the Indian are unknown." Wendell Phillips, the fiery abolitionist famed for his condemnations of southern slaveowners, became equally outspoken after the Civil War in denouncing the army's "extermination policy" toward American Indians.[68]

In response to such concerns, on June 20, 1867, Congress created a commission to investigate conditions among the Indians. The Peace Commission's first report, submitted in January of 1868, documented widespread abuse of the nation's Indian peoples, which the commissioners attributed to the fact that most Indian agents achieved their positions through political patronage rather than knowledge of Indian affairs. In place of the current spoils system, the commission recommended that Indian policy be turned over to the one institution of American life that seemed above reproach: the ministry.

In 1869, Congress therefore created a Board of Indian Commissioners, made up of prominent evangelicals and humanitarians, to oversee the nation's "Indian problem." That same year, the newly elected Ulysses S. Grant appointed his former military secretary, Ely Parker, a Seneca from upstate New York and the man who had taken down the terms of surrender at Appomattox in 1865, as commissioner of Indian affairs. For the first time in U.S. history, an Indian was to direct the agency responsible for the nation's indigenous peoples.[69]

Grant's approach to Indian affairs was popularly known as the "Peace Policy" after a remark that the new president supposedly made to a delegation from the Society of Friends not long after his election. "If you can make Quakers out of the Indians it will take the fight out of them," Grant reportedly stated. "Let us have peace." The "Peace Policy" broke with a number of previous federal practices, especially by attributing conflicts with Indian peoples to avoidable American injustices rather than to some inherent Native American "savageness." Still, backers of the policy imagined a quite specific form of peace with Indian peoples. One reason for placing religious denominations in charge of Indian policy, in fact, was not simply ministers' supposedly greater imperviousness to corruption but also the desire to remake Indians along the lines of how Americans liked to imagine themselves: as Christian, capitalist citizens of the United States.[70]

"Let us have peace": a drawing from Harper's Weekly *of 1870, celebrating Grant's Indian policy. Grant is pictured shaking hands with a visiting delegation of Lakota Indians made up of Red Cloud, Spotted Tail, and Swift Bear.*

The commissioners' concern for the well-being of Indian peoples thus led them to endorse deep intrusions into Indian culture. In its 1869 report, the commission called for abandoning the treaty system, which had treated Indian tribes akin to sovereign nations, and suggested instead that the proper "legal status of the uncivilized Indians should be that of wards of the government." Eventually, it was hoped, Indians would sunder all connections with their tribes and these communities would vanish altogether. In a departure from the prior policy of removal, the commission also recommended the creation of reservations. These were to be located far from Anglo population centers so as to isolate Indians from all outside influences other than the missionaries now in charge of Indian life. This arrangement, however well-intentioned, distanced Indians from their traditional homelands; it also undercut the ability of Indian peoples to sustain themselves through trade or temporary employment off the reservation. Finally, the commissioners called for supplanting Indian languages, practices, and religion through intensive instruction in English, Euro-American models of agriculture, and Christianity. The imagined result of such policies may not have been physical extermination but it was, in essence, cultural extermination.[71]

Indeed, one of the great ironies of the "Peace Policy" was that the program was marred by almost constant hostilities. This was not only the case in Arizona, where war with the Apaches continued apace, but also in the Great Plains and on the West Coast, where the army soon found itself embroiled in campaigns against the Lakota, Cheyenne, and Modoc Indians. In retrospect, such a turn of events should not be surprising, for, wrapped within its professed humanitarianism, the "Peace Policy" retained a germ of violence. Implicitly, in defining the terms of peace, the commissioners had also set the conditions for war. As Grant observed in a less well-remembered comment on the "Peace Policy," "Those who do not accept this policy will find the new administration ready for a sharp and severe war policy." Those Indians who accepted reservations, added Commissioner Parker, deserved to be "assisted in agricultural pursuits and the arts of civilized life." Those found off the new reserves, however, "would be subject wholly to the control and supervision of military authorities." The "Peace Policy," in short, promised a U.S.-dictated peace on the reservations—and war everywhere else.[72]

The "Peace Policy" took root slowly in Arizona. In 1869, the same year as Parker's appointment as commissioner of Indian affairs, Lieutenant Colonel John Green of the U.S. Army complained of the ongoing confusion over how to treat the Apaches he encountered on his patrols, who gave little indication of being hostile. "The Apaches have but few friends, and, I believe, no agent," reported Green. "Even the [army] officers, when applied to by them for information, cannot tell them what to do. There seems to be no settled policy, but a general policy to kill them wherever found." The cavalry officer Camillo Carr echoed Green's concerns. During the late 1860s, he recalled, "[t]here was no reservation to which the Apaches could be sent when they came in and it was impossible to hold and guard them as prisoners, so the game of see-saw, fight and palaver, was indefinitely continued." Not until 1870 did federal authorities create Fort Apache, the first Apache reservation. Officials intended to collect all of Arizona's Apaches into this single locale, but the reserve attracted few Indians other than those already inhabiting the area.[73]

Despite its limited initial effect, the "Peace Policy" nonetheless fostered bitter resentment among many settlers. Americans in Arizona—many of them former Confederate sympathizers with little patience for the ex-abolitionists guiding federal Indian policy—saw the program as creating a most peculiar state of affairs. Post–Civil War Arizona, such settlers maintained, was a place where "all was reversed." Instead of the Indians being confined to reservations, it was Americans who were limited to Tucson and the few other locales where their numbers were sufficient to protect them from Apache attacks. Rather than aiding pioneers in developing the territory's rich natural resources, federal authorities seemed preoccupied with the well-being of a group of "savages." That the federal government had secured northern Sonora from Mexico, surveyed the border, and dispatched soldiers, judges, and other officials to the territory counted for little. Many Americans in Arizona saw themselves as victims of the federal government, and the Apache Indians who had been subjected to brutal army campaigns for close to a decade as, oddly enough, the allies of those same authorities. "[T]he Indian and the Government," contended one correspondent to the *Weekly Arizonan* in 1869, "maintain the present harmony in the project of crushing out the settler."[74]

Those who put forth this position had little trouble recasting the "Peace Policy" from a humanitarian program into one of unmitigated violence. Their consideration of violence did not extend to the warfare that the policy justified against Indian peoples, but rather fastened upon what settlers viewed as the toleration of attacks on Americans by Indians who escaped reprisal by settling upon the new reservations championed by reformers. "[T]he mistaken philanthropists of the East," editorialized the *Weekly Arizonan*, "have not the most remote conception of the Apache character. . . . The effect of their policy is terrible on this far West border; and these men who are pleading for soft measures with the Apaches are guilty of the blood of the murdered pioneers of Arizona and New Mexico."[75]

To support their accusations, the *Weekly Arizonan* compiled a list of the attacks conducted by the Apache in Pima County during the period from July 1869 to July 1870 (the southernmost county in Arizona, Pima County at the time included Tucson, Tubac, and most of the rest of the Gadsden Purchase). In a single year, the newspaper reported, Apaches killed forty-seven men, wounded six, carried one "Mexican boy" into captivity, and stole over five hundred head of livestock. Faced with this "record of horrors," asserted the newspaper, who would dare "condemn any measure whatsoever which may be resorted to by the pioneer for the protection of his property and the punishment of the common despoiler"?[76]

FRANK LESLIE'S ILLUSTRATED NEWSPAPER.

GOVERNMENT   RESERVATION

WHAT TO DO WITH THEM.

Our Artist comes to the help of the Indian Department, which, according to a contemporary, "is puzzled to know what to do with the captured Apaches."

"What to do with them": nineteenth-century cartoon decrying what many at the time viewed as the federal government's pampering of the Apache.

IN FEBRUARY OF 1871, a small group of Apache women waving a scrap of white material approached the U.S. Army fort located at the intersection of the San Pedro River and Aravaipa Canyon. Originally called Fort Aravaypa when it was first established in 1860, the encampment had gone through numerous transformations during its short existence. Renamed Fort Breckenridge for the then vice president just weeks after its founding, it was torched by retreating Union forces at the outset of the Civil War, only to be reoccupied by members of the California Column in 1862. In 1865, it had been rechristened Camp Grant in honor of the Civil War hero and future supporter of the "Peace Policy," Ulysses S. Grant. From the fort's location atop a small rise overlooking the San Pedro River, the army was able to monitor a number of crucial routes through Arizona Territory—the new wagon trail that Americans had blazed from Tucson to Santa Fe as well as an Apache trail "many yards wide" in the San Pedro Valley, long a major north-south corridor for Apache raiding into Sonora.[77]

Speaking through the fort's translators, the women explained to the camp's commanding officer, Lieutenant Royal Whitman, that they were engaged in a familiar borderlands undertaking: searching for a missing child. The son of one of the women in the group had been captured along the Salt River a few months earlier and was thought to be residing among the Americans. Although unable to locate the boy, Whitman, a thirty-seven-year-old Civil War veteran from Maine, nonetheless made sure that the women were well treated during the two days they spent at the fort. About a week later, the women returned to trade for pieces of manta—canvas cloth that the women used for their outfits—and to report that the leader of their band would like to talk to Whitman. The lieutenant responded positively to this request, and so a few days later Whitman found himself engaged in a conference with a man who proclaimed himself to be the head of some 150 members of "the Aravapa Apaches." This figure, who Whitman would come to know by the names "Es-him-en-zee" or "Es-cim-en-zeen," explained that his people lived in dread of American attack. Exhausted and hungry, Es-him-en-zee and his band wanted to come down from the mountains and settle in Aravaipa Canyon.[78]

Es-him-en-zee's request placed Whitman in an awkward position. Although the goal of the "Peace Policy" was to move all Apaches to reservations, the only official reservation in Arizona was Fort Apache, located some eighty miles to the north. When Whitman suggested this option to Es-him-en-zee, however, the leader declined, claiming to be ill at ease with the place and its inhabitants. Not knowing what else to do, but believing that he was supposed to encourage peaceful interactions whenever possible, Whitman offered to let Es-him-en-zee and his followers collect at Camp Grant. Whitman's troops would furnish the Indians with food and other supplies while the lieutenant contacted his superiors for guidance. Whitman quickly composed a detailed report asking the commander of the Department of Arizona, Colonel George Stoneman, for instructions. After six weeks of anxious waiting, however, the letter was returned with no other comment than to note that Whitman had not followed proper military procedure by attaching a summary of the report on the outside fold.[79]

The absence of any clear commands from his supervisors forced Whitman to improvise his own "Peace Policy." Initially, he gathered the Apaches less than half a mile from Camp Grant's adobe houses and dusty parade ground. Soldiers counted the Apaches every other day, only issuing rations (one pound of beef and one pound of flour or corn per Indian) to those who were in camp. To develop what the former abolitionist saw as a necessary spirit of enterprise among Es-him-en-zee's followers, Whitman instituted a policy of hiring Apache women to gather hay for the army's livestock. In exchange, the women were issued tickets that they could redeem with the post's contractor for manta and "such little articles as they desired." Intent on using the ticket system as a training ground for wage labor, Whitman even negotiated with local ranchers for tribe members to harvest barley from farms along the nearby San Pedro River once the crop was ripe.[80]

Over time, the number of Apaches gathered at Camp Grant expanded from the initial hundred or so followers of Es-him-en-zee to over five hundred. Well aware that without any official approval for his behavior he would be held accountable for any problems that arose, Whitman did his best to keep the Apaches "continually under supervision," spending so much time in their camp that, in his words, he came "to know the faces of all the men, but also the women and children." Once the lieutenant felt assured that the Apaches were honoring the terms of their agreement with him—remaining near the fort and ceasing all raiding, not only on local settlers but throughout Arizona and Sonora—he extended the count for rations to once every three days and issued passes for small groups to leave the post for a few days to gather mescal from the surrounding hillsides. As the seasons changed to early spring and the water in Aravaipa Creek began to diminish in the heat, Whitman even allowed the Apaches to move their camp farther up the canyon, closer to the source of the spring feeding the stream and to the sites where the Apaches intended to plant their crops, until Es-him-en-zee and his followers were situated some five miles upstream from the military's base at Camp Grant.[81]

While Whitman's transformation of Camp Grant into a de facto Indian reservation may have gone uncommented upon by his military supervisors, it had not escaped the attention of the territory's civilian population. To many settlers, Whitman's efforts epitomized the naiveté of federal Indian policy. The lieutenant, who had only arrived in Arizona in November of 1870, may have imagined that the promises of Es-him-en-zee were an unprecedented development in the region's bloody Apache relations. But longtime settlers knew that peace treaties had been negotiated before with Apache bands in Aravaipa Canyon, the first dating all the way back to the modified "calico treaty" the

U.S. Army had made in 1859. None of these agreements had proven enduring, and settlers doubted this most recent arrangement would be any different. Indeed, most Americans in the territory pronounced it a transparently
temporary expedient. "They [the Apache] have just gathered in their harvest
of blood and need a short season of repose," explained a correspondent to the
Weekly Arizonan, "and the sheltering arms of a fanatical Indian policy are ever
ready to receive them."[82]

What rendered federal policy all the more misguided to most settlers was
the coeval conduct of the military. In 1870, in recognition of its difficulties
controlling the Gadsden Purchase, the army had created a separate Department of Arizona. But the department's new commander, Colonel Stoneman,
anxious to avoid the "hot, sickly town of Tucson," promptly relocated his
command to Los Angeles, California. Stoneman compounded his seeming
indifference to conditions in the territory by announcing in late 1870 that he
planned to streamline operations by closing almost half of the military posts
in Arizona.[83]

To settlers who believed themselves vulnerable to Apache attack almost
anywhere in the territory, the colonel's plans seemed out of touch with reality. So too were the claims that Stoneman put forth in his official report for
1870: the "Apache nation" was "nearly harmless"; Indian affairs were "in as
satisfactory a condition as can reasonably be expected." If anything, contended
outraged residents, recent years had witnessed an escalation of hostilities with
Apaches. "[E]very citizen of Arizona knows, that the last three years constitute the bloodiest page in the history of Arizona," maintained the *Weekly Arizonan* in January 1871.[84]

As much as Americans in Arizona might complain about federal med-
dling in their affairs, they found the prospect of federal disengagement even
more disconcerting. During the early months of 1871, "a large number . . . of
prominent citizens" in the territory held a series of public meetings in Tucson, Arizona's most populous town and its new capital, to discuss "the Indian
question." One of the initial goals of these meetings was to compile what the
settlers believed to be a proper record of conditions in the territory—the truth
about the "savage war" that existed in Arizona. Toward this end, officials took
affidavits from dozens of self-proclaimed "pioneers" describing recent Apache
depredations. These accounts were then printed at the territory's expense in

a pamphlet bearing the doleful title *Memorial and Affidavits Showing Outrages Perpetrated by the Apache Indians, in the Territory of Arizona during the Years 1869 and 1870.*[85]

Over its thirty-two pages, the pamphlet offered scores of brief narratives of the injuries Apaches had inflicted upon Arizona's settlers.

John Miller, *sworn*: Resides in Pima County. In July, 1869, the Apache Indians murdered a man by the name of Culver, while plowing in his field, and drove away his two horses. In September, 1869, they stole from a neighbor, named Hartzel, two horses. In October, 1869, they stole two horses from witness. All of which depredations were committed on the San Pedro River.

In May, 1870, they killed a United States soldier at the Cienega Station, and a cow belonging to witness, in sight of the station.

On July 9th, 1870, they attacked the Cienega Station and killed two men; and witness had to abandon the station on account of said hostilities. That said station is located on the southern overland mail road, twenty-five miles east of Tucson. Has lived in Arizona eight years, and has never known the Indians more hostile than now.

James Lee, *sworn*: Has resided in Tucson since 1856. On October 10th, 1870, witness, with a party of four others, pursued the Apache Indians that had stolen stock; overtook and had a fight with them, and was obliged to retreat, after one of the party was severely wounded.

Witness is part owner in a valuable silver mine located near Tucson, but is prevented from working the same on account of the hostility of the Apache Indians.

Depredations have been more frequent by the Apaches in the last year than during his residence in the Territory.

Taken together, this chorus of affidavits generated a condensed history of Arizona in which settlers risked losing not only life and property, but the very hallmarks of the civilization that they sought to bring to the region: mail and other expressions of literacy, home and family, livestock, mines, and other forms of capital. Unsurprisingly, this record of loss was also a history that admitted few moral ambiguities. The pioneers included no mention of settler violence against the Apache and expressed little doubt as to the rightness of their effort to "subdu[e] our hostile foe, and thereby reclaim from the savage one of the most valuable portions of our public domain."[86]

Finally, the affidavits traced a history of deteriorating conditions. Most every account closed by arguing that Apache hostility was increasing; the repetition of this observation evoked a territory on the brink of crisis. This may, of course, have been simply a strategic ploy in a pamphlet designed to pressure the federal government into investing greater military resources in the territory. But the drumbeat of doom seems to have persuaded more than a few settlers to believe their own rhetoric. As winter gave way to spring—and as Whitman's experiment at Camp Grant with Es-him-en-zee's followers began to gain momentum—the citizens of Arizona continued to debate the Indian threat in their midst.

During one public meeting in March of 1871, those assembled elected to send five delegates to discuss Arizona's military situation with Colonel Stoneman during one of his infrequent tours of the territory. A two-hour conference between the delegates and Stoneman a few days later, however, did little to assuage the settlers' concerns. Stoneman pled an inability to do much more than he already had, given the priorities of the "Peace Policy" and the limited resources available to him. The colonel noted that one-tenth of the entire armed force of the United States was already posted to Arizona and that residents were unrealistic to expect further military deployments. To those meeting with him, Stoneman's underlying message was, in the words of the delegates' chairman, William Oury, "[t]hat we can expect nothing more from him . . . if anything further is expected we must depend upon our own efforts for its consummation."[87]

If the settlers did decide to resort to their own efforts, Oury was just the sort to lead them. Born in Virginia in 1817, he had left home in his teens and drifted toward Texas, then still a province of Mexico. His wanderings soon thrust him into a remarkable number of the borderland's best-known events. In 1836, when only nineteen, Oury found himself stationed in the Alamo in the midst of the Texas Revolution. With the former mission surrounded by Santa Anna's army, William Travis dispatched the young Oury with a message asking Sam Houston for reinforcements, an order that made Oury one of

"Uncle Billy": William Oury, Tucson dairy man, school board member, future sheriff, and participant in the Camp Grant Massacre.

the last Americans to escape the Alamo alive. After Texan independence, Oury participated in yet another spectacular borderlands disaster: the so-called Mier Expedition of 1842, in which some three hundred Texans raided deep into the contested border zone between Mexico and the Republic of Texas. Many of the intruders were eventually captured by Mexican troops and sentenced to death, an order that was modified to decimation—the killing of every tenth man. Oury and his compatriots drew lots from an earthen jar, with a black bean symbolizing death and a white bean pardon. Those who drew black beans were shot at dusk; Oury and the other prisoners were marched in chains to Mexico City. After his release and return to Texas, Oury joined a new organization called the Texas Rangers, at the time a paramilitary group designed to protect their new nation against "all enemies of Texas." When war between the United States and Mexico broke out in 1846, Oury and his fellow rangers promptly joined the U.S. Army as it fought its way through northern Mexico under General Zachary Taylor.[88]

For a man whose prior experiences with Mexicans were overwhelmingly hostile, Oury's next step was unexpected: following his discharge from the

U.S. Army in 1848, he settled in Durango, Mexico, one of the towns he had marched through as a prisoner after the Mier Expedition. There he courted and married Inez García, a nineteen-year-old Mexican. The next year saw the newlyweds join the Gold Rush to California. By 1856 they had made their way to Tucson, where Oury found employment as an agent for the Overland Mail Company.[89]

Here, in the newly acquired lands of the Gadsden Purchase, Oury flourished. Joined by his brother Granville, he established a large dairy farm and became a prominent figure in Tucson. Although his and his brother's ardent Confederate sympathies sparked controversy at the outbreak of the Civil War, he quickly accommodated himself to the Union reoccupation of the territory in 1862—so much so, in fact, that two years later, Governor Goodwin appointed Oury the first mayor of Tucson, to serve while the town was reorganized into a municipality. Not long afterwards, Oury became active in the effort to establish free public schools in Tucson, sitting for several years on the town's school committee. Fluent in Spanish, he also worked upon occasion as a translator at the courthouse. So prominent had Oury become by 1870 that the marriage of his eldest daughter, Dolores, included as guests many of the leading civilian and military figures in Arizona (including the army band from Camp Grant) and was covered in the popular journal *Overland Monthly*.[90]

The selection of Oury as the leader of the "Committee of Public Safety" in early 1871, then, was little more than a continuation of "Uncle Billy's" already established role in the community. As chairman of the delegates elected to meet with Stoneman, Oury would describe his group's meeting with the colonel to the local Tucson newspaper, the *Arizona Citizen*, in early April of 1871. Less than a month later, Oury, despite claiming that he "did not wish to be [voted] captain," would emerge as one of the leaders of the Camp Grant Massacre.[91]

Between these two incidents lies but a short path, but it was far from an inevitable one. Looking back, many participants in the attack, including Oury himself, would come to describe early 1871 as a rising crescendo of Indian raids, the tracks of which consistently led back to Camp Grant, climaxing in an event so atrocious that it demanded retribution: the slaying of Leslie B. Wooster, a twenty-eight-year-old settler from Connecticut, and his wife at their ranch near Tubac on March 20. "[T]he work of death and destruction was kept up with ever increasing force," recalled Oury, "until the slaughter of Wooster and wife in the Santa Cruz above Tubac so enflamed the people that an indignation meeting was held in Tucson . . . and it was determined to raise a military company at once."[92]

In Oury's depiction, the attack became an unavoidable response to Apache raiding, with the killing of Wooster and his wife the final breaking point. Reading the sources from this period, however, one is struck by how minor a role the deaths of Wooster and his spouse in fact played in events prior to the assault on Camp Grant. The first public mention of their slayings appeared in the *Arizona Citizen* and its crosstown rival, the *Weekly Arizonan*, on March 25, 1871. The article in the *Citizen*, entitled "A Few Days' Record," contained five different accounts of Apache killings during the past week, from "an Indian unprovokedly run[ning] a lance through the heart of Perry Redmond" at Fort Apache to the murder and robbery of two unnamed herders for the Hinds & Hooker freighting company. The details about Wooster appeared at the end of the article, and his death and her supposed kidnapping received less coverage than most of the other stories. The treatment in the *Weekly Arizonan* was much the same. Wooster's death appeared at the end of an article bearing the headline "Indians! Indians!!" that featured several of the same murders discussed in the *Citizen*, along with detailed accounts of the livestock and other goods the Apache had recently stolen from settlers in southern Arizona.[93]

The shifting depiction of the woman later described as "Mrs. Wooster" is even more telling. She was a twenty-year-old woman from Sonora named Trinidad Aguirre, who had apparently become involved with Wooster without the blessing of civil or ecclesiastical ceremony. Perhaps because of their less than entirely proper relationship, the initial report in the *Citizen* simply listed Aguirre as "a woman" and offered no suggestion of any link, romantic or otherwise, between her and Wooster: "On the 20th, L.B. Wooster was killed at his home near Tubac, and a woman taken prisoner." The *Weekly Arizonan* was similarly circumspect, almost to the point of being misleading, although it did at least report Aguirre's first name (albeit misspelled): "A Mexican woman named Trinedad, employed at the ranch, was captured and carried into captivity."[94]

Little in the documentary record, in short, indicates that the deaths of

Wooster and Aguirre struck an unusually powerful chord among the territory's settlers when they first occurred. Only in later retellings of events leading up to the massacre did Aguirre acquire in death a status denied her in life. She would go from being Wooster's nameless Mexican mistress to the respectable "Mrs. Wooster," her Anglo husband's beloved spouse. (Indeed, in some subsequent versions, she would be recast not only as Wooster's wife but as the pregnant mother of his unborn child.) Equally important, Aguirre retroactively came to provide one of the key pieces of evidence linking the Indians at Camp Grant to recent attacks in southern Arizona. "Wooster's wife had some very peculiar jewelry, which was well known by many of the people of Tucson," recalled Francis Goodwin a decade and a half after the Camp Grant Massacre. According to Goodwin, someone named Joseph Speedy "saw an Indian squaw in the sutler's store at Camp Grant with a breastpin which he knew had belonged to Mrs. Wooster, and after quietly looking around among the Indians found many other articles which had belonged to the illfated Wooster family."[95]

This all sounds quite convincing—until one notices that the documentary record offers little support for these assertions either. Aguirre's distinctive brooch, for example, is first mentioned in a May 6 article in the *Arizona Citizen*—almost a week after the Camp Grant Massacre had already taken place. Nor would her jewelry, on closer examination, seem to provide the conclusive proof that those who supported the attack sought. Aguirre's pin was a modified $2.50 gold piece, a far from unusual form of jewelry in the borderlands, where many inhabitants transformed the precious metals in Mexican and American coins into forms of adornment. So marginal, in fact, would the brooch prove as an item of evidence that, during a subsequent governmental investigation into the attack, witnesses, when required to testify under oath, suddenly claimed that they "saw no jewelry of Mrs. Wooster's" at Camp Grant at all.[96]

So Trinidad Aguirre may never have been Mrs. Wooster, resplendent in her distinctive jewelry. But as the lone female to die in an Apache raid in the weeks prior to the massacre at Camp Grant, she proved a potent symbol for Arizona's settlers as they sought to justify their actions to the outside world. With just a few minor adjustments, Aguirre could be fit into the familiar story of the vulnerable white woman—the very embodiment of home, civilization, and the future of the white race itself—imperiled by dusky savages. Aguirre's insertion into such narratives was the last, subtle transformation that she would experience after her death: her liminal racial status as a Mexican woman from a humble, immigrant background would be resolved, and, as "Mrs. Wooster," she would take the place usually reserved for white womanhood. So strong would this impulse prove, in fact, that in at least one newspaper account, she was referred to as the "white woman lately murdered at Tubac."[97]

By elevating Aguirre's death, settlers hoped to create an impression of horrific crisis, one which legitimated the massacre at Camp Grant as an act of self-defense, undertaken not only to protect settlers' livelihoods but to preserve the honor of their women. This portrayal of the attack, however, emerged only in retrospect, occasioned by the notoriety that the mass murder of women and children subsequently produced. Viewed in the days leading up to April 30, 1871, the massacre appeared far more ordinary than extraordinary. Ever since the outbreak of hostilities with the Apache, Anglo settlers had held public meetings to build popular support for civilian anti-Apache campaigns and had enlisted Pimas, Papagoes, and Mexican Americans as scouts and allies. The assault on Camp Grant followed this same pattern. Sometime after being voted the leader of the "Committee on Public Safety," Oury was contacted by Jesús María Elías to discuss a mutual campaign against the Apache. (The two had known each other since at least 1862, when Oury had recorded several land sales for Jesús María and his brothers.) The plan the men agreed upon— surprising an Apache encampment at dawn—was a familiar tactic, and, as Conner's experiences during the Civil War demonstrate, the possibility that the attackers might kill large numbers of women and children was, for many settlers, not a source of great unease.[98]

Still, the proposed attack on Camp Grant did present one significant divergence from other civilian campaigns against the Apache. Previous attackers had operated with the support, either tacit or actual, of the U.S. or Confederate army. This time, however, the campaigners were targeting Apaches under the care of the military. Even though Whitman had acted with only vague instructions from his supervisors, Camp Grant remained a U.S. Army installation and Whitman a lieutenant in the Third Cavalry and the fort's acting commander. An attack on the Apache at Camp Grant would therefore be construed as an assault not only on the Indians but on one of the territory's most potent symbols of federal power.[99]

Perhaps for this reason, although some eighty-two Americans had signed a pledge to take the field against the Apache during public meetings in Tucson, many developed second thoughts. On April 28, the date selected for the attackers to collect surreptitiously outside of Tucson, only a handful of Americans—six according to Oury—appeared, in contrast with far larger numbers of Papagoes and Mexicans. Two other Americans, Samuel Hughes and Hiram Stevens, both among the most prominent merchants in the territory, declined to participate in person but contributed vital support. Hughes, a Welshman who first arrived in the Gadsden Purchase in 1858 and the current adjutant general of the territory, furnished the raiders with a wagonload of Sharps and Spencer carbines from Arizona's armory along with ammunition and other provisions. And in response to a last-minute request from Oury, Stevens, Hughes's brother-in-law and the post trader at Fort Huachuca and Camp Crittenden, dispatched several men to watch the main road from Tucson to Camp Grant and stop "any and all persons going towards Camp Grant until 7 o'clock a.m. of April 30th, 1871."[100]

From this point onward the attack unfolded much as planned. Guided by Jesús María Elías, the party journeyed for two days to Aravaipa Canyon. Then, according to Oury, as the attackers neared the Apaches' suspected campsite shortly before dawn, they divided. The Americans and Mexicans crept to the top of the steep bluffs overlooking Aravaipa Canyon, armed with their new carbines, to shoot any escaping Apaches; the Papagoes charged up the canyon floor. Even in the midst of this deadly assault, the physical arrangement of the participants in Oury's presentation mirrored how the Americans liked to imagine their place in the borderlands: themselves well above the savage Indians on the canyon floor, orchestrating events and asserting their dominance not through the crude clubs of the Papago but rather by means of the latest machinery that their industrialized society had to offer.[101]

THE NNĒ̄

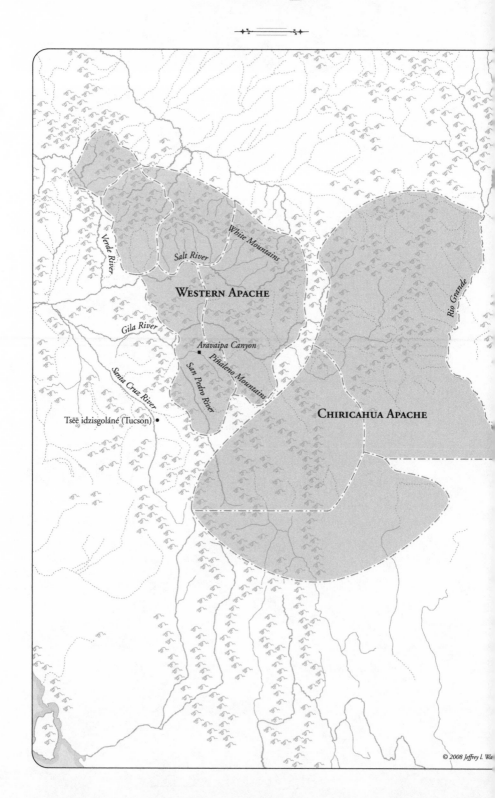

Verde River

White Mountains

Salt River

WESTERN APACHE

Gila River

Aravaipa Canyon

Piñaleno Mountains

Santa Cruz River

San Pedro River

Tsēē idzisgoláné (Tucson) •

Rio Grande

CHIRICAHUA APACHE

© 2008 Jeffrey L. Wa...

THE NNĒ̱Ē

OR CENTURIES, THE PEOPLE who call themselves the Nnē̱ē (the "Human Beings" or "People") managed with considerable success to evade not only Spanish, Mexican, and American military forces, but the newcomers' historical archives as well. Because of the resulting sparseness of the documentary record, many facets of the Nnē̱ē past remain subject to dispute even today. Outside scholars, for instance, have tended to interpret the paucity of Apache artifacts in archaeological digs and the limited mention of the Apache in the earliest Spanish sources as proof that the Nnē̱ē did not arrive in the borderlands until the mid-1500s. But many of the People view such absences as instead illustrating long-standing Nnē̱ē traditions of self-preservation: erasing all traces of their campgrounds and avoiding potentially threatening intruders.[1]

Those written sources from the sixteenth century on that do discuss the Nnē̱ē pose their own interpretive challenges. Almost all these materials were produced not by the Nnē̱ē but by Spanish, Mexican, and American record-keepers. For many Nnē̱ē, such documents thus speak more to how they were viewed by outsiders—as *'O:b, "indios bárbaros,"* or "Johnny Apache"—than they do to the rich cultural practices and intimate family ties at the core of the People's existence. History, explains Eva Tulene Watt, an elder of the White Mountain Apache, should be "stories about our relatives." Properly done, "[t]here's lots of Apaches in there and all they were doing, so you can see what happened to them and know what they were thinking. It's like their tracks, lots of tracks." Yet only rarely have these tracks and the people who made them found their way onto the written page. "Lots is missing in those books because there's hardly no Indians in there. You can't see hardly nothing in there about how we used to live."[2]

There is no easy solution to this palpable absence, especially when seeking to understand events that took place well outside the memories of present-day Nnēē. Although Western Apache oral traditions preserve much of the People's past, the passage of time has eroded certain features of the historical record, as has the Nnēē preference for avoiding any mention of unpleasant events or the names of deceased family members. As a result, the apparently conflicting statements that members of the People offered to the pioneering anthropologist Grenville Goodwin in the early twentieth century—"This I am telling you was told me by my grandmother, and before she told it to me she heard it from her grandmother, and before that her grandmother heard it from another old person"; "We don't remember our grandparents' times, just as you White people don't"—both contain important truths as to the continuities and silences in the Nnēē past.[3]

Still, by paying close attention to existing oral accounts and creatively rereading the available documents with a sensitivity to Nnēē cultural practices, it is possible to construct something akin to a preliminary draft of Western Apache history. The result may not reveal as much of the Nnēē social world as Mrs. Watt might like—the individual tracks, as it were, may be indistinct in places—but it nonetheless traces the main trails the People traversed across the landscapes of the past.

ALTHOUGH THE APACHES' name for themselves—the People—calls to mind a single, unified group, for much of their history the Nnēē might better be described as a constellation of distinct communities. Each community stood at the center of its members' world yet possessed subtle connections outwards to other groups of Nnēē. The basic unit of daily life was the family, an institution that was organized matrilineally among the People. Upon marriage, men typically took up residence near their wife's family and were expected to contribute to their in-laws' support—a situation that the Nnēē mediated through the custom of "mother-in-law avoidance," in which a son-in-law and mother-in-law almost never addressed one another directly or inhabited the same dwelling. Several such extended families gathered together as a *gotah* (family cluster) under the leadership of a headman or *nohwá goyą̄ą̄hí* ("the one who is wise for us"). The headman exercised authority less because of hereditary ties—indeed, as a result of the matrilineal nature of Nnēē society, the *nohwá goyą̄ą̄hí* more often than not was an outsider who had married into the family—than out of respect for his demonstrated wisdom and experience.[4]

These family clusters were, in turn, arranged into local groups. Each group claimed a specific territory and was presided over by a chief selected from among the local headmen. As with the *nohwá goyą̄ą̄hí*, these chiefs did not possess absolute authority over their followers, but rather led by displaying the qualities—generosity, eloquence, industriousness—prized by the People. Above all, through his prowess in hunting, raiding, and other activities, a chief demonstrated mastery over some of the *diyịh*, or supernatural power, that, in the People's view, suffused the universe. This supernatural power often assumed quite distinctive forms: "Horse Power," for example, gave one skill in managing horses, "Running Power" allowed one to cover great distances quickly, and "Enemies-Against Power" protected one from harm while on raids or on the warpath. Little noticed by outside historians, given their preoccupation with the male leader's role in warfare (a position not necessarily filled by the chief but instead by the man with the most developed "Enemies-Against Power"), an equally important figure for each local group was the "Head Woman," who served as a source of advice and who coordinated activities such as wild-food gathering, a significant source of subsistence for the People.[5]

Although the Nnēē possessed no formal organization beyond that of the local group, communities inhabiting adjoining territories often came, through intermarriage, joint ceremonies, and other forms of contact, to share cultural similarities and to think of themselves as distinct from People elsewhere. Ironically, it was frequently through these loose social arrangements that the People were best known to outsiders, who (inappropriately) termed them "tribes," despite their absence of a unified political structure. By the nineteenth century, there existed some twenty of these groupings (later designated bands by anthropologists) among the Western Apache dwelling to the north of Tucson alone. When one considers that each of these bands contained several local groups—and that the Western Apache were but one portion of a vast galaxy of Athapaskan peoples with common linguistic and cultural features spanning

The People: Nn̠ēē family outside their gow̠ąh *at the turn of the century.*

the borderlands—we can begin to appreciate the tremendous diversity that has characterized the People throughout their history. Although the Western Apache predominated to the north of Tucson, the other notable Apache community in the region was the Hák'ą́yé, or Chiricahua Apache, who inhabited the mountains near the Sonora-Chihuahua border and whose members in the nineteenth century included the figure known as Guyaałé ("The Yawner"), or Geronimo.[6]

Woven through these overlapping structures of family cluster, local group, and band was the People's clan system. All Western Apache belonged to one of approximately sixty clans, membership in which was, as with one's family, determined matrilineally. Unlike the geographically defined local groups and bands, clans were arranged around the countervailing principle of kinship. Even if they belonged to different communities, members of the same clan were expected to regard one another as relatives and to come to one another's assistance, generating bonds that, by bridging different family clusters and local groups, helped counterbalance the fragmentation that the People's dispersed social structure might otherwise foster.[7]

Clans ordered not only the People's family relations but their history as well. Each clan possessed an organizing narrative that linked the members of that clan to specific origin sites and, in many cases, to other clans through a common ancestor or shared geography. Many of these legends located the clans' origins to the north of the People's nineteenth-century homeland and traced a series of journeys through which the Nnēe came to inhabit their current domain. The wealth of detail in these narratives demonstrates that far from being the rootless nomads imagined by outsiders, the People inhabited a space replete with specific places, each evoking distinct moments in their history. The tale recounted to the anthropologist Grenville Goodwin in the 1930s is typical:

> Some people started from *gùtálba kòwà* ("dance camp") and came south this way to *`mbú' sìzín* ("owl standing"). They moved on from there to *tlùk'à dàdèsgai*, then on to where two hills come up together and where there is an old stone house. Then they moved to *lèyìt'ú* ("water in ground") and then to *tséyàná'ìlt'o'* ("he smokes under a cliff"). From here they went to where three white cottonwoods stood at the place called *t'ìs'ò'á'* ("cottonwood standing alone"); and from there they came to *tsé'ìjò jtcò'* ("large rock slide"), where there is a big rock with a trail going through it. Then they went on to *sísnàsndì'é* ("belt given away"), where there was a stone house. From that place they went to *t'ìst'é'd 'n'áyé* ("cottonwood extending to the water") above *mú'sìné* ("owl song"). The people settled in these different places, where canes were growing and there were cliff dwellings. Then all came down together. Now at the last place they became *t'ìst'é'd 'n'áid 'n* ("cottonwoods extending to the water people"). Before that they had no name.[8]

Such legends offer a number of insights onto the Nnēe's distant past. The north-south trajectory described in many clan origin tales complements current linguistic evidence, which places the Nnēe in the Athapaskan or Na-Déné language family. The most varied forms of Na-Déné are found far to the north of the borderlands, suggesting that at some point the ancestors of the Apache, over a process of many generations, may have migrated from more northern latitudes into the People's current homeland.[9] The clan legends also hint at the incorporation of members of other indigenous communities into the Nⓝēē, for the People recognized connections between their own clans and those of neighboring groups such as the Yúdahá ("Above People," or Navajo), Tséká'kiné ("House on Top of Rocks People," or Hopi), and Nasht'izhé ("Enemies Painted Black," or Zuni).[10]

While the clan legends are the most telling window into the People's deep past, written sources from the sixteenth and seventeenth centuries document Western Apache trading relationships with agricultural groups such as the Pueblo and Hopi along with more intimate forms of mixing. Spanish record-keepers in the late 1600s frequently wrote of encountering encampments of hundreds of "Apaches, Jocomes, and Janos . . . confederated together" or spoke of the fact that the "Janos, Jocomes, Mansos, Sumas, Chinarras, and Apaches have united." Although one should be wary of applying current tribal names to past band structures (especially ones that well may have been recorded inaccurately by non-Apache outsiders), it is possible that over the course of their migration into the region, Athapaskan speakers absorbed a number of pre-existing communities, making the present-day People an amalgam of indigenous groups. Such incorporation, either through intermarriage or the seizure of captives, may explain how it was that the Western Apache (unlike the Chiricahua Apache, who rarely farmed) came to adopt the corn-bean-squash agriculture practiced by the region's sedentary populations.[11]

Despite the addition of these crops, the Western Apache continued to derive the bulk of their sustenance from hunting and gathering. During the summer and fall, women and children collected seeds, acorns, roots, and wild plants in the mountains. In the winter, when cold weather drove them to lower elevations, the People turned to their preeminent source of wild food, the mescal or agave cactus. The Nⓝēē pried the mescal plant from its roots and buried it in a large earthen pit lined with mesquite branches. At sunrise, a specially selected woman would light the wood on fire, starting from the pit's eastern side and reciting a prayer that Coyote had taught to the People. After the fire had been allowed to burn for two days, the women would pound the now-tender mescal into thin sheets. Dried and wrapped in bear grass, these sheets could last for over a year, making them a durable, easily transportable food.[12]

Initially, men's main contribution to subsistence was through hunting, an activity that took place in the early spring, before the People's crops were ripe, and in the autumn, when animals' meat and hides were at their best. Beginning in the late seventeenth century, however, Nnee men began to raid their neighbors for food during these same seasons, particularly for the previously unknown large mammals—the *dzaneezí* ("his ears long and slender," or mule), *túlgaiyé* ("white belly," or donkey), *ĺįį́* (horse, a word likely derived from the People's word for dog, *ĺíchání*)—that accompanied Spanish entry into the region.[13]

The Spanish considered the People's taking of their livestock a hostile act from the very beginning. It is less clear, however, that the Nnee at first viewed such behavior as theft. Unaccustomed to treating animals as private property, the People may have looked upon the horses, sheep, cattle, and goats outside Spanish settlements as little more than an unusual new form of wild game. Moreover, since some of these animals escaped Spanish control early on, many Nnee may have encountered feral horses or cattle well before actual Spaniards. Under such conditions, taking these animals may have seemed more akin to hunting than to raiding—a trend that the tendency of the People to eat the *dzaneezí, túlgaiyé*, and *ĺįį́* rather than use them for transportation would have reinforced.[14]

Because of the Spanish response to their activities, however, the Nnee eventually came to view the taking of livestock as an activity that might best be translated as "to search out enemy property." When a local group's supplies ran low, an elder, often an older woman, might suggest the need to seek livestock or other goods for the well-being of the community. This comment served as an invitation for a man who had served on past raids to volunteer to lead an expedition. The man would publicly announce the intended target and time of departure. All males who had completed the necessary training—a period of tutelage under an older man in the proper way to behave while on attacks against the *Nnaa ch'iidn* ("Enemy ghosts," the raiding and warfare term for enemy)—were free to join or decline as they saw fit. Those who decided to participate, however, were expected to follow the commands of the raid's leader for the duration of the expedition without complaint.[15]

Raiding parties tended to be small and to place a priority on speed and stealth. Raiders would journey surreptitiously toward a chosen locale, frequently waiting until a full moon made nighttime operations easier. Palmer Valor, a Western Apache who participated in several raids in the 1800s, recalled that in their quest for mobility, it was not unusual for the Nṉee to travel for days in a row without halting for food or rest, during which time they might cover hundreds of miles. Even for men who had trained since childhood for such expeditions, the experience could prove grueling. Valor recollected one raiding party in which, when they finally stopped to butcher and eat one of their mounts, "[s]ome of the men, while they still had meat in their mouths and were sitting there chewing it, went to sleep right there. This was because we had been traveling steadily for five nights and days . . . never stopping to sleep or eat."[16]

Since the objective of such expeditions was to seize needed supplies, raiders attempted to avoid confrontations. Not only did pitched fights risk alerting others to the People's presence; unduly violent raids might drive away those from whom the People derived their support. "If cattle or horses were conveniently left in corrals some distance from the houses," explained the Hák'áyé member James Kaywaykla, "the inhabitants were not disturbed. And never did we take all the herds. We did not care much for cattle, and we took care to leave enough horses so that the Mexicans could raise more for us."[17]

In contrast with these efforts to avoid conflict during raids, the Nṉee goal during war was to inflict fatalities, as the People's term for warfare ("to take death from an enemy") indicates. Such expeditions, intended to avenge Nṉee deaths, included not only the members of a local group but all those related via clan ties to the deceased. Because they mobilized a wider social base, war parties tended to be far larger than raiding parties, sometimes including as many as two hundred men, along with a shaman who used his knowledge of *diyjh* to guide the expedition to a successful conclusion.[18]

In addition to "taking death from an enemy," war parties also sought to seize captives. If young, these outsiders might fill roles left vacant by deceased family members. As one of the People, Joseph Hoffman, explained, captured children "were divided among the women whose relatives had been killed. . . . This is called *gegodza'* ['to be paid back'], and when it was done they [the family members of the deceased] felt all right again." Similarly, women might be incorporated into Nṉee groups through intermarriage. Adult males, however, were viewed as too dangerous for such policies. Occasionally, such individuals might be held as hostages, to be exchanged for captured members of the People or traded for "horses, knives, and other things they [the Nṉee] want." But often a captive male was called upon to provide a more violent form of retribution, one in keeping with the central place of women in the People's social structure. After being made to dance during the Nnee victory celebration, the prisoner would be turned over to a female relative of the person for whom the war party had been organized.

> [I]f a woman's relative was killed in Mexico then the woman relative closest to that man, maybe his sister, would be avenged by a war party sent down to Mexico. If any prisoner was brought back she would be the one in charge of killing him. But the women who helped her do it would not have to be all of the same clan. They could be of any clan.
>
> The woman in charge had the first shot . . . then after her each woman had her chance shooting, or with a spear, to see who would finally kill him.[19]

To outsiders, the People's raiding and warfare could appear indistinguishable. Raids frequently led to the killing of opponents or to Nnee deaths that needed to be avenged through warfare. Warfare was often accompanied by the seizure of goods. But to the Nnee, each activity was distinct. The motivation for each was different, as was their manner of organization. If any similarities between the two existed, it was that during both sorts of expeditions the participants followed a set of practices designed to protect them from danger. "From the time the war party started until it got back," recalled one Nnee, "the men in the party had all kinds of *gudnlsi* ['taboos'] to observe. Mostly, these were about how they had to talk. There were sacred names for many things, and a man had to know these and use them, for if he didn't something bad would happen to him and to all the other men that were with him."[20]

When these Nnee traditions first arose is now lost to the mists of time, although as early as the 1730s one Spanish observer noted that the People gathered in small groups "to plunder" but "in large numbers to mount a major attack." Nevertheless, there is little question that raiding and warfare assumed a more prominent place among the Nnee in the aftermath of the People's encounter with the *Innaa* (the term for Enemy, which was applied to Spanish, Mexicans, Anglo Americans, and other outsiders at various moments in the People's history). To the Nnee, the *Innaa* represented both great promise and great peril.

The Europeans' strange animals, metal tools, and durable fabrics were useful resources in an environment where scarcity was a frequent fact of life. Yet gaining access to these goods, either through trade or raiding, exposed the Nꞑēē to great risks, for the *Inꞑaa*, the People soon discovered, were far more relentless opponents than any other community the Nꞑēē had heretofore encountered. A heightened body of rituals around raiding and warfare may have therefore arisen as a way of bringing order to these processes, which had become simultaneously more rewarding and more perilous following the *Inꞑaa*'s appearance.[21]

One glimpse of how the People made sense of these early encounters with the *Inꞑaa* comes to us through several oral accounts recorded in the opening decades of the twentieth century. The Nꞑēē possessed an intricate cycle of stories, of which the tales touching on the coming of the Enemy constitute only a fragment. Telling these stories in the proper way constituted a central feature of the People's oral culture. "In the old days when a person got ready to be told a story," recalled Her Eyes Grey, a White Mountain Apache born in the early nineteenth century, "from the time the storyteller started no one there ever stopped to eat or sleep. They kept telling the story straight through till it was finished." Some stories, especially those focusing on the foibles of Coyote, were a frequent source of amusement; others, describing the origins of certain powers "in the beginning," were sacred or mythic (so much so, in fact, that they were sometimes considered too powerful to share with women and children and only told on winter evenings, when dangerous powers such as the sun, snakes, and insects were less prevalent); others might be considered historical accounts from "long ago."[22]

For all the diversity of genres, the stories were united by an impulse to instruct—to explain why the world was as it was and what the proper forms of behavior for the People were. One version of the mythic tales of "the beginning" given to Goodwin hints at how the People conceptualized the differences between themselves and the *Inꞑaa*. In this particular narrative, Sun presents his son, Monster Slayer, one of the Nꞑēē's cultural heroes, with a choice between two landscapes:

Then Sun set up two mountains, one on the east and one on the west.
The one on the east side was brown and barren. The one on the west
side was covered with plants of all kinds and ripe fruits. "Which one

do you want?" Sun asked the boy. The boy went up on the mountain to the east, but he found it all barren ground. Then he went up on the mountain to the west and found lots of ripe fruits and good things to eat. "Which one do you want?" asked Sun. "That one to the east has nothing on it and I would get hungry. I will take this one to the west," the boy said. Then Sun said, "All right, there is nothing fit to eat there, but you will have to eat it anyway. Those grasses are no good to eat, but you will have to eat them just the same." The boy's father moved the hill to the west to one side and the hill to the east he moved over that way. From the hill to the east came lots of horses, mules, burros, cattle, sheep, goats, all such animals. They were on that hill.[23]

The second narrative, told by a different speaker, depicts this same process— the arrival of livestock and Europeans—within the genre of a historical tale from "long ago."

The people were poor. They set fire to the material at the base of the sotol stalks and when the fire was burned down, hunted in the ashes for the singed mice that were left. They picked them up and ate them. They lived on these. They were poor....

Then they found out there were white men living somewhere. They also discovered that white people had something to live on. The Indians began to live by stealing. They stole burros, horses, and cattle and brought them home.

After that they used the thick skin from the hips of burros and horses and made soles for their moccasins. Cowhide is also thick and they used that for the moccasin soles. They made the tops of soft dressed deerskin which they sewed on. In this way they came to have moccasins.

Before this they were poor but now they lived well. They had sinew and rawhide made from cow's skin. They were happy.

They said that stealing from those who lived on the earth was a grand way to live. They did not go around in this country but went to white people's houses. The white people would run away and the Indians would pick up their blankets. They lived by going to war. Then they would come back where their homes were.[24]

"Slayer of Monsters went to his father, Sun, and got a horse from him": mounted Nṇēē, photographed in the early 1900s by Edward S. Curtis.

Despite the obvious challenges in interpreting oral accounts recorded centuries after the events they describe, both tales evoke a telling mix of sentiments: the allure that the *Innaa*'s horses, mules, and cattle had for the Nṇēē; the People's puzzlement as to why these valuable animals were given to the Enemy rather than to themselves; and an awareness of the central role livestock played in triggering conflicts between the People and other groups. As one Western Apache, Henry Irving, observed in the early twentieth century, "We were getting on all right, but Slayer of Monsters went to his father, Sun, and got a horse from him. From that time on trouble started."[25]

PARADOXICALLY, at the same time that the confrontation with the *Innaa* transformed certain features of the People's culture, making raiding and warfare more prominent, it reinforced other customs. The People's preference for mountainous terrain, for instance, which likely arose because it gave the

Nnēē access to a broad range of ecological zones while also providing relief from the region's punishing summer heat, also came to protect them from *Innaa* assault. The mountains' rugged geography slowed intruders; their visual high ground made it possible to see pursuers long before they arrived in the People's campsites; and their caves and canyons furnished an abundance of hiding places where the Nnēē could cache food, weapons, and other supplies for use in some future time of need.[26]

In much the same way, what seemed to the *Innaa* to be a fragmented and chaotic social structure became for the People a source of strength, its very divisions vital to Nnēē survival. The People's low population density and diffuse political authority rendered them less vulnerable to losing their population in a single blow or becoming paralyzed by the loss of a particular leader. These same patterns also inhibited the diseases and other dislocations that accompanied the Enemy's arrival in the region, while the People's openness to incorporating outside women and children, as they likely did with the Janos, Jocomes, Sumans, and other groups, helped maintain population levels in an era of heightened mortality.

The People's flexible blend of old and new left them well suited to the disruptions of European colonialism. Indeed, not only did the Nnēē preserve their autonomy in the face of the Enemy's arrival; they expanded their sphere of operations, developing raiding corridors deep into Spanish-ruled Sonora and Chihuahua. The success of such raids and the People's other efforts to remain beyond the margins of *Innaa* control, however, transformed them into the targets of the Enemy's efforts at extermination in a way that the Sáíkiné (Tohono O'odham) never experienced. Nnēē evasion of this intended annihilation—and the People's exercise, in turn, of violence against the Spanish—speaks volumes as to the brutal forces shaping the borderlands at this time.[27]

Whatever their other limitations for Apache history, Spanish records contain a detailed portrait of these early conflicts between the Nnēē and the *Innaa*. In the 1690s, according to Spanish sources, mounted *Innaa* troops launched the first of several prolonged campaigns against the People, pursuing them in their mountain homelands for months at a time, rather than making a single raid in the manner of the Sáíkiné. These expeditions not only produced what were likely to have been unprecedented casualties among the People (close to seven hundred in the first seven years, "not counting a multitude who were

taken prisoners"); they destroyed the food supplies and other property the fleeing Nṇēē left in their wake. Those People who survived the Enemy's attacks
were thus left impoverished and at possible risk for starvation—a situation,
ironically, most easily remedied through renewed raids on *Inṇaa* settlements,
thus reinforcing the region's cycle of raids and counter-raids.[28]

During these initial contacts, the Nṇēē could not have failed to notice the
grisly fate that awaited those People unfortunate enough to fall into *Inṇaa*
hands. The Enemy appeared to make a habit out of killing and dismembering
captives, removing ears, heads, and other body parts, and leaving the victims'
corpses hanging in Nṇēē campgrounds. Often, those killed in this way were
the most vulnerable members of the People's communities, such as children or
the aged, who were less capable of fleeing *Inṇaa* attackers. During one expedition in 1695, for example, the *Inṇaa* surprised a large camp of Nṇēē that had
gathered to share in the horses and cattle taken in a recent raid, capturing five
elderly men and women. The prisoners informed the Enemy that they "had
gone to hunt livestock because the people were hungry"—a comment that
both reinforces the notion that the Nṇēē initially viewed seizing the new animals in their midst as more akin to hunting than to stealing and hints at the
disruptions caused by previous Spanish campaigns. Nevertheless, the *Inṇaa*
shot the five captives the following morning "and left [the bodies] hanging on
a gallows of three posts."[29]

A similar pattern carried across subsequent encounters. Almost a century
after these five elders were executed and their bodies left as warnings to the
Nṇēē, the *Inṇaa*, following a variety of "Indian tracks," launched a campaign
along Tɬʼohkʼaʼá tū biɬ nlịị ("The Water Flows with Cane," or Aravaipa Creek),
territory the People had recently acquired after displacing the Sobaipuri
Sáíkiné. The Enemy stumbled upon several of the People's abandoned mescal pits and camping sites in Aravaipa Canyon before capturing and beheading a Nṇēē woman and child. Two years later, during an expedition against
the Nṇēē on the San Pedro River abutting the canyon, the *Inṇaa* captured "a
woman and two boys." That evening, while the prisoners' kin, hidden in the
brush outside the *Inṇaa* encampment, watched in horror, the Enemy killed the
three captives and cut off their ears, prompting the Nṇēē "to shriek at them
[the Enemy] from the woods."[30]

As these haunting cries convey, there was much that the People found terrifying about the *Innaa*. Accustomed to treating captured women and children as potential future members of their community, the Nnēē viewed the Enemy's habit of killing and dismembering such prisoners as unusually savage. The public exhibition of Nnēē corpses was even more horrifying: according to the People's beliefs, the denial of a proper burial to the dead provided material for witches and released a ghost that might return to trouble its relatives.[31]

THE CONVENTIONAL ACCOUNT of the colonial period credits the Spanish with inaugurating a more peaceful state of affairs along Nueva España's northern frontier in the 1780s with the Gálvez reforms that created the *establecimientos de paz* at Tucson and other presidios. An alternative, Apache-based reading of this era, however, would situate the initiative for peace with the Nnēē. Alongside the expected raids and attacks, one finds repeated references in the historical record to delegations of the People, often led by Nnēē women, attempting to mitigate the violence between themselves and the *Innaa*. Early on, the People incorporated the European symbol of the white flag or, on occasion, the related images of a cross or even the Virgin of Guadalupe—who as a female may have resonated with one of the central figures of Nnēē spirituality, Changing Woman—as a device for signaling to the Enemy their desire to enter into peace talks. On April 30, 1757, for instance, an elderly Nnēē woman bearing a black wooden cross appeared at the Janos presidio expressing a desire for peace. A week later, three more of the People, displaying a similar cross, made a similar visit to the fort, and the next month a band of Nnēē agreed to set up camp outside Janos.[32]

Such measures were often short-lived because of the People's concerns about betrayal. In keeping with this pattern, the group at Janos became alarmed a week or so after their arrival and slipped away one night without notifying the Spanish. But as a result of such attempts to normalize relations with the *Innaa*, well before Gálvez's policy shift, one can locate groups of Nnēē dwelling among the Spanish. In the 1730s, groups of the People lived briefly at Fronteras and Janos, and a 1775 report from Tubac revealed in passing the presence of a Nnēē family among the other settlers at the presidio. What may have changed in the 1780s, then, was not the People's desire to reach an accommodation with the *Innaa*, but rather Spanish receptivity to Nnēē delegations, especially the Spaniards' willingness to contemplate a relationship that incorporated a greater degree of Apache autonomy than the previous policy of submission to the mission had allowed.[33]

Those bands of the People whose territories brought them into the closest proximity to Enemy settlements grappled most directly with the dilemmas the *Innaa*'s presence posed. In the Tucson area, the band dwelling in the vicinity of Aravaipa Canyon, which may have been the group later known among the Western Apache as the Tsézhiné ("Black Rocks People") and whose lands, with the dispossession of the Sobaipuri in the 1760s, had grown to incorporate much of the San Pedro River, developed extensive relations with the inhabitants of Tsēē idzisgoláné ("Rocks Which Have Many Dips," or Tucson). In January 1793, the Nṉēē leader Nautilnilce ("He Misses the Enemy's Chest") along with fifty-one followers from Aravaipa Canyon established a camp outside of Tucson where they were "taken care of with distinction." Nautilnilce was given a new set of clothes and rations of beef, grain, tobacco, and brown sugar for his band members. Unlike the temporary character such arrangements often assumed, this one proved enduring: three years later, the number of People at Tsēē idzisgoláné had grown to over a hundred and eighty. Nautilnilce and his followers settled just to the north of Rocks Which Have Many Dips along the Santa Cruz River, where they cultivated a few crops. Visitors reported that the Nṉēē, having begun to master Spanish, greeted them with "the Ave María Santísima" and that "there is no instance of their having hurt anyone."[34]

While Nautilnilce's band may not have harmed Tsēē idzisgoláné's residents, their relationship with other groups of the People was more ambiguous. Upon his arrival at Tucson, Nautilnilce presented to the *Innaa* as a token of "good faith" the ears of eight Nṉēē his band had recently killed, and like many other *apaches de paz*, he acceded to Enemy requests to fight those People who had yet to settle among the *Innaa*. Nautilnilce soon joined a scout during which he killed seven Apaches and brought their heads back for the fort's commander. Although outsiders sometimes found it odd that the People would take up arms "against their countrymen" in this manner, such an interpretation overlooks the fact that in a world where the primary allegiances were to one's clan and local group, intense rivalries between Nṉēē communities were as common as close allegiances. According to accounts from the pre-reservation era, disagreements springing from personal misunderstandings could trigger violent feuds among the People. Nautilnilce and his followers may have opted to seek refuge among the *Innaa* during one such conflict to shield themselves from retaliation. Settling among the Enemy in this way would not only have offered the People protection; it allowed them to enlist *Innaa* violence to their own ends, as Nnēē scouts could now guide the Spanish toward Nautilnilce's rivals.[35]

The highly personal character of the People's world manifested itself in the *establecimientos de paz* in other ways as well. From the People's perspective, whatever peace agreements they reached during this time were not between "the Apache" and "the Spanish," but rather between individual Nnēē and *Innaa* communities. Moreover, to the People, peace was not so much a one-time agreement as an ongoing relationship, grounded in personal, face-to-face interactions. Under these conditions, the rations of meat, grain, and other goods that the *Innaa* supplied to the People served not only to meet Nnēē material needs but also to establish networks of amity and mutual obligation. Rations thus functioned much as gift-giving did among the People, in which generosity was prized, leadership expressed through the ability to meet the needs of one's followers, and wealth reckoned more through social relations than the accumulation of goods.[36]

Over time, the growing Nnēē population of Tsēē idzisgoláné rearranged the landscape of the Western Apache. In February 1819, a Pinal Apache leader named Chilitipagé ("Licentiously, He Starts Off to War") entered into a series of negotiations that eventually brought him and some 236 of his followers to Rocks Which Have Many Dips. (Known to the Spanish as the Pinals for the pine-covered mountains they frequented, these People usually called themselves *T'iisibaan* after the "Cottonwoods in Gray Wedge Shape" where their band once lived.) Concerned about previous hostilities between themselves and Chilitipagé's followers, many of Tucson's *apaches de paz* relocated to the presidio of Santa Cruz. Five months later, however, a delegation of twelve *apaches de paz* leaders returned to Tsēē idzisgoláné "with the object of making a complete reconciliation with the Pinal Indians who have recently been admitted to peace." This "reunion" seems to have succeeded, for records show no subsequent hostilities between the two bands.[37]

As a result of such negotiations—both between the People and the *Innaa* and within the People themselves—by the opening decades of the nineteenth century a significant portion of the closely related Tsézhiné and T'iisibaan bands had settled in Tucson. Ironically, however, at the very moment these accommodations were reached, the Enemy proved unable to support such a large population of Nn̄eē. If the People were little more than spectators in the war for Mexican independence that marked the 1810s and '20s, they could not escape the decline in rations this decade of unrest unleashed. (Indeed, on several occasions in 1826, hungry members of Tucson's *apaches de paz* made it a point to drive cattle from the village's herds to their camps and slaughter the animals "in front of everyone.") The cessation of rations in 1832 only exacerbated these tensions, fracturing the Nn̄eē population anew. While over four hundred of the People elected to remain at Tsēē idzisgoláné, becoming the germ of an *apache manso* community under the leadership of a Nn̄eē called Antuna, others left Tucson and returned to their mountain haunts.[38]

This Nn̄eē departure from Rocks Which Have Many Dips may be recorded in one of the People's clan legends: "Long ago, they say, a part of the Apache Mansos living near Tucson came up along the San Pedro River. Somewhere near its juncture with the Gila River they met people of the Arivaipa and Pinal bands. They joined them, saying, 'We are called *ságùné* and have come to live with you.'" With its reliable water supply and flourishing stands of agave, saguaro, and other foodstuffs, Aravaipa Canyon would have held numerous attractions for the People, as it had for the Sobaipuri before them. Many Nn̄eē who left Tucson in the opening decades of the nineteenth century thus appear to have resettled in the canyon under the leadership of a chief known to the *Inṉaa* as Chiquito.[39]

Throughout the early 1830s, Chiquito and Antuna sent emissaries (a role typically filled by Nn̄eē women) between their encampments in an attempt to reduce friction between the two groups. The chiefs faced what had fast become an explosive situation: as some of the People turned to seizing from the *Inṉaa* the supplies they had once received as rations, the Enemy, in turn, encouraged the *apaches mansos* (now known among the People as the Bāāchii, a seeming corruption of the Spanish word *apache*) to retaliate against the raiders. By 1831 at least two casualties between the communities had occurred, the first when Chiquito's group killed a man escorting a group of female emissaries from Antuna's camp, the second when one of Antuna's followers retaliated by killing a headman from Chiquito's camp. The following year, this faltering effort to prevent a wider conflict was disrupted in more spectacular fashion: the Sección Patriótica launched its surprise attack (in which Antuna apparently did not participate) on several groups of People meeting in Aravaipa Canyon, leading to the deaths of Chiquito and seventy other Nn̄ē̄ē̄ as well as the capture of thirteen Apache children.[40]

Even this devastating assault did not end the People's desire to remain in Aravaipa Canyon. Four years after Chiquito's slaying, a large group of T'iisibaan under the chiefs Navicaje and Quiquiyatle reached an agreement with the *Innaa* at Tucson in which they agreed to settle at Łee ndlį̄į̄ ("Flows Together," or the meeting place of the San Pedro River and Aravaipa Canyon) under much the same conditions as during the *establecimientos de paz* era. In keeping with this agreement, a year later the People at Flows Together warned the inhabitants of Tucson of an attempt among the Chiricahua Apaches to organize a war party to avenge the death of their chief Tutijé ("The One Like the Killdeer Bird"). Among the targets of the intended attack were not only Tucson's *Innaa* but also Antuna and the Bāāchii, who had escorted the captured Tutijé to his public execution in Arispe, Sonora.[41]

S UCH MOMENTS OF INTER-APACHE rivalry and Nn̄ē̄ē̄-*Innaa* cooperation reveal the fluid character of hostilities during this era. The "partial peace" that predominated across Mexico's northern frontier is perhaps best viewed as an extension of the personalized worldview of the People, in which relations between communities reflected individual experience rather than, in the manner of the *Innaa*, some grand scheme as to the relation between "savage" and "civilized" peoples. Thus at the same time that the Nn̄ē̄ē̄ raided into Mexico, they also strove to develop amiable relations with particular *Innaa* villages, where they could trade for alcohol, tobacco, fabric, ammunition, or other supplies. If such exchanges evinced the familiarity with European goods that the People had acquired through the *establecimientos de paz*—many Nn̄ē̄ē̄, for instance, began to outfit themselves in shirts or dresses of "unbleached cotton or calico" manta during this time—they did not necessarily signal deeper changes in Apache culture. Tobacco from southern Sonora, for example, was prized because of its importance in Nn̄ē̄ē̄ healing ceremonies and other rituals rather than for the recreational uses to which the Enemy put it.[42]

The desire to trade that brought the People to *Innaa* towns, however, also rendered them vulnerable to attack. While the Nṉeē doubtless already possessed a reservoir of tales about *Innaa* brutality from their experiences with the Spanish, these stories took on new meaning amid the renewed violence of the mid-1800s, becoming what one folklorist has termed "narratives of horrors." The defining feature of such narratives was the mass murder of the People in a supposedly peaceful *Innaa* village. Seeking trade, a party of Nṉeē would visit a Mexican town, where they would be received cordially, often with gifts of alcohol. Once lulled into a false sense of security—a condition exacerbated by the disorienting effects of the liquor—the defenseless People found themselves under attack from "our treacherous friends[,] the Mexicans."[43]

Different towns provided the setting for these tales, depending on each band's experiences. But such narratives of horrors circulated widely, shared not only between groups of Nṉeē but with outsiders as well. Upon encountering a group of American fur trappers in the 1820s, for example, one "indignant" Nṉeē community described how "a large party of their people had come in to make peace with the Spaniards, of which they pretended to be very desirous; that with such pretexts, they had decoyed the party within their walls, and then commenced butchering them." Almost three decades later, one of the leaders of the Chiricahua Apache, Mangas Coloradas (Gandazisłichíídń, or "The One with Reddish Sleeve Covers"), offered a similar tale of his encounters with *Innaa* trickery:

> Some time ago my people were invited to a feast; aguardiente, or whiskey, was there; my people drank and became intoxicated, and were lying asleep, when a party of Mexicans came in and beat out their brains with clubs. At another time a trader was sent among us from Chihuahua. While innocently engaged in trading . . . a cannon concealed behind the goods was fired upon my people, and quite a number were killed. Since that, Chihuahua has offered a reward for our scalps, $150 each. . . . How can we make peace with such people?

The prevalence of such episodes led Jason Betzinez, "an eyewitness to the Casas Grandes massacre" in which Mexicans attacked him and his fellow Hák'áyé after giving them liberal supplies of liquor, to conclude that the history of this era was little more than "a series of treacherous attacks made upon us by whites or Mexicans."[44]

In keeping with the People's belief that historical accounts should instruct, Nṇēē stories of Mexico as "a land of treachery" imparted lessons both obvious and subtle. Most immediately, the tales reinforced Nṇēē beliefs in the perils of trusting those outside one's clan or local group. The apparent generosity of others, these stories suggested, often masked an ulterior motive. Many accounts also contained a pointed critique of the deleterious effect that alcohol had upon the People, clouding their judgment and rendering them liable to deception.

THE UNANTICIPATED ARRIVAL in the 1820s and '30s of the newcomers whom the People came to call *Inṇaa shashé* ("Bear Enemy") for their hairy bodies only heightened the era's volatility. If these Anglo trappers, by exchanging guns, metal tools, and liquor with the Nṇēē, enabled the People to avoid the dangers of trading with Mexican villages, the Bear Enemy could nonetheless prove as treacherous as their Mexican counterparts. Some were not above using their familiarity with the People to engage in surprise attacks of their own, no doubt generating new narratives of horrors among the People about the dangers posed by outsiders and alcohol consumption.[45]

Such encounters decimated several Nṇēē groups, especially among the Hák'ą́yé, whose homeland straddled the main routes into northern Mexico and who consequently had the most regular contact with the Bear Enemy. In contrast, many Western Apache came to view the small parties of Bear Enemy entering their homeland as a useful resource. Members of the T'iisibaan fondly recalled the yearly visits of a man known to them as Shash bich'ahn ("Bear Hat" for the fur cap he wore) who supplied them with gunpowder, lead, and other hard-to-secure items. John Rope, who as a young boy witnessed the arrival of a party of American traders, remembered his group's chief taking measures to protect the men from harm:

> Once in a while these men brought knives and metal hoes to trade. During one of their visits to us, some of our men (not chiefs, just common men) talked among themselves, "Let's kill these white men and take all their guns away from them." But one of them told the chief what they

had decided to do. When the traders were about to leave, this chief sent word among the people to come together at one place and meet. He spoke to them, "Don't talk about killing these traders any more. I don't want to hear of it. They bring us guns; they bring us axes; they bring us everything we need. This is how we get the things that we use. When you kill these white men, it will not make men of you. They are our friends, and they are also the friends of the Navaho." [46]

When the tensions between the Bear Enemy and the Mexicans erupted into open war in the 1840s, the People's experience of this conflict, as with their experiences of the Bear Enemy, varied considerably. Given the limited fighting in Sonora between the two nations, some of the Nn̲ēē, especially the Western Apache, may not have been aware of the war at all. Others, especially the Hák'ą́yé, who lived closer to the new, evolving border, were quick to note the differences between the American mode of warfare and their own. As one observed to a group of American soldiers whom he encountered in 1846, "You fight for land; we care nothing for land; we fight for the laws of Montezuma and for food." If what this man meant by the phrase "the laws of Montezuma" remains elusive—it may be a misinterpretation on the part of American recordkeepers—the larger meaning of his comment was clear. This Nn̲ēē recognized that whereas the Americans engaged in warfare to claim territory and subjugate peoples, he and his fellow local group members sought movable goods and revenge. The People made little attempt to claim absolute control over the spaces where their raids took place, nor did they endeavor to eliminate rival groups, since enemy property served as a valuable resource to be seized during raids. In fact, in a subsequent encounter with Americans, one of the People labeled Sonora the "Apache Rancho," for the livestock that it provided his people and contended that the Nn̲ēē "allowed the Sonorans to live, simply for the purpose of raising and herding stock for the Apaches." [47]

The People found the *Inn̲aa* style of peace as curious as its mode of warfare. At the war's conclusion, a group of Americans mapping the new international boundary encountered Gandazislichíídń (Mangas Coloradas) and his followers. The *Inn̲aa* attempted to explain "the war between the United States and Mexico, and its results" to the chief, only to discover that "he pretty well understood already" much of the recent conflict, having observed—and, upon occasion,

Nnēē and Nakaiyé: Western Apache with Mexican captive.

met with—various participants in the combat. What Gandazisłichíídń and the other People found harder to understand was why the Americans were now the Mexicans' allies, let alone why they claimed the right to dictate relations between Mexicans and the Nnēē. The People, reported the surveyors, "could not comprehend why we should aid them [the Mexicans] in any way after we had conquered them, or what business it was to the Americans if the Apaches chose to steal their [the Mexicans'] mules, as they had always done, or to make wives of their . . . women, or prisoners of their children." [48]

As hard as the Nnēē found it to understand why the end of hostilities between Mexico and the United States had any bearing on the People's inter-actions with Mexico, they nonetheless proved willing to forge agreements with the Americans trickling into the region, especially when such pacts were solidified through the distribution of trade goods. "The first time that our people had anything to do with the White people," remembered Palmer Valor, "was when we went to meet a White officer who issued some clothes to us. He also gave us some big brass kettles, red blankets, and some copper wire for making bracelets. A whole pile of things he gave to us. Besides those things he gave us about thirty head of cattle. That's the way the White people first started to make friends with us." Other Nṉee recalled these rations, too, along with a promise or threat of sorts: "After issuing corn, copper wire, and red cloth, the white *Nant'an* [chief] said, 'We have taken this country away from the Mexicans. Now we are going to build a fort in your country so you will stop killing each other.' " [49]

Although such agreements helped secure a tenuous peace for much of the 1850s, by the early 1860s relations between the People and the *Inṉaa* had deteriorated into open hostility. Unlike the Enemy, who often pointed to the misunderstanding between Lieutenant George Bascom and Gúchį́į́sh ("His [Prominent] Nose," better known as Cochise) as the event triggering the conflict between themselves and the Nṉee, the People, in keeping with their diffuse social structure, appear to have had varying interpretations of what led to the heightened violence of the 1860s. For many Chiricahuas, the deaths of Cochise's family members in 1861—an incident that came to be known among them as "cut the tent" for Gúchį́į́sh's manner of escape—did indeed lead them to go to war to avenge their relatives' deaths. But for the Western Apache, the experience of the Hák'ayé, a community with whom their local groups sometimes had strained relations, while illustrative of the perils of trusting the *Inṉaa*, did not require a change in behavior. In fact, so marginal was the Bascom-Cochise incident among the Western Apache that it does not even appear in any of their surviving oral accounts from this period.[50]

Instead, a rereading of American documents of this time against the available Nṉee testimony suggests that relations between the Enemy and those People closest to Tucson—the Tsézhiné and the T'iisibaan—were shaped, much as they had been during the Spanish and Mexican eras, by a series of encounters in and around Aravaipa Canyon. Moreover, rather than the inevitable slide into hostilities that most *Inṉaa* believed occurred whenever "savagery" and "civilization" encountered one another, this period witnessed not an immediate explosion of violence triggered by a single event but instead a fluid process of negotiation. Often the leaders of these encounters were not the male warriors that have dominated most *Inṉaa* histories but rather women and elders—figures whom one Nṉee illuminatingly defined as "talk carriers" and whose role it was to travel between communities and mitigate conflict.[51]

The Tsézhiné and the T'iisibaan achieved their first recorded agreement with Americans in the spring of 1859. Negotiations opened in March, when two of the Black Rocks People visited the Enemy's main camp, waving a white flag to request a parley with the fort's officer. The two sides agreed to meet for a more extended talk two weeks hence at Cañada del Oro, a canyon thirty miles northeast of Tucson. Just days before the chosen date, however, delegates from the People returned to request that the meeting be moved north to Aravaipa Canyon, where a majority of their community was then camped.[52]

The *Innaa* refused this change of venue and insisted in meeting in Cañada del Oro on the chosen date. Upon the Enemy's arrival, the People, "fear[ing] treachery," kept a cautious watch. After surveying the Enemy for a day, the People sent out three representatives while the rest of the Nnee "hover[ed] upon the distant hill tops," studying how their compatriots were received. Only once they were convinced that there was little risk of a surprise attack did eight hundred or so Tsézhiné and T'iisibaan descend to the canyon floor for two days of negotiations.[53]

The agreement that emerged out of this exchange differed little from those the People had secured during the Mexican era of "partial peace." In exchange for pledging not to kill or raid any Americans, the Black Rocks People and Cottonwoods in Gray Wedge Shape People were promised safe passage throughout the territory as well as regular distributions of food and other supplies. The Tsézhiné and the T'iisibaan followed up this agreement by selling a large amount of livestock seized in Mexico to the *Innaa* and making a number of journeys to Tucson to bargain "for blankets, &c."[54]

As with other "partial peace" agreements, this negotiation did not signify a total end to hostile relations with outsiders, but rather an effort on the People's part to secure friendly relations with those Enemy living closest to Nnee homelands while leaving the People free to continue raids farther afield. The result was an uneven pattern of accommodation and violence. In the months after the treaty, observers in the Tucson vicinity noted that the Black Rocks People and Cottonwoods in a Gray Wedge Shape People, in accordance with their agreement, had "frequently met Americans, and not interrupted them in any way," even when there were only a few *Innaa* "and the number of Indians was large." At the same time, however, raids on livestock continued on the Nakaiyé ("Those Who Walk Around," or Mexicans) across the border in

Sonora and even at a few mines on the U.S. side of the recently created and poorly marked international boundary.[55]

Although it is unclear which local groups participated in these latter raids (or even whether the offending groups realized they were in the United States rather than Mexico), in the winter of 1859 the Enemy, considering the treaty from the Cañada del Oro defunct, launched a campaign against the People living near Aravaipa Canyon. A surprise *Innaa* attack captured twenty or so children, leading the Black Rocks People to dispatch a delegation of two older women to reestablish amicable relations between themselves and the Enemy. The *Innaa* responded, however, with another expedition into the People's territory. Warned of the campaign by a T'iisibaan woman at Tucson, one of the People's leaders hailed the approaching attackers from a high point not far from the Gila River. In Spanish, accompanied by "emphatic gestures" and, when this effort to communicate in a foreign tongue failed him, with words in his native language, the man expressed his distress at the *Innaa*'s invasion. "What have you come here for?" he reportedly asked his would-be assailants. "I thought we were good friends. Did we not visit Tucson and Tubac, and go on an excursion to the Fort to see you all? We sat by your fires in friendship, and ate of your bread; and now you come to kill us, our wives and our children." The man's words, however, did not dissuade the *Innaa* from pursuing the People for the better part of a day before abandoning their campaign.[56]

The following month a band of People seized an American woman and her eleven-year-old Mexican servant from their home in the foothills of the Santa Rita Mountains. This was an unprecedented development: in the six years since the Enemy claimed sovereignty over the region, never before had the People taken an *Innaa* woman captive. At the same time as this unusual incident, an Apache elder arrived in Tucson to try to arrange a new truce. Through this elder, as well as two Nnēē prisoners released as negotiators, the *Innaa* demanded the release of the female captives. Although the Black Rocks People denied any involvement in the incident, they nonetheless promised to help find the women. A few weeks later, having secured the Mexican servant from the group that captured her, they released her during a parley in Aravaipa Canyon in exchange for the two dozen Tsézhiné women and children seized in earlier attacks by the *Innaa*.[57]

Whatever joy the Black Rocks People experienced at being reunited with their imprisoned family members, however, likely dissipated soon afterwards.

Tūdotł'ish sik̯án ("Blue Water Pool"): Camp Grant as it appeared in 1870.

Little more than a month after the exchange of captives in Aravaipa Canyon, the *Innaa* began to construct a fort at Tūdotł'ish sik̯án ("Blue Water Pool," not far from the junction of the San Pedro River and Aravaipa Canyon). We do not know what the Black Rocks People termed the new settlement that had suddenly sprung up in the middle of one of the most fertile portions of their homeland—a locale they had struggled to control for close to a century and which defined their very group identity. But over the next few years, as they occupied, abandoned, and then reoccupied the spot at the canyon's mouth, the Enemy would give it several names: Fort Aravaypa, Fort Breckenridge, Camp Stanford, and, finally, in 1865, Camp Grant.[58]

T O THE NNEE, the growing violence of this period was not confined solely to raids and war expeditions against the *Innaa* but intersected with ongoing conflicts between the People themselves. Western Apaches thus described

Jésus María Elías's 1863 attack on the N̲n̲ee̅ in Aravaipa Canyon in a way that emphasized how an unfortunate clan feud had, in fact, set the stage for the assault. According to Her Eyes Grey, "two young men who were cross-cousins and close friends" were joking around one day when one "by accident" pulled down the other's breechcloth, exposing his genitals. "Because of this, the other got mad and killed him right there." Realizing the gravity of what he had done, the young man, who was from the Bìszáhé clan ("Adobe Cut Bank or Edge of Cliff Dwelling People"), fled with many of his clan members to the Black Rocks People in Aravaipa Canyon.[59]

The dead man was from the T'é'nádòljàgé clan ("Descending into the Water in Peaks People"). Following custom, three of his kinspeople, setting out to avenge his death, managed to surprise their clansmember's murderer early one morning while he was out tracking a deer. In the ensuing confrontation, however, the man shot and killed one of the T'é'nádòljàgé before being dispatched himself. Perceiving themselves to be unlucky for having lost another of their relatives, the members of the Descending into the Water in Peaks People quickly retreated, leaving their opponents to bury the bodies. The Bìszáhé placed the two men in the same grave, saying, "They have both died together, and our people and the *t'é'nádòljàgé* always used to be close friends before. It still should be that way, so we will bury them together."[60]

Now that each clan had shed blood, the Bìszáhé hoped that they might achieve a reconciliation that would allow the two groups to live together as before:

> Not long after that [the murderer's death] they made a raid down into Mexico and brought back some horses and cattle. On their return they talked together: "One person has been killed on each side now, so that makes us even. But then another man was killed and we will have to pay for him. That way we will make peace and become close friends just as we were before all this happened."
>
> They decided that the animals they had on hand were not sufficient to satisfy the dead man's relatives, and so they made another raid to the south. They told their families to wait for them at a certain place close to the head of Arivaipa Canyon. They returned to them with several head of cattle. They posted guards to see that the Mexicans did not trail

and attack them, but these guards found no sign of any pursuers. All the same, the Mexicans and Apache Mansos had banded together and started out to follow them.

About three days after that the people held a big dance. They did not know it, but the Mexicans and Apache Mansos had surrounded the place and had their guns trained on them. Right there they attacked and killed a great many of the people—men, women, and children. Those who were wounded they later killed with stones. There were a lot of Apache Mansos in the party with the Mexicans. It was a terrible thing, for they shot the people down like cattle. They caught them in a blind canyon and many could not get out. Those who managed to escape later gathered together on top of a hill. They returned to bury their dead when the enemy had gone.

Many *bìszáhé* clanspeople had been killed, and it was all because of that *bìszáhé* man killing the youth who pulled off his gee string [breechcloth]. They all thought it was the *t'é'nádòljàgé* clanspeople who had brought about this catastrophe by using *gò'*ndì* [a supernatural power often used on enemies] on them. They must have had men who sang and prayed that some evil would befall them and sent their power against them to cause all this. Their power must have been strong. Because of this the *bìszáhé* people were able to make peace with the *t'é'nádòljàgé* people. They had killed two of the *t'é'nádòljàgé*, but in time the *t'é'nádòljàgé* had caused the death of many *bìszáhé* by using their power on them. That is how the thing ended and those people were able to return to their homes on White River once more.[61]

If this story served in part to instruct the People as to the dangers of losing one's temper, it offers a number of additional insights into Nnee interpretations of the past. While the Enemy make an appearance, the central characters of this drama are not T. T. Tidball or Jesús María Elías but the Nnee, and it is the People's concerns (and, above all, their appeals to supernatural power) that ultimately shape the course of events. The narrative also evokes the divided character of Nnee society. Not only could there be feuds between different clans; there was also deep suspicion of the Bāāchii communities in Tucson and Tubac. Perhaps the most obvious measure of this tension can be found in the fact that Her Eyes Grey placed the *apaches mansos*, a group that Mexican-American folklore about the 1863 attack does not mention at all and that in U.S. Army documents appears as only a single individual ("Lojinio, the Apache boy, who so successfully guided . . . Captain Tidball"), at the forefront of the killings.[62]

Innaa documents suggest that the total number of Bāāchii in the mid-nineteenth century was modest: an 1860 report tallied approximately 150 *apaches mansos* "in the immediate vicinity of Tucson," while a territorial census in 1869 recorded seventy-seven "tame Apaches," thirty-two men and forty-five women. Yet as invisible as the Bāāchii may have been for most non-Apaches, they loom large in the People's accounts from the era.[63] In most of these stories, the Bāāchii functioned both as a shadowy threat and a community that inverted proper norms of Nnēē behavior.

> One time, my relatives had an Apache Manso captive. He was captured and raised among our people. He was a boy about twelve or fifteen years old, old enough to know his own mind. Then he ran off back to his own people in Tucson. When this boy ran off to Tucson he saw all Whites and Mexicans in Tucson. He knew now where our people lived most of the time. So they appointed him a leader for the Mexicans. From that time on there were a lot of attacks on our people because this captive knew where our people would be at different times of the year. He knew where all the springs were and where our people camped.[64]

Although the Bāāchii's roots can be traced to the bands that settled in Tsēē idzisgoláné during the Spanish era, they received periodic infusions of Nnēē throughout the nineteenth century. To the People, the Bāāchii appear to have offered a refuge for those who violated community mores or who inhabited the margins of their local group. In one case from the mid-1860s, for example, a Nnēē husband and wife who arrived in Tucson, seeking to join the *apaches mansos*, turned out to have become involved with one another without parental approval, prompting their flight. Another member of the Bāāchii reported that she had left her original band because other Nnēē "killed her mother, her husband & her boy," presumably in a clan feud or in a dispute over witchcraft. Others may have seen the Bāāchii as offering individual preservation at a time

of tremendous violence and chaos. After a group of the People, fearing a surprise attack, fled from the Enemy in 1866, one Nnee, perhaps exhausted by
the constant danger posed by soldier and civilian patrols, stayed behind and
informed the *Innaa* that he "want[ed] to go to Tucson and live with the tame
Apaches."[65]

The Baachii had a vexed relationship with other Nnee groups, doubtless
because of the profound risk the Baachii presented to the People. The Enemy
attempted to harness the cycles of revenge between the Baachii and rival Nnee
communities to their own ends, distributing food and "very liberal" gifts
to the *apaches mansos* and even offering bounties for every Apache scalp the
Baachii brought back to Tucson. But more often than not, the Baachii seem to
have pursued hostilities against other bands of People in accordance with their
own customs. As one Baachii told a U.S. official, "We need no urging from
the great captain of the whites to turn our feet towards the mountains where
live our murderous brethren, while we have left to us the widows and children
of our own braves who have fallen by their hands; we only live now to avenge
their wrongs."[66]

As such comments imply, the Baachii aspired to more than a mere mer-
cenary existence on the fringes of the Enemy's towns. In 1866, a delegation
of Baachii chiefs paid a visit to Arizona's Indian agent to demand their own
land. During the Spanish and Mexican era, the leaders explained, they had
farmed along the Sonoita River near Tubac, only to be displaced in the past
few years by "white settlers." They now insisted that a permanent plot contain-
ing "good wood, water, and soil for cultivation" be set aside for them, either in
the Sonoita valley or along the nearby San Pedro River, which some Baachii
apparently still regarded as part of their original homeland.[67]

I F THE BEHAVIOR OF EACH GROUP was radically different from one
another, the Black Rocks People and the Baachii shared the common challenge of adjusting to the *Innaa*'s presence. In May of 1862, the Enemy reoccupied its military base at Tūdotł'ish sikán ("Blue Water Pool"), transforming
the heart of Tsézhiné territory, Aravaipa Canyon, into a source of danger.
Within months of the fort's reestablishment, local Nnee would attempt "little by little" to negotiate with the newcomers in their midst. Soon afterwards,

however, the army, because of the then ongoing war against the Confederacy, abandoned the fort. Even without a permanent *Innaa* presence in Aravaipa, however, the People's camps in the canyon remained vulnerable. Unable to capture or kill the People in large numbers, the Enemy initiated a policy of destroying whatever crops and "mescal, dried beef etc." they could locate. In 1864, for example, the *Innaa* launched a raid during which soldiers "set fire to everything" at Aravaipa Canyon, "effecting a complete destruction of the crop, huts, etc." For its part, Nnee oral tradition records that there "came a time" when the leaders of the Tsézhiné "stopped their people from coming down here to the Little Running Water to plant crops," presumably because of the dangers involved.[68]

A subsequent set of negotiations that took place in 1866 after the *Innaa* reestablished their post at Tūdotł'ish sikán demonstrates the very different ways that the People and the Enemy had come by this time to think about peace. In December, a delegation from the Black Rocks People and Cottonwoods in Gray Wedge Shape People held a meeting with the *Innaa* not far from Tūdotł'ish sikán. Pronouncing himself "happy" to "come back to the spot where we were born and where we played as children," Askinenha ("Angry, He Is Snoring"), a chief of the Tsézhiné, sought an agreement that would allow him and his people to settle in Aravaipa, safe from attack and starvation. "[W]e have been living upon herbs and grass," stated Askinenha. "[W]e now wish to change our manner of living." Added Askevanche ("Angry, He Is Selfish"), a T'iisibaan chief: "[W]e require some few oxen, some ploughs, and some food to maintain ourselves and children and wives." [69]

In response, the Enemy offered his own vision of peace. The *Innaa* would allow the People to settle near Aravaipa, "assist you with food," and "remove the danger from your wives and children." But if the Enemy thought that the People had not fulfilled their pledges, "soldiers by the thousands will come to hunt you down, drive you from one mountain to another, burn your rancherias, your mescal and other property and take your wives and children away from you."[70]

Not surprisingly, the chiefs evinced considerable wariness in the face of such vows. "[W]e do not wish to settle with our families right away at the post," explained Askinenha, who doubtless planned on bringing in most of his followers once he was better able to gauge the Enemy's intentions. Askinenha and the other chiefs also tried to educate the *Innaa* as to the migratory nature of Nnēē subsistence, which made it impossible for the People to confine them-selves solely to Aravaipa Canyon. "[O]ur principal food is mescal . . . we can therefore not be expected to be and remain in the valley all the time. . . . [W]e wish to go and come when we please, for we must go for mescal, must hunt the deer and visit the mountains."[71]

These arguments seemed to convince the Enemy, for they promised the Black Rocks People and the Cottonwoods in Gray Wedge Shape People "safety in all parts of this Territory." To signal their acceptance of the agreement, the *Innaa* distributed red ribbons to the People, which each band member was sup-posed to wear to indicate their participation in the peace accord. That evening, the Nnēē celebrated the treaty by holding a ceremonial dance; the next day, they recognized the Enemy's traditions by having the agreement read aloud to them and by making their marks on a piece of paper. The People then pro-posed following up the treaty with an exchange of captives. In exchange for a "white child" whom they had held for two years, the Nnēē asked the Enemy to help secure the release of an unusual eight-year-old Apache boy—a mute with "a double little toe on one foot"—seized two months earlier by the Sáíkiné.[72]

What happened over the next few weeks is only partially recorded, but it must have renewed the People's belief in the untrustworthy character of the *Innaa*. Despite Nnēē efforts to explain their seasonal migrations to the Enemy, the *Innaa* soon insisted that the People remain at Łee ndlįį (Flows Together). Any of the People found away from the river junction would, the Enemy informed them, be "shot on sight." Possibly outraged at the *Innaa*'s attempt to enforce such impossible rules on them or perhaps fearing that such threats pre-figured a general attack, the People fled to the mountains to the north of Ara-vaipa Canyon. Within a matter of weeks, the Enemy, in accordance with their earlier threats to "punish and destroy" the Nnēē, dispatched several hundred *Innaa* and Sáíkiné in pursuit of the People. A group of the People attempted to hail the invaders from a nearby hilltop, waving a white flag and shouting "Ami-gos." But the attackers destroyed the Nnēē's newly planted crops and killed several People anyway. Among the casualties was one of the chiefs who, just a few months before, had participated in the treaty at Łee ndlįį.[73]

Much as the "narratives of horrors" of the 1830s and '40s had instructed the People as to the perils posed by the Mexicans and the "Bear Enemy," so too must these later encounters with American military and civilians have produced their own cautionary tales. Bits and pieces of these narratives surface in comments that the Nṉēē offered during the tense negotiations of the 1860s and '70s. At one parley, for example, members of the People voiced the suspicion that the Enemy was interested not in peace but rather in exterminating them. "They said that the Zuñis had told them that after the Navajoes surrendered we had killed all the men, and left none alive but the women and children, of whom we made slaves," observed one *Inṉaa*, who found himself incapable of "disabus[ing]" the People of this not entirely inaccurate description of the bitter campaign that forced the Navajo onto New Mexico's Bosque Redondo Reservation. During another encounter, a Nṉēē elder proclaimed that "he was opposed to making peace. The whites were only doing it to kill them." Although the Enemy tried to persuade the People otherwise by offering them a cow, the Nṉēē remained "apprehensive of treachery." That night, apparently convinced by the elder's warnings, they slipped away, leaving behind burden baskets and other goods in their haste to escape what they believed to be an imminent massacre.[74]

With such stories guiding the People and *Inṉaa* raids devastating Nṉēē subsistence, the struggle between the two groups grew increasingly desperate. While the People, fearing ghost sickness, almost never took body parts as trophies in the manner of their Tohono O'odham, Mexican, and American foes, this did not stop them from stripping naked and mutilating those they killed—in part as a protest at *Inṉaa* mistreatment of Nṉēē dead, in part in an effort to intimidate their opponents, and in part as a show of outrage. "They [the People] used to spear a man three or four times through the body after he was dead, just to show how much they hated him," recalled one Nṉēē.[75]

Equally prevalent was the destruction of *Inṉaa* property. Some of these acts—the surreptitious burning of haystacks and buildings, the destroying of bellows and other mining equipment—had the obvious objective of encouraging the Enemy to abandon specific locations. Others are harder to interpret. After a Nṉēē raid on one Anglo homestead, the entire contents of the house was left "on the ground outside, in heaps of broken rubbish. Not far from the door stood a pile made of wool, corn, beans, and flour, and capping the whole a gold watch hung from a stick driven into the heap." In another instance, "[t]he sides of the house were broken in and the court was filled with broken tables and doors, while fragments of crockery and iron-ware lay mixed in heaps with grain and the contents of mattresses." It may be that through such exuberant destruction of the trappings of *Innaa* existence—buildings, furniture, food, kitchenware, timepieces—the People hoped not only to signal the fragility of the Enemy's presence but also to mock *Innaa* notions of property and propriety, the very essence of the civilization that the Enemy claimed to be bringing to the borderlands.[76]

And yet many of the People came to realize that such efforts could not displace the even greater violence of the *Innaa*. As one Nṉēē chief acknowledged when trying to arrange a truce in 1866, "the Apaches could not fight successfully, they would all be killed if they did not make peace." The dilemma facing the People by the early 1870s was therefore as terrifying as it was stark. Could the Enemy be relied upon to make a lasting peace, one that would protect the Nṉēē from starvation and surprise attack? Or was it better to flee to the mountains and hope to evade the Enemy there?[77]

I N FEBRUARY OF 1871, several groups of the People, led by the T'iisibaan chief Hashkēē bá nzį́n ("Angry, Men Stand in Line for Him") and a man known to the *Innaa* as Captain Chiquito, responded to the perilous position in which their community found itself by sending a group of female elders to initiate negotiations with the Enemy at Blue Water Pool. (Captain Chiquito's name was derived from the Spanish word for "small"; whether he had an Apache-language name or was related to the former *apache de paz* leader Chiquito who was killed in Aravaipa Canyon in 1832 is unknown.)

Non-Apache histories have typically presented these negotiations as an exceptional occurrence—a rare attempt by a Nṉēē leader to convince his followers to abandon warfare. As we have seen, however, for more than a decade the Tsézhiné and the T'iisibaan had been dispatching "talk carriers" to the *Innaa* in an effort to diminish the violence between themselves and the Enemy near Aravaipa Canyon. In addition to the 1859 pact and Askinenha's and Askevanche's 1866 truce, *Innaa* records document repeated delegations of People "asking permission . . . to come in and make peace" with the Enemy at Blue Water Pool, only to be dismissed and, in one case, pursued and killed. There is little evidence, in short, to suggest that Hashkēē bá nzį́n acted on his

*Hashkēē bá nzín ("Angry,
Men Stand in Line for Him"):
Chief of the T'iisibaan
("Cottonwoods in Gray Wedge
Shape People," or Pinal Apaches).*

own in initiating negotiations or that by telling the Enemy at Blue Water Pool
that "his people had no home, and could make none, as they were at all times
apprehensive of the approach of cavalry," he was doing anything other than
articulating—as it was a chief's duty to do—the collective fears and desires of
his followers.[78]

The paramount hope the Black Rocks People expressed through Hashkēē
bá nzín was familiar from past negotiations: the desire to inhabit Aravaipa
Canyon in safety. "Our father and their fathers before them have lived in these
mountain[s] and have raised corn in this valley," Hashkēē bá nzín informed
the *Innaa*, explaining why his band did not want to join the Dziłghá'é ("On
Top of the Mountain People," or White Mountain Apache) at Fort Apache as
the Enemy suggested. "We are taught to make mescal our principal article of
food, and in summer and winter here we have a never-failing supply. At the
White Mountains there is none, and without it now we get sick. Some of our
people have been in . . . for a short time at the White Mountains, but they are
not contented, and they all say, 'Let us go the Aravapa and make a final peace
and never break it.'"[79]

The next few months appear in Nnéé oral accounts as a time of plenty and tranquillity. As the Western Apache woman Bi ja gush kai ye ("The One Whose Ears Look Like Cactus") told the anthropologist Grenville Goodwin years later:

[We] heard there were lots of Indians living down close to *tu dn tl ij si kun* [Blue Water Pool] and drawing rations there. So we went down there again and camped at *nadn lit choh* [Big Sunflower Hill, Malpais Hill on San Pedro River] where the rations were being issued. That was the first time I ever saw flour, sugar, or coffee. . . . We had lots of rations, flour, sugar, coffee, meat. We had no bags to put them in, so had to dump all into our burden baskets. They gave us corn also. Later on we went back for rations again, and this time when we moved away a lot of people came with us. . . . Some *sli na ba ja* [Some Who Hunt on the Horse, a White Mountain Apache band] had heard that there were rations being given over here, and so had come over also.

Now we lived close to San Pedro. The women used to go out and cut hay and sell it to the soldiers for their horses. For this, they would get a red ticket on which they could draw rations or get calico and other things.[80]

For all their detail as to events in Aravaipa, the People's accounts of this period offer little commentary on happenings outside the canyon. The surviving narratives never mention Tséé idzisgoláné (Tucson) or the heated controversy that the Apaches' presence generated among the town's residents. Nor do Nnéé stories engage one of the central accusations the *Innaa* lodged against them: that the People in the canyon made surreptitious raids despite their professed peace agreement.

This silence can be interpreted in multiple ways. It may prove, as the Nnéé maintained at the time, that they were not involved in attacks. Or it may reflect a desire to cover up an embarrassing truth. As Bi ja gush kai ye's account highlights, the People in Aravaipa came from several local groups, not all of which may have felt obligated to observe whatever agreement Hashkéé bá nzín had worked out with the *Innaa*. Given the People's tendency to forge partial peace agreements with Mexicans and Americans alike, it is possible that some of the Nṉēē at the canyon conceptualized their treaty in their usual localistic terms. Lieutenant Whitman later recalled that "[t]heir [the Apaches'] understanding when they first came in was, that they were at peace only with Camp Grant, and not with Arizona." When the *Innaa* encouraged the People to serve as scouts against other Apache bands, a few agreed, "provided that in turn they should be assisted in an expedition upon Sonora." Was this evidence that the Nṉēē in Aravaipa Canyon hoped to impose their vision of partial peace on the *Innaa* at Camp Grant? Or was it a clever way of declining to join the Enemy's campaigns, as the People suspected that the *Innaa* would reject their proposal out of hand?[81]

Still, when questioned before the massacre about the deaths of Wooster and his "wife," Hashkēē bá nzį́n pointed out that the couple's murders, which took place over a hundred miles away from Blue Water Pool, corresponded with a ration day at Camp Grant. This contention prompted the military to check their records, which indeed revealed "there were more Indians on the Reservation [when Wooster and Aguirre were killed] than at any other time." Whatever their involvement with other raids, Hashkēē bá nzį́n and the T"iisibaan likely had nothing to do with the deaths that the *Innaa* would later use to justify the mass murder of women and children in Aravaipa Canyon.[82]

If conventional historical records provide little insight into how the People viewed their treaty, they tell us even less about what the four to five hundred Nṉēē camping in Aravaipa on April 29, 1871, may have been contemplating as the shadows began to lengthen across the canyon floor early that evening. Apache oral sources suggest that many among the People were preparing for a healing ceremony or a celebratory dance, and that the gender divisions central to these rituals explain the predominance of women and children killed the following morning. Such accounts, however, come to us from the massacre's survivors. The scores of Nṉēē who would be dead within a few hours left behind no records of their final moments—only a vast and desolate silence that haunts the canyon even today.[83]

PART TWO

JUSTICE

December 11, 1871. A warm winter sun beats down on the adobe buildings and packed-earth plazas of nineteenth-century Tucson. For the past few days, the town has hummed with energy, its dusty streets and stores crowded not only with its usual three thousand or so residents, but also with large contingents of Tohono O'odham and vecinos *from San Xavier del Bac and other nearby villages. Voices speaking Spanish, English, and O'odham hang in the desert air, mingling with the noise of passing wagons and oxcarts bound for Guaymas, Hermosillo, and other settlements across the border in Sonora.*

The event drawing these visitors to Tucson is not the Fiesta de San Agustín or another of the festivals that make up the usual rhythm of community life along the border. Rather it is the unprecedented trial of one hundred locals—Anglos, Tohono O'odham, and Mexicans alike—in U.S. District Court on charges that with "malice aforethought {they} did kill and murder" the Apache dwelling in Aravaipa Canyon.[1]

Sensing history in the making, an itinerant photographer has shown up to record the proceedings. During a break in the testimony, he sets up his equipment—a large, hooded camera, a box of fragile glass plates, a mobile darkroom. The resulting image captures the accused arrayed in the plaza facing the courthouse: the Anglo participants together with their counsel, his hand tucked inside his jacket, at the center of the frame, staring resolutely into the camera; the vecinos *crowded to the rear; and the O'odham lining the courthouse's adobe walls, as much on the margins of the photo as they are in the proceedings inside the courtroom. The scene is indeed historic: this collective portrait*

of the accused participants in the Camp Grant Massacre remains the earliest known
photograph of Tucson and its inhabitants.

D
ESIGNED TO UNEARTH the truth about the Apache deaths near
Camp Grant, the trial that unfolded in Tucson in December 1871
brought to the surface a different, unintended reality: the existence of stark divides in how the varied inhabitants of the borderlands narrated
the events surrounding the massacre. If to the region's military commander,
Colonel Stoneman, "[t]he murder of those hostages in camp was an act of war
against the United States," to many of the region's residents, it was not clear
that the killing of Apache women and children in Aravaipa Canyon constituted a crime at all. Not until October 1871, following six months of prod-
ding from federal authorities, culminating in threats to impose martial law in
the territory, did the U.S. district attorney for Arizona, W. C. Rowell, arrest
the alleged ringleaders of the massacre—Jesús María Elías, Juan Elías, and
William Oury—along with four other suspects. The men all pled not guilty,
as would the ninety-three other men arraigned with them two months later in
U.S. District Court in Tucson.[2]

The ensuing trial, held in the very same courthouse where some of the
meetings to organize the attack on Camp Grant had taken place in the spring
of 1871, represented the first time in Arizona territorial history that the
killing of an Apache by a non-Apache led to the prosecution of the accused
perpetrators. It also boasted a number of other unusual features. Rather than
determine the individual guilt or innocence of each suspect, it was agreed to
try only Sidney DeLong (an alleged member of the attacking party and the
mayor of Tucson) and let whatever judgment he received be applied to the
rest of the defendants. (Why DeLong, who played only a marginal role in
the Camp Grant Massacre, became the lead figure in the prosecution is not
entirely clear, but it may have been because of his prominent position in Tucson's local government.) In addition, the suspects were represented by both
Granville Oury, "Uncle Billy's" brother, and J. E. McCaffry, Pima County's
district attorney.[3]

The trial's opening on December 6 attracted a crowd of observers to Tuc-

"Not guilty": Camp Grant Massacre trial participants outside Pima County Court House in December of 1871.

son's mudbrick courthouse, constructed within the walls of the former presidio in 1868. Over the next five days, the audience, which included not only a significant portion of Tucson's Mexican and Anglo population but "nearly 100 Papago Indians," would hear from an array of witnesses, each presenting their version of the killings in Aravaipa Canyon.[4]

Reminding his audience that as a veteran of the Civil War he "had seen . . . battlefields before," Lieutenant Royal Whitman highlighted, in his role as a witness for the prosecution, the extraordinary violence visited upon the Apache women and children:

I saw the dead bodies of several women that I recognized. . . . [T]wo were lying on their backs entirely naked and shot through the breast apparently with pistol balls. . . . I saw the dead bodies of children—perhaps six. They had died apparently by gunshot wounds. . . . I recollect one child perhaps two years of age with the arm nearly cut off. Besides [an]

old man . . . the only other dead body of a male was a boy perhaps sixteen years of age.[5]

Ascención, a captain among the Desert People and the lone O'odham to
testify at the trial, spoke about the long-running cycle of raids and counter-
raids between his people and the Apache:

> The Papagoes are at war with the Apaches; have so been since I was
> born. . . . If I was alone among the Apaches they would kill me.
> They would do so with any of my tribe. We would look for nothing
> else. . . . The Apaches are now and have been always in the habit of
> stealing stock from us. When stock has been stolen from us by the
> Apaches we follow on the trail and try to recover the stock.[6]

Although none of the attack's supposed ringleaders—the Elías brothers
and William Oury—testified, a parade of Anglo and *vecino* defense witnesses
offered evidence designed to link the Apache at Camp Grant to an assortment of local killings and thefts. A woman named Gertrude McWard told of
seeing a dress "with black silk trimmings" that had once belonged to "Mrs.
Wooster" in the possession of an interpreter's wife at Camp Grant in July 1871.
The German immigrant Fritz Contzen, who came to Tucson in the 1850s as
a member of the U.S. Boundary Survey, swore that the saddle that a *vecino*
named Concepción Biella had secured a few months before from an Apache in
Aravaipa Canyon was the property of a mail rider killed by Apaches outside
Tucson the previous year. Rais Mendoza, a *vecino* from San Xavier del Bac, and
Francisco Carillo of Punta de Agua contended that they attacked the *ranchería*
in Aravaipa Canyon only because the Apaches who stole the Elíases' stock in
early April had left tracks heading in that direction—and that in pursuing
these raiders, the Elíases killed an Apache from Camp Grant with a distinctive missing front tooth.[7]

The defense testimony was intended to establish an incontrovertible link
between the Apaches in Aravaipa and the recent depredations, but it raised
almost as many questions as it answered. Even if Trinidad Aguirre's dress or
the mail rider's saddle was as distinctive as McWard and Contzen claimed,
for example, might not the Apaches at Camp Grant have acquired them just

as their present owners had, via trade? Moreover, given that neither of these items was identified until midsummer, how did they justify a massacre carried out in April? The story of the Elíases chasing Apache raiders and killing one of them seemed equally uncompelling at second glance. Any tracks leading from the Elíases' ranch to Aravaipa Canyon would have been more than two weeks old by the time of the massacre and virtually impossible to locate during the party's nighttime approach, even for a skilled tracker like Jesús María. (Indeed, Carillo admitted as much in his testimony, stating that in the darkness, the attackers had been limited to "follow[ing] the direction the trail had been leading.") The defense witness José María Yesques undermined this narrative even further when, under cross-examination, he described talking to the Apache with the telltale missing tooth several months after the Indian's supposed death. Other testimony at the trial revealed the embarrassing fact that Rowell, the district attorney directing the prosecution, not only had advance knowledge of the attack but participated in several of the public meetings leading up to the massacre, where he spoke in favor of the settlers' launching "a war" against hostile Apaches.[8]

Although their presence haunted the proceedings in ways spoken and unspoken, the one group not in attendance at the trial was the Apache. The murdered Nṉēē, their names unknown to the federal government, were listed in court documents simply as "John Doe Apache," "Mary Doe Apache," and "Susan Doe a female Apache." For their part, those Nṉēē still alive—Hashkēē bá nzín, Captain Chiquito, and their followers—spent most of the time prior to the trial hidden in the inaccessible peaks above Aravaipa Canyon in hopes of eluding further attacks. Even after reaching an agreement with U.S. negotiators in September to return to the juncture of Aravaipa Creek and the San Pedro River, none of the Apache survivors of the massacre were invited to take part, either as witnesses or observers, in the very event designed to achieve justice for their people's deaths.

On December 11, after several days of competing testimony, the presiding judge, John Titus, remanded the case to a jury made up of twelve Mexican Americans and Anglos from Tucson. In his charge to the jurors, Titus all but exempted the O'odham from his court's jurisdiction on the basis that "both the Apache and Papago nations are tribal organizations with codes of their own concerning peace and war. . . . By the barbarous codes of both nations, the slaughter of their enemies, of all ages and sexes, is justifiable." He then proceeded to offer self-defense as a plausible explanation for all of the defendants' actions:

> The government of the United States owes its Papago, Mexican, and American residents in Arizona protection from Apache spoliation and assault. If such spoliation and assault are persistently carried on and not prevented, by the government, then the sufferers have a right to protect themselves and to employ force enough for the purpose. It is also to be added that if the Apache nation or any part of it persists in assailing the Papagos, or American, or Mexican residents of Arizona, then it forfeits the right of protection from the United States.

Presented with such narrow grounds on which to base their decision, the jury needed only nineteen minutes to return a verdict of not guilty.[9]

The acquittal of William Oury, Jesús María Elías, Juan Elías, and their fellow suspects marked the end of any official effort to seek redress for the Camp Grant Massacre. The speed of the jury's decision and the seeming conclusiveness of its verdict led one local newspaper, the *Arizona Miner*, to declare all debate over the murders in Aravaipa Canyon to be over as well: "Thus has justly ended the much-talked-of 'Camp Grant Affair.'" But even though the U.S. judicial system had passed judgment on the attackers' actions, the contest over the event's meaning remained far from finished. The struggle had now simply shifted—from the courtroom to the realm of historical memory.[10]

PART THREE

MEMORY

POST-1871 ARIZONA-SONORA BORDERLAND

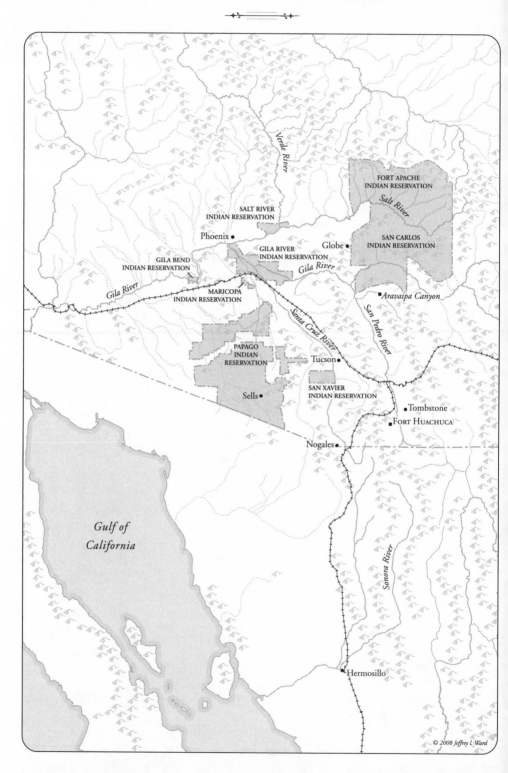

Verde River

FORT APACHE
INDIAN RESERVATION

Salt River

SALT RIVER
INDIAN RESERVATION

Phoenix •

Globe •

SAN CARLOS
INDIAN RESERVATION

GILA BEND
INDIAN RESERVATION

GILA RIVER
INDIAN RESERVATION

Gila River

Gila River

•Aravaipa Canyon

MARICOPA
INDIAN RESERVATION

San Pedro River

Santa Cruz River

PAPAGO
INDIAN
RESERVATION

Tucson •

Sells •

SAN XAVIER
INDIAN RESERVATION

• Tombstone

■ FORT HUACHUCA

Nogales •

Gulf of
California

Sonora River

• Hermosillo

© 2008 Jeffrey L. Ward

THE O'ODHAM

O N THEIR RETURN from 'Al Waiphia on the morning of April 30, 1871, the O'odham took care to follow the purification rituals necessary for all those who had come into contact with the *'O:b* for the first time. "[A]t the foot of the mountain in the Santa Cruz River Valley, they met this man," recollected one of the Desert People. "He had water, bread and pinoche [a parched grain drink] in a wagon. The young men only pretended to drink and wash themselves with the water. The old men could eat and drink, but the young men had to fast. They came back and had a big dance at Comobabi [Mulberry Well]."[1]

Only one of the People's calendar stick keepers found it necessary to make reference to the event that outsiders would soon come to call the Camp Grant Massacre, and he touched upon few of the issues that the *Milga:n* considered so important about the episode. The stick keeper made but passing reference to the existence of a U.S. Army base near 'Al Waiphia, and he included no acknowledgment that the *'O:b* had reached a truce with the soldiers at Aravaipa Canyon. Nor did the stick contain a tally of the number of deaths or mention the fact that most of those killed were women and children, although it did reference the taking of captives: "The People brought some children back and kept them as their own. When they were grown, and able to work, they were sold in Sonora for a hundred dollars a piece."[2]

Other communities' calendar sticks focused on different incidents altogether.

1870–71: For the second time in the memory of Indians, snow fell on their country and lay on the ground. Although it was light and melted away in two days, it was considered of historic value.[3]

1870–71: The first canal at Tempe was built by the Mormon settlers.

1870–71: The Apaches had come to the river at Santan for water and some Pimas discovered their trail and set off in pursuit. They failed to inflict any injury upon the enemy and retired with one of their own number mortally wounded.

At this time a Pima was killed at Ta-atûkam by the Apaches. These two corpses were burned.

Another Pima was killed during the year at Tempe by the Apaches, and his body was buried.[4]

As always, in keeping with their chronicle format, such records offered no suggestion that the events of 1871 possessed any greater import than those of preceding or following years.

Two developments in the attack's aftermath, however, signaled to the People that the *Milga:n* did not regard this raid as they had other expeditions against the *'O:b*. The first was the trial in Cuk Şon in December 1871 of the attack participants. Those Tohono O'odham who had taken part in the assault, according to their federal Indian agent, "came forward to a man voluntarily to respond to the charge of murder." The People nonetheless expressed confusion as to why killing Apaches—an act usually encouraged by American officials and civilians alike—had incurred such displeasure. "In regards the action taken by the Papago Indians in the Camp Grant Massacre," commented the agent, "I would most strongly urge upon you the belief that nothing but the best of motives induced these people to lend themselves to the affair. . . . [A]re we to find fault with these Indians for aiding in a transaction which they were given to believe was of service to these people [of Tucson] and to the Government itself[?]"[5]

The second unusual development was the arrangement of a peace conference at Little Springs in the spring of 1872. This was an unprecedented undertaking: for the first time, U.S. officials invited representatives from the

"You are the Pima who killed me years ago": Luis Morago (right), the Akimel O'odham translator, with fellow tribe member Kawadk Totşagï ("Shield Like Foam").

O'odham, Apache, and Mexican communities to negotiate with one another. Few O'odham could recall ever having an extended, face-to-face parley with the *'O:b*. "The Papagoes and Apaches have been at war as they express it themselves since they were born and they cannot easily be brought to think of the Apaches other than as enemies," explained the Tohono O'odham agent. But, he added, "I cannot express to you the satisfaction displayed by these Indians at the idea the time might come when the only enemy they have ever feared, indeed ever had, would be silenced in friendship." [6]

In late May of 1872, in a shady cottonwood grove along the San Pedro River, some forty-two River People and fifteen Desert People met with the surviving leaders of the Apaches at Camp Grant. Although seated apart, many of the participants nevertheless recognized one another. One of the translators for the River People, Luis Morago, found himself greeted "in high glee" by an *'O:b* whom he had knocked unconscious during an earlier raid, who told him in Spanish, "You are the Pima who killed me years ago." [7]

The meeting opened with the *'O:b* making a number of dramatic speeches. Placing a stone on the ground in front of the *Milga:n* organizers, one of the

Enemy chiefs promised to "make a peace as lasting as the rock." When it came his turn to respond, Francisco Galerita, a captain among the Tohono O'odham at Wa:k (San Xavier del Bac) and a probable participant in the recent massacre at Aravaipa, expressed his support for a new era of peace—provided the *'O:b* halted their aggressions on the People:

> If you Apaches will comply with your promises, I will never tread your soil again with evil intentions. If I have done so in the past, it was because I was provoked by your robbing. I obey the orders of my superiors: if you will do the same, and comply with your promises, we will dig a hole in the ground, and bury every thing—all our past differences—in it, and be as if no differences had occurred between us. . . . We are friends. If you want to come to Tucson, do so; and you can traffic with us and visit us without fear.

The Akimel O'odham chief Mawid Kawadk ("Lion Shield," known to the *Milga:n* as Antonio Azul) likewise counseled that peace would require his People and the Apache to overlook past outrages: "[N]ow they were at peace, let everything therefore be forgotten."[8]

Whatever other meanings the People may have assigned to this unusual conference remain difficult to determine. At least one community recorded it in their calendar stick: "1871–72: The symbols simply state that peace was made with the Apaches." But Mawid Kawadk, despite his willingness to forget the past, expressed some doubt as to the *'O:b* leaders' sincerity, and in the months following the peace conference conflict with the Enemy did not dissipate completely. In August and again in October of 1872, Tohono O'odham from Wa:k complained to American officials that Apaches had once again stolen livestock from them. If the People were to be restrained from going on punitive raids, the O'odham insisted "that they be recompensed for their loss."[9] In later years, the People renewed their campaigns against the *'O:b*, both on their own and alongside American soldiers.

> 1872–73: It was during this winter that the United States soldiers and the Pima, Maricopa, and Apache scouts surrounded the Superstition Mountain Apaches at the "Tanks" and rained bullets into their ranks until not a single man remained alive.[10]

Mawid Kawadk ("Lion Shield"):
Antonio Azul as he appeared in 1872.
The distinctive headdress was made
out of woven cotton and covered the
chief's long hair.

1873–74: A band of Enemies came to [Black Base] and stole horses. A
man of the People, who lived there, came to [Standing Water] to ask
help in chasing them. [Standing Water] held a meeting all night and
the next morning they started.[11]

DESPITE THE CONTINUING conflict with the Apache, this period also
witnessed a slow fracturing of the alliance between the People and *Milga:n*.
Given the dispersed nature of the People, this process happened at different
times in different places. The Akimel O'odham were among the first affected.
To the River People, the decades after 1871 became known as the "years of
famine," for it was in these years that American settlers moved upstream of
the O'odham settlements on the Gila and diverted the river to their own fields.
With the water upon which their once-flourishing agriculture depended gone,
the River People's status as the region's leading farmers, the sellers of millions
of pounds of wheat and other foodstuffs, soon withered in the harsh desert
sunlight.

Not surprisingly, Akimel O'odham calendar sticks from these years chronicle a people beset by multiple woes. Some migrated to the outskirts of the recently founded town of Phoenix in search of fresh sources of water, while others sunk into intracommunity conflicts, economic crisis, and disease.

1872–73: For several years the Pimas had had little water to irrigate their fields and were beginning to suffer from actual want when the settlers on Salt River invited them to come to that valley. During this year a large party of Rso'tûk Pimas accepted the invitation. . . . The motive of the Mormons on the Salt was not wholly disinterested, as they desired the Pimas to act as a buffer against the assaults of the Apache.

1875–76: In this year sickness prevailed in the village of Rsânûk, apparently the same as in 1866, when the principal symptom of the disease was shooting pains through the body. Two medicine-men were suspected of having caused the trouble by magic means, and they were killed to stop the plague.

1877–78: A party of Pimas went to the Kwahadk' village to drink tizwin [a fermented corn drink], and in the quarrel which ensued the Casa Blancas killed two men of Santan. Some time afterwards the Gila Crossing people drank tizwin, and one of their number was killed by a man from Salt River.[12]

In addition to this rising intervillage conflict, relations between the Akimel O'odham and adjoining settlers teetered on the brink of open warfare on several occasions during the 1870s, as starving River People, brandishing weapons at any protesting *Milga:n*, helped themselves to their new neighbors' crops and livestock.[13]

For the Tohono O'odham, who would receive a small reservation encompassing the lands near Wa:k in 1874, tensions with outsiders would not peak for another decade. But by the mid-1880s, with the Apache increasingly confined to reservations and southern Arizona's cattle herds expanding, "[t]here were white men here and there on our land . . . as there had never been," remem-

"Years of famine": abandoned fields outside an Akimel O'odham community in the early twentieth century.

bered the Tohono O'odham María Chona. A particular flashpoint was the region's limited water holes—especially those outside the Tohono O'odham's new reservation, which the Desert People still continued to claim as theirs by right of prior possession.

> 1884–85: At White Well (back of Roadside Mine), the Mexicans dug a well close to the old one that belongs to the People, and which had been there since the creation. The Indians had been given water by Elder Brother, who stuck his rod into the side of the mountains and made water come out. All such water belongs to the Indians. The Mexicans, after they had dug their well, would not let the Indians drink out of their old one. . . . This almost caused a war between the Mexicans and the Coyote people.[14]

The People's homeland constricted in other ways, too, during these years. Mexico and the United States began to exert greater control over their national domains, transforming the borderline that had lain dormant in the People's midst for almost half a century into a tangible reality. By the late nineteenth century, Tohono O'odham migrating between their traditional lands in Mexico and the United States found themselves accused of smuggling. Officials on both sides of the line arrested the Desert People or confiscated what they purported to be stolen livestock, leading on April 14, 1898, to what would be the last armed conflict undertaken by a Tohono O'odham community: a raid across the border on the village of El Plomo to free several relatives imprisoned by Mexican authorities and recover their cattle and horses. Five of the Desert People would die in the ensuing shootout before the survivors retreated back across the international boundary.[15]

If the El Plomo skirmish signaled the end of the O'odham tradition of village-based warfare, memories of the People's long struggles with the *'O:b* lingered on, preserved in the chronicles of the calendar stick keepers and other palpable reminders of the violence of the past. "Some of the old warriors are badly scarred from encounters with the Apaches," noted a visitor to the People in 1893. "[T]hese are much respected by the young, who listen in the village council house to their winter evening tales of former exploits." "My mother told me the Iron Stand massacre story frequently, for it was in her village where it occurred," recalled James McCarthy, a Tohono O'odham born in 1895. "The Apache killed the very young and the old, burned the village, stole the horses, and carried off the young girls. . . . She often told of María, a young Papago girl, who was taken to an Apache village, but she escaped. After many adventures and hardships she made her way back home. When I was young I met María, who was then an old woman."[16]

With violence against the *'O:b* relegated to the realm of memory for the first time in centuries, some O'odham communities opted to preserve the traditions that had long surrounded warfare through the staging of mock conflicts. *Sisiakam* constructed imitation Apaches out of straw so their young men could "kill" them and learn the rituals of the *gidahim*.[17]

> 1894–95: [Standing Water] had a meeting and it was said: "We're going to have a ceremony as we used to do before going on the warpath." This they did so the young men could know how it used to be, although there

was now no more war. So the men went out to the southeast, whence the Enemy used to come and camped for the night, and a medicine man worked to find where the enemy were. He said they were close on the other side of the hill, so two men were sent over there to make grass effigies. They made two and put skirts on them like men and they set them in a brush enclosure. The war party sent two scouts to circle around that enclosure and they named two boys who were to be the killers. These two would be purified and they would learn the old speeches which can be spoken only by Enemy Slayers. So, when the order was given, they clubbed the effigies and a messenger was sent to announce the killing. From far off he began shouting the names and every family danced in front of his own house. The boys were purified and then they held the scalp dance.[18]

If the People managed, through such practices, to retain the ceremonies that had served for centuries as communal touchstones, the end of warfare proved more difficult to manage when it came to outsiders. Upon occasion, the People still evoked their onetime military alliance with the *Milga:n.* In the early 1900s, for example, a group of Tohono O'odham chiefs, seeking to resolve a dispute over reservation boundaries, wrote the commissioner of Indian affairs to remind him that "[f]rom the time of the Gadsden Purchase until the late eighties the Papagos have been the main allies of the United States in fighting the enemies of peace, the enemies of Tucson."[19]

But with their resource base beset by a growing array of threats—increasing numbers of ranchers and miners, a more stringently monitored international boundary—a few of the People came to question how much they had in fact benefited by assisting the *Milga:n.* "Sometimes I have heard thoughtful Papagos say with a tinge of bitterness that it would have been better for them if they had taken up arms against the whites," commented one observer. "They would have been better off: the United States government would have been forced to recognize their rights."[20]

Echoes of this disquiet appear in the People's shifting memories of the 1872 peace parley with the Apache. Over time, the account of one Tohono O'odham calendar stick keeper, José Santos, began to suggest that the *'O:b,* through their

"The main allies of the United States": Tohono O'odham cowboys at the turn of the century.

intransigence toward the Americans, had secured much better treatment than the People. By the early 1900s, Santos's description transformed the rock the *'O:b* chief had used during negotiations from a symbol of peace into a sign of Apache stubbornness:

> [The U.S. official] advised the Enemy to stop warring. But the Enemy chief said it had been given him from the beginning, he could not change his ways. Then the agent for the People said: "You should be friendly with the People, they are peaceful."
>
> But the Enemy was still determined. He said it had been so since creation. He said the Enemy had been the first to speak, the first to drink cold water. That is why they are so fierce. That chief had a rock as big as his fist. He slammed it on the table and said he would not change. The agent said: "If you disobey the law, the law will kill off the Enemy. Soldiers will come. The other Indians will help." The Enemy chief said: "If you'll give me food and all I ask, I'll stop."
>
> The White man agreed. He promised a wagon and horses to the

chief, and food and clothes for all the tribe. That was why the Enemy got so much.[21]

As with other events, different O'odham communities remembered this episode in their own ways. The Akimel O'odham elder Anna Moore Shaw dwelled upon another facet of the negotiations in her retelling of the 1872 peace parley.

A council was held to resolve many important matters. One of the topics was marriage. An Apache chief declared, "When one of your Pima boys decides to marry one of our Apache girls, he must bring money, horses, and other valuable gifts to her parents."

Chief Azul emphatically shook his head in the negative: "No! No! It is not right! It would be the same as buying your daughter. The families on both sides must bring gifts to the young couple to help them start their home. We Pimas call this custom *kih shondath* (house foundation)."

In a similar manner Antonio Azul's good judgment helped iron out many other differences between the two tribes. Peace was declared, and the mountains never again rang with the yells of angry warriors.[22]

Although *Milga:n* transcripts of the 1872 conference document no discussion of intermarriage, Shaw's inclusion of an image suggestive of a new era of Pima-Apache cooperation nonetheless reveals a truth of sorts. With raiding between the O'odham and the *'O:b* over, and the two groups subjected to a similar regimen of reservations, boarding schools, and wage labor, many O'odham had begun to believe that they had more in common with their former Apache opponents than they had previously recognized.

The Akimel O'odham George Webb, who, like Shaw, was born in the 1890s and thus possessed no direct experience of warfare with the *'O:b*, made a similarly telling observation on how many in his community now chose to remember the violence between the O'odham and the Apache. "Sometimes you hear people say: 'Those Apaches were bad,'" he noted.

I don't know. They are peaceful people today, doing a good job with their livestock. In the early days they did cause the Pimas, and others, some trouble. We had plenty from our farms and those Apaches only had what they could hunt over their wild mountains. Sometimes they would come down and raid us and we fought them back away from our settlements and then left them alone. They never tried to drive us off our land and away from our homes. We never tried to drive them out of their own country. But the white man did.[23]

LOS VECINOS

OR JUAN AND JESÚS ELÍAS and their fellow *vecinos*, there was much
that initially seemed familiar about the events that followed the attack
on the Apache in Aravaipa Canyon. After destroying the Indians'
encampment, the raiders, in keeping with Mexican custom, rewarded those
who had assisted in the raid with captured Apache children and livestock
before hastening home. Some Apache captives ended up with prominent *Tucsonenses* such as Leopoldo Carrillo, who enrolled his newly baptized *criada* in the
Tucson convent school; others were sold into communities across the border
in Sonora. Upon reaching the outskirts of Tucson, the *vecinos* separated, bearing both booty and tales of their success against the Apache home to family
and friends. So enthused were many *vecinos* that they envisioned the attack in
Aravaipa Canyon as the prelude to an extended, *mexicano*-organized campaign
against Apache elsewhere. "A large number" of *vecinos*, reported the *Arizona
Citizen*, were "anxious to follow up the Grant raid" by attacking Cochise but
were obliged to wait until after the May wheat harvest.[1]

What may at first have seemed like little more than an unusually successful assault on the Apache, however, soon became a much more notable event.
As accounts of the killings spread beyond Tucson to newspapers on the east
and west coasts, *americano* reformers began to critique the massacre participants for their slaughter of women and children, while federal officials, especially those in the army and the Office of Indian Affairs, decried the attack as
an assault on their authority over Indian affairs. In contrast with the region's
prior ruler, México, which had seldom possessed the ability to discipline those

who acted in variance with its Apache policy, the U.S. government initiated an investigation of the murders—a process that culminated several months later in the arrest of the massacre's alleged ringleaders: William Oury, Juan Elías, and Jesús María Elías.[2]

Not long before his arrest, Juan issued the Elías brothers' only public statement about the attack. Recognizing Juan's considerable experience in tracking Indians and his status "as an honored member of the last Arizona legislature," a group of settlers persuaded him to release a deposition defending the killing of the Apache at Camp Grant. Juan did not mention his wounding by Eskiminzen's and Capitán Chiquito's followers in 1867 or Wooster and his "wife," but instead emphasized the raid upon the Elías ranch on April 12. Juan maintained that the Apaches had driven his cattle toward Aravaipa and that after the April 30 attack, the party had found in the canyon a horse belonging to Leopoldo Carrillo that had been stolen from Tucson sometime earlier. The net effect of this testimony was to portray the attack at Camp Grant as a proportionate response to deliberate Apache provocations, although it required one to overlook some inconvenient realities: a key piece of evidence—Carrillo's horse—was not located until after the murders, and most of those killed were not stock thieves but sleeping women and children.[3]

This deposition represented one of the few *vecino* ventures into the spirited debate unfolding in the English-language press in the latter half of 1871 over the morality of what some were beginning to call the "Camp Grant Massacre." In part, this absence may reflect little more than linguistic barriers. Although both Juan and Jesús could read and write Spanish, they remained far less fluent in English. Lacking a ready command of this second language, a far from essential skill in the nineteenth-century borderlands, neither Juan nor Jesús may have been completely aware of the controversy surrounding the killing of the Apache in Aravaipa Canyon—or, if they were, they may not have felt they possessed the facility to intervene in a discussion taking place in the leading English-language journals of the day.[4]

But it is equally possible that such debates did not interest them. Throughout their lives, *Tucsonenses* like the Elíases had manifested a concern first and foremost with the local community over such abstract collectivities as the nation-state, be it México or, now, the United States. Since Tucson evinced little critique of the raiders from either *vecinos* or *americanos*—indeed, Jesús was selected to represent the region's Mexican residents at the region-wide peace conference held along the banks of the San Pedro River in 1872 and Juan was reelected to Arizona's Legislative Assembly the following year—the Elíases may have felt no pressing need to make a public explanation of their actions.[5]

Mexican memories of the attack thus circulated at the local level, their emphasis more on the actions of familiars than on national debates over federal Indian policy. Unsurprisingly, *vecinos'* stories emphasized the valor of the participants and the belief that the attack was justified by clear evidence of Apache raiding. "Men in those days did not know what fear was," recalled Juan Téllez, whose father took part in the massacre. In the aftermath of the raid, Téllez maintained, his father found a yoke of oxen "and this proved that it was the Aravaipa Indians who were doing the stealing and killing."[6]

The recollections of Jesús Elías's daughter, Alvina, extended such tropes by recasting the massacre as a story not about the destruction of families but rather about its inverse: the rescue of a woman and her restoration to her relatives. In an interview years after the killings, Alvina dwelt not on the events leading up to the attack but rather on an unusual incident that occurred in the midst of the assault itself. Unlike most *americano* descriptions of the massacre, which placed the Papagoes on the canyon floor and the Americans and Mexicans on the cliffs above, firing down on those who managed to escape the Papagoes' clubs, Alvina's version suggests that Jesús (and presumably much of the rest of the party) had in fact engaged the Apache at close quarters among their wickiups. During the assault, Jesús had been about to shoot what he thought was a young Apache woman when the girl cried out to him in Spanish, "Don't kill me. I am not an Indian. I am a captive." Taking a closer look at the girl, Jesús realized that although she was dressed in Indian clothing and "somewhat tanned," she had "grey eyes and a clear complexion." Anxious to protect what he now realized was a young *mexicana*, Jesús reached out and placed his hat upon her head "so that the other men would not shoot her." Once the raid was over, Jesús brought the girl back to his home in Tucson, where overjoyed relatives from Sonora soon reclaimed her.[7]

For all their tales of valor, Téllez's and Alvina Rosenda Contreras's narratives contained hints of disquiet as well. In her account of the rescue of the Mexican captive, Alvina unintentionally confirmed one of the more unsettling

features of *vecino* raids against the Apache: the killing of female noncombatants was a not unexpected feature of such attacks. After all, Jesús planned to
execute the unarmed girl, and he feared that those with him might attempt
to do the same unless he took some step to distinguish her from the surrounding Apaches. Téllez's account grappled with this question even more directly.
As the attackers made their way back from Camp Grant, Téllez maintained,
they ran into an Apache mother and daughter returning to Aravaipa Canyon.
The men shot the woman, but it was not her death but what happened next
that seemed to disturb Téllez. One of the *vecinos* on the raid began to lead the
Apache girl off by her hand, "for he was going to keep her." But as he did so,
a man named "Placido Soza [came] up with his gun and shot her." Whether it
was the killing of a child or Soza's insult to another man's honor that was most
egregious about this episode is never made clear in Téllez's account. But in
either case, his memory of the massacre managed simultaneously to convey an
image of justified revenge and of violence edging into uncontrolled chaos.[8]

Such fears about violent excess lurked in Alvina's narrative as well, linked
to the racial dilemmas confronting *vecinos* in the late nineteenth century. At
first glance, her tale offered a comforting resolution: for all the momentary
confusion that might exist in distinguishing a Mexican from an Apache, in
the end, there remained clear physical markers separating the two. Apaches
might upon occasion use their facility in Spanish to deceive *vecinos*, but the
"grey eyes" and "clear complexion" of the girl that her father rescued during
the massacre left little doubt as to her true status: a Mexican captive, the victim of an earlier Apache raid on her people. Yet the fact that her father and his
compatriots came within a few seconds of killing a fellow Mexican—as well
as the lack of clarity, no matter how brief, over the categories *gente de rázon*
and *india bárbara*—hinted at the violent and unsettled world that such stories
hoped to keep at bay.

If the attack helped to solidify the reputation of the territory's *vecinos* as
Indian fighters, the benefits from this arrangement were both unevenly distributed and short-lived. Amid the controversy unleashed by the massacre, the
federal government reshuffled the military control of the territory, replacing
the impolitic commander of the Department of Arizona, George Stoneman,
with Lieutenant Colonel George Crook. Crook was fresh from a campaign
against the Paiute in the Pacific Northwest that had won him a reputation

as the army's premier Indian fighter. His success derived primarily from his reliance on native scouts, and Crook immediately proposed the same plan for Arizona. The territory's governor tried to convince the commander that in Arizona it was the *vecino* population who best "knew the country, the habits and mode of Indian warfare." But after a brief experiment with Mexican scouts, Crook decided instead to encourage the members of different Apache bands to fight one another. This policy displaced *vecinos* from the position as military guides and auxiliaries that they had occupied ever since 1857, much to the disapproval of Juan Elías: "The Apache scouts are, in my opinion, very unreliable and they should not be employed at all to fight their own race."[9]

Among the rest of the *americano* population in Arizona, the notion of *vecinos* as uncommonly knowledgeable trackers and Apache fighters proved more enduring. But this image coalesced around only a few, exceptional figures, such as the Elías brothers, rather than around *vecinos* as a whole. In the years after 1871, the Elíases would receive acclaim on several occasions for using their tracking skills to help solve local mysteries. In 1878, for example, the stagecoach between Tucson and Florence found itself bedeviled by a series of holdups. When the local Anglo sheriff twice proved unable to follow the robber's track, Juan Elías took command of the search. Noting a distinctive crooked hoof mark left by the thief's horse, Elías quickly trailed the man to the house of one of his accomplices. The following year, when two miners were found murdered in their camp in the Santa Rita Mountains, Juan again stepped forward to lead the posse investigating their deaths, much to the relief of Tucson's *Daily Star*, which praised "[t]he judgment of such experienced frontiersmen as Elias."[10]

As the *Daily Star*'s choice of language suggests, Juan's and Jesús's postmassacre careers demonstrate how "frontiersman" and the related term "pioneer"—products of an *americano* ideology of national expansion—proved sufficiently malleable that at least a few *vecinos* could inhabit them as well. The essence of the Anglo-American notion of the frontier, after all, was that of civilizing a wild landscape, and the paradigmatic figures were those of the farmer, the cowboy, and—as demonstrated by the popularity of "Buffalo Bill" Cody, who leapt to fame in 1869—the scout. In post-annexation Arizona, it was difficult to overlook the fact that many of these roles were filled by the region's *vecinos*. The fit was by no means perfect: *vecinos* also risked being subsumed,

"Experienced frontiersman" and family man: Juan Elías with his wife and children,
circa 1890.

in stereotype as well as in reality, into the position of "peons," whose subservi-
ent status represented the antithesis to the imagined freedom of the frontier.
But American frontier images were capacious enough that at least a few *vecinos*
were, by virtue of their class position or civic activities, able to find themselves
sharing an identity of sorts with their *americano* neighbors.[11]

The clearest marker of this shared status came in 1884, with the creation
of the Society of Arizona Pioneers, an association of settlers that functioned
in its early years as something of a hybrid mutual aid association, social club,
and historical society. Of the 283 early members of the group, thirty-three
(almost twelve percent) bore Spanish surnames—and of the remaining Anglo-
American members, fully half were married to Mexican women. Many members of Tucson's original Mexican merchant elite, such as Leopoldo Carrillo
and Estevan Ochoa, appeared on the society's rolls as did, of course, both Jesús
and Juan Elías. For all the deep connections between "pioneer" imagery and
American nationalism, the organization adopted an evenhanded policy of
commemorating both U.S. and Mexican holidays, with its members marching

through Tucson to celebrate not only the Fourth of July and Memorial Day but also *el Cinco de Mayo* and Mexican independence on September 19.[12]

For Tucson's *vecinos*, part of the appeal of joining the Pioneers' Society was doubtless strategic: the opportunity that it offered to ally oneself with well-placed members of the town's Anglo community and to ensure that the contributions of Arizona's *mexicano* population in wresting the territory from the Apache were not overlooked. But this self-identification as "pioneers" may also have resonated with the northern Mexicans' sense of themselves as *Norteños*, whose long exposure to the hardships of the borderlands had instilled in them not only a more self-sufficient character than that of southern Mexicans but also a whiter, more Spanish background, one shaped by Indian-fighting rather than the *mestizaje* (European-Indian intermarriage) that prevailed in central México.[13] It spoke volumes as to this shared frontier identity that when the Sonoran immigrant Carlos Velasco founded Tucson's leading Spanish-language newspaper in 1878, he titled it *El Fronterizo*. While this term might be translated as closer to "border" than "frontier," Velasco's inaugural column spoke of Americans' and Mexicans' shared experiences as frontier or border peoples (*"pueblos fronterizos"*), and *El Fronterizo* was as prone to describing the Apache as "savages" and "implacable enemies of humanity" as were its counterparts in Arizona's English-language press.[14]

The similarities between Anglo and Mexican notions of the frontier, however, could not obscure the declining fortunes of many in the Mexican community by the closing decades of the nineteenth century. For many, the shift came as rapidly as an onrushing locomotive: in 1880, the Southern Pacific Railroad extended its tracks into Tucson and soon began regular shipments of freight and passengers to town. Almost overnight, the railroad ruptured the long-standing circuits of exchange in the region, shifting the dominant flow of trade from its north-south axis between Arizona and Sonora to an east-west orientation that linked Tucson to California and the Atlantic seaboard. Unable to compete with the low-cost goods and transportation that the new railroad offered, the Mexican merchant elite witnessed its once-central role in Tucson's economic life destroyed—a situation perhaps best symbolized the following year when an incoming Southern Pacific locomotive ran over a Tully & Ochoa mule train. By 1883, the venerable firm, once the largest enterprise in southern Arizona, was out of business, along with many other Mexican-American companies.[15]

This economic and social displacement was mirrored on the physical level by the relocation of the Fiesta de San Agustín. The same year that the railroad began to make its march toward Tucson, a number of residents, complaining of the "large number of objectionable people" that the festival brought to the village, urged the town's council to move the fair outside the town's limits. To resolve the ensuing controversy, the town council reached a compromise: half the festival would be held in the old Plaza Militar and the other half would take place in Levin's Park, a beer garden on the outskirts of town owned by the German immigrant Alex Levin. In subsequent years, the fiesta would move completely to Levin's Park and then to Carrillo's Gardens, another private park even farther outside town, before being discontinued altogether sometime in the early 1900s.[16]

Even the scattered Apache outbreaks of the mid-1880s provided *vecino* Indian fighters with only a temporary opportunity to reassert a central role for themselves in community affairs. When a handful of Chiricahua Apaches led by Geronimo fled the San Carlos Reservation in 1885, Juan Elías, then forty-eight years old, and his younger brother Tomás, supported by contributions from the territory's ranchers, put together "a party of fifteen or twenty determined Mexican volunteers" to pursue them. "In Don Juan Elias, they have an experienced leader, bold, brave and yet discretely cautious," reported the *Arizona Daily Citizen.* "Every resident of Pima county possesses the most unbounded confidence in him and they feel that this force placed in the field by the cattlemen will prove the most effective against the Indians of any that has yet taken up the trail." But with the army continuing Crook's policy of relying on Apache scouts and many others in town supporting the organization of a company of "Tucson Rangers," Juan now found himself less the leader of a popular community response than a hired gun of sorts for local stockmen.[17]

It is tempting to interpret such incidents as evidence that *vecinos* such as the Elíases had become prisoners of the odd amalgam of American and Mexican frontier ideologies circulating in the borderlands by the close of the nineteenth century, compelled to commit fresh acts of violence against the Apache to curry favor with the increasingly dominant *americanos.* Yet the path that Juan and his brothers charted in their later years revealed a far different reckoning with the burdens of the region's past. The most striking of these developments came from Jesús Elías, who, toward the end of his life, recalled his daughter Alvina, became "very good friends" with the Apache leader Capitán Chiquito—the very man Jesús believed had commanded the raiders who shot his brother Juan in 1867, and who four years later lost two of his wives, along with scores of his relatives and followers, in the attack Jesús led on the Apache camp in Aravaipa Canyon. Jesús's daughter remembered the chief as a regular guest at their house in Tucson. When Capitán Chiquito took another wife, Jesús bought several bolts of brightly colored material so that Alvina's mother and aunt could make some dresses for the Apache's new spouse; in addition, Jesús bestowed a "good horse, a saddle, and all sorts of fine trappings" upon the couple. Not to be outdone, Capitán Chiquito brought his new baby girl to show Elías when it was born, along with gifts of his own for Elías's family: "a cane covered with blue and white beads and a doll made of buckskin."[18]

And so it was that Jesús Elías, a man who had, by his own reckoning, lost six of his family members to Apache attacks and who had led raids that resulted in the deaths of hundreds of Apaches, spent his final years exchanging pleasantries with one of his former adversaries. The sense that *vecinos* developed in the nineteenth century of Apaches as uniquely intimate enemies—unseen yet all-seeing foes haunting the shadows of Mexican life—had not prevented the occurrence of episodes of great brutality during this time. Indeed, it may well have exacerbated Mexican violence by making it seem that the only way to stop the elusive Apache was through overwhelming demonstrations of force.[19]

But this same peculiar intimacy may have made reconciliation easier as well. During his childhood in turn-of-the-century Tucson, Alberto S. Urías, the descendant of local *vecinos*, recalled that passing Apache Indians regularly helped themselves to water from his family's well in a curious exchange. "We had a little table outside . . . and they always used to leave a little token on the table—a bowl of pinole, beef jerky, corn tortillas. They never spoke, except to my grandmother, because she could speak the Apache language." Urías did not reveal how his grandmother acquired her knowledge of Apache. Had there been an Apache *criado* in her household, as among the Elíases, when she was a child? Was she herself a onetime captive—either a *vecina* who had been held for a while by an Apache band or a captured Apache who married into

Tucson's Mexican community, as apparently happened with several of the children seized during the massacre at Camp Grant? Nor did Urías explain the mystery of what his grandmother spoke to their Apache visitors about. Was it simply casual greetings? Or did they discuss people, possibly even family members, that they both knew? If such questions are now unanswerable, they nonetheless evoke a lost landscape of intimate interactions between *vecino* and Apache societies that was replaced over time by increasingly separate, if less antagonistic, worlds.[20]

For the Elías brothers, several events in the closing decades of the nineteenth century may have facilitated their reconciliation with the Apache. After the U.S. government created a reservation for the Papago at San Xavier del Bac in 1874, Jesús María Elías, Juan Elías, and Tomás Elías, all of whom had ranched in the area for several decades, found their land claims preempted by the Department of the Interior. When the Elíases and some thirty other *vecino* families refused to leave, U.S. marshals forcibly evicted them in 1881. For good measure, the marshals burned the *vecinos'* houses and fences, much to the dismay of *El Fronterizo*, which saw such displacements as violating the terms of American annexation: "Were not all the inhabitants of Arizona, whether Indians or Mexicans, equally protected by the Gadsden treaty, in their person and property, and if so were not the Mexican families in their ancient possessions as much entitled to their property as the Papagos?"[21]

The Elíases' unfortunate interactions with the federal government continued in later years. In 1892, Juan Elías filed an Indian Depredation Claim with the federal government seeking compensation for the hundreds of animals he had lost to Apache raiders after 1854, when the Apache were supposedly under the control of the United States. Testifying in the case forced Juan, his brothers Tomás and Jesús, and many of their neighbors to recount the long history of raids and counter-raids between themselves and the Apache Indians. They now did so, however, in a context in which their ultimate opponent was no longer the Apache but rather the U.S. government. Unsympathetic federal judges allowed only $1,680 of Juan's $21,650 in claims (of which Juan had to turn over $250 to his Anglo lawyer to pay his fees), and the government's attorneys proved less than gentle in their questioning of him. They took pains to point out that he did not speak English well and had not been born a citizen of the United States, and they seemed confused when he referred to the agreement that naturalized his citizenship by its Mexican terminology, the Treaty of La Mesilla, rather than by its American name, the Gadsden Treaty, until an irate Juan volunteered to fetch a copy of the treaty from his house.[22]

Despite having lived amid great violence, Jesús and Juan would both die peacefully at home within a few months of one another in 1896. Each man received respectful obituaries in Arizona's newspapers, but only the English-language press noted the roles both had played in the attack on the Apaches near Camp Grant in 1871.

Today the end came to a brave man. Jesus Maria Elias, one of the oldest and most noted of Arizona frontiers men, a daring Indian fighter and government scout. He came of a family of famous fighters. . . . He was captain of the expedition that wiped out the renegades at old Fort Grant. His brother Juan was also in that celebrated conflict.[23]

In the early days of Arizona's history, when the Apaches were a constant menace, by night and by day, to the safety of those brave men who were determined to live here, Juan Elias was always in the front rank of those who sought to rid the country of her bitterest enemies. His record is one of exceptional bravery and many of his comrades who are yet living, proudly point to him as the personification of manly courage. He was one of those present at the famous Fort Grant massacre, and almost times without number he made his presence strongly felt in repelling the vicious assaults of the murderous Apaches.[24]

In spite of such praise for the former "daring Indian fighters," by the time of the brothers' deaths, the Elías family's once-vast herds and landholdings had slipped from their grasp. "In days ago," the *Arizona Citizen* remarked on Jesús's passing, "he was well to do but misfortune came and he died a poor man"—so much so, in fact, that the Society of Arizona Pioneers appears to have paid Jesús's funeral expenses, as it often did for impoverished members.

Joining the pioneers in turning out en masse for the Elíases' funerals were the members of a new group whose presence underscored the recent changes in Tucson. For many of the town's Mexican Americans, the most important organization in their lives by the turn of the century was no longer the Arizona Pioneers'

*The Spanish-American Alliance: a gathering of Alianza Hispano-Americana members
in southern Arizona at the turn of the century.*

Society, with its nostalgic invocations of the territory's early years, but rather
the more outspoken Alianza Hispano-Americana (Spanish-American Alliance).
Founded in 1894 by several Mexican-American members of the Pioneers' Society, the Alianza took on some of the functions of earlier *mutualistas* (mutual aid
societies), including the "Mexican Society for Mutual Benefit" created by Estevan Ochoa and Juan Elías in 1875, which offered their members support in case
of family tragedy. Under the guidance of Leopoldo Carrillo's son-in-law, Ramón
Soto, the Alianza adopted a more avowedly political agenda, urging its members
to support Mexican candidates at the polls as a way to contest the rising tide of
discrimination facing Tucson's Mexican-American community.[25]

The politics of the new organization were perhaps most clearly demonstrated by the Alianza's conscious selection of the novel term *hispano-americano*
to describe its members. Rather than the localistic label *vecino* that had predominated earlier, which translated literally as "neighbor" and included no
reference to ethnicity, the word *hispano-americano* stressed the bearer's U.S.
citizenship and white, "Spanish" background—shifts that underscored how

americano ideas of race and nationalism had become inescapable realities in Mexican-American Arizona. From its base in Tucson, the Alianza spread to much of the rest of the borderlands. With some 17,000 members at its peak in the early twentieth century, the alliance would become the first national organization for people of Mexican descent and an important precursor to later Mexican-American civil rights organizations.[26]

In keeping with such transformations, *Tucsonenses'* memories of the nineteenth century began to shift as well. This changing sense of the past seldom manifested itself within the books or lectures that were the hallmarks of the historical profession in the early twentieth century. North of the border, Mexican Americans found the academic institutions that served as the gatekeepers for historical scholarship largely closed to them, while south of the border, Mexican historians constructed a vision of their nation's past that, confining itself to the current international boundary, made little reference to onetime Mexican lands and peoples in Arizona.[27]

For southern Arizona's Mexican Americans, the most vivid representations of the past were thus contained not in published histories, but rather in the songs and stories passed informally from one generation to the next. Tales about the long-running confrontation with *los apaches*—of babies hidden under washtubs during Apache raids, of family members from Tucson's presidio leading expeditions against the Apache, of the site where Tully & Ochoa teamsters had perished in an Apache ambush—continued to be a prominent feature of such accounts.[28] Over time, however, many Mexican-American memories began to dwell on a different, if no less wily, opponent: American settlers and the U.S. government. Describing his family's experiences in Tucson, Alberto Urías hinged his narrative not on the conflict with *"indios bárbaros"* that had been so central to prior Spanish histories of the region (and which would continue to be important in Mexican histories of Sonora and Chihuahua) but rather on the shift in landownership that followed U.S. annexation. "My grandfather, Juan Urías, was born in 1817 in what was called Barrio San José, near the old Mission of San Cosme which was located at the foot of 'A' Mountain," Urías recollected.

> He used to have land along the Santa Cruz River—he was a farmer.
> My grandfather also owned six sections of land where Casa Adobes is

now. . . . He had a little adobe house right there on the way to Florence.
A man named Walters took possession of his land, because in the old
days the people did not have land titles. So the judge decided in the
American's favor, and my grandfather lost all his land. . . . There were
a lot of Mexican people who had ranches in those days—many of them
lost the rights to their land.

With numerous Mexican Americans, like the Elíases, losing ranches to American settlers or to new federal institutions such as the Papago reservation, the
intertwined themes of prior habitation and illicit dispossession ran through
many of their recollections. Mexican Americans found themselves nostalgic
for a vanished agrarian past and torn between asserting a right to their land
through violent conquest or critiquing such forcible dispossession altogether.[29]

It was perhaps in the realm of folklore that Mexican Americans created
their most enduring response to this dilemma. The raw material came from a
familiar source: the tale of Joaquín Murrieta. With many Sonorans who took
part in the California Gold Rush either returning to their home state or resettling in Arizona, the story of Joaquín's mistreatment and subsequent revenge
against his oppressors spread throughout Mexican communities on both sides
of the border. In the process, the narrative of Joaquín's life began to take on
features that extended it beyond the brief years of the Gold Rush. Some in
Sonora claimed that Joaquín was descended from a long line of Apache fighters
from Fronteras (or was it Pueblo de Murrieta? or Las Trincheras?). The Mur-
rietas, it was said, had "raised stock, mined and fought Indians for 100 years"
in Sonora, honing the skills that would make Joaquín such a fearsome opponent when crossed in California. Others asserted that Murrieta had outwitted
his attackers, escaping his final ambush to deliver his loot to fellow Mexicans before dying of his wounds or, in a slightly different version, to retire in
comfortable anonymity elsewhere in the borderlands—scenarios that reflected
what *mexicanos* must have considered far more satisfactory resolutions than the
standard American account, which ended with Murrieta's death, mutilation,
and exhibition throughout California as a common criminal.[30]

These memories of Murrieta coalesced sometime in the late nineteenth century into a number of *corridos* (folk ballads). Like the later accounts of Joaquín's

life, these songs focused not on Murrieta's death at the hands of an Anglo posse but rather on his triumphs over his *americano* oppressors.

Cuando apenas era un niño	When I was just a child
huérfano a mí me dejaron.	I was left an orphan.
Nadie me hizo ni un cariño,	No one cared for me,
a mi hermano lo mataron,	they killed my brother
y a mi esposa Carmelita,	and the cowards murdered
cobardes la asesinaron.	my wife Carmelita.
. . . .	. . . .
Yo soy aquel que domina	I am the one who dominates
hasta leones africanos.	even African lions.
Por eso salgo al camino	This is why I set out on the path
a matar americanos.	to kill Americans.
Ya no es otro mi destino.	Now my destiny is no other.
¡Pon cuidado, parroquianos!	Beware, countrymen!
Las pistolas y las dagas	Pistols and daggers
son juguetes para mí.	are toys for me.
Balazos y puñaladas,	Shootings and stabbings,
carcajadas para mí.	laughable for me.
Ahora con medios cortados,	Now with their means cut off,
ya se asustan por aquí.	they're afraid around here.
No soy chileno ni extraño	I'm neither a Chilean nor a foreigner
en este suelo que piso.	on the ground that I walk upon.
De México es California	California is Mexico's
porque Dios así lo quiso,	because God wanted it that way,
y en mi sarape cosida	and in my sewn serape
traigo mi fe de bautismo.	I carry my baptismal certificate.
. . . .	. . . .

Me he paseado en California	*I traveled throughout California*
por el año del cincuenta,	*in the year fifty {1850},*
con mi montura plateada,	*with my silver-plated saddle,*
y mi pistola repleta.	*and my pistol loaded.*
Yo soy ese mexicano	*I am that Mexican*
de nombre Joaquín Murrieta.	*named Joaquín Murrieta.* [31]

If the *corrido de Joaquín Murrieta* was ostensibly about events that had happened in the 1850s, few could miss the contemporary implications of a composition about *americano* oppressors brought low by a valiant Mexican with a pistol and dagger in his hands, a song that ended with the singer proudly proclaiming, "I am that Mexican named Joaquín Murrieta." Because of its appeal as a symbolic corrective to Anglo discrimination, the *corrido* proved wildly popular among Mexican Americans in the Southwest. For many years, however, those who played the song in public in Arizona mining towns risked being arrested by Anglo law enforcement agents; the *corrido de Joaquín Murrieta* was also forbidden on Arizona radio stations.[32]

Despite such efforts to silence it, the *corrido* endured as a counternarrative to then dominant Anglo stories about the "winning of the West." The stories that Mexicans and Mexican Americans told one another about Joaquín called into question many of the arguments *americanos* had long used to justify their dominance over the borderlands. Rather than bringing civilization to a primitive frontier environment, Americans appeared to be doing much the opposite: acting as agents of disorder who destroyed family, property, and lives, much like *los apaches* and other *indios bárbaros*.[33]

And yet in sustaining this fugitive historical account of righteous Mexican retribution to American aggression, the *corrido de Joaquín Murrieta* committed a certain erasure as well. As a fluid folk form that first evolved in México sometime in the early nineteenth century, *corridos* often borrowed elements from previous ballads. The *corrido de Joaquín Murrieta* seems to have been no exception: with its distinctive six-line stanzas, the song appears to be based on an even older *corrido* entitled *Mañanas de los cahiguas* ("Morning of the Cahigua Indians") that depicted an Apache attack on Zacatecas in 1853. According to the *corrido*, a "terrifying" Apache captain on whom the government has placed a five-hundred-peso reward for his head attacks several towns; Mexicans kill many of the raiders, and the rest of the Indians flee "all the way to Tucson." This earlier history of violent encounters with the Apaches, then, in which *vecinos* in Tucson such as the Elíases played such a central role, is quite literally supplanted in the *corrido de Joaquín Murrieta* by a focus on the wrongs committed by Anglo Americans. It was not that the knowledge of these previous interactions with the Apaches vanished altogether from the Mexican-American community. But at a time when most Apaches were safely confined to reservations and Anglo social and economic dominance over the territory was becoming ever more manifest, such memories seemed increasingly out of place—the remnants of a remote and distant past that offered few lessons for the years ahead.[34]

THE AMERICANS

A S THEY BREAKFASTED after the massacre, Oury and the other Americans, content in "a work well done," reportedly made a pact with one another: "never to tell anything about it [the massacre] or tell the name of anybody that took part in it." Despite this supposed agreement, however, the participants' efforts to control the story of the murders in Aravaipa Canyon quickly proved elusive. Part of the problem was that as much as Oury and the Americans with him may have hoped to keep their roles in the attack secret, they never intended for the massacre itself to be unknown. Among its central purposes had been to issue public statements to the federal government and the region's Apache peoples—and such statements could only operate if knowledge of the massacre became widespread.[1]

To the federal government, the raiders intended the dead Apache women and children littering Aravaipa Canyon to serve as incontrovertible evidence of the violent conditions predominating throughout Arizona—even though, ironically, to generate this proof, they had to reverse what they insisted was the normal state of affairs, in which Apache "savages" assaulted unsuspecting Anglo settlers. To the Apache, the attackers hoped to send a different but no less emphatic message. Arizona's Apaches, the massacre suggested, were vulnerable to retribution anywhere in the territory. The Indians might trick representatives of the U.S. government into believing their peace declarations, but the settlers knew that the only language the Apache understood was one of violence and vengeance.

Yet once the assault became public, it invited other interpretations as well.

"Bloody retaliation": the early offices of the Citizen *(right).*

The first commentaries came from the Tucson press, which seemed to know a suspiciously large amount about a deed committed under a supposed vow of silence. A few days after the attack, on May 6, 1871, the *Tucson Citizen* issued an article bearing the headline "Bloody Retaliation" that described, without mentioning the names of those involved, the main details of the attack, including the number killed and captured (which it put at eighty-five dead, "28 children prisoners, and seven escaped"). Although the *Citizen* hesitated to label the attack "unreservedly commended," it termed the deaths "excused or justified" on grounds of self-defense. Blame for the raid, according to the *Citizen*'s editor, lay not with the people of Arizona, who had exhibited "patient endurance," but rather with the Apaches for committing countless atrocities under an "assumed peace arrangement" and with the federal government for its failure to offer the territory's settlers "just protection."[2]

As the first press account to appear on the deaths at Camp Grant, the *Citizen*'s article profoundly influenced most initial coverage of the event. Within a matter of days, many leading newspapers, from the *Alta California* and the *San Francisco Chronicle* in the West to the *New York Times* and the *New York Herald* in the East, republished the *Citizen's* article verbatim on their front pages. Soon millions of those who had never strolled Tucson's hot, dusty streets would be familiar with the story of Wooster, his wife, and her distinctive breast pin, the deceptive practices of the cruel Apache, and settlers' forbearance in the face of Indian atrocities and federal inaction. With their knowledge confined to information from the *Citizen*, these other papers tended to echo settlers' interpretation of the event. Journals such as the *Alta California* thus spoke of the Apache deaths as "[o]ne of the most important victories ever achieved by the white men over the savages in Arizona" and called for the federal government to take a more aggressive approach toward Indian affairs, including, "if necessary to that end, the extermination of the Apaches." [3]

If participants and their supporters had the initial advantage in presenting their account of the attack, those who disagreed with the massacre managed to challenge the emerging consensus within a matter of weeks. One of the most influential of these counternarratives came from the man who had been in command of Camp Grant at the time of the incident, Lieutenant Royal Whitman. As he told the story, at about 7:30 a.m. on the morning of April 30, just as he was sitting down to breakfast, he received a message from the commander at Fort Lowell informing him of the rumor that a suspiciously large number of men were absent from Tucson and intended to attack Camp Grant. (This was precisely the message that Oury had feared might disrupt their plans, if the two men that Stevens dispatched had not delayed the riders from Fort Lowell.) Whitman rushed his interpreters to the Apaches' campground to warn them of the possible threat. But they arrived too late. The interpreters were unable to find a single living Apache, only "[t]he camp . . . burning and the ground strewed with . . . dead and mutilated women and children." [4]

Whitman's depiction of the army's efforts to bury the dead Apaches and coax the traumatized survivors back into camp became not only the basis for later governmental reports but also fodder for the popular press. The lieutenant did not dispute the basic facts presented in earlier versions of the assault: the date of the attack, the origins of the attackers, or the number of dead and missing, which most placed at at least one hundred. But he harnessed these details to a very different narrative. Rather than including any reference

to Wooster and his "wife," for example, Whitman commenced his account
with the peace agreement between Es-him-en-zee's band and the U.S. Army,
thereby transforming the killings from an act of retribution to an agreement
betrayed. Likewise, the lieutenant closed not as the *Citizen* had done, with calls
for the improved protection of settlers, but with quite different symbols of
vulnerability: the murdered women and children at Camp Grant; the Apache
youngsters fated to a life of "debauched captivity" as prostitutes.[5]

Whitman's version encouraged at least a few journals to alter their view of
the incident. "A few days since," asserted the editor of the *San Francisco Chronicle*, "advices were received of the killing of a number of Indians of both sexes at
Camp Grant Reservation, Arizona Territory."

> These advices justified the attacking party . . . alleging that those killed,
> instead of being peaceably inclined, were deceiving the agents of the Gov-
> ernment, only awaiting a favorable moment to perpetrate deeds of pillage
> and murder. From official news, since received, it seems that this was but
> another massacre, in cold blood, of inoffensive and peaceable Indians who
> were living on the Reservation under the protection of the Government.

Almost immediately, then, the attack produced two opposing narratives
within the Anglo-American community, each structured around divergent
assessments of the categories of victim and perpetrator. As these two narratives confronted one another, they moved not toward a more nuanced understanding of the incident but rather toward a more polarized one as both sides
sought to buttress their respective position by clinging to the figures of innocent victim and malevolent perpetrator all the more fiercely.[6]

It was at this moment, for example, that those who disapproved of the
attack began to use the much more charged label of massacre—the "Indian
Massacre," the "Arizona Massacre," or, finally, the term that is most common
today, the "Camp Grant Massacre"—to describe what had happened at Aravaipa Canyon. In so doing, they were both tapping into and transforming a
familiar narrative mode. Americans in the latter half of the nineteenth century had become accustomed to view massacres as a regular feature of their
western frontier. Typically, however, when they spoke of an "Indian massacre," Americans meant an atrocity in which Indians were the perpetrators.

The popular press abounded with lurid examples of such horrors, from the "Oatman Massacre" by the Apache of a family on their way to California, to the "Indian Massacre of 1862," when the Sioux in Minnesota with "blood-dripping hatchets" had killed scores of settlers, to the "massacre by Indians of three officers and seventy-eight soldiers" outside Fort Philip Kearney in Wyoming some five years later. What seemed to distinguish a massacre from any other violent encounter was not the number killed (indeed, commentators often applied the term to events in which only two or three people died) but rather the cruelty of the attackers, who in their "savage hatred" left behind a "tale of horror to curdle one's blood." Above all, massacre suggested a deed that bore little resemblance to a legitimate military encounter but was rather prosecuted through deceit upon an unsuspecting and often defenseless foe. "What, indeed, is the distinction between civilized and savage races but this," asked a correspondent for *Putnam's Magazine* in 1870, "that one carries on war as if it were murder; the other under rule and with human pity?"[7]

By calling what had happened in the early-morning hours of April 30 a massacre, critics were thus turning prevailing notions of virtuous settlers and brutal Indians on their head. This anxiety that the categories of civilization and savagery had begun to collapse upon themselves ran through many accounts of the killings at Camp Grant. "Arizona at the best is a sort of borderland between barbarism and civilization," maintained a correspondent for *Every Saturday.* "But even for Arizona," what happened at Camp Grant was an act "of unparalleled ferocity and malignity":

> [W]hatever the wrong of the red men at either point in the matter of robbery, the retaliatory acts were wholly indefensible, whether in law, justice, humanity, or common decency. In a word, they were the acts of brutal ruffians—embracing not alone murder, but pillage, outrage of women and girls, and deeds so horrible and revolting that they cannot be publicly mentioned.

Commentators brooded over the humiliation of the federal government's having its military post at Camp Grant violated and pondered whether the inhabitants of Arizona "insist[ed] that the Apaches shall be exterminated" out of a crass desire for military contracts.[8]

For their part, Arizona's settlers were quick to insist that any confusion over the categories of civilization or savagery resided in the minds of eastern reformers. What happened at Camp Grant remained little more than the "so-called massacre," the "alleged massacre," or, as most came to refer to it, the "Camp Grant affair." Settlers even refashioned one of the most unnerving features of this "affair"— the deaths of a large number of women and children—into evidence not of the brutality of the raiders but rather of the treachery of the Apache, who supposedly had left their women and children in the relative safety of Aravaipa Canyon while the men were "off roaming about committing . . . deeds of murder and theft."[9]

To many in the West, the "Camp Grant affair" represented not the reversion to barbarism warned about by eastern reformers but rather an act designed to aid the march of progress. "[T]he 'Camp Grant Massacre,'" maintained Tucson resident John Spring, "was the result of the Government's neglect and the long and patient suffering of a body of pioneers who tried to bring civilization into a heretofore wild country." A Colorado newspaper likewise termed the massacre a "victory for peace" akin to many other recent mass murders of Indian peoples in the western United States:

> We give to this act of the citizens of Arizona most hearty and unqualified endorsement. We congratulate them on the fact that permanent peace arrangements have been made with so many, and we only regret that the number was not double, or three times as many. Camp Grant is the last of those victories for civilization and progress, which have made Sand creek, Washita, the Piegan fight, and other similar occurrences famous in western history. It is just and right, and was fully demanded by the circumstances of the time.

"To the frontiersman familiar with the Apache character and history, [the Peace Commission's] touching picture of the poor Apaches, so intensely anxious to live on terms of peace and friendship with their white neighbors, will appear like a satire of the finest description," concluded the *Arizona Miner*.[10]

G IVEN HOW DISCUSSIONS of the killings at Camp Grant quickly evolved into debates over the "Peace Policy," it was perhaps inevitable that those directing federal Indian policy would soon pass judgment on the attack. The president himself set the tone, defending his vision of Indian affairs in an interview shortly after news of the killings reached the East Coast. "My policy is peace," Grant told a journalist for the *New York Herald.* "When I said, 'Let us have peace,' I meant it." Although he acknowledged that the Apaches were "warlike," Grant also asserted that, as his former secretary and now commissioner of Indian affairs, Ely Parker, a member of New York's Seneca tribe, demonstrated, Indians could "be civilized and made friends of the republic." Viewing events in Arizona as an attack not only on the Apache but also on his policy as a whole—"murder, purely"—the president vowed to "investigate the massacre of the Apaches at Camp Grant and be just to all concerned."[11]

Events on the ground in Arizona, however, soon revealed some of the hidden fault lines within federal Indian policy. Not long after the new commander of the Department of Arizona, George Crook, reached the territory, hired fifty Mexican scouts, and began his first efforts at tracking the Apache across Arizona's forbidding mountains and desert valleys, his plans were put on hold by the arrival of Vincent Colyer, secretary of the Board of Indian Commissioners. Seeking to avoid "the perpetration of further outrages like the Camp Grant massacre," the Peace Commission had appealed to President Grant to delay Crook's campaign until Colyer was given the opportunity "to bring these roving Apache Indians upon suitable reservations, and to feed, clothe, and otherwise care for them." Sharing a belief in this "desirable object," Grant issued orders for Colyer to be given "enlarged powers" and the assistance of the War Department.[12]

As one of the first members of the Peace Commission to set foot in Arizona, Colyer found himself the target of a torrent of abuse in the territorial press. To the *Arizona Citizen,* the commissioner was a "hypocrite, and accessory before the fact to murder," engaged in a "war upon American citizens." To the *Arizona Miner,* he was a "self-conceited idiot" and an "egregious ass." Colyer was only slightly more popular with Crook and his staff. Although decorum demanded that he support the secretary, Crook complained privately that Colyer had "interfere[d] with my operations" and grumbled to his superiors that "if this entire Indian question be left to me . . . I have not the slightest doubt of my ability to conquer a lasting peace with this Apache race in a comparatively short space of time."[13]

Such utterances have led some historians to paint a stark contrast between Colyer and Crook, in which the former emerges as a befuddled idealist and the latter a hard-nosed realist. In his 1889 history of Arizona and New Mexico, for example, Hubert Bancroft decried Colyer as "an ultra fanatic," while he presented Crook as "energetic" and "effective." Distinctions doubtless existed between the two men: as Colyer himself observed during his trip to Arizona, "The general and I differed somewhat in opinion as to the best policy to be pursued toward the Apaches." A number of these tensions, however, were more administrative than philosophical. In 1849, Congress had transferred responsibility for Indian affairs from the War Department, where they had resided ever since the nation's founding, to the newly created Department of the Interior. Even decades later, many in the military still resented the intrusion of what they regarded to be corrupt civilians into the army's proper sphere. Indeed, Crook and his junior officers looked upon Colyer as little more than a tool of the "Indian Ring," despite the fact that the Board of Indian Commissioners had been specifically created to combat profiteering in Indian affairs.[14]

Other disagreements between Colyer and Crook were more over means than ends. Colyer believed that the Apaches, as demonstrated in their interactions with Whitman at Camp Grant, possessed an "eager desire for peace" that only needed the establishment of reservations to flower. Crook, for his part, thought most Apaches an "impudent lot of cut-throats" who would have to be driven militarily onto reserves. Both, however, shared the vision of bringing peace to the borderlands by confining Indian peoples to reservations and converting them to Christianity and an agricultural lifestyle. There is little evidence that in dispatching Crook to Arizona in May and Colyer to the same territory in July, President Grant saw himself as radically altering his approach to the Apache within just a few months. Rather he doubtless viewed the soldier and the reformer as the twin faces of the same program.[15]

The "Peace Policy," after all, had never advanced a purely pacific stance toward Indian peoples. It did imply, however, that the deployment of violence was only legitimate after the effort to establish peace (or the United States' version of it) had first been attempted. Thus, Captain Guy Henry, who served in the Third U.S. Cavalry under Crook at the time of Colyer's visit, viewed both Crook and Colyer as embodying the mixture of belligerence and forbearance that lay at the heart of the "Peace Policy." Crook, in Henry's words, was "a man of character, a soldier (and necessarily a Christian and a gentleman) selected for solving the Indian problem, not by killing all, as people imagine, but . . . punishing the bad, causing the rest to be put on reserves and taught the advantages of civilization in farming, raising stock, etc." Colyer was likewise "a gentleman and Christian, and one in whose views every army officer will coincide (that is, do all you can first to civilize the Indians; that failing, kill the bad ones)."[16]

To Colyer, what made the Camp Grant Massacre such a "disgrace" was that it impeded acceptance of the civilized lifestyle that the Apaches so clearly desired. The commissioner's conclusion flowed out of a reading of Arizona's history that emphasized the peaceful interactions that had initially taken place between Anglos and Apaches. "When the Americans first came among them . . . ," noted Colyer, "the Apaches received them as friends." But "the natural gravitation towards barbarism which seems inherent in human nature when left unrestrained, as in the life on the border," had led Americans "to treat the Apaches as incumbrances [sic] to be exterminated." The result had been a brutal war that, despite costing "a thousand lives and over forty millions of dollars" during the past decade, had brought the borderlands no closer to peace. Economics, as well as morality, thus dictated that the United States seek another path. "[T]hese Indians still beg for peace, and all of them can be placed on reservations and fed at an expense of less than half a million dollars a year, without the loss of life."[17]

During his tour of Arizona, Colyer met with Apache leaders at the forts scattered throughout the territory. During his stay at Camp Grant, he parleyed for several days with Es-him-en-zee as well as the leaders "Esce-nela" and "Captain Chiquito." One afternoon he even rode out with Es-him-en-zee to look over the massacre site, only to discover that, because of summer floods along Aravaipa Creek and the actions of scavengers (animal and, possibly, human, for several Aravaipa Apache skeletons eventually made their way to U.S. museum collections), the "skulls of the Indians, with their temple-bones beaten in" were once more visible on the canyon floor. In his wake, Colyer left behind several new reservations, designed to make this institution at last an integral feature of Indian policy in the borderlands.[18]

The reserve Colyer created at Camp Grant was roughly a twenty-mile by twenty-mile square, bounded on the north by the Gila River and the east by the foothills of Mount Graham, with Aravaipa Canyon at its heart. Although this new reservation displaced a few settlers along the San Pedro River, much of its terrain was, in Colyer's words, "a barren waste, yielding nothing that the white man cared for, but considerable food, such as mescal, mesquite beans, and cactus fruit, of which the Apaches were very fond."[19] Perhaps most important, the new reserve promised "good natural boundar[ies]." Unable to discern Indian intentions, federal officials had turned to location to determine Apache treatment. "We carefully instructed the chiefs about these boundaries," Colyer reported, "impressing it upon them that they must not go beyond them; that while within these limits they would be protected and fed; if they went beyond they would become objects of suspicion, and liable to be punished by both citizens and soldiers."[20]

According to Grant's secretary of war, William Tecumseh Sherman, the only way now for the Apache "to escape war" was to collect at Colyer's new reserves and "remain thereon." Following the 1872 peace conference, events unfolded much as Sherman had envisioned. Crook launched a devastating campaign, employing multiple units and Apache scouts (instead of Mexicans as before), on all those Apaches not yet on reservations. After several sharp encounters—none of which came to be called massacres, although at the "Battle" of Salt River Cave troops killed seventy-six men, women, and children trapped in a cave with the loss of only one Pima auxiliary—Apache resistance collapsed. By April 1873, almost all the Apache residing within Arizona could be found on one of the three reservations designated for them, wearing the mandatory metal identity tags designed by Crook. These badges simplified what had been for Americans a bewildering Apache band structure to a fixed system of symbols and numbers that enabled reservation authorities to monitor their new captives. Through such measures, Crook bragged, he had brought to a close a history of "Indian war that has been waged since the days of Cortez."[21]

A T THE SAME TIME that the Camp Grant Massacre was reshaping national Indian policy, it was also reverberating through Tucson. Despite the perpetrators' supposed vow of secrecy, it was soon an open secret as to which Americans had been involved in the massacre. Besides Oury, the other names whispered about town as potential participants were Sidney R. DeLong, James Lee, Charles Etchells, David Foley, and D. A. Bennett. With the exception of the last two participants, who appear in the 1870 census as a thirty-seven-year-old miller from Arizona and as a thirty-one-year-old miner from New York State, both with no appreciable property, all the others were members of Tucson's entrepreneurial or craftsman elite. DeLong, for example, was the former merchant at the U.S. Army's Camp Crittenden and ex-editor of the *Weekly Arizonan*. In 1870 he had become a partner in the territory's most important freighting firm, Tully & Ochoa, which was promptly renamed Tully, Ochoa & DeLong. According to the federal census from that same year, he owned $135,000 of property, which made him one of the wealthiest men in Pima County. Etchells was the proprietor of one of Tucson's biggest blacksmith shops, where he employed several Anglo and Mexican-American assistants and engaged in the profitable sideline of constructing wagons especially suited to Arizona's rocky roads. Lee, an Irish immigrant, owned a mine and a ranch outside of Tucson as well as the largest building in southern Arizona, which housed a steam flour mill known as the Eagle Mill, where he likely employed his fellow miller, Foley.[22]

Nineteenth-century commentators, prone to see the borderlands as a site of degeneration where civilization could be lost as well as gained, typically blamed frontier violence on "desperate characters" who had fled to the nation's periphery to escape "civilized society." Those implicated in the assault on Camp Grant, however, were more likely to be at the forefront of Tucson's civic and economic life than the "vagabonds of different nationalities" implicated in newspaper accounts. Moreover, with the possible exceptions of Bennett and Foley, about whom little is known, and DeLong, who was single at the time, all the other attackers were connected not only to Tucson's Anglo community but through marriage to Tucson's far larger Mexican community.[23]

This civic involvement only deepened in the massacre's aftermath. Just weeks after the massacre took place, Tucson, newly incorporated as a municipality, held its first election for mayor. DeLong won. In the same election, Oury and Hughes (who as the territory's adjutant general had lent the weapons and ammunition for the attack on Camp Grant) were elected to the town's four-person governing council. The new council's treasurer was none other than Hiram Stevens, who had dispatched the men who prevented the messengers from Fort Lowell from reaching Camp Grant ahead of the attackers. Stevens would go on to serve in the Arizona legislature and to be elected territorial delegate to the United States Congress. For their parts, Oury and Hughes would be reelected to Tucson's council in 1872. The next year, Etchells would join them on the council—a position he would hold, off and on, for the next five years, in addition to serving as a trustee for the public schools—while Oury would be voted Tucson's sheriff from 1873 to 1877.[24]

No records remain of these early electoral campaigns, making it is impossible to gauge the extent to which the Camp Grant Massacre influenced the proceedings. But it is quite clear from the surviving documentation that Tucsonites seldom viewed participation in the attack as a blot on one's character—and may even have considered it a marker of suitability for office. Arizona newspapers routinely described those suspected of taking part in the assault in glowing terms. In the words of a correspondent to the *Arizona Miner* who knew several participants, the killers were "good citizens and humane, generous-hearted men." The *Arizona Daily Citizen* lauded Etchells in 1879 as "one of Tucson's best and most solid citizens." Oury would be remembered a few years later as "brave, generous and intellectual," someone who "never did a mean act"; DeLong termed "upright and agreeable"; and Lee celebrated for his "big heart."[25]

This warm embrace of the American participants in the massacre made further attacks on Indian reservations appear not only possible but probable. Just three months after the attack on Camp Grant, the residents of Grant County, New Mexico, held a public meeting at which they vowed to recover their livestock "by force" from the Apaches receiving rations at Cañada Alamosa "even if it be at the sacrifice of every Indian man, women [*sic*], and child, in the tribe." Added B. Hudson, a member of the group: "if we are to be forever at the mercy of these thieving murderous Apaches, who have a 'house of refuge' at Alamosa . . . the citizens of this county are determined to put a stop to it, and if they carry out their programme *the Camp Grant massacre will be thrown entirely in the shade, and Alamosa will rank next to Sand Creek.*" Similarly, as tensions between white settlers and the Pima Indians rose following the Pimas' appropriation of crops and livestock from the newcomers' fields, the *Arizona Citizen* predicted that "unless the Indian agent stops these robberies soon, there will be

"Upright and agreeable": Sidney R. DeLong, voted mayor of Tucson just weeks after the Camp Grant Massacre.

such a blood letting of the Pima kind as will cause a greater howl in the East than did the few drops shed near Camp Grant a short time ago."[26]

WITH CROOK'S CAMPAIGN apparently having solved the "Apache problem," settlers soon released a torrent of booster literature designed to attract new immigrants and capital to Arizona. In works such as *Arizona as it is; Or, the Coming Country* and *The Hand-Book to Arizona: Its Resources, History, Towns, Mines, Ruins and Scenery*, boosters forged a narrative of Arizona as a place of tremendous natural wealth, access to which had been stymied for decades by the "terrible struggle with the Apache."[27] At the same time, to avoid alarming potential investors, such works described the Apaches' current confinement to reservations not as the outcome of any particular military or civilian action (indeed, the deaths at Camp Grant never appeared in any of this literature, either as "massacre" or "affair") but rather as the inevitable outgrowth of the clash between "savagery" and "civilization." "The survival of the fittest holds here as elsewhere," claimed *The Resources of Arizona*, "and the dominant race has asserted itself."[28]

The event the booster literature all pointed to with breathless enthusiasm was the imminent arrival of the transcontinental railroad. In 1880, the Southern Pacific Railroad completed construction of a rail line from California to Tucson, connecting the town to "the fiery annihilator of time and space" that had already transformed so much of American life. To mark the railroad's arrival, Tucson held a daylong celebration, complete with firing of cannons and music courtesy of the Sixth Cavalry Band. The centerpiece of the festivities was a speech by none other than William Oury, who had been selected to give the town's official "address of welcome" to the Southern Pacific's visiting dignitaries. For what was supposed to be a celebratory event, Oury struck a somber note, his words anticipating the melancholy triumphalism that would suffuse the historian Frederick Jackson Turner's "frontier thesis" a decade later:

> The pioneers of Arizona have spent the best years of their life in preparing the way for that progress which we now see consummated. . . . Here, then, arises the question: What are you to do with us? The enterprise of such men as now surround me has penetrated every nook and corner of our broad land, and we have no frontier to which the pioneer may flea [*sic*] to avoid the tramp of civilized progress. . . . [O]ur last request is that you kindly avoid trampling in the dust the few remaining monuments of the first American settlements of Arizona.[29]

Oury's allusion to the potential displacements that the railroad would bring to his generation of settlers proved all too accurate. Within a year, Tucson, which had been a village of 3,500 in 1872, would boom to more than 9,000 residents. This rapid growth upended long-standing patterns of deference in the town, for many of these newcomers had little idea who "Uncle Billy" was or of the central role that he and his compatriots had played in Tucson affairs. Moreover, the railroad's arrival imperiled the economic standing of the participants in the Camp Grant Massacre. With the railroad now the main form of transportation, there was little need to freight goods from Sonora as Hughes, Stevens, and DeLong had done, to buy the specialized wagons that Etchells built for this specialized trade, or to grind flour at Lee's mill rather than importing it from elsewhere. On the demographic level, the growth in population that followed the railroad's arrival stabilized the gender ratio in the American community. Intermarriage between Anglo men and Mexican or Mexican-American women tapered off, casting a slightly disreputable light upon the leaders of an earlier generation, almost all of whom, having married women of Mexican descent, now found themselves fretting as to the place their children would occupy in Tucson's new social order.[30]

It was under these circumstances that Charles Poston convened a meeting in Tucson on January 31, 1884, to create a "Pioneer Association." The stated goal of the proposed organization was to bring the earliest settlers in Arizona together in "a Moral, Benevolent, Literary, Scientific Association." But the organization's implicit purpose—to shore up its members' waning social and political influence—was revealed in a passage in its certificate of incorporation: "to advance the interests and perpetuate the memory of those whose sagacity, energy and enterprise induced them to settle in the wilderness and become the founders of a new state."[31]

One of the first challenges the organizers faced in creating their association was determining who, in fact, qualified as a "pioneer." Those at the meeting agreed that the criterion should be time of residence in the territory. Why not, proposed Jacob Mansfield, select April 30, 1871—the date of the Camp Grant Massacre—as the dividing line? "[T]his was a time when the people of Arizona protected themselves from the Indians," he observed, and so all those who were living in Arizona on or before this date deserved to be considered pioneers. William Oury, also at the meeting, objected to Mansfield's use of the word "massacre," saying the attack had been "a necessary defense against murderous Indians." After what the board minutes only refer to as "long arguments," it was agreed to sidestep the contentious Camp Grant "affair" by making January 1, 1870, the date by which all those who wished to be considered pioneers had to be resident in the territory. But there are hints that the Camp Grant Massacre left its imprint on the association nonetheless. The pioneers agreed that the "annual celebration of this society shall take place on the first day of May in each year"—in other words, on the anniversary of the day after the attack. Even more telling, the pioneers elected William Oury as their first president. Over the years, others involved in the massacre, such as Samuel Hughes, Charles Etchells, Hiram Stevens, and Sidney DeLong, would serve as officers as well.[32]

The "Society of Arizona Pioneers" functioned in its early years as a peculiar amalgam of benevolent organization, policy advocate, and historical society.

Members, who were supposed to refer to one another as "Brother," created a "Widow and Orphan Fund" to support the families of deceased pioneers, a "Pioneer Relief Fund" to help members in financial distress, and adopted the custom of visiting one another when sick and of serving as pallbearers at one another's funerals. In 1885, when the Chiricahua Apache leader Geronimo fled the San Carlos Reservation, revealing that the "Apache problem" was far less resolved than Crook and the boosters had predicted, members of the society seized upon this event in an attempt to recapture their role as community leaders with "long experience" in Indian matters. The pioneers called several public meetings on the "[d]isastrous troubles [that] have again fallen upon the Territory" that bore more than a passing resemblance to the gatherings that had preceded the killings at Camp Grant over a decade earlier.[33]

As before, a list of civilian volunteers for action against the Apaches was drawn up, the governor declared his "complete sympathy with any movement which will result in permanent relief from Indian barbarities in this territory," and the distribution of rifles and ammunition was proposed. Ultimately, however, the aging pioneers contented themselves with issuing appeals to the federal government in favor of "the speedy and absolute removal of the Apache Indians from our Territory." In the meantime, in its role as a fledgling historical organization, the association rented out a section of the Tucson public library where it began to build a collection of books and newspapers, and at the suggestion of "President Oury," the members at their monthly meetings commenced delivering brief "historical reminiscences" to all those assembled, the texts of which were then filed among the society's documents.[34]

One of the first of these reminiscences was given by Oury himself. "Uncle Billy's" subject matter was, to no one's surprise, a defense of the killings at Camp Grant in 1871. Although he delivered his talk in front of a local audience, Oury doubtless directed his comments toward the national debate still swirling around the attack. In 1880, George Manypenny, the former U.S. commissioner of Indian affairs, had published a memoir that decried the "merciless and barbarous" Camp Grant Massacre and expressed his horror that the attack "was approved by men of prominence and influence in the territory." Two years later, the reformer Helen Hunt Jackson released a history of U.S. Indian policy entitled *A Century of Dishonor*. A highly critical account of the United States' treatment of Native Americans, Jackson's book could arguably be considered the progenitor of the revisionist approach to American Indian history. Its narrative condensed the history of U.S.-Indian relations into one vast tale of white atrocity. "It makes little difference," she contended, "where one opens the record of the history of the Indians; every page and every year has its dark stain." Making extensive use of the reports that Whitman had submitted to his superiors in 1871 (as had Manypenny before her), Jackson held up the Camp Grant Massacre as a model of the "treachery and cruelty" that typified the American treatment of Indians.[35]

Oury's response came on April 6, 1885. In Tucson's Pioneer Hall, before "a large gathering of pioneers and their friends," he delivered a speech on "one of the events most important in its results to the peace and progress of our Apache cursed land": the "so-called Camp Grant massacre." The narrative that Oury presented contained elements familiar to most of his audience, as portions of it had been rehearsed for years in newspaper accounts of the killings and in the trial of the participants. "[N]oble Wooster" and his wife made their inevitable appearance, as did Whitman as a representative of a misguided federal Indian policy, all assembled by Oury to demonstrate the "carnival of murder and plunder" that the Apache had committed in the months leading up to the attack. Given his effort to underscore the horrors the Apache had perpetrated, Oury spent little time on the killings he and the other participants (none of whom he referred to by name, other than Jesús Elías) had committed at Camp Grant. Similarly, he made no mention of the large number of women slain in the raid or the probable rape of several Apache women in the moments before their deaths, only noting that "not an adult Indian [was] left to tell the tale."[36]

The crux of Oury's speech came at the end. As he closed his effort "to fully vindicate those who were aids and abettors" in the deaths of the Apache at Camp Grant, he portrayed the massacre as the point from which the region's current peace and prosperity flowed. "Behold now the happy result immediately following that episode. . . . [N]ew life springs up, confidences restored and industry bounds forward with an impetus that has known no check in the whole fourteen years that have elapsed since that occurrence." The pioneers had not been motivated by primitive bloodlust as their critics charged but rather, Oury suggested, by the desire to create the same civilization so celebrated by Jackson and Manypenny—only such reformers were too naive to realize that it could not be established without violence.[37]

As in Oury's speech to mark the arrival of Tucson's railroad, the sense that the pioneers were both cause and victim of the region's recent changes saturated his narrative. The massacre of the Apache at Camp Grant, in Oury's telling, became an awful duty that the pioneers had been required to perpetrate in order to usher in civilization. Yet this same progress now left the pioneers socially and economically displaced and subjected their past deeds to harsh new criticism. Oury thus ended his talk with a challenge, not only to the concept that what had taken place at Camp Grant should be termed a "massacre," but for all those who enjoyed Arizona's current conditions to acknowledge that they too were complicit in the attack. "In view of all these facts, I call on all Arizonians to answer on their consciences: Can you call the killing of the Apaches at Camp Grant on the morning of April 30th 1871 a massacre?"[38]

Oury's speech was reprinted the following morning on the front page of the *Arizona Daily Citizen*, appearing alongside a column describing the imminent death of the architect of the "Peace Policy," ex-president Ulysses S. Grant, from terminal throat cancer. Seemingly unaware of the ironic juxtaposition of these two articles, the Tucson press predicted that Oury's account, coming as it did from a recognized participant, "will be accepted in future as the correct statement of the affair."[39]

If this acceptance was never as total as the newspaper expected and Oury doubtless hoped, numerous factors did ensure that Oury's version enjoyed a long afterlife. During the closing decades of the nineteenth century, the Society of Arizona Pioneers, with its growing collection of reminiscences from Oury and other early settlers, underwent a gradual conversion into the official caretaker of Arizona's historical record. In 1897, the Arizona Legislative Assembly provided the organization, now renamed the Arizona Pioneers' Historical Society, with funding and designated it the trustee of Arizona's territorial records. In 1901, DeLong became the society's president and, the following year, its first historian, responsible for writing a history of Arizona based on the records of the Pioneers' Historical Society.[40]

DeLong's work, released in 1905 as *The History of Arizona from the Earliest Times Known to the People of Europe to 1903*, closely echoed the portrayals of the Apache ("the determined foe of all civilization") and the killings at Camp Grant ("an event . . . that compelled the general government to . . . take these Indians under her immediate control") long advanced by the Pioneers' Society.

Although Oury had passed away in 1887 at his Tucson home—his ensuing funeral was reportedly the largest the community had ever seen—the publication of DeLong's book extended the reach of "Uncle Billy's" reminiscences through time and space, and the growing status of the Pioneers' Society as Arizona's official historical organization imbued Oury's words with a certain authority. Indeed, several histories written in the 1910s uncritically excerpted or paraphrased Oury's account in its entirety to describe nineteenth-century relations with the Apache, demonstrating the extent to which Oury's memories and the historical record had merged into one and the same.[41]

Nonetheless, in the shadow of Oury's death, a peculiar new set of memories about the massacre began to emerge. Throughout the early 1900s, numerous individuals came forward to unmask themselves as one of the last surviving members of the secret cohort of Americans who had participated in the Camp Grant Massacre. In 1910, for example, a man named Theodore Jones released a vivid account of the massacre in which he recounted his close relationship with Wooster and told how, riding alongside Oury and the Papago, he had avenged his friend's death at Camp Grant. Likewise, in 1916, an Arizona resident named John Cady published a book entitled *Yesterday's Arizona* that placed him next to Oury and DeLong as they scouted the scene of Wooster's murder, planned the attack on Camp Grant, and faced trial in Judge Titus's courtroom.[42]

For all Jones's and Cady's invocation of familiar episodes of the massacre, abundant evidence indicates that neither of these men took part in the terrible deeds they described. Instead, building on Oury's well-known recollections, they invented stories that cast them as central actors in the event. Given the tattered veil of secrecy that still surrounded the massacre's participants, Jones's deception might never have been recognized had not the *Arizona Daily Star*, catching wind of his story, checked with DeLong, the last known Anglo participant in the massacre. DeLong informed the paper that "Jones was not of them nor had he ever been. He was a clerk for E.N. Fish and that is all that is remembered of him." As for Cady, there is little proof that he was in Arizona in 1871, let alone a participant in the massacre. He does not appear in the 1870 federal census of Tucson or in the 1881 and 1883–84 directories of the town. Nor is his name featured among those tried for the attack in 1871 or as a founding member of the Society of Arizona Pioneers in 1884. If this were not

The crossroads of past and present: DeLong Street in Barrio Anita, with the high rises of downtown Tucson in the background.

sufficient to raise one's suspicions, it should be noted that Cady, perhaps having learned from Jones's public humiliation, did not reveal his role in the massacre until after DeLong passed away in 1914. As the Tucson resident George Roskruge recalled with some bemusement in the 1920s, "Sidney DeLong told me again and again that he was the last man alive who went on the Camp Grant massacre, but since his death both Bill Cady and Dave Dunham have told me that they were on that trip also."[43]

The fact that men would willingly place themselves at an atrocity they did not commit reveals a great deal about the pull that the Camp Grant Massacre continued to exert on Arizona's Anglo residents well into the twentieth century. This influence made itself felt in places like Tucson in ways both large and small. At the turn of the century, when Samuel Hughes developed some of his land into a residential area that came to be known as Barrio Anita, he named many of the new neighborhood's streets after his old friends—many of whom also happened, of course, to be participants in the Camp Grant

Massacre. Thus Tucson soon sported a DeLong Street, a Hughes Street, and an Oury Street, all of which bordered a new city park created in 1913 and named for William Oury.[44]

Over this same period, the Pioneers' Society continued its evolution into a mainstream historical society, moving in 1928 to the campus of the University of Arizona, broadening its membership requirements, and eventually conceiving of itself as a "research center." In 1971, exactly a century after the Camp Grant Massacre, the organization became the Arizona Historical Society.[45]

In spite of—or, perhaps, because of—this shift toward an ostensibly more scientific and objective study of Arizona's history, it was also during this era that the massacre began to disappear from the consciousness of many Americans. There are numerous interlocking reasons for the growing silence about the Apache deaths at Camp Grant. For those who wanted to recall the Apache wars, the campaigns of the 1880s against Geronimo provided a much less ambiguous set of stories to contemplate. Geronimo's seemingly implacable efforts to resist American domination raised few of the troubling issues that Es-him-en-zee's experiences offered, in which a potentially sincere attempt at peace was met with federal bumbling and civilian atrocity. Moreover, as the last Indian leader to surrender to U.S. authorities, Geronimo became an object of fascination for U.S. audiences in a way that Es-him-en-zee could never be. By the turn of the century, Geronimo could be found in everything from plays (*The History of Geronimo's Summer Campaign*) to magazine articles ("Effacing the Frontier") to the popular autobiography that he dictated shortly before his death (*Geronimo's Story of His Life*, published in 1907).[46]

For many other Anglos, who preferred to view their history as a story of Euro-American progress, the Indian wars had become something of an embarrassment. In 1908, when Orick Jackson published *The White Conquest of Arizona*—a book that, as its title made all too clear, treated the arrival of white Americans as the defining event of Arizona's history—he effaced all references to the Camp Grant Massacre altogether. To Jackson, the image of white men like Oury, Etchells, Lee, and Hughes, married to Mexican women and only able to avenge themselves against the Apache through an alliance with the territory's Mexicans and Papagoes, fit poorly with the narrative of white mastery that he sought to tell. Although not all historians were as obvious in

"Effacing the frontier": Geronimo leading a delegation of American Indians in Theodore Roosevelt's inaugural parade.

their biases, the tendency to see Anglos as the primary actors in the region's historical drama not only bleached the polyglot character of the early U.S. borderlands out of many studies; it also rendered an episode like the Camp Grant Massacre a problematic and therefore marginal event.[47]

Equally common was the desire, shared with the earlier wave of booster histories, to gloss over the less pleasant aspects of Arizona's history. The strange career of Arizona's first textbook of state history for schoolchildren exemplifies this impulse. The textbook, written by a longtime Arizona civics teacher and self-described pioneer named Ida Flood Dodge, went through two iterations. The first, *Arizona Under Our Flag*, was published in Tucson in 1928 after first being serialized in the *Arizona Daily Star*. This version included a three-page discussion of the "tragical" Camp Grant Massacre that echoed the conventional pioneer narrative established by Oury and DeLong. A year later, a New York–based

Aravaipa without the Apache: Augustus Thomas's play Arizona: A Drama in Four Acts.

publisher, Charles Scribner's Sons, released a revised edition of Dodge's book for national distribution. Entitled *Our Arizona*, this volume contained no discussion of the Camp Grant Massacre at all, only a note in the introduction that the author had attempted to present Arizona's history in a style suitable for children and "unencumbered by sensational or gruesome details." In place of a discussion of the massacre, one thus found a largely abstract depiction of the conflicts between the Apache and settlers. "Our government tried to put an end to the warfare, but the problem was difficult to solve. . . . Sometimes the attempts made proved worth while [*sic*]. Sometimes they failed." [48]

Most popular literature paralleled this trend of avoiding the disturbing brutality that had marked Arizona's Apache wars. In his long-running play *Arizona*, which first appeared in Chicago in 1899 and was later revived on Broadway in 1913, where it helped establish a tradition of Western-themed theatrical melodramas, Augustus Thomas offered a vision of Arizona from which the Apache had been totally erased. Although set at Camp Grant and opening with a scene of "the mountains that wall in the Aravaipa valley . . . in

The New West: "Old Tucson" stage set.

bold relief against the hot summer sky of Arizona," the play had no Apache characters in it at all, let alone any mention of the horrifying events that had taken place in Aravaipa Canyon in the 1860s and '70s. Instead, the work that critics hailed for its "melodrama, love, and patriotism" focused on the romantic foibles that ensued on a remote army outpost when Anglo women were in short supply.[49]

Clarence Budington Kelland adopted a similar storyline a few decades later in his best-selling 1939 novel *Arizona.* Although Kelland's book did include some Apaches, including Cochise, as bit players, and incorporated portraits of such real-life pioneers as Charles Poston, Estevan Ochoa, and William Oury's brother Granville, the plot centered on a romantic triangle concerning the fictional Phoebe Titus, "the first white woman ever to marry in Tucson." When Columbia Pictures decided to capitalize on the novel's popularity by turning it into a movie starring William Holden and Jean Arthur, the filmmakers went to Arizona to consult with members of the Pioneers' Society. To capture an authentic look for the film, Columbia even constructed a replica of nineteenth-century Tucson in the desert outside of town. Over the following decades, Columbia and other studios would use this stage set—dubbed "Old Tucson"—as a backdrop for countless westerns starring everyone from Frank Sinatra to Ronald Reagan, Jimmy Stewart, John Wayne, Paul Newman, and Clint Eastwood. In the process, Arizona's desert scenery and facsimile Tucson became the archetypical western landscape for generations of movie-watching Americans.[50]

It is tempting to conclude that the story of the Camp Grant Massacre ends for most Americans here, lost amid a simulated western past valued only for its entertainment value. Yet submerged as it may be beneath the virtual reality of "Old Tucson" and other popular reimaginings of the American West, history nonetheless survives—quiet, to be sure, but not altogether silent. The accounts that Oury, DeLong, and the other perpetrators produced, documenting the atrocity at Camp Grant, have endured for more than a century, carefully filed away in the archives of the organization that the participants helped establish. In its new guise as the Arizona Historical Society, the Pioneers' Society remains in Tucson, only a few short miles, in fact, from "Old Tucson." To the extent that the massacre has managed to avoid being forgotten among the Anglo-American community, it is in large part because Oury and his compatriots, the people who might seem to have the most to hide, created the means to ensure its survival.[51]

THE N<u>N</u>ĒĒ

T HE FIRST RESPONSES of the People to the massacre on April 30, 1871, illuminate the very limits of human expression. Not only were many N<u>n</u>ēē, their bodies sprawled amid the burning *gow<u>a</u>h* along Aravaipa Creek, silenced by death; Western Apache traditions favored not speaking in the face of intense despair and instead using nonverbal displays of grief such as cutting one's hair or burning a deceased family member's possessions. Survivors' initial refusal to articulate their losses left a deep impression on the first outsiders to reach the massacre site. "Many of the men, whose families had all been killed, when I spoke to them . . . were obliged to turn away, unable to speak, and too proud to show their grief. The women whose children had been killed or stolen were convulsed with grief. . . . Children who two days before had been full of fun and frolic, kept at a distance, expressing wondering horror."[1]

In those stories about the attack that N<u>n</u>ēē survivors did tell over time, the massacre manifested itself much as it must have been experienced in real life: as a sudden, unexpected intrusion, disrupting not only the People's existence but also the ceremonies that guided their spiritual life. Bi ja gush kai ye ("The One Whose Ears Look Like Cactus") narrated the deaths of her people as follows:

> While we were there [Aravaipa Canyon], the uncle of my husband got sick in our camp. So my husband said, "Let's take him about a mile

down the valley and sing over him there at the camp of a big medicine man called *ni ba bi je ji.*" So they did, and down there they sang over him all night, till almost dawn.

Just about dawn, some Mexican men came out over a hill above our camps. Now we heard a shot. Then there were lots of Mexicans, *se kine* [Tohono O'odham], and Americans all round us. They must have killed about one thousand of us, I guess. Only a few of us got away, up on the mountains.²

M-ba-lse-slā ("Coyote, Two Dead Ones Lying There") also depicted the killings as disturbing a ritual event:

Now some men said that they would give a dance to celebrate their coming into the agency. The dance was to be tomorrow night, and notice was sent out to the different camps along both sides of the Arivaipa. They started in the next evening to give their *tl-e gû-chi-ta'sl* [night dance]. They danced all through the night and almost till sunrise.

There was a big ridge above their camps, and one on the other side too. During the night a big bunch of Mexicans and Papagoes had got up on these ridges, and surrounded the camp completely. The Mexicans and Papagoes [. . .] fired on them while they were still dancing. They killed a lot of people this way. They all scattered. . . . I ran into an arroyo. I had my bow and arrows, and I pointed at them as if I was going to shoot. This scared some Mexicans and Papagoes back, who were after me. I ran on, trying to get away, but four of them followed me, but they did not kill me or hit me. In those days we Apaches could run fast. . . . I ran in behind some rocks, below an overhanging bluff finally, and hid there. They shot at me, but could not hit me those four enemies. They four were afraid to come close. I shot arrows at them. Finally they ran away, and left me. I ran on up the side of the mountain, to the top, and stayed there. Some others who had gotten away were on top of this mountain also. It is called *m-ba ma-gu'sl î-he.* The sun was getting really low now. We stayed on top of this mountain all night. The next day one man went back to [the] place where we had been dancing. He found lots of dead Apaches there.

Some of the women and girls who had long, nice hair, they had cut a round place right out of the scalp, leaving the hair on, and taken it away with them. I don't know why they did this.[3]

M-ba-lse-slā also described the preliminary efforts to negotiate with the Enemy over the People's deaths at the place the Nnēē came to call Gashdla'áchoh o'āā, or "Big Sycamore Stands There," for the large tree shading Aravaipa Creek.

Next day, the people who had gotten away, and were hidden in different places over the mountains, started to call one another together. When they had all gathered, they sent that same man who had been back to the dance ground and 15 others, down towards Camp Grant. When they were near the camp, they stopped, and rested on some level ground. Then their two head men, Captain Chiquito and *haské bahnzin*, went and talked with the agent, telling him all that had happened. The agent said he didn't know that this massacre had taken place at all. The Officer said that those Mexicans and Papagoes would never come back, and that even if they did, the soldiers there at Camp Grant would know about it first. The Officer said that up till this time they had been good friends, and had gotten along all right. This was why he had sent out for them to come in and talk. He sent me up to bury the dead for the Apaches, and he gave out rations to those who had survived. He told them to come back, and settle down again. The band did so, and made their camp on the Arivaipa River, about one mile from the soldiers, so that they would be near them, and have protection.[4]

In these early parleys, one point emerged paramount: the fate of the twenty-nine children seized during the massacre. "Get them back for us," one Nnēē exhorted the Enemy. "[O]ur little boys will grow up slaves, and our girls, as soon as they are large enough, will be diseased prostitutes to get money for whoever owns them. . . . Our dead you cannot bring back to life, but those that are living we gave to you, and we look to you, who can write and talk and have soldiers, to get them back."[5]

The *Innaa* at Blue Water Pool vowed to protect the survivors from further attack and to recover the People's missing children. Subsequent events, however, soon called the Enemy's promises into question. Six weeks after the massacre, Hashkēē bá nzį́n, who had lost two wives, five children, and scores of followers in the attack—the only survivor among his immediate family being his two-and-half-year-old daughter, whom Hashkēē bá nzį́n had carried to safety during the assault—suddenly found himself and his relatives threatened once again. An army patrol from Fort Apache stumbled across him and the remaining members of his *gotah* in the upper reaches of Aravaipa Canyon and, believing them to be hostile, charged their camp. No one was killed in the ensuing chaos, but afterwards Hashkēē bá nzį́n went to Blue Water Pool and bade the *Innaa* leader there a formal farewell. Next, as if to underscore his turn away from the peace process, the chief killed one of the first *Innaa* he encountered, a white rancher living near Aravaipa with whom he had become friendly. Then, after hiding the remaining members of his family in the mountains above Aravaipa Canyon, Hashkēē bá nzį́n led a raid against the Sáíkiné in an unsuccessful bid to reclaim the children captured during the massacre.[6]

Meanwhile, news of the killings in Aravaipa, apparently carried by fleeing survivors, spread among neighboring Nṉēē bands. In mid-May, many of the Dziłghą́'é (White Mountain Apache), fearing that they might be the next group massacred, abandoned their reservation at Fort Apache. The following month, *Innaa* delegates to the Chiricahua Apache found Gúchį́į́sh more reluctant than ever to settle on a proposed reserve near the Mexican border. "Nothing was said in regard to the outrage at Camp Grant," reported an observer, "but . . . Cochi[se] knew of it, and was influenced by it to some extent." Elsewhere, army officers reported that "several of the Apache Chiefs" had informed soldiers at various military posts that the Nṉēē knew the identities of those who had murdered the People in Aravaipa Canyon.[7]

In September of 1871, Hashkēē bá nzį́n, Captain Chiquito, and almost three hundred of their followers, "carrying white doe skins for flags [of truce]," returned to Blue Water Pool for another round of negotiations. In the transcript of the encounter, Hashkēē bá nzį́n, who likely had had local newspapers translated to him with help from Mexicans or literate captives among the Apache, demonstrated a keen awareness of the accounts of the massacre already circulating in the Enemy press: "They [the People] believe these Tucson people write for the papers and tell their own story. The Apache have no one to tell their story." Although Hashkēē bá nzín and the People expressed fears of another attack ("They think that as soon as the commissioner [Colyer] has gone these people will return again and try to massacre them"), they nonetheless deflected the *Innaa*'s continued suggestions to move to Fort Apache. Because of the People's refusal to abandon their Aravaipa homeland, the *Innaa* eventually responded by creating a reserve for them in the vicinity of Blue Water Pool.[8]

In addition to making clear his People's desire to remain in Aravaipa, Hashkēē bá nzín also took pains to underscore for the Enemy the tremendous loss of life the Nnēē had suffered. His role as leader, the chief maintained, no longer held much meaning after the deaths of so many followers. "If he [Colyer] had seen him about three months ago, we would have seen him [Hashkēē bá nzín] a captain. Then he had a band of seventy men, but they had all been massacred; now he has got no people. . . . He never had much to say, but this he could say, he likes this place [Aravaipa Canyon]. He has said all he ought to say, since he has no people anywhere to speak for. If it had not been for the massacre, there would have been a great many more people here now; but, after that massacre, who could have stood it? It was not possible for any man to have stood it." Hashkēē bá nzín and Captain Chiquito concluded the encounter by conducting Colyer to Big Sycamore Stands There to survey the massacre site, where scores of Nnēē lay once more exposed to the elements, along with "camp utensils, the clothing, and blankets . . . also the bundles of hay that the women were bringing in." The sight of these decaying remnants of his community moved Hashkēē bá nzín to tears.[9]

Captain Chiquito, Hashkēē bá nzín, and their followers soon settled on the grounds of their new reserve in Aravaipa Canyon (although, noted one observer, "[t]hey no longer encamp in very large numbers lest they be surprised again"). Around this time, Hashkēē bá nzín also remarried, taking as his spouses three daughters of Santos, an Aravaipa Apache leader. Yet for all these changes, neither Hashkēē bá nzín nor the other members of his group forgot about the Nnēē children stolen from them on April 30. By the Black Rocks People's reckoning, twenty-nine of their youths had been seized; of these, two had escaped back to the Tsézhiné, leaving twenty-seven still unaccounted for. One of Hashkēē bá nzín's last comments during his September parley with the Enemy had been to express his pleasure at the *Innaa*'s renewed promises to return the youngsters to the People: "It seems to him now as if he had his children in his own hands." Similarly, when a new *Innaa* (General O. O. Howard) called upon the Black Rocks People the following spring, the redemption of their children was one of the first points the People raised with him. Much as they had with Colyer before, the Tsézhiné, strove to impress upon their visitor the human costs of the massacre, conducting the *Innaa* to Big Sycamore Stands There and showing him "a little girl, eight or nine years of age," who had survived the Camp Grant Massacre but was "wounded under her ear and in her side."[10]

The concerns the People voiced during this latest meeting, which extended not only to their missing children, but also to creating a lasting peace with the Sáíkiné and the "citizens who were annoyed by their presence," prompted the *Innaa* to organize an unprecedented new round of negotiations the following month with representatives from almost all the communities in the borderlands. Held along the San Pedro River in the spring of 1872, the conference was attended by Hashkēē bá nzį́n, Santos, and Captain Chiquito, among others. Santos opened the negotiations by "[a]rizing and going before the General [Howard] and laying a small stone on the floor." Santos stated that "he did not know how to read or write, this is his paper (pointing to the stone), and he wants a peace that will last as long as that stone lasts." Another of the People, Eskelpeldotendi, who prefaced his comments by swearing "before God and the Virgin Mary," explained that "the peace they wanted is that which will permit them to go to Tucson and wherever they wish without danger"—a pointed critique of the geographic limits that the reservation system imposed on the People. For his part, Hashkēē bá nzį́n appears to have alluded to the People's mythic tale about Sun and Monster Slayer in an effort to explain the longstanding tensions between the Nṇēē and the Sáíkiné: "In the first place, there were two nations. Two of them had possession of two small hills. The Papagos and Apaches were . . . originally friends. Then they were hostile; now the time has come when they shall be friends [again]."[11]

These initial expressions of the People's desire to make a lasting peace were well received (the only tense point being when Hashkēē bá nzį́n accused Jesús María Elías, the representative for the Mexican-American population, of looking "as if he was trying to intimidate them"). As the conversation turned to

"A peace that will last as long as that stone lasts": Santos during his trip to Washington, D.C., in 1872.

the still unresolved status of the Nnēē children, however, the mood of the conference darkened. More than a year after the massacre and despite repeated promises to locate the People's offspring, the Enemy produced only six (four girls and two boys) of the twenty-seven missing children. Even more disappointing, the lead *Innaa* negotiator, General Howard, swayed by settler claims that the Apache children were better off in "civilized," Christian households, suddenly imposed a new condition: he would only return those Nnēē whose parents were alive to care for them.

Hashkēē bá nzín responded by stressing both the losses and survivals surrounding the Camp Grant Massacre: "when General Howard was here before, he [Hashkēē bá nzín] showed the General where one hundred and thirty of his people had been killed. These children had lost their fathers and mothers." Nevertheless, Hashkēē bá nzín reminded the *Innaa*, the children still "had relatives" among the Black Rocks People. At this point, one Nnēē man attempted to lead a captive, his sister, away by the hand. Her tears and apparent

252 SHADOWS AT DAWN

unfamiliarity with the People after more than a year among the Enemy, however, caused Howard to intervene. Frustrated, Hashkee bá nzín reiterated that
the captives "were theirs (his people's) and they wanted them"—indeed, the
"object of his making this treaty had been to get these children back."[12]

Dusk and ill-humor having descended upon the negotiators, the parley was
suspended until the following morning. Santos again opened the talk, implor-
ing the translator, a Baachii named Manuel Duran, to present his words as
accurately as possible: "Santos said he knew Manuel (the interpreter) when he
was a boy, and had known his father when a boy; and he asked it as a favor
of Manuel to do the interpreting well; that his people might get the children
back." In the end, however, the only compromise the two sides could agree
upon was to have the six children remain at the army base at Blue Water
Pool under the care of an *Innaa* governess—a measure that did not return
the youths to their families but that did not leave them among their captors
either.[13]

Despite the determined efforts of the Black Rocks People to reclaim their
relatives, the trail of the other twenty-one captured children vanishes at this
point. Most of their final tracks point toward Sonora, where many were apparently sold to families in the vicinity of the town of Altar (although other stories
place at least a few captives in prominent Anglo and Mexican households in
Tucson). While these youths survived the massacre, they spent the remainder
of their lives apart from their relatives. As a result, whatever memories they
retained of the Camp Grant Massacre remained inaccessible to the rest of the
People and, because of the secrecy surrounding the children's sale, undocu-
mented by Mexican and Anglo archivists. The captured children thus represent an absence of another sort in the historical record—one linked not to
murder but rather to dispossession and exile, of voices not erased but silenced
nonetheless.[14]

A similar absence defines at least one other Apache perspective on the
massacre. Scattered clues suggest that at least a few Baachii took part in the
attack in Aravaipa. Not only was the canyon familiar to them—in 1869, some
Baachii served as guides for *Innaa* forces at Blue Water Pool—but in June
1871, amid the controversy following the massacre, a "tame Apache" named
Eugenio Chiqui submitted an affidavit stating that "I was with the expedition

that attacked the Indians near Camp Grant, April 30th." Similarly, Manuel Duran, the interpreter during the 1872 peace conference, reportedly sold a six-year-old Nnee girl days after the massacre, and on the second day of the parley, an event he had attended with great reluctance, he unexpectedly disappeared. He materialized back in Tucson several days later with the explanation that, fearing the vengeance of the Black Rocks People for what he had done to them, he had fled to Tucson. Duran never specified what his past misdeeds might have been, but surely participating in the Camp Grant Massacre would have constituted an act for which the T'iisibaan and the clan members of the dead would have both sought revenge.[15]

And so it may be, just as in the 1863 attack on the People in Aravaipa Canyon, the Baachii played a role in the 1871 massacre as well. We may never know for certain: the most illuminating testimony as to the *apaches mansos'* participation in the 1863 assault, after all, was produced by the People themselves, and many of these potential witnesses perished in the Camp Grant Massacre. But it is not outside the realm of the possible that the massacre bore the imprint of the tensions that existed both between Apaches and non-Apaches and between different Apache bands. If this was indeed the case, it adds one more layer to the oddly intimate violence of the nineteenth-century borderlands. Not only may there have been Apaches on both sides of the era's worst atrocity—the Apache participants in this episode were familiar with one another and perhaps even grew up together, as Santos's reference to knowing Manuel and his father as young boys would seem to suggest.

Ironically, not long after the 1872 peace negotiations, the Baachii, like the captive T'iisibaan children, vanish from the historical record. The Baachii had received only minimal attention from the Office of Indian Affairs in the years after the Gadsden Purchase: they were never assigned an Indian agent, or, for that matter, granted the territory along the San Pedro or Sonoita rivers that they requested in 1866. Lacking federal recognition or a permanent land base, the Baachii community appears to have been gradually absorbed into southern Arizona's Mexican population. Commentators in Tucson described the group as "work[ing] in the same manner as, and . . . upon an equality with the Mexican peons," celebrating the village's Catholic feast days, and possessing "intimate associations with the Mexican people." Apache oral tradition likewise supports a scenario of gradual assimilation into the Mexican community: informants in the early twentieth century described the Bāāchii as a people who, having become like the *Inṉaa*, they no longer recognized as related to them. "They have a little town. They raise corn. They are more like Mexicans."[16]

Much like those Nṉēē killed or kidnapped at Camp Grant, then, the Bāāchii represent another Apache voice from the massacre lost to contemporary historians. Lacking further evidence, it is impossible to tease out responses to the questions of motivation and complicity that Tucson's Bāāchii community presents. Did the Bāāchii join the raiders in keeping with Nṉēē norms governing feuds and clan vengeance? To curry favor with influential Mexicans and Americans in Tucson, perhaps with the hope of improving their claim to lands along the San Pedro or Sonoita rivers? For money or other material rewards? Could Duran's sale of a captive girl afterwards be viewed as a gesture of compassion, an effort to rescue a young child, one with whose parents Duran may have even been acquainted? With the Bāāchii's tracks having faded, only the questions they raised linger on, unanswered.

O THER SURVIVORS of the Camp Grant Massacre left clearer trails across the years. Shortly after the negotiations in 1872, Santos served as the T'iisibaan's representative in a delegation of Arizona Indians to Washington, D.C., where he met with President Grant and the commissioner of Indian affairs, and toured a navy yard, penitentiary, and school for deaf children. In February of 1873, Hashkēē bá nzịn and Captain Chiquito led their followers north to the new reserve Howard had created for them at the intersection of the San Carlos and Gila rivers, a locale that would come to be known as San Carlos Reservation.[17]

That the Black Rocks People would move away from Aravaipa Canyon, having struggled to retain a presence there for over a century, may seem something of a surprise. But given the canyon's proximity to Tucson, the People's fear of another massacre remained palpable, leading the Nṉēē to camp next to Blue Water Pool rather than farther upstream in the canyon as before. This forced proximity to the army soon manifested noticeable drawbacks. "[B]eing prevented from hunting they [the People] collect around the post, and get mixed up with the soldiers," observed Hashkēē bá nzį́n. "Sometimes the soldiers kick them and throw stones at them; this makes trouble." In addition, the water at Blue Water Pool proved a fertile breeding ground for the malaria-carrying mosquitoes that were inadvertently introduced into the People's homeland with European colonization. Under these conditions, relocating to the more remote locale of San Carlos may have seemed like a wise decision, one that protected the People from vigilantes, soldiers, and disease alike. Moreover, for a community used to making extended journeys to raid or gather foodstuffs, moving away from the canyon in no way symbolized the surrender of their rights to Aravaipa—even though the Innaa came to perceive their actions in this light.[18]

San Carlos soon proved to be far from the comfortable home the Black Rocks People anticipated. Not only did it too harbor malaria and other diseases; the Innaa undertook a policy of concentrating the region's disparate Indian communities in this single location, including the Mbachii yūmaa (Yuma), Gōōn (Yavapai), and the Hák'áyé (Chiricahua Apache)—peoples with whom the Western Apache, themselves divided into contesting groups, possessed only limited or uneasy relations. The ensuing tensions placed Hashkēē bá nzį́n, Captain Chiquito, and their followers in a perilous position. Initially, according to the Enemy, Hashkēē bá nzį́n was supposed to be "chief over all the eight bands" confined to San Carlos. But friction—including occasional violence—between the communities on the reserve propelled each group to separate portions of San Carlos. By 1873, Captain Chiquito would find himself in the territorial prison on charges of harboring fugitives and trading in stolen livestock. The following year, the Innaa would blame Hashkēē bá nzį́n for the ongoing unrest on the reservation and lock him in San Carlos's guardhouse.[19]

Somehow, Hashkēē bá nzį́n managed to escape from his jail cell a few days later and flee with many of his followers, triggering the flight of several other bands from the reservation. During the outbreak, a number of Nnēē made their way back to Aravaipa Canyon, where, in probable revenge for the massacre there three years before, they murdered a group of Mexicans who had recently settled near Tūdotł'ish sikán. The army launched an aggressive pursuit, attacking all Apaches found off the reservation. But it soon settled upon a more effective policy: exploiting the tensions between different Apache communities, the military paid scouts from those Nnee bands that remained on the reservation to kill escapees and bring in their heads. The army then exhibited these gruesome trophies among the People to deter further breakouts.[20]

Although Hashkee bá nzín and his followers eluded the worst of this campaign, the Apache-on-Apache violence the army had unleashed led them to surrender in San Carlos a few months later. Upon regaining custody of Hashkee bá nzín, the army riveted chains onto the chief's ankles and sent him to "new" Camp Grant, which had been moved to the foot of Dził nchaa si'án ("Big Mountain," or Mount Graham). Here, while making adobes with several other imprisoned Nnee, Hashkee bá nzín met the latest of San Carlos's many agents. Known among the Innaa as John Clum but called Tazhii ("Turkey") by the Nnee for his strutting style of walking, the agent had Hashkee bá nzín and his family returned to the reservation, where the chief again resumed a leadership role.[21]

In 1877, when Tazhii left for a new post, Hashkee bá nzín, apparently having learned from prior experience what a change in administration might foretell for him, decided to leave the reservation as well. "If there should be trouble here again I will be blamed," he reported. "I want to live at peace and make my own living and raise things for my family to eat. . . . I will go down to the Rio San Pedro and take some land where no one lives now, and I will make a ditch to bring water to irrigate that land. I will make a home there for myself and my family and we will live like the other ranchers do."[22]

Hashkee bá nzín's move precipitated the return of perhaps as many as one hundred Black Rocks People to the familiar geography of Łee ndlíí ("Flows Together"). With the closing of "old" Camp Grant, these lands had become part of the public domain, and so Hashkee bá nzín and several other Nnee took out homesteads in accordance with the General Allotment Act of 1887. By the late 1870s, Hashkee bá nzín had a thriving farm of some 140 acres along the San Pedro River. Although superficially similar to that of his Mexican and Anglo neighbors, with its adobe buildings, barbed wire, irrigation ditches, and crops of Old World and New World origin (barley, corn, watermelon, and pumpkins), the homestead also betrayed unmistakable Nnee influences. Rather than

Tazhii ("Turkey"): John Clum seated at center with a delegation of Apaches from San Carlos, including Hashkēē bá nzín (second row, far left) and Captain Chiquito (second row, second from left).

constituting the dwelling place of a single nuclear family as among the *Innaa*, the ranch and vicinity was inhabited instead by Hashkēē bá nzín's *gotah* of six to eight interconnected families, demonstrating the continued importance of the matrilineally organized family for the People.[23]

Captain Chiquito, who was, as one of his descendants, Wallace Johnson, recalled, "rich in wives," followed a similar pattern, taking out an allotment in Aravaipa Canyon with his six spouses, each of whom inhabited her own *gowah*. Captain Chiquito's camp became the nucleus around which other Nnēe established farm sites of their own. Remembered one of the People, James Nolin, "Chiquito was recognized as sort of Chief of the Indians on this Arivapa Canyon near San Pedro. [T]his camp extends along the canyon several miles, his own family camp was just a part of this big camp." Like Hashkēē bá nzín,

"Chief of the Indians on this Aravaipa Canyon": Captain Chiquito and one of his wives in the mid-1870s.

Captain Chiquito became a successful commercial farmer, renowned for his delicious peaches and figs.[24]

In a series of letters dictated to and translated by his children (who had learned English in school), Captain Chiquito offered a poignant defense of his People's return to Aravaipa. "I love my land here at the Arivaipa Canyon and wish to live well and happy," stated the chief, adding, "These Indians [in Aravaipa], they don't belong to San Carlos, they belong to San Pedro Country." Yet despite the deep emotional bond between Captain Chiquito's band and Aravaipa Canyon that these letters illuminate, they fail to answer the deeper question of how the People responded to resettling the lands where their relatives were murdered in 1871. In many cases, the proximity of their new homes to the massacre site was striking: while Hashkeē bá nzín's homestead and those of several other Nnēē families were located a few miles below Blue Water Pool, Captain Chiquito's farm embraced the lands around Big Sycamore Stands There. Other of the People, while not taking out homesteads, made annual trips into the canyon to gather acorns, saguaro fruit, and other wild foodstuffs. How the Nnee reconciled such behavior with their cultural inhibitions about coming into contact with the dead is unclear. But the People had previously returned to Aravaipa after the killings of their kinfolk there in 1832 and 1863, despite what observers at the time reported to be "a great number of skeletons" scattered across the canyon floor. It may be that Aravaipa's ecological riches or the tug of other, happier memories outweighed the concerns about disturbing Nnee remains. Or that once ceremonially purified—a custom that usually involved the use of tobacco or corn pollen to ward off the spirits of the deceased—the canyon's bones and gravesites no longer posed as great a peril as they might have otherwise.[25]

A further Nnee attempt to grapple with the legacy of the Camp Grant Massacre can be witnessed in the behavior of Captain Chiquito. In the late nineteenth century, the chief became reacquainted with Jesús María Elías, most likely during Chiquito's trips to Tucson to market produce from his farm in Aravaipa Canyon. Such visits were not unusual at the time: several of the Nnee making annual visits to Aravaipa also stayed with Mexican families, sometimes for several weeks, the two groups communicating through whatever odd phrases of Spanish and Apache they shared.[26]

Still, Captain Chiquito's rapprochement with Jesús Elías may have possessed an undercurrent of unresolved tension. One reason for Captain Chiquito to introduce his new wife and child to his onetime rival, after all, could have been to show Elías that despite the slaying of two of Captain Chiquito's wives at the Camp Grant Massacre, his family had survived and was, in fact, growing. This same message may have been implicit in at least one of the gifts that Captain Chiquito gave to Elías: the "cane covered with blue and white beads" remembered by Jesús's daughter. Similar canes were a prominent feature of the Na'i'ees ("Sunrise Ceremony/Changing Woman Ceremony"), the rite marking the passage of all Nnee girls into adulthood and, given the centrality of women to Nnee family and clan structures, one of the People's most important rituals. The cane stood for long life: the girl was to keep it to serve her in old age. Might Captain Chiquito, in presenting Elías with an object that symbolized Apache longevity, been marking a triumph of sorts over those who had tried to destroy him and his kinfolk in 1871?[27]

I N LESS THAN A DECADE, Hashkeē bá nzín, Captain Chiquito, and their followers would find their attempts to respond to the dislocations of the Camp Grant Massacre—the return of the Nṉeē to their lands near Aravaipa Canyon, the demonstration to old foes such as Elías of the People's survival— imperiled by many of the same forces that had led to the original massacre. For several years, Inṉaa ranchers along the San Pedro had accused Hashkeē bá nzín and his relatives of stealing livestock from them. Finally, in late 1887, a local sheriff attempted to arrest Hashkeē bá nzín and twenty-seven of his followers on charges of cattle theft. The threat of "150 citizens coming with pistols" stirred up disquieting memories for Hashkeē bá nzín, who fled to the relative safety of San Carlos. Following this encounter, in which he lost an entire year's harvest along with all his animals, Hashkeē bá nzín refused to return to his homestead ever again, telling officials on San Carlos that "I would not be safe there." He instead remained on the reservation, where he took up a farm near the Gila River.[28]

Even this change could not insulate Hashkeē bá nzín from further disruptions. One of the chief's daughters was married to a young Nṉeē with the probable name of Hashkeē biṉaā nteel ("Angry, Wide Eyes"). A onetime scout for the U.S. Army and policeman on San Carlos, Hashkeē biṉaā nteel—known to the Inṉaa as the "Kid"—had by most measures accommodated himself well to the reservation era. When another Nṉeē killed his father in 1887, however, Hashkeē biṉaā nteel, in keeping with the People's customs of vengeance, shot the supposed murderer. This slaying set in motion an unlikely chain of events that ended with Hashkeē biṉaā nteel fleeing into the mountains as a tsétahgo ("among the rocks," or outlaw). Repeatedly eluding the Apache and Anglo lawmen dispatched after him, Hashkeē biṉaā nteel was rumored to appear from time to time in Aravaipa Canyon, his supposed birthplace, as well as on San Carlos, where he kidnapped women to help him around his camp.[29]

Embarrassed by their failure to capture Hashkeē biṉaā nteel, to whom every unsolved murder or robbery in southern Arizona was soon attributed, the army in 1891 arrested those it suspected to be accomplices of the "Kid." Hashkeē bá nzín, as Hashkeē biṉaā nteel's father-in-law, was among those seized, as was Captain Chiquito, who was thought to lead the local group into

Captives in exile: Hashkēē bá nzį́n and family members in Mount Vernon, Alabama.

which Hashkēē bi̱na̱a̱ nteel had been born in the late 1850s. Together with perhaps as many as a hundred of their followers, the two chiefs were shipped to Mount Vernon, a military camp in the humid swamplands of southern Alabama, where they were imprisoned alongside Guyaałé (Geronimo) and the other Hák'áyé (Chiricahua Apache)—the very people with whom many Western Apaches had had such a strained relationship on San Carlos.[30]

Not until December of 1894 would Hashkēē bá nzį́n and Captain Chiquito see San Carlos again. Their returns to Arizona took place in secret because of army fears that *Inṉaa* vigilantes might attack the chiefs and their families. Hashkēē bá nzį́n stayed on San Carlos, where he died little more than a year after his return. But Captain Chiquito, who would take the surname Bullis, reoccupied his homestead near Big Sycamore Stands There. In exchanges with officials at San Carlos, Captain Chiquito, claiming that he "was born upon this land," insisted that "I want to die right here [in Aravaipa]." In keeping with his vow, he remained at his canyon farm until his death in 1919.[31]

What became of the elusive Hashkēē binाā nteel is less clear. Considerable evidence from *Innaa* archives and Nnēē oral tradition alike suggests that one or more groups of the People survived in Sonora's rugged, sparsely inhabited Sierra Madre Mountains well into the twentieth century. Intriguingly, one such refugee appears to have been the former captive in the Elías household, José María Elías: Sonoran authorities tried to arrange a peace treaty with an Apache band led by a man bearing this name in late 1888, and stories from remote Mexican pueblos tell of visits from *el apache Elías* and his descendants into the 1930s.[32]

Many Nnēē believe that Hashkēē binाā nteel joined these refugees and lived out his days south of the border. His uncanny ability to evade U.S. authorities and his imagined life of freedom in Mexico transformed him into a symbol of resistance for many on San Carlos, albeit one tinged with unease given the Kid's propensity to seize young women from the reservation. Given these tensions, the song by which the Nnēē memorialized the Apache Kid was as much a meditation on the costs of the renegade's separation from the People as a celebration of his way of life.[33]

> *Anah, hiyu, Anah, hiyu*
> *Oh, they say I was involved*
> *Yes, they say I was involved*
> *But, I was not*
> *Now they want to send me far away*
> *Yes, they want to send me far away*

Unlike such efforts by the People to probe the ambivalent, evolving meanings of San Carlos, outside scholars have treated the coming of the reservation as the end not only of armed conflict between the Nnēē and the *Innaa* but of the People's history itself. Most studies of the Apache close with the surrender of Guyaałé (Geronimo) in 1886, on the apparent assumption that nothing of note happened after the Apache suffered military defeat and the Hák'áyé were shipped into captivity in Florida and Alabama. "Those books make you think that after the fighting was done, everybody was just lying around doing nothing, just waiting around for rations," observes White Mountain Apache elder

"Just waiting around for rations": ration day on San Carlos in the late nineteenth century.

Eva Tulene Watt. "That's not true. *Lots* was going on. See, people were busy every day—going here, going there, doing this, doing that."[34]

"Doing this, doing that" meant not only the births, marriages, illnesses, deaths, joys, and sorrows that made up the Nnēē life cycle but also the long, uneven process by which the groups confined on San Carlos began to conceive of themselves as a unified tribe and of their reservation as a shared homeland. As many Nnēē soon discovered, although open warfare with the *Innaa* might have ended, the challenge of protecting their resources and autonomy remained. Indeed, the People's new reservation proved all too vulnerable to Enemy assault: in 1876, trespassing *Innaa* miners carved the town of Globe out of San Carlos's western fringes after finding silver there; in 1896, a 70,000-acre "mineral strip" along the reservation's southern boundary was leased to *Innaa* investors and ranchers; and in the 1920s, Coolidge Dam was constructed on the San Carlos River, flooding much of the reservation's best farmland and

"There is no land for us": view of Coolidge Dam in 1928. The rising waters from the dam flooded the original agency buildings as well as much of the most productive farmland on the reservation.

forcing over six hundred Black Rocks People who had settled in the vicinity to move. (Even worse, the impounded water went not to the Apache but rather to the *Innaa* settlements around Phoenix and to the Nṉēē's old rivals, the Sáíkiné.)[35]

As the People on San Carlos mobilized to resist these threats to their reservation, many used history to support their positions. In 1930, Gila Moses, in a public statement that he asked to be written down for the commissioner of Indian affairs, reminded the San Carlos Indian agent and his fellow Nṉēē of the promises made to the People during the 1872 peace negotiations:

When I was a boy they made a treaty at old Fort Grant. There was army there and [a] camp and I became scout. There was Indian scout called Santo and there was a captain and he and Santo went to Washington and they come back from there and they sent all the Indians over there to where they call old San Carlos. Santo and Captain [Chiquito] they promise us that it was going to be headquarters at San Carlos . . . and that we will live there all our life. . . . That time General C[r]ook and Grant promised that there is a good reservation set aside for the Indians, maybe you Indians have other land outside, north, east, or south or west, but we are going to cut a land for you Indians to live on and they promised this reservation being cut for you, belongs to you and we are not going to be put off reservation. . . . So they told us that this is for your cattle, sheep, goats, horses and White settler[s] can not go on reservation.[36]

Another San Carlos tribal member, Mike Nelson, also invoked the 1872 agreement to underscore his frustrations with Coolidge Dam:

We are friends with the Government. . . . We are friends since 1872. Since 1872 the Government used to help us but now [it is] just like they are throwing us away. . . . We Indians live[d] at San Carlos on our farms but now we do not have any farms. Another thing. Looks like these Indians are all going to die this winter or starve this winter. These Indians feel this way. We used to live on farm[s] and plant crop[s] but now I wish to plant some crop but I can not cause there is no land for us, no farm land for us.[37]

In addition to relying upon Nnee oral tradition, with its remarkable recall of treaty negotiations from almost a half century before, some of the People were not above lecturing officials from their own history books. When a group of U.S. senators came to San Carlos in 1931 as part of a survey of conditions on Indian reservations, tribal member Manuel Victer, seeking to dispel what he saw as unduly negative stereotypes of the Nnee, resorted to reading aloud to the visitors from a work by Tazhii (John Clum), the agent who had secured Hashkee bá nzín's release in 1874 and who had since fashioned a role for himself as a historian of the Apache:

It states here by Mr. [C]lum, and there is the terrible Apache Indian as he really is. . . . (reading): "He is admitted to be the greatest fighting soldier ever produced by any race at any period of history. . . . He is industrious, patient, loyal. He is honorable, square, and faithful, and burns his enemy at the stake. He stuck to his friends, white or Indian, and does not take into account the cause or the consequence." There is the Apache Indian. . . . Everything that is written there is the truth.

The lesson of the *Innaa*'s own histories, Victer told the visitors, was that the Nnē̄ē deserved greater control over their lives: "If the reservation really belongs to us Apache Indians here, we want all the Apaches to get the work and to be employed anywhere here in the agency or the school, not sent away to be employed off the reservation. . . . We want our own Indians to be encouraged here to build up homes for themselves, to see what they can do for themselves."[38]

There was one feature of the past, however, that the People rarely discussed in such encounters with the *Innaa*: the maelstrom of violence that had engulfed them and the Enemy in the 1860s and '70s. The People might refer to events along the periphery of this conflict: the 1872 peace conference; Nnē̄ē service as scouts against other groups; tribe members' participation in later wars such as the Philippine Insurrection. The San Carlos Apache might even point out that the *Innaa*'s current prosperity could be attributed in no small part to their possession of lands that had once belonged to the People, as John Rope did in 1930: "These White people they live off of [the] reservation they should thank us cause they have lots of things on that land that we used to own." But the armed confrontations between the People and the *Innaa*—not to mention atrocities such as the Camp Grant Massacre—were subjects that the Nnē̄ē seldom raised in their interactions with outside authorities. Perhaps the People were already sensitive to *Innaa* images of them as warlike savages and feared that revisiting this history of conflict might only reinforce such caricatures. Or perhaps the People acted out of respect for the Nnē̄ē custom of not discussing issues that might exacerbate others' despair (if so, Hashkē̄ē bá nzín's violation of this norm in his negotiations with Colyer and Howard, when he conducted both to the massacre site and pointedly reminded the latter that "one hundred and thirty of his people had been killed" in Aravaipa Canyon, highlights the urgency that the People felt about the return of their children). But above all it may be that the carnage had been so overwhelming that many of the People could find no suitable way to articulate their experiences to the *Innaa*, leading them to avoid the subject altogether.[39]

"They have lots of things on that land that we used to own": Ga'an *("Mountain Spirit Dancers") from San Carlos taking part in a parade in Globe in 1910.*

These same tensions manifested themselves within Nṉēē society, albeit on a different register. While a portion of the People preferred to frame their history in terms of cultural practices—ceremonies, language, and the like—rather than dwell upon past unpleasantness, other Nṉēē struggled to make sense of the warfare that had consumed them throughout the nineteenth century.[40] By the turn of the century, the People's approach toward the Camp Grant Massacre was thus suspended between two countervailing tendencies: to elide past misfortune and to draw lessons from historical events. Some survivors of the Camp Grant Massacre, hoping to shield others from the distress that discussing such an atrocity might invite, remained circumspect in their discussion of the killings of their people—so much so that in a few cases even their own descendants, despite participating as youngsters in trips to Aravaipa to gather wild foodstuffs, were not told what had happened in the canyon. Over the twentieth century, even these periodic journeys began to taper off with increased Apache reliance on store-bought foods and medicines, and *Innaa* harassment of off-reservation Nṉēē—as one Apache, Wallace Johnson, put it, "We used to travel

freely, now you see [signs saying] 'No Trespassing.'" As a result, many Nn̄ēē
came to have less and less direct experience of the Aravaipa Canyon, further
limiting a younger generation's knowledge of its history.[41]

Yet even in the face of such challenges, there were those People who managed not only to preserve the story of the massacre but also to distill patterns
of meaning out of its violence and chaos. Unlike the survivors' accounts, which
stressed the attack's interruption of Nn̄ēē ceremonial life, these later narratives
emphasized the warnings that preceded the attack. Johnson, whose mother
survived the massacre as a young girl, but whose grandmother was killed in
the attack, told the story of the massacre as follows:

> My mother used to tell me that they went up there, dancing . . . you don't
> suspect anything, that's how they went up there. I don't know why those
> guys just turned against the Indians. The army said they'd give them food
> to use at the dance and somehow they ganged up on them. And they told
> one guy, he used to live right up here, and now he died, old man, he used
> to tell me that he was a little boy that time and he was sent up there to
> tell the people "You're going to be killed tonight." But they don't believe
> him. He [was] just a kid, they think he [was] just kidding, but if older ones
> go up there, maybe the army's gonna catch them, too, see, that's why they
> send a little boy, you know they go anywhere, you see, you don't suspect
> them. So he came there but nobody believed it. He used to cry when he
> told me about this. I don't know how he got out of it . . . he used to sing.
> Yeah, if they had believed that little boy they would have been saved.[42]

This focus on unheeded warnings moved even more to the foreground in the
account of the massacre told by Jeanette Cassa, the longtime coordinator of
the San Carlos Elders' Cultural Advisory Council, who was a generation or so
younger than Johnson.

> As the men from Tucson were coming, an Apache scout saw them head-
> ing toward Camp Grant. He found a little Apache boy and told him to
> run back to where the Apache were camped near Camp Grant and warn
> them to run away. The boy did so, but when he told the people they did
> not believe him because he was so young and so stayed where they were.

That night, however, a medicine man had a dream, a vision, about what was going to happen. He warned the people and told them to gather near some cliffs where they were camped. They had gathered for a dance to celebrate something. Some stayed and danced, while others left for the safety of the mountains. After the dance by the cliffs on the flood-plain, the people just collapsed where they were. The next morning the events happened. Manuel Jackson saw his mother get knocked down with a piece of wood and killed. He hid in the branches of a wickiup. It was the Anglos and Papagoes who did this, but afterwards the Mexicans came and took children and women—and anyone else alive—captive.[43]

If the need to be attentive to possible warnings served as the underlying theme for these later accounts of the massacre, the particular lesson to be drawn could still vary depending on the teller. To some, the massacre taught the dangers of not arising with the dawn; to others, the value of telling the truth (in this version, the young boy's warning was not believed because of his previous lies). Still others emphasized how their spiritual practices helped the People cope with the attack's aftermath. Della Steele recalled a family story about how her mother's older sister had eluded her attackers during the Camp Grant Massacre by hiding in a hollow space at the base of a tree. Although her family members discovered her alive two days later and brought her back to their camp, it was because "they had a medicine man sing and pray for her . . . [that] she actually survived."[44]

In each of these versions the People occupied center stage in the unfolding drama. But they never served as the sole authors of history: the ultimate force driving events lay less with the Nnēē or their rivals than with the *diyíh* animating the universe. This emphasis on spiritual power enabled even disturbing narratives to incorporate a reassuring premise: far from being mere helpless victims, the Nnēē could shape events by following appropriate practices.

Intermingling history and spirituality in this way, however, meant that any effort to share Nnēē history with non–tribal members posed a troubling dilemma: to what extent were the People willing to discuss the religious contexts that shaped their narratives of the past? Despite a widely shared desire to limit intrusions into one of the People's last autonomous realms, some latter-day Nnēē, echoing Hashkēē bá nzín's 1871 complaints that "these Tucson people . . . tell their own story" and Manuel Victer's 1931 wish to depict the "Apache Indian as he really is," felt an obligation to challenge inaccurate *Innaa* historical interpretations. For those who accepted this burden, the Camp Grant Massacre was especially useful. Not only was it one of the greatest atrocities the People had experienced under U.S. rule; it also helped undermine *Innaa* stereotypes of violent Apaches and peace-loving settlers. In the early 1980s, members of the San Carlos Apache and the White Mountain Apache tribes, prompted by a concern that "there's nothing in the history books about what happened here," held a series of memorial services of "Peace and Brotherhood" at Aravaipa Canyon on the anniversary of the massacre to which outsiders, including the U.S. military, were invited. ("We're a conquered nation under the U.S. government," explained one of the organizers, Salton Reede Jr. "We thought the government should be represented here.")

The Nn̲ēē were not above making pointed demands at these events. "Every incident like this must be paid for," observed Philip Cassadore, a former member of the San Carlos Tribal Council. "We're asking the U.S. government to open up this case again and see what can be done to give restitution to the surviving relatives of [Hashkēē bá nzín]." Many of the People, however, chose to commemorate the massacre through tribal songs and dances, or to put forth pleas that Apaches and non-Apaches alike not forget what had become for many in both communities a little-known incident. In 1984, Winema Dewey, a great-great-granddaughter of Hashkēē bá nzín, admitting she had only learned of the massacre a few years before, urged, "We should come together and try to make an effort . . . [to] understand what happened here. . . . We shouldn't try to bury it." [45]

Such calls to unearth the history of the Camp Grant Massacre demanded that the People engage *Innaa* modes of historical presentation. In the 1990s, for example, a group of elders from San Carlos, assisted by the tribe's historian, Dale C. Miles, led a successful effort to have the massacre site placed on the Park Service's National Register of Historic Places (although, in deference to Apache sensibilities, the precise location of the massacre remained obscured).[46] And in 1995, the San Carlos Apache Tribe opened the San Carlos Apache Cultural Center, its first museum, in a former café on Highway 70, one of the main routes through the reservation, to educate outsiders and tribe members alike as to "the history of this proud nation." [47]

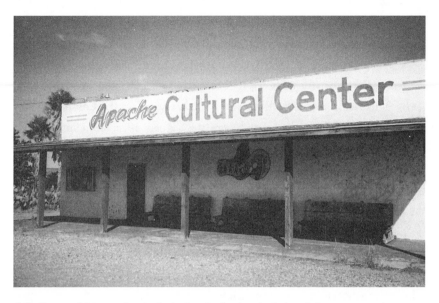

"The history of this proud nation": the San Carlos Apache Cultural Center.

The center's emphasis on the vast sweep of Nnēē history—from stories from "long ago" to the present day—rendered the bitter warfare that marked the encounter between the People and the *Innaa* little more than a brief chapter in a much longer tale. Yet to illuminate the People's experiences in the 1800s, the museum's exhibits focused on a single, paradigmatic incident: the Camp Grant Massacre.

In contrast to the popular conception created by the Spanish, Mexicans, and Americans, Apaches were not war-like bloodthirsty savages. We raided for food only during times of shortage. Wars were waged not as random acts, but were generally well-planned campaigns for redress against injustices against us.

The gun and the horse expanded the range, success, and reputation of our raiding and warfare.

Tensions quickly rose in the 1870s as settlers demanded more and more of our territory. We were increasingly unable to carry on our traditional movements with the seasons to hunt, gather, and collect those things that kept us clothed, fed, sheltered, and happy. We resisted by increasing raids on their farms, ranches, and towns. This was a course of action taken out of necessity by countless other American Indian cultures across North America, but led to increased conflict . . . and bloodshed.

This rising tide of violence and hatred resulted in the Camp Grant Massacre. In the early morning hours of April 30th, 1871, a group of Anglo-Americans, Mexicans, and Tohono O'odham from Tucson slaughtered over 140 unarmed Aravaipa Apache living peacefully five miles outside of Camp Grant, a military establishment north of Tucson. The tragedy illustrated the lack of an organized federal policy to protect Indians against vigilante groups and led directly to the creation of the San Carlos Indian Agency in 1872.[48]

The center's displays reveal the continuing evolution of Nⁿēē ways of thinking about the massacre. What had once been the experience of particular families and bands, an event often shielded from others because of its disturbing nature, has at the cultural center become a shared public heritage, one linked to the very origins of the San Carlos Apache Tribe.

The museum also imparts an even more fundamental message. Not every passing *Innaa* may notice the modest two-room building at the side of the highway as they hasten through San Carlos in their air-conditioned cars on their way to Phoenix, Las Cruces, and points elsewhere. But the museum's existence testifies to the fact that in the face of centuries of *Innaa* efforts to exterminate, silence, or forget them, the People continue to survive. Their stories of the past, it turns out, have only begun to be told.

EPILOGUE

August 2, 2003. Holding a sacred staff adorned with feathers, a relay of Nṉēē participating in a "sacred run" to protect Dził nchaa si'án ("Big Mountain," or Mount Graham) makes its way into Aravaipa Canyon. Members of the group initiated their run outside Tucson several days earlier, gradually making their way north through the Arizona summer heat. Now evening is falling, and it has begun to grow dim. One after another, the runners move forward with the staff, venturing deeper into the canyon amid the gathering darkness. Beyond them in the distance looms the runners' final destination, Mount Graham, where after a ceremony the next morning, the staff will join several others atop Dził nchaa si'án.[1]

WHEN THE DAWN BREAKS nowadays over Aravaipa Canyon, the bright Arizona sun illuminates a landscape that bears the passage of more than a century and a quarter since the Camp Grant Massacre. The army base at the junction of the canyon and the San Pedro River has long since vanished, its adobe buildings melting away in the summer rains and its parade grounds replaced by "Aravaipa Villa" RV park and a branch campus of Central Arizona College. The lower canyon, originally claimed in the 1880s and '90s by Anglo and Mexican-American ranchers, has in recent years experienced a gentrification of sorts, giving way to rustic second homes and bed-and-breakfasts.

The rest of the canyon, for the first time in centuries, has no permanent

"National wilderness": present-day entrance to Aravaipa Canyon.

human presence at all. Since 1969, the federal Bureau of Land Management (BLM), in association with the Nature Conservancy, has overseen thousands of acres in and around Aravaipa, first as a "primitive area" and then, since 1984, as a "national wilderness." One of the last free-flowing streams in the Sonora Desert, Aravaipa Creek has become a crucial refuge for numerous endangered species as well as a favorite spot for hikers seeking a respite from the ever-growing sprawl of Arizona's booming sunbelt. The odd juxtaposition of the canyon's troubled history with its oasislike present evokes Kurt Vonnegut Jr.'s poignant observation: "Everything is supposed to be very quiet after a massacre, and it always is, except for the birds."[2]

Most contemporary visitors to the canyon have little knowledge of Aravaipa's violent past. Although the massacre site lies several miles downstream from the BLM's and Nature Conservancy's holdings, the groups' policy of preserving the canyon as a wilderness—"an area where . . . man himself is a visitor who does not remain," in the words of the BLM's 1988 management plan for the canyon—has helped solidify public perceptions of Aravaipa as untouched nature. As Patrick O'Neill, the ranger in charge of the canyon's bucolic west entrance, informs me during one of my visits to Aravaipa, "far more people come out here for nature than for history."[3]

One can note many such locales across the region—sites where present-day developments seem at first glance to have overwhelmed any trace of the past. Much of the land surrounding the onetime O'odham village of Cewagï— where Luis Oacpicagigua surrendered to Spanish authorities in 1752, where Juan and Jesús María Elías passed their childhoods during the tumultuous early years of the Mexican Republic, and where Nnēē raiders murdered Leslie Wooster and Trinidad Aguirre in 1871—has been reborn as the Tubac Golf Resort and Spa, a vast, faux-adobe complex abutting a complex of surreal green, sprinkler-fed fairways. The plot along the Santa Cruz River, just to the north of the onetime presidio of Tucson, settled by Nautilnilce and other *apaches de paz* from Aravaipa Canyon in the 1790s, has undergone a similar transformation. In a peculiar twist of fate, the lands where Tucson's *apache manso* community once resided were reborn at the turn of the last century as Oury Park. Then, as "Uncle Billy" in turn faded into obscurity, the park acquired yet another title, being renamed in 2001 in honor of two longtime Barrio Anita residents, David G. Herrera and Ramon Quiroz.[4]

As much as such locations may seem to stand as monuments to amnesia—to the erasure of an often disturbing history of violence and dis-possession—they are perhaps better understood through the metaphor of the palimpsest: an artifact that, beneath its dominant text, retains other, less discernible forms of expression. Despite the prevailing notion today of Ara-vaipa as pristine wilderness, for example, the canyon in fact contains numerous Apache efforts to affirm its human history, most of them, it turns out, hidden in plain sight. In addition to the San Carlos Apache Tribe's placement of the massacre site on the National Register of Historic Places in 1998, the location along Aravaipa Creek where Nnēē women and children were killed in 1871 remains in Apache hands. Having inherited the land Captain Chiquito home-steaded in the late nineteenth century, members of the Bullis family hold the title to their ancestors' property even today. And in the opening years of the new millennium, participants in the "Mount Graham Sacred Run," organized by some on the San Carlos Apache Reservation to protest the University of

History submerged: the Tubac Golf Resort and Spa.

Arizona's construction of a network of powerful observatories on top of Dził nchaa si'án ("Big Mountain"), included Aravaipa Canyon as part of their route in a conscious effort to educate younger Apaches about the massacre.[5]

The persistence of such fugitive understandings of the past serves as an important reminder that the dominant interpretation of the past often enjoys its status not because of its superior historical accuracy but because of its proponents' social power. It was, after all, because of their access to the printed page and their ability to form a historical society that Oury and his fellow pioneers were able to publicize their exculpatory narrative of the "Camp Grant Affair," one that supplanted not only the accounts of Nnēē survivors of the massacre but those of the attack's Mexican-American and Tohono O'odham participants as well. A similar pattern played itself out across the American West in the nineteenth century. As Anglo-American settlers assumed greater dominance throughout the region, their activities became *the* western story, enshrined in countless speeches, publications, and pioneer societies. If this process of conquest and commemoration seldom silenced other communities altogether, it frequently relegated their stories of the past to obscurity or even called into question these other tales' historical validity.[6]

To recognize in this way that history often reflects social power need not negate the validity of the historical undertaking. Indeed, at its best, by holding the actions of the powerful up to scrutiny, history serves not as the handmaiden of power but rather as a counterbalance (albeit often a belated one) to power's distortions and manipulations. Resurrecting unfamiliar stories from the past—as this book endeavors to do—can assist such goals by detailing the alternative ways of thinking and feeling that the dominant narrative has long obscured. Perhaps the best measure of history's power is that those marginalized from the predominant historical interpretation have seldom rejected the notion of history itself, but rather sought to articulate their own visions of the past through calendar sticks, *corridos,* or institutions like the San Carlos Apache Cultural Center.[7]

Yet as we unearth the stories long buried beneath the dominant account of the past, we confront once again the question that opened this book: how to understand the deaths that took place in Aravaipa Canyon on April 30, 1871? As we have seen, the murder of these Apache women and children was just one fragment of the maelstrom of violence that swept over the Sonora-Arizona borderlands. This violent storm would touch Aravaipa Canyon on more than one occasion, and it would leave silence, death, and ruptured narratives among all the region's communities. But only one group—the Nnēē—was the subject of stories justifying their extermination. If to some such tales merely spoke of a time when the Apache no longer posed an obstacle to Spanish, Mexican, or American projects in the region, this vision of a peaceful agrarian order nonetheless contained a dark, dystopian inner core: the willingness to contemplate a world where no Apache existed at all.[8]

Still, to collapse the stories running through the Camp Grant Massacre into a single tale of genocide—of "acts committed with intent to destroy, in whole or in part, a national, ethnical, racial or religious group," in the words of the 1948 United Nations convention on genocide—possesses its own perils. Not because such an account misstates the violence directed against the Apache, but because it risks reducing the stories about an event like the Camp Grant Massacre into a narrative solely about the actions and intentions of the incident's perpetrators. The ability of many Nnēē to elude the exterminatory violence directed toward them from the seventeenth century onwards and to undertake raids, war parties, and peace negotiations of their own is a no less important story—indeed, for the Apache, this tale of survival is arguably the preeminent narrative to be told about their past.[9]

In the end, then, the Camp Grant Massacre, like so much of the past, is best understood as a palimpsest of many stories. A multitude of narratives flows into and out of the events of April 30, 1871: tales of genocide; tales of the Mexican north and the American West, of O'odham and Nṉéé home- lands; tales of survival, accommodation, and cultural reinvention. Not only do these narratives offer different interpretations of the past, but those who told them expressed themselves through a variety of formats: the mnemonic calendar stick chronicles of the Tohono O'odham; the missionary reports, fam- ily stories, and songs of the Spanish and Mexicans; the oral histories of "long ago" of the Apache; the lectures and books of the Anglos. We can judge these accounts for their faithfulness to an always incomplete historical record, and we can acknowledge that all attempts to narrate the past are at once processes of remembering and forgetting, in which the creation of a coherent story is achieved by prioritizing certain events over others. But we cannot confine our- selves to a single one of these narratives without enacting yet another form of historical violence: the suppression of the past's multiple meanings.

Given the obstacles to merging these fragile and diverse forms of story- telling into a single tale, it is, paradoxically, by venturing in the opposite direction—by listening for the silences between accounts; by discovering what each genre of recordkeeping cannot tell us—that we can capture most fully the human struggle to understand our elusive past. What this past asks of us in return is a willingness to recount *all* our stories—our darkest tales as well as our most inspiring ones—and to ponder those stories that violence has silenced forever. For until we recognize our shared capacity for inhumanity, how can we ever hope to tell stories of our mutual humanity?[10]

Acknowledgments

THE VOLUME that you hold in your hands would not have been possible without the many people who generously shared their time and insights with me. My first thanks go to family and friends in Arizona and Sonora, who introduced me when I was just a toddler to the region that features so prominently in this work and who have welcomed me during my return visits over the ensuing decades. Not all of them have understood my desire to unearth some of the more difficult moments in their region's past, but I hope they realize that I did so out of a deep affection for the communities on both sides of the border that first took root during these childhood trips.

Although I would like to imagine that this book will open up new avenues for understanding, I also want to ensure that it provides more tangible benefits as well. Toward that end, a portion of the royalties from this book will be donated to the San Carlos Apache Tribe Cultural Center and to the White Mountain Apache Cultural Center and Museum to facilitate both tribes' efforts to tell their histories as they see fit. (Indeed, I would urge that all those wanting to learn more about the events contained within this book visit both these institutions, along with the Arizona Historical Society in Tucson and the newly opened Tohono O'odham Nation Cultural Center and Museum in Topawa, Arizona.) I am grateful to Herb Stevens, the manager of the San Carlos Apache Tribe Cultural Center, and Ramon Riley, the cultural resource director for the White Mountain Apache Tribe, for their friendship and their efforts to teach me the basics of Apache culture and history—in particular, for Herb's permission to use the quote from the center's exhibit that appears on pages 271–72 of this text and for Ramon's sage advice to me to "just tell the truth." The San Carlos Apaches' first tribal historian, Dale Miles, did me the enormous favor of reading an entire rough draft of my manuscript. Readers who examine my sources will note several times at which I lean heavily upon Dale's thoughtful essays on Apache history in forming my interpretations of events; more difficult to discern, but even more important, is the impact that our many conversations have had on my text. It goes without saying that whatever errors in the interpretation of Apache culture that remain in this book are entirely of my own making and are in no way a reflection upon Herb's, Ramon's, and Dale's knowledge.

Almost anyone who writes about the American West cannot escape the deep influence of Howard Lamar, William Cronon, John Mack Faragher, and Patty Limerick on the field. In my case, this influence is especially apparent. Howard, Bill, and Johnny played an incalculable role in my intellectual development, first as graduate school mentors and now as friends and colleagues. I am deeply grateful for their continued support, comradeship, and, not least of all, their cheerful production of the countless letters of recommendation that academia demands. In early 2005, Johnny invited me to speak about the Camp Grant Massacre at Yale's Lamar Center for the Study of Borderlands and Frontiers. His and Howard's enthusiasm for what was then a rather inchoate project (along with some encouraging words from Marni Sandweiss, at the time a visiting scholar at the center) lent me the confidence to see this project through to its completion. In a memorable conversation at the 2007 Western History Association annual meeting, Bill Cronon helped me grasp the deeper narrative and ethical issues that this project raised. I was never lucky enough to take a class with Patty Limerick, but I feel as if I were one of her students nonetheless. The intellectual ferment that she instilled around the "New Western History" first revealed to me the stakes involved in studying the American West, and her support has been fundamental to my growth in the years since.

One of the great pleasures in completing this project has been joining an expanding cohort of scholars exploring the United States' and Mexico's intertwined histories, many of whom were generous enough to comment on various drafts of this book. My first thanks, as always, go to Sam Truett, who gave my project a rigorous reading based on his deep knowledge of the Sonora-Arizona borderlands. Katie Benton-Cohen, Ben Johnson, Ari Kelman, and Ben Madley likewise all cast a critical eye on versions of this project, as did Ann Fabian, who was kind enough to pass along some information gleaned from her own forthcoming project on Native American remains. Seth Pilsk and Keith Basso each shared with me a few words of wisdom based on their considerable knowledge of Apache culture as I began this project. Bud McKanna was most helpful in answering some questions relating to early murder trials in Arizona. Gerry Cadava shared his thought-provoking material on the making of the movie *Arizona,* Matt Babcock generously shared some of his findings on the *apaches de paz,* and Jared Farmer provided some useful insights on "haunted" landscapes.

In southern Arizona, Brad Rawlings generously lent me his clippings related to the recent controversy over Camp Grant and the Sam Hughes School. Rick Leis, Steven Dowdle, and Gil García patiently answered my questions as to the Coalition of Prayer Network's reconciliation campaign in 1996.

Special thanks go to Ian Record and Chip Colwell-Chanthaphonh. When I began this project, I was puzzled that more than a century after it took place, there was still no book-length scholarly study of the Camp Grant Massacre. It was thus a pleasure to discover several years into my research that Ian, Chip, and I all had complementary works in progress. Through example and exhortation, both Ian and Chip have nudged me toward a deeper reckoning with Apache perspectives on the past. Chip in particular has been uncommonly generous in sharing contacts and sources with me, and I can only hope that my attempts to reciprocate have proven half as helpful as his efforts on my behalf.

Although I already thanked both in the Note on Terminology, it bears mentioning once again the linguistic contributions of William de Reuse and Colleen Fitzgerald. Not only have both spared me from far more misuses of Apache and O'odham than I care to contemplate, but they have also opened my eyes as to how much a knowledge of language can further one's understanding of history. (In so doing, they illustrated the wisdom of one of Ramon Riley's other admonitions: "to understand Apache history, you have to learn the language.")

My colleagues at Brown were extremely helpful at countless stages of this project. The late—and dearly missed—Jack Thomas gave an early draft of this project one of his famous close readings. I am thankful to Omer Bartov for encouraging me long ago to contemplate expanding what was at first only an idea for a short article into a book-length study and to Doug Cope for tolerating my countless questions about Mexican colonial history with the good humor that is his trademark. Carolyn Dean led a remarkable Pembroke Seminar on "The Language of Victimization" in 2005–06 that opened my eyes to the ways in which a variety of disciplines have approached the questions of representation, memory, and trauma—a seminar in which my colleague Maud Mandel was a most enlightening participant. Matt García and Michael Vorenberg did me the favor of reading a rough draft of my manuscript, despite their busy schedules. Evelyn Hu-DeHart not only read my work with her usual enthusiasm but was generous enough to use her considerable contacts in the Sonoran history community on my behalf, putting me in touch with the tremendously helpful Aaron Grageda of the Universidad de Sonora in Hermosillo. Many other members of the department provided the companionship vital to preventing one from becoming lost in the often rather isolating world of scholarship.

Whether they know it or not (and I suspect most do not), my students at Brown have over the years taught me a tremendous amount about the historical process. I feel privileged to teach at an institution with such gifted young people. In particular, as undergraduate teaching and research assistants during the summer of 2004, Linda Evarts and Susan Oba provided invaluable assistance in this project (indeed, Susan is becoming something of a mainstay in the Penguin History of American Life series, having also assisted my former colleague Jim Campbell on *Atlantic Crossings*). During the course of her extended career at Brown (which until recently was longer than my own!), Jen Edwards has taught me a great deal about humor, community involvement, and Native history alike. I look forward to her new career in documentary filmmaking with great anticipation. Chan Hee Chu, George Conklin, and Alex Hughes helped me create the Web site featuring a number of documents related to Camp Grant.

As this book entered into its final stages, it benefited tremendously from a thought-provoking workshop on narrating Native American history that Rachel St. John and Melinda Lowery organized at the Radcliffe Institute for Advanced Study with an uncommonly talented group of scholars: James Brooks, Lisa Brooks, Colin Calloway, Lizbeth Cohen, Sasha Harmon, Barbara Krauthamer, Jean O'Brien, Michael Witgen, and my colleague Matt García. In an offhand comment made during a group discussion at Radcliffe, Walter

Johnson provided one of the images that proved to be central to *Shadows at Dawn*'s conclusion. Thanks are due too to Brown's new Cogut Humanities Center, where as a faculty fellow in the spring of 2008 I was able to think through some of the final issues related to this book.

I am deeply grateful to the organizations that provided the funding that allowed me the time to devote to this project. The National Endowment for the Humanities provided an invaluable fellowship to the Huntington Library in 2001–02. I am thankful to the Huntington's able director, Roy Ritchie, for his assistance in making my fellowship possible under unexpectedly difficult circumstances, Peter Blodgett for his expert guidance through the library's vast Western American holdings, and to the gifted collection of historians with whom I shared the Huntington—Peter Mancall, Mary Ryan, Susan Johnson, Camille Guerzon, Hal Barron, Bill Deverell, Gary Gallagher, and Joan Waugh, among others—for providing such a stimulating intellectual environment. I especially treasure the fact that during my brief stay at the Huntington I had the opportunity to know Clark Davis, whose wit and warmth were so memorable to all who came into contact with him. I am also deeply indebted to the American Council of Learned Societies for a fellowship in 2005–06 that gave me a release from teaching, without which I could never have written up my findings. Brown University's Office of the Vice President for Research generously provided a Richard B. Salomon Faculty Research Award in 2006 that facilitated the final research in Tucson, Hermosillo, and San Carlos so essential for this project.

In addition to the helpful staff at the Huntington, I benefited from the assistance of archivists and librarians at the Southwest Museum in Los Angeles, the Arizona Historical Society (especially Debbie Newman, Chrystal Carpenter Burke, and Jim Turner), the Beinecke Library (above all, the inimitable George Miles), the National Archives in Washington, D.C., and Laguna Niguel, the National Museum of the American Indian (Lou Stancari), the Arizona State University Library (Brian E. Davis), and Brown's own John Carter Brown Library. Diane Drobka of the Bureau of Land Management was most helpful in putting me in contact with Patrick O'Neill of the Aravaipa Canyon ranger station and in making copies of the oral interviews that Diana Hadley took for her detailed history of Aravaipa Canyon. Diana was, in turn, generous enough to allow me to quote from her interviews in this work. My thanks to all. *Estoy tambien muy agredecido a Benjamín Alonso Rascón, el gran sabio del Archivo General del Estado de Sonora.*

I feel very lucky that Gordon Wood and Patty Limerick introduced me to the Penguin History of American Life, with its unique emphasis on innovative historical narration. One unexpected bonus of joining Penguin's series was connecting with Scott Moyers, who proved to be just as gifted an editor as my dear friend Gordon Kato had promised. I am just sorry that Gordon did not live to see the publication of this book. After Scott's departure for the world of agenting, Laura Stickney deftly assumed command of the editorial process. For her part, Geri Thoma has proven the comforting advisor and advocate that every writer hopes for in an agent.

I cannot even begin to express the crucial role that my family has played in my life. Thanks to you all: Dad, Grace, Victor, Allison, Chess, Victoria, Leonard, Evangelen, Michelle, Dean, Karla, and Ainara. Finally, I dedicate this book to the people who would be the heroes in all the stories of my life: Marie and Jason.

Glossary

KEY:

AP. = APACHE
O. = O'ODHAM
SP. = SPANISH

'a paču: enemy: the Zuni word from which the Spanish derived the term "Apache."

Akimel O'odham: O. "River People": O'odham term used to describe community members living along the Gila River. Often known to outsiders as the Pima.

'Al ṣonag: O. "Place of the Small Spring": Tohono O'odham term for a location on the upper Santa Cruz River, near the present-day U.S.-Mexico border.

'Al Waiphia: O. "Little Springs": Tohono O'odham term for Aravaipa Canyon.

Alianza Hispano-Americana: Sp. "Spanish-American Alliance": turn-of-the-century Mexican-American self-help organization, founded in Tucson in 1894.

Alta California: Sp. "Upper California": the Mexican province that is now the U.S. state of California.

apaches de paz: Sp. "peace Apaches": Spanish term for Apaches who took up residence in Spanish villages.

apaches mansos: Sp. "tame Apaches": Mexican term for Apaches who took up residence in Mexican villages.

Arizónac: Sp. Spanish silver mining center on the upper Santa Cruz River in the late 1700s.

Askevanche: Ap. Hashkēē baa nchị, or "Angry, He Is Selfish"?: leader of the Pinal Apache in the mid-nineteenth century.

Askinenha: Ap. Hashkēē ń'iłháh, or "Angry, He Is Snoring"?: leader of the Aravaipa Apache in the mid-nineteenth century.

Bāāchii: Ap. Western Apache term for "tame Apaches" inhabiting Mexican settlements.

babawï oodham: O. "bean eater": possible origin of the Spanish term for the Tohono O'odham ("Papago").

bahidaj-sitol: O. the sweet syrup the O'odham produce from the fruit of the saguaro cactus.

baile: Sp. dance.

bando: Sp. a government-published broadside, designed to be read aloud.

bárbaro: Sp. "barbarian": Apaches and other "uncivilized" Indians.

Bi ja gush kai ye: Ap. Bijaa hoshgaiyé, or "The One Whose Ears [Look Like] Cactus"?: Western Apache survivor of the Camp Grant Massacre.

Biszáhé: Ap. "Adobe Cut Bank or Edge of Cliff Dwelling People": Western Apache clan. The present-day spelling of the clan's name would be *Biszáhé* or *Biszáhá.*

casta: Sp. "caste": a person of mixed Spanish, Indian, and/or African ancestry.

Cewagï: O. "cloud": the Tohono O'odham village that became Tubac.

Chilitipagé: Ap. Jiłí dibáhé, or "Licentiously, He Starts Off to War"?: Apache leader at Tucson in early 1800s.

compañía volante: Sp. "flying column": a roaming patrol of soldiers designed to control Indians along the frontier.

corrido: Sp. folk ballad.

coyote: Sp. "coyote": a person of mixed Indian and African ancestry. Often used interchangeably in Sonora with *mestizo.*

criado: Sp. "one who is raised": a servant, often a captive Indian.

Cuk Şon: O. "Black Base": the Tohono O'odham village that became Tucson.

diyįh: Ap. supernatural power.

dzaneezí: Ap. "his ears long and slender": Western Apache term for mule.

Dził nchaa si'án: Ap. "Big Mountain": Mount Graham.

Dziłghá'é: Ap. "On Top of the Mountain People": Western Apache term for the White Mountain Apache.

establecimientos de paz: Sp. "peace establishments": Spanish term for settlements inhabited by *apaches de paz.*

frontera: Sp. frontier or border.

Gandazislichíídń: Ap. "The One with Reddish Sleeve Covers": probable name of the Chiricahua Apache leader known to outsiders as Mangas Coloradas.

Gashdla'áchoh o'āā: Ap. "Big Sycamore Stands There": the site in Aravaipa Canyon where the Camp Grant Massacre took place, later part of Captain Chiquito's homestead.

gente de razón: Sp. "people of reason": Spanish term for peoples of European origins or acculturated to European norms.

gente sin razón: Sp. "people without reason": Spanish term for peoples not of European background and/or not acculturated to European norms.

gidahim: O. war campaign.

gobernador: Sp. "governor": the Spanish and Mexican term for chiefs among the O'odham.

Gōōn: Ap. Western Apache term for Yavapai Indians.

gotah: Ap. "family cluster": a number of extended families living together, usually related matrilineally to one another.

gowah: Ap. "house" or "home": a canvas or brush shelter, often known to outsiders as a wickiup.

Gúchíísh: Ap. "His [Prominent] Nose"?: possible name of the Chiricahua Apache leader known to outsiders as Cochise. A potential alternative interpretation might be Guchizh, or "His Wood"?

gudnlsi: Ap. taboos.

guerra de fuego y sangre: Sp. "war of fire and blood": a confrontation in which the most extreme military measures take place.

Guyaałé: Ap. "The Yawner": Apache name of the Chiricahua leader known to outsiders as Geronimo.

Hák'ąyé: Ap: Western Apache term for the Chiricahua Apache. The Chiricahua were also known in some Western Apache dialects as the *Ha'iąhá,* or "Sunrise People," because they lived to the east.

Hashkēē bá nzín: Ap. "Angry, Men Stand in Line for Him": Pinal Apache leader during the latter half of the nineteenth century. Known to outsiders as Eskiminzin, Eskimizen, Es-him-en-zee, and Es-cim-en-zeen, among other names.

Hashkēē binąā nteel: Ap. "Angry, Wide Eyes": San Carlos Apache scout turned outlaw, known to outsiders as the Apache Kid.

Hia-Ceḍ O'odham: O. "Sand People": O'odham term for those living near the Gulf of California. Sometimes known to outsiders as the "Sand Papago."

Huhugam: O. "Vanishing People": O'odham term for the onetime residents of the ancient abandoned towns along the Salt and Gila rivers. Borrowing the O'odham's terminology, modern archaeologists usually call these people the Hohokam.

I'itoi: O. "Elder Brother": the O'odham cultural hero.

Innaa: Ap. "Enemy": Western Apache term for non-Apaches, particularly in current usage Anglo Americans.

Innaa shashé: Ap. "Bear Enemy": Western Apache term for early Anglo traders, so called for their hairy bodies.

Kełtł'ah izláhé: Ap. "Rope Under Their Feet People": Apache term for Akimel O'odham or Tohono O'odham.

kiho: O. basket.

Kui Tatk: O. "Mesquite Root": Tohono O'odham village.

Łee ndlįį: Ap. "Flows Together": the place where the San Pedro River and Aravaipa Canyon meet.

łįį': Ap. horse.

ma:kai: O. doctor or healer (plural: *mamakai*).

Mawid Kawadk: O. "Lion Shield": an Akimel O'odham chief known to Americans and Mexicans as Antonio Azul.

Mbachii yūmaa: Ap. Western Apache term for Yuma Indians.

M-ba-lse-slā: Ap. Mba' silāā, or "Coyote Two Dead Ones Lying There"?: Western Apache survivor of the Camp Grant Massacre.

mestizo: Sp. "mixed": a person of Spanish and Indian ancestry.

Milga:n: O. Anglo American.

mulato: Sp. a person of Spanish and African ancestry.

Na'í'ees: Ap. "Sunrise Ceremony/Changing Woman Ceremony": the rite marking the passage of a Nṉēē girl into adulthood.

Nakaịyé: Ap. "Those Who Walk Around": Western Apache term for Mexicans.

Nasht'izhé: Ap. "Enemies Painted Black": Western Apache term for Zuni.

Nautilnilce: Ap. *Nṉaa bitíl ńyiłsiih*, or "He Misses the Enemy's Chest"?: leader of Apache community in Tucson in late eighteenth century.

Nawait-'I'idag: O. "Wine Drinking Ceremony": summer ritual among the O'odham designed to bring the summer rains. Celebrated using liquor made from the fruit of the saguaro cactus.

nixora: Sp. a detribalized Indian, often originally a captive. In New Mexico, the comparable term was *genízaro.*

Nṉaa ch'iidn: Ap. "Enemy ghosts": Western Apache raiding and warfare term for opponents.

Nṉēē: Ap. "People" or "Human Beings": Apache term for themselves. Alternative spellings, depending on dialect, include Ndee and Indé.

nohwá goyą̄ą̄hí: Ap. "the one who is wise for us": the male leader of a group of interrelated Apache families.

Norteños: Sp. Northern Mexicans.

Nowa:l: O. Nogales

Nueva España: Sp. "New Spain": Spanish term for their colony in Mexico.

Oacpicagigua: O. 'Uagpig Gigia, or "Brain Splicer"?: leader of the 1751 Tohono O'odham revolt against the Spanish.

'O:b: O. "Enemy": O'odham term for the Apache.

'O:bad: O. Opata Indian.

O'odham: O. "People": Pima or Papago term for themselves.

pi ha'icu: O. "nothing": possible origin of the Spanish term for the Akimel O'odham ("Pima").

piloncillo: Sp. brown sugar.

Pimería Alta: Sp. "upper Pima land": Spanish term for the area of what would today be Sonora and Arizona where speakers of the Pima language predominated.

pinole: a drink made from parched ground grain.

presidio: Sp. fort.

Provincias Internas del Norte: Sp. "Interior Northern Provinces."

pueblo: Sp. town or village.

ramada: Sp. a shade arbor, usually built of poles.

ranchería: Sp. a hamlet or rural settlement. Often used by Spanish, Mexicans, or Anglo Americans to refer to an Indian encampment.

rancho: Sp. ranch.

Sáíkiné: Ap. "Sand House People": Western Apache term for Akimel O'odham or Tohono O'odham.

Sección Patriótica: Sp. "Patriotic Section": organization dedicated to fighting the Apaches, created in northern Sonora in 1832.

siakam: O. "Enemy Killer" (plural: *sisiakam*).

Sonorense: Sp. "Sonoran": a Hispanic resident of Sonora.

Tazhii: Ap. "Turkey": Apache nickname for John Clum, the San Carlos Reservation agent in the 1870s.

T'é'nádòljàgé: Ap. "Descending into the Water in Peaks People": Western Apache clan. The present-day spelling of the clan's name would be *Ténádoljagé.*

T'iisibaan: Ap. "Cottonwoods in Gray Wedge Shape People": the Western Apache community that inhabited the mountains around the Gila River. Often known to outsiders as the Pinal Apache.

Tł'ohk'a'á tū bił nlįį̄: Ap. "The Water Flows with Cane": Aravaipa Creek.

Tohono O'odham: O. "Desert People": O'odham term for community members inhabiting the Sonora Desert of Arizona and Mexico. Often known by outsiders as the Papago.

Tsēē idzisgoláné: Ap. "Rocks Which Have Many Dips": Tucson.

Tséká'kiné: Ap. "House on Top of Rocks People": Western Apache term for Hopi.

tsétahgo: Ap. "among the rocks": Western Apache term for an outlaw or renegade tribe member.

Tsézhiné: Ap. "Black Rocks People": the Western Apache community that inhabited Aravaipa Canyon. Often called by outsiders the Aravaipa Apache.

Tucsonense: Sp. "Tucsonian": a Hispanic resident of Tucson.

Tūdotł'ish sikán: Ap. "Blue Water Pool": A site just upstream from the juncture of Aravaipa Canyon and the San Pedro River. It would become the location of the U.S. Army base known as Camp Grant.

túlgaiyé: Ap. "white belly": Western Apache term for donkey.

Tutijé: Ap. Dúúdehé, or "The One Like the Killdeer [Bird]"?: Chiricahua Apache leader in the early 1800s.

vecino: Sp. "neighbor": the landholding resident of a village.

Wa:k: O. "Standing Water": the Tohono O'odham village that became San Xavier del Bac.

wickiup: an Anglo-American term used to describe any small Indian shelter built of brush.

Yúdahá: Ap. "Above People": Western Apache term for Navajo.

Notes

FOREWORD

1. Patricia Nelson Limerick, *The Legacy of Conquest: The Unbroken Past of the American West* (New York: W. W. Norton, 1987), 259.

INTRODUCTION

1. The number of Apaches killed in the attack is controversial even today, as Chip Colwell-Chanthaphonh explores in "The Camp Grant Massacre in the Historical Imagination." I have selected here to use the number given in Dale Curtis Miles and Paul R. Machula, *History of the San Carlos Apache*, 15, which echoes contemporary Apache tallies of the massacre.

2. There are signs of a promising new wave of studies of violence and American Indians. See Ned Blackhawk, *Violence Over the Land*; Jeff Ostler, "The Question of Genocide in U.S. History" (paper in possession of the author); and Benjamin Madley, "Patterns of Frontier Genocide, 1803–1910." The term "age of extremes" comes from E. J. Hobsbawm, *The Age of Extremes.*

3. For thoughtful recent assessments of the Bear River and Wounded Knee massacres, see Kass Fleisher, *The Bear River Massacre and the Making of History*; and Jeff Ostler, *The Plains Sioux and U.S. Colonialism.* Because massacres tend to be chaotic events, the casualty totals for these events are estimates rather than exact counts. I have used here what seem to be the most commonly accepted totals. Other, equally reasonable estimates might give a slightly different order of magnitude.

4. For more on the role of ordinary people in mass murder, see Christopher R. Browning, *Ordinary Men.* My thinking here is also indebted to Jill Lepore, *The Name of War*, xxi.

5. Primo Levi, *The Drowned and the Saved*, 84.

6. Elaine Scarry, *The Body in Pain*, 5. See also the essays in Saul Friedlander, ed., *Probing the Limits of Representation.*

7. Vizenor quoted in Thomas King, *The Truth About Stories*, 32; Eric R. Wolf, *Europe and the People Without History*, 4, 21. For a variety of recent works defending Native American oral culture, see Donald L. Fixico, *The American Indian Mind in a Linear World*; Angela Cavender Wilson, "Grandmother to Granddaughter"; and Devon Mihesuah, *Natives and Academics.* For more on narrative and historical judgment, see William Cronon, "A Place for Stories"; and Michel-Rolph Trouillot, *Silencing the Past*, 2.

8. For a thoughtful discussion of the place of insider and outsider perspectives in ethnohistory, see Daniel Richter, "Whose Indian History?" 387–93. For more on competing notions of temporality and space in historical narration, see Walter Johnson, "Time and Revolution in African America,"

148–67; David Harvey, *Justice, Nature and the Geography of Difference*, 222–23; and James Goodman, *Stories of Scottsboro*.

9. John Demos, "Afterword: Notes From, and About, the History/Fiction Borderland."

10. Until recently, there were no book-length histories of the Camp Grant Massacre. The first is Chip Colwell-Chanthaphonh, *Massacre at Camp Grant*. There are, however, a number of essays and book chapters exploring various facets of the event. In chronological order, these would include: George P. Hammond, "The Camp Grant Massacre"; James R. Hastings, "The Tragedy at Camp Grant in 1871"; Dee Brown, *Bury My Heart at Wounded Knee*, 201–6; J. Phillip Langellier, "Camp Grant Affair, 1871"; J. C. Alexander, "Massacre at Camp Grant"; Richard Waterfall, "Vengeance at Sunrise"; and Larry McMurtry, *Oh What a Slaughter*, 119–27. The massacre has also served as inspiration for a number of novels: Don Schellie, *Vast Domain of Blood*; Elliot Arnold, *Camp Grant Massacre*; Sinclair Browning, *Enju*; and Chelley Kitzmiller, *Embrace the Wind*.

A Note on Terminology

1. Willem J. de Reuse, *A Practical Grammar of the San Carlos Apache Language*; Albert Alvarez and Kenneth Hale, "Toward a Manual of Papago Grammar."

Part I
Violence: The O'odham

1. Grenville Goodwin, *The Social Organization of the Western Apache*, 86; Willem de Reuse (personal communication, 8/6/06); Roberta J. Stabel, "The Natural Setting," 11–17.

2. For more on the area's ecology, see Frederick R. Gehlbach, *Mountain Islands and Desert Seas*, 1–20; and Michael F. Logan, *The Lessening Stream*.

3. For more on *akĭ-ciñ* farming, see Kirk Bryan, "Flood Water Farming," 416–28.

4. Ruth M. Underhill et al., *Rainhouse and Ocean*, 17–22; Ruth M. Underhill, *Singing for Power*, 151–56; Henry F. Dobyns, *The Papago People*, 6–8; Winston P. Erickson, *Sharing the Desert*, 12–13. Erickson's work was written with the cooperation of the Tohono O'odham to serve as a textbook for the nation's schools.

5. Robert K. Thomas, "Papago Land Use West of the Papago Indian Reservation," 365, 370; Scott O'Mack and Eric Eugene Klucas, *San Xavier to San Augustín*, 39–40. Padre Kino noted in his memoir that some O'odham villages were "very hostile," having engaged in open warfare with one another. *Kino's Historical Memoir of Pimería Alta*, I:123–24.

6. Bernard L. Fontana, for example, has observed that "[t]he history of the Papago Indians of necessity begins with the documentary period of Hispanic history." Fontana, "History of the Papago," 137. See also David E. Doyel, "The Transition to History in Northern Pimería Alta," 139–58.

7. Underhill et al., *Rainhouse and Ocean*, 18–19.

8. Frank Russell, "The Pima Indians," 206–30; Donald Bahr, ed., *O'odham Creation and Related Events*, 5–53; Dean Saxton and Lucille Saxton, *O'othham Hoho'ok A'agitha*, 1–10; and Donald Bahr, *Pima and Papago Ritual Oratory*.

9. Lynn S. Teague, "Prehistory and the Traditions of the O'odham and Hopi"; Donald Bahr et al., *The Short Swift Time of Gods on Earth*; Roger C. Echo-Hawk, "Ancient History in the New World"; Bahr, *O'odham Creation and Related Events*, 5; Anna Moore Shaw, *A Pima Past*, 2.

10. Daniel T. Reff, *Disease, Depopulation, and Culture Change in Northwestern New Spain*, esp. 168–79. See also Ann L. W. Stodder and Debra Martin, "Health and Disease in the Southwest before and after Spanish Contact," and Daniel T. Reff, "Contact Shock in Northwestern New Spain." Both are found in John W. Verano and Douglas H. Ubelaker, eds., *Disease and Demography in the Americas* (Washington, D.C.: Smithsonian Institution Press, 1992).

11. Reff, *Disease, Depopulation, and Culture Change*, 111; Reff, "Contact Shock in Northwestern New Spain," 271; Richard A. Pailes, "An Archeological Perspective on the Sonoran Entrada," 177–89.

12. Quoted in Herbert Eugene Bolton, *The Rim of Christendom*, 397. See also Edward F. Castetter and Willis H. Bell, *Pima and Papago Indian Agriculture*, 74, 114, 118–19; and Paul H. Ezell, *The Hispanic Acculturation of the Gila River Pimas*, 32–36.

13. *Kino's Historical Memoir of Pimeria Alta*, I:119; Harry J. Karns, trans., *Unknown Arizona and Sonora*, 39, 78, 81–82. For a model of the recasting of colonial America as a "New World" for all of its participants, see James H. Merrell, *The Indian's New World*.

14. Bolton, *Rim of Christendom*, 265–67. An eloquent explanation of the ambiguities of colonialism on the fringes of empire can be found in Richard White, *The Middle Ground*, xi.

15. Thomas E. Sheridan, "The Columbian Exchange," 58–59; David Rich Lewis, *Neither Wolf nor Dog*, 131–32; and Donald Bahr et al., *Piman Shamanism and Staying Sickness*.

16. Lewis, *Neither Wolf nor Dog*, 134; Ruth Underhill, *Social Organization of the Papago Indians*, 99–100. For more on the trade in iron tools, see Jacobo Sedelmayr to Andrés Xavier García, June 15, 1748, in *Before Rebellion*, 17–18.

17. *Kino's Historical Memoir of Pimeria Alta*, I:113–14; Logan, *The Lessening Stream*, 48–51.

18. Report of Jacobo Sedelmayr, in *Before Rebellion*, xxviii; see also Sheridan, "The Columbian Exchange," 58.

19. Underhill et al., *Rainhouse and Ocean*, 114. See also Alphonse Pinart, "Vocabulario de la lengua Papaga (1879)." BANC MSS M-M 487, Bancroft Library. For Apache trade networks, see Neal Salisbury, "The Indians' Old World," 457.

20. Bahr, ed., *O'odham Creation and Related Events*, 20–21. I updated the wording of this passage slightly, substituting "Akimel O'odham" for "Pima" and "Shaman" for "Doctor" for reasons of consistency.

21. Karns, trans., *Unknown Arizona and Sonora*, 46–50, 78, 81.

22. Underhill et al., *Rainhouse and Ocean*, 89.

23. Underhill, *Social Organization*, 131–36; Ruth M. Underhill, *Papago Indian Religion*, 167–85; and Bernard L. Fontana, ed., "Jose Lewis Brennan's Account of Papago 'Customs and Other References.'" For examples of formalized duels, see *Kino's Historical Memoir of Pimeria Alta*, I:179–81, and Shaw, *A Pima Past*, 12.

24. Underhill, *Social Organization*, 132.

25. George Webb, *A Pima Remembers*, 33; Underhill, *Social Organization*, 136–38; Underhill, *Papago Indian Religion*, 192–210; Ezell, *Hispanic Acculturation*, 87–89. In some O'odham communities, these rituals were not limited to those who had touched an enemy but also included those who had come into close proximity with them, "breathing their breaths." Shaw, *A Pima Past*, 62.

26. Bahr, *O'odham Creation and Related Events*, 22.

27. Karns, trans., *Unknown Arizona and Sonora*, 46–50, 78, 81. For an early, detailed nineteenth-century account of O'odham cleansing rituals, see F. E. Grossman, "The Pima Indians of Arizona," 416–18. Healing and disease are discussed in Frances Densmore, *Papago Music*, 101–17; and Underhill, *Papago Indian Religion*, 265–301.

28. Underhill et al., *Rainhouse and Ocean*, 89–90; Underhill, *Social Organization*, 137.

29. Shaw, *A Pima Past*, 11–13; Russell, "The Pima Indians," 47; Webb, *A Pima Remembers*, 25; Underhill, *Social Organization*, 128–29.

30. Report of General Juan Fernández de la Fuente, 1695, in Thomas H. Naylor and Charles W. Polzer, eds., *The Presidio and Militia on the Northern Frontier of New Spain*, I:617; Karns, trans., *Unknown Arizona and Sonora*, 54, 59. For examples of the Akimel O'odham killing their shamans in the nineteenth century, see Russell, "The Pima Indians," 50, 52, 55, 59, 60,

31. Report of General Juan Fernández de la Fuente, 1695, in Naylor and Polzer, eds., *The Presidio and Militia on the Northern Frontier of New Spain*, I:606–7, 618; *Apostólicos afanes de la Compañía de Jesús escritos por un padre de la misma sagrada religión de su provincia de México*, 257; *Kino's Historical Memoir of Pimeria Alta*, I:144–45; Edward H. Spicer, *Cycles of Conquest*, 125–26.

32. Report of General Juan Fernández de la Fuente, 1695, in Naylor and Polzer, eds., *The Presidio and Militia on the Northern Frontier of New Spain*, I:637–38; *Kino's Historical Memoir of Pimeria Alta*, I:146–47; Erickson, *Sharing the Desert*, 30.

33. Treutlein, trans., *Missionary in Sonora*, 124; Pfefferkorn, *Sonora*, 264.

34. Bernard L. Fontana, "Pima and Papago: Introduction," 134.

35. George P. Hammond and Agapito Rey, eds., *Obregón's History of Sixteenth Century Explorations in Western America*, 164, 194; Report of Jacobo Sedelmayr, 1750, in *Before Rebellion*, 27; Karns, trans., *Unknown Arizona and Sonora*, 102. For more on the different terms used for the O'odham, see Fontana, "Pima and Papago: Introduction," 134; and Philip Burnham, "O'odham Linguist Comes to Washington," *Indian Country Today*, January 4, 2006.

36. Treutlein, trans., *Missionary in Sonora*, 167.

37. Ibid., 120, 124.

38. The Pima Rebellion of 1751 has received considerably less scholarly attention than the Pueblo Revolt of 1680. For leading summaries, see Erickson, *Sharing the Desert*, 38–48; Roberto Mario Salmon, "A Marginal Man"; and Thomas E. Sheridan, *Landscapes of Fraud*, 46–52. For useful primary sources on the revolt, see Juan Nentvig, *Rudo Ensayo*, 113–14; Report of Juan Antonio Balthasar, in Charles W. Polzer and Thomas E. Sheridan, eds., *The Presidio and Militia on the Northern Frontier of New Spain*, II:407–25; and Diego Ortiz Parrilla, "Correspondence with Officials, 1752." WA MSS s-834 P248, Beinecke Library, Yale University.

39. Matson, trans., *Before Rebellion*, xii–xiii; Oacpicagigua quoted in Sheridan, *Landscapes of Fraud*, 47–48.

40. Erickson, *Sharing the Desert*, 40–43; Spicer, *Cycles of Conquest*, 129–30; Sheridan, *Landscapes of Fraud*, 48–49. For a list of those killed in the attack in Sáric, consult the documents placed online by the Tumacácori National Historical Park: Project 2000, http://www.nps.gov/applications/tuma/detail2 .cfm?Event_ID=6055 (accessed 3/15/06).

41. Erickson, *Sharing the Desert*, 44–46; Spicer, *Cycles of Conquest*, 129–30; Bernard L. Fontana, *Of Earth and Little Rain*, 55; William Bright, *Native American Placenames of the United States*, 515. According to Bright, O'odham words that are now written using "c" the O'odham pronounced more like "t" in the eighteenth century, thus explaining the Spanish spellings of Tubac and Tucson. For a description of the fight between Luis's forces and the Spanish, see http://www.nps.gov/applications/tuma/detail2 .cfm?Event_ID=3534 (accessed 3/15/06).

42. Henry F. Dobyns, *Spanish Colonial Tucson*, 66, 86, 93, 102–6, 110, 115, 129; Bright, *Native American Placenames*, 515, 516; Cynthia Radding, *Wandering Peoples*, 256–63; and Henry F. Dobyns, "Military Transculturation of Northern Piman Indians, 1782–1821."

43. John L. Kessell, ed. and trans., "San José de Tumacácori—1773," 311.

44. *Kino's Historical Memoir of Pimería Alta*, I:169–71; Joseph C. Winter, "Cultural Modifications of the Gila Pima, 72–74; T. J. Ferguson and Chip Colwell-Chanthaphonh, *History Is in the Land*, 67.

45. James E. Officer, *Hispanic Arizona*, 39–40; Nentvig, *Rudo Ensayo*, 73; Erickson, *Sharing the Desert*, 51–52; Bright, *Native American Placenames*, 420.

46. Treutlein, trans., *Missionary in Sonora*, 166–67. My thoughts on indigenous space owe a great deal to the provocative essay by Michael Witgen, "The World Beyond the Atlantic" (in possession of author).

47. Shaw, *A Pima Past*, 85; Webb, *A Pima Remembers*, 3, 17.

48. Ruth M. Underhill, *A Papago Calendar Record*, 6, 12; see also *Arizona Daily Star*, May 25, 1941.

49. Russell, "The Pima Indians," 40.

50. Underhill, *A Papago Calendar Record*, 19.

51. Ibid., 13, 18. See also Peter Nabakov, *A Forest of Time*, 156–63; and Hayden White, "Narrativity in the Representation of Reality," in *The Content of the Form*, 4–24.

52. For more on Tohono O'odham involvement in the unstable Sonoran politics of the 1830s and '40s, see Bill Hoy, "War in Papaguería."

53. John Demos, *The Unredeemed Captive*, 214.

54. Underhill, *A Papago Calendar Record*, 19.

55. Russell, "The Pima Indians," 44.

56. Underhill, *A Papago Calendar Record*, 20.

57. Ibid., 23.

58. Russell, "The Pima Indians," 45.

59. Ibid., 46.

60. William H. Emory, *Report on the United States and Mexican Boundary Survey*, I:95, 117.

61. Ibid., I:96. For the translation of "American," see Dean Saxton, Lucille Saxton, and Susie Enos, *Dictionary: Papago/Pima-English, O'othham-Mil-gahn*, 110.

62. Emory, *Report on the United States and Mexican Boundary Survey*, I:96; Erickson, *Sharing the Desert*, 74–77.

63. Russell, "The Pima Indians," 46; Underhill, *A Papago Calendar Record*, 26. For a list of

captains among the Pima and Papago, see *Annual Report of the Commissioner of Indian Affairs, 1858,*
559–60.

64. For distribution of gifts, see *Annual Report of the Commissioner of Indian Affairs, 1859,* 721–24. For
examples of early O'odham joint campaigns, see *Annual Report of the Commissioner of Indian Affairs,
1857,* 587; and Constance Wynn Altshuler, ed., *Latest from Arizona!* 50–51.

65. Underhill, *A Papago Calendar Record,* 26.

66. Charles D. Poston, *Speech on Indian Affairs Delivered in the House of Representatives,* 6; J. Ross Browne,
Adventures in the Apache Country, 110; John Nicolson, ed., *The Arizona of Joseph Pratt Allyn,* 109–10;
Annual Report of the Commissioner of Indian Affairs, 1859, 719. For more on crop sales, see *Annual
Report of the Commissioner of Indian Affairs, 1867,* 162; James F. Rusling, *Across America,* 369–70; and
A. G. Brackett, "Arizona Territory," 170.

67. *Annual Report of the Commissioner of Indian Affairs, 1859,* 720; William A. Bell, *New Tracks in North
America,* 175–76; Michael James Box, *Adventures and Explorations in New and Old Mexico,* 262–64;
Los Angeles Star, June 13, 1857; and *Weekly Arizonian,* April 21, 1859. For more on the saguaro
harvest, see Gary Paul Nabhan, *The Desert Smells Like Rain,* 25–31.

68. *The War of the Rebellion,* Series 1, L:138–39, 825, 928–31, 1052; Russell, "The Pima Indians,"
48–49.

69. Underhill, *A Papago Calendar Record,* 28.

70. A. T. Kilcrease, "Ninety-Five Years of History of the Papago Indians," 301. This calendar stick
record is also reprinted in William M. Tatom, *The Papago Indian Reservation and the Papago People.*
Black vomit is usually suggestive of yellow fever.

71. James H. Carleton to William McCleave, March 15, 1862; James H. Carleton to Richard C. Drum,
May 24, 1862, in *The War of the Rebellion,* L:899, 932, 1094–95; *Annual Report of the Commissioner of
Indian Affairs, 1862,* 34, 239; Russell, "The Pima Indians," 51.

72. *Annual Report of the Commissioner of Indian Affairs, 1867,* 163; *Annual Report of the Commissioner of
Indian Affairs, 1866,* 113; *Annual Report of the Commissioner of Indian Affairs, 1862,* 34; John G.
Bourke, "General Crook in the Indian Country," 657; *Annual Report of the Commissioner of Indian
Affairs, 1868,* 142.

73. Brackett, "Arizona Territory," 169; Camillo C. C. Carr, "The Days of the Empire—Arizona, 1866–
1869," *Journal of the United States Cavalry Association* 2:4 (March 1889): 3–22, in Peter Cozzens, ed.,
Eyewitnesses to the Indian Wars, 33.

74. Underhill et al., *Rainhouse and Ocean,* 126–29; Underhill, *Social Organization,* 133–38; Underhill,
Papago Indian Religion, 192–93; Underhill, *A Papago Calendar Record,* 40.

75. *Annual Report of the Commissioner of Indian Affairs, 1868,* 142; Neil Carmony, ed., *The Civil War in
Apacheland,* 86; Altshuler, ed., *Latest from Arizona!* 150.

76. Russell, "The Pima Indians," 51; see also the depiction of this event in Shaw, *A Pima Past,* 84–85.

77. Russell, "The Pima Indians," 52.

78. Ibid.

79. *Weekly Arizonan,* September 17, 1870.

80. Thomas, "Papago Land Use," 376.

81. Underhill, *Social Organization,* 133. See also Ruth M. Underhill, "The Autobiography of a Papago
Woman," 13.

82. Underhill, *A Papago Calendar Record,* 34–35.

83. Thomas, "Papago Land Use," 385–90. A somewhat similar version of this story is recorded in
Underhill, *A Papago Calendar Record,* 29–30. The possible translation for *tewas* was provided by
Colleen Fitzgerald (personal communication, 8/29/07).

84. Thomas, "Papago Land Use," 391–92.

85. Underhill, *A Papago Calendar Record,* 36–37; Thomas, "Papago Land Use," 371–72. For reasons
of consistency, I have adjusted Underhill's translations of Tucson and San Xavier del Bac to their
current understandings.

86. Underhill, *A Papago Calendar Record,* 36–37; Erickson, *Sharing the Desert,* 51. Some of the residents
of San Xavier del Bac described themselves as Sobaipuris until the 1930s. See Bernard L. Fontana,
"Report of Bernard L. Fontana Before the Indian Claims Commission," 165.

87. Underhill, *A Papago Calendar Record*, 37. The brevity with which the O'odham discuss the actual act of killing is discussed in Underhill et al., *Rainhouse and Ocean*, 125.

VIOLENCE: LOS VECINOS

1. For an example of how the Spanish mapped upper Sonora at this time, see the reprint of Father Kino's 1705 map in *Kino's Historical Memoir of Pimería Alta*, 4; and José Antonio de Alzate y Ramírez, "Nuevo mapa geographico de la America Septentrional, perteneciente al Virreynato de México, 1768." John Carter Brown Library, Brown University.
2. Thomas Richards, *The Imperial Archive*, 6–7; Fintan Warren, "Jesuit Historians of Sinaloa-Sonora."
3. Randall H. McGuire, ed., *Ethnology of Northwest Mexico*, xiii.
4. Roberto Mario Salmon, *Indian Revolts in Northern New Spain*, 65 n.4; and David J. Weber, *The Spanish Frontier in North America*, 78.
5. Officer, *Hispanic Arizona*, 32; Report of General Juan Fernández de la Fuente, 1695, in Naylor and Polzer, eds., *The Presidio and Militia on the Northern Frontier of New Spain*, I:583–84, 597, 608; Spicer, *Cycles of Conquest*, 125–26; Tirso González to Juan de Palacios, July 28, 1696, in *Correspondencia del P. Kino con los Generales de la Compañía de Jesús, 1682–1707*, 42–44.
6. Report of General Juan Fernández de la Fuente, 1695, in Naylor and Polzer, eds., *The Presidio and Militia on the Northern Frontier of New Spain*, I:585–86, 657; Max L. Moorhead, *The Apache Frontier*, 16.
7. Byrd H. Granger, *Arizona Place Names*, xv; Bright, *Native American Placenames*, 47; *Apostólicos afanes de la Compañía de Jesús*, 230; Officer, *Hispanic Arizona*, 31–32.
8. Francisco Moyano, "Liber de statu animarum hujus populi Sancti Antonio de Oquitoa, 1796 Oct. 20," 2. WA MSS s-1542 m8731 (1796), Beinecke Library, Yale University. For more on Sonoran ethnic categories, see Radding, *Wandering Peoples*, 357–62.
9. Ignaz Pfefferkorn, *Sonora*, 284–85; Peter Stern and Robert Jackson, "Vagabundaje and Settlement Patterns in Colonial Northern Sonora," 461–81.
10. Report of General Juan Fernández de la Fuente, 1695, in Naylor and Polzer, eds., *The Presidio and Militia on the Northern Frontier of New Spain*, I:585–86; Morris E. Opler, "The Apachean Culture Pattern and Its Origins," 385. Technically, Sonora would remain part of the province of Nueva Vizcaya until 1733, at which point it would become part of the new province of Sinaloa and Sonora. This new unit would in turn be transformed into the state of Occidente following independence in 1824. Not until 1830 would this state divide into the current Mexican states of Sonora and Sinaloa. Rather than chart the ebb and flow of all these administrative changes, however, I have for simplicity's sake termed the area that became Sonora by this name throughout much of this chapter. For more on landscapes of order and fugitive landscapes in the making of Sonora, see Samuel Truett, *Fugitive Landscapes*; and Donald E. Worcester, "The Beginnings of the Apache Menace of the Southwest."
11. Report of General Juan Fernández de la Fuente, 1695, in Naylor and Polzer, eds., *The Presidio and Militia on the Northern Frontier of New Spain*, I:585, 651, 657; Juan Nentvig, *Rudo Ensayo*, 82. For a similar depiction of increasing hostilities in the 1760s, see Luis María Belderrain's report in Kieran McCarty, ed. and trans., *Desert Documentary*, 73–74, 76. A revisionist interpretation of the Apache threat during this time can be found in Sara Ortelli, *Trama de una guerra conveniente*.
12. Kessell, ed. and trans., "San José de Tumacácori—1773," 310–11; José Ortega, ed., *Historia del Nayarit, Sonora, Sinaloa y ambas Californias*, 534, 553. This is a reprint of a work published anonymously in Barcelona in 1754.
13. Karns, trans., *Unknown Arizona and Sonora*, 47, 75, 78; Alfred Barnaby Thomas, ed. and trans., *Teodoro de Croix and the Northern Frontier of New Spain*, 137–38.
14. Not all of these presidios were exclusively intended to counter the Apache threat; those in the interior, such as Buenavista and Pitic, were also designed to watch over internal threats such as the Yaqui and the Seri. Martha Ortega Soto, "La colonizacion española en la primera mitad del siglo XVIII," 162–66.
15. Donald C. Cutter, ed. and trans., *The Defenses of Northern New Spain*, 74; Weber, *Spanish Frontier*,

204–20; Thomas, ed. and trans., *Teodoro de Croix and the Northern Frontier of New Spain*, 224; and Ana María Alonso, *Thread of Blood*, 15–17.

16. *Apostólicos afanes de la Compañía de Jesús*, 442; Odie B. Faulk, "The Presidio: Fortress or Farce?" 67–76; Spicer, *Cycles of Conquest*, 238.

17. Thomas, ed. and trans., *Teodoro de Croix and the Northern Frontier of New Spain*, 144–45; and Report in Kieran McCarty, *Desert Documentary*, 44, 46.

18. Report in Kieran McCarty, *Desert Documentary*, 44, 46; O'Mack and Klucas, *San Xavier to San Agustín*, 47; and Phelipe de Neve, Plan of Operations, February 22, 1784, in Alfred Barnaby Thomas, ed. and trans., *Forgotten Frontiers*, 253.

19. Diego Miguel Bringas de Manzaneda y Encinas, *Father Bringas Reports to the King*, 67, 74; James Brooks, *Captives and Cousins*, 6, 8; Weber, *Spanish Frontier*, 307–8; Ignacio Zuñiga, *Rapida Ojeada al Estado de Sonora*, 6 n.5.

20. Officer, *Hispanic Arizona*, 76. The Guevavi baptismal records are available online through the National Park Service's "Mission 2000" website: http://www.nps.gov/applications/tuma/search.cfm (accessed 1/13/06). For records of Beldarrain's activities, see Event IDs 401, 402, 1114, 1115, and 1217.

21. Henry F. Dobyns et al., "What Were Nixoras?"; Weber, *Spanish Frontier*, 308; and Pfefferkorn, *Sonora*, 29.

22. Pfefferkorn, *Sonora*, 149–50.

23. William B. Griffen, *Apaches at War and Peace*, 99–100; Bernardo de Gálvez, *Instructions for Governing the Interior Provinces of New Spain, 1786*, 38, 41, 43; Daniel S. Matson and Albert H. Schroeder, eds., "Cordero's Description of the Apache, 1796," 350; and Elizabeth John, *Storms Brewed in Other Men's Worlds*, 444–45. For more on the relation between the *apaches de paz* program and the *moros de paz* program in North Africa, see Elizabeth John, ed., and John Wheat, trans., *View from the Apache Frontier*, 7.

24. Gálvez, *Instructions for Governing the Interior Provinces of New Spain*, 34; Max L. Moorhead, "Spanish Deportation of Hostile Apaches," 205–20; Christon I. Archer, "The Deportation of Barbarian Indians from the Internal Provinces of New Spain, 1789–1810."

25. Zuñiga, *Rapida Ojeada*, 14 n.10, 14–15; Michael F. Logan, *Desert Cities*, 28–29; Thomas E. Sheridan, *Los Tucsonenses*, 14. For figures as to the total *apaches de paz*, see Griffen, *Apaches at War and Peace*, 87, 267; and Ricardo León García and Carlos González Herrera, *Civilizar o exterminar*, 142–43.

26. Officer, *Hispanic Arizona*, 88.

27. Alan Knight, *Mexico: The Colonial Era*, 283–92; Officer, *Hispanic Arizona*, 84.

28. José María Tornel, *Memoria del secretario de estado y del despacho de guerra y marina*, 83; Pedro García Conde, *Memoria del secretario de estado y del despacho de guerra y marina, 1845*, 27–28; and David J. Weber, *The Mexican Frontier*, 108.

29. Ramón Ruiz to ?, June 2, 1833 (Folio 396, Expediente 8, 1833), and José María Elías González to Commander of the State of Occidente, June 23, 1835 (Folio 33312, Expediente 22, 1835), Fondo Ejecutivo, Ramo Apaches, Archivo General del Estado de Sonora; Zuñiga, *Rapida Ojeada*, 21; Griffen, *Apaches at War and Peace*, 125, 131; McCarty, ed. and trans., *A Frontier Documentary*, 34–35.

30. Josiah Gregg, *Commerce of the Prairies*, 202–3; John E. Durivage, "Through Mexico to California," 211–12; Cave Couts, "Journal, 1846–1848," 32. CT 2541, Huntington Library. For the Tucson census, see McCarty, ed. and trans., *A Frontier Documentary*, 50. For another account of an enduring "partial peace," see R. W. H. Hardy, *Travels in the Interior of Mexico*, 459–60.

31. John G. Bourke, *On the Border with Crook*, 120; Gregg, *Commerce of the Prairies*, 202–3. For further accounts of this trade, see Dwight L. Clarke, ed., *The Original Journals of Henry Smith Turner*, 82; and Philip St. George Cooke, "Journal of the March of the Mormon Battalion, 1846–1847," 137.

32. Emory, *Report on the United States and Mexican Boundary Survey*, I:86; the quote "beating them against rocks" comes from Ralph A. Smith, "Indians in American-Mexican Relations before the War of 1846," 54. John Russell Bartlett, *Personal Narrative of Explorations and Incidents in Texas, New Mexico, California, Sonora, and Chihuahua*, I:267–68, 306; John C. Cremony, *Life Among the Apaches*, 39; William B. Griffen, *Utmost Good Faith*, 77, 84–85; Griffen, *Apaches at War and Peace*, 211–14, 238.

33. Juan Nepomuceno Almonte, *Memoria del ministerio de estado y del despacho de guerra y marina, 1846*, 34; Manuel Robles, *Memoria del secretario del estado y del despacho de guerra y marina, 1852*, 56–57; Mariano Arista, *Memoria del secretario del estado y del despacho de guerra y marina, 1849*, 10. For more on Mexicans' sense of geographic vulnerability, see Raymond B. Craib, *Cartographic Mexico*, 25.

34. Although the modern-day term among Mexicans for U.S. citizens is typically *norteamericanos* or *estadounidenses*, in the nineteenth century, the usual term was *americanos*. See John C. Reid, *Reid's Tramp*, 67.

35. Vázques quoted in John L. Kessell, *Friars, Soldiers, and Reformers*, 305; Bartlett, *Personal Narrative*, II:292. See also García Conde, *Memoria del secretario de estado y del despacho de guerra y marina, 1845*, 29; Ralph A. Smith, "Mexican and Anglo-Saxon Traffic in Scalps, Slaves, and Livestock, 1835–1841," 98–115; and Officer, *Hispanic Arizona*, 266. The conflation of Indian and American threats to Mexico is explored in detail in Brian Delay, "Independent Indians and the U.S.-Mexican War."

36. Mariano Arista, *Memoria del secretario de estado y del despacho de guerra y marina, 1850*, 14–18; Mariano Arista, *Memoria del secretario de estado y del despacho de guerra y marina, 1851*, 33, 38–39; Tornel, *Memoria del secretario de estado y del despacho de guerra y marina, 1844*, 83; and Weber, *The Mexican Frontier*, 110.

37. Tornel, *Memoria del secretario de estado y del despacho de guerra y marina, 1844*, 53; Arista, *Memoria del secretario de estado y del despacho de guerra, 1849*, 11. See also Almonte, *Memoria del ministerio de estado y del despacho de guerra y marina, 1846*, 33; and León García and González Herrera, *Civilizar o exterminar*, 168. For another reference to the desirability of exterminating the Apaches, see Juan Nepomuceno Almonte, *Memoria del ministerio de guerra y marina, 1841*, 35.

38. Gobierno supremo del estado de Occidente: Decree No. 158, June 5, 1830; Gobierno supremo del estado de Occidente: Decree No. 149, March 31, 1830. Don Jesús José Aguiar Collection, MS 916, Arizona Historical Society. Occidente was the short-lived precursor state to Sonora. See also Weber, *The Mexican Frontier*, 115–16; and Alcalde of Tucson to ?, May 31, 1829 (Folio 46, Expediente 1, 1829). Fondo Ejecutivo, Ramo Apaches, Archivo General del Estado de Sonora.

39. Joaquín Vicente Elías to Governor of Sonora, May 21, 1832 (Folio 283, Expediente 7, 1832); "Triunfo sobre los apaches," July 6, 1832 (Folio 316, Expediente 7, 1832); Joaquín Vicente Elías to Governor of Sonora, June 19, 1832 (Folio 307, Expediente 7, 1832); Joaquín Vicente Elías to Governor of Sonora, June 21, 1832 (Folio 307, Expediente 7, 1832). Fondo Ejecutivo, Ramo Apaches, Archivo General del Estado de Sonora. See also Kessell, *Friars, Soldiers, and Reformers*, 284.

40. "Triunfo sobre los apaches," July 6, 1832 (Folio 316, Expediente 7, 1832); Custagio Martínez to Governor of Sonora, June 17, 1832 (Folio 300, Expediente 7, 1832); Joaquín Vicente Elías to Governor of Sonora, June 19, 1832 (Folio 309, Expediente 7, 1832). Fondo Ejecutivo, Ramo Apaches, Archivo General del Estado de Sonora. See also Kessell, *Friars, Soldiers, and Reformers*, 285–86. Kessell and I differ somewhat in our reading of Martínez's first name. For a description of the role of *bandos* in northern México, see Andrés Reséndez, "An Expedition and Its Many Tales," 121–50.

41. *Gobierno supremo del estado de Sonora, decreto número 85* (Arizpe, 1835). Pinart print No. 435, Bancroft Library, University of California at Berkeley; Stuart F. Voss, *On the Periphery of Nineteenth-Century Mexico*, 69–70; and Smith, "Indians in American-Mexican Relations before the War of 1846," 44. For later scalp bounties, see *Weekly Arizonan*, December 31, 1870; *Weekly Arizona Miner*, July 1, 1871; and Charles Drew to William Clinton, Jan. 5, 1870, in *Annual Report of the Commissioner of Indian Affairs, 1869*, 108.

42. Almonte, *Memoria del ministerio de guerra y marina, 1841*, 35.

43. Rafael Elías González to Minister of the Interior, September 20, 1837, in McCarty, ed. and trans., *A Frontier Documentary*, 57; Cooke, "Journal of the March of the Mormon Battalion," 147, 153 n.189, 159–60. The reference to "Apache barbarians" comes from José Elías, "Secretaría del gobierno de Sonora circular" (Ures: N.p., 1846). Pinart Print No. 794, Bancroft Library, University of California at Berkeley.

44. Luis Redondo, "El Vice-Gobernador del estado de Sonora" (Ures: Impr. del estado en Palacio, dirigida por J.P. Siquieros, 1847). Pinart Prints, No. 886a. See also Luis Redondo, "El Vice-Gobernador del estado de Sonora" (Ures: Impr. del estado en Palacio, dirigida por J.P. Siquieros, 1847). Pinart Print No. 884. Bancroft Library.

45. García Cubas quoted in Craib, *Cartographic Mexico*, 25. Hernández Silva, "Sonora y la guerra con Estados Unidos," 490–93; Hubert Howe Bancroft, *History of Arizona and New Mexico, 1530–1888*, 475. For more on the impetus that the loss of territory gave to the study of Mexican history, see Richard Griswold del Castillo, *The Treaty of Guadalupe Hidalgo*, 114–21.

46. Paul Neff Garber, *The Gadsden Treaty*, 25–33, 102–3; Hilario Gallego, "Reminiscences of an Arizona Pioneer," 78. For Mexican reconnaissances of the Gila and Salt rivers, see Long, *Desert Cities*, 31–32.

47. Voss, *On the Periphery of Nineteenth-Century Mexico*, 110; José Francisco Velasco, *Noticias estadísticas del estado de Sonora*, 316–17; and Robles, *Memoria del secretario de estado y del despacho de guerra y marina, 1852*, 56.

48. Hernández Silva, "Sonora y la guerra con Estados Unidos," 495; Velasco, *Noticias estadísticas*, 254. Ramírez is quoted in Logan, *Desert Cities*, 31.

49. "Reminiscences of Juan I. Téllez," 87; Report of D. Fergusson, November 12, 1862, in *The War of the Rebellion*, Series 3, Vol. III, 32; Robert C. Stevens, "The Apache Menace in Sonora, 1831–1849," 221; Bartlett, *Personal Narrative*, I:266.

50. "Interview with Carmen Reuteria Lucero, Dec. 24, 1927." Folder 3, Charles Morgan Wood Papers, MS 881, Arizona Historical Society. See also "Reminiscences of William Fourr," 69. Luis Aboites Aguilar and Victor Orozco discuss the contrast northern Mexicans drew between nomadic and sedentary peoples in "Nómadas y sedentarios en el norte de México: Elementos para una periodización" and "El conflicto entre apaches, rarámuris y mestizos en Chihuahua durante el siglo xix," both in Marie-Areti Hers et al., eds., *Nómadas y sedentarios en el norte de México*, 613–21, 683–92.

51. Arthur Woodward, ed., *Journal of Lt. Thomas W. Sweeny, 1849–1853*, 83. See also William Bausman, "Reminiscences of the United States and Mexican Boundary Survey." DA 5, Huntington Library; and Cremony, *Life Among the Apaches*, 10.

52. Velasco, *Noticias estadísticas del estado de Sonora*, 239; *Memoria del estado de la administración pública, 1870*, 23; and Leonard Pitt, *The Decline of the Californios*, 54–57.

53. For more on Murrieta, see Susan Johnson, *Roaring Camp*, 25–53; and Ireneo Paz, *Life and Adventures of the Celebrated Bandit Joaquín Murrieta*.

54. Garber, *Gadsden Treaty*, 100–101; Angela Moyano Pahissa, "The Mesilla Treaty," 10–12.

55. Garber, *Gadsden Treaty*, 102–4; *The Treaties Between the United States and Mexico*, 10–11, 28.

56. Garber, *Gadsden Treaty*, 152–53; Manuel Olasagarre, *Cuenta de la percepción*.

57. Browne, *Adventures in the Apache Country*, 159; and Charles D. Poston, "Reminiscences," 1A. FAC 308, Huntington Library.

58. Although there has been no corresponding study for the Treaty of La Mesilla, it is estimated that some 3,500 Mexicans migrated south with the new border created by the Treaty of Guadalupe Hidalgo rather than live in the United States. See Martín González de la Vara, "The Return to Mexico," 50–51.

59. Velasco, *Noticias estadísticas*, 240; O'Mack and Klucas, *San Xavier to San Agustín*, 79.

60. Officer, *Hispanic Arizona*, 162, 284–97. For more on Ramírez, see Teodoro Ramírez to Rafael Elías González, September 6, 1837, in McCarty, *Frontier Documentary*, 55–56.

61. Box 1, Folder 4, 46. Charles Morgan Wood Papers, MS 881, Arizona Historical Society.

62. Altshuler, ed., *Latest from Arizona!* 117. See also *Weekly Arizonan*, October, 22, 1870, and December 31, 1870; and *Memoria del estado de la administración pública*, 23.

63. These statistics come from *Federal Census—Territory of New Mexico and Territory of Arizona*, 89th Congress, 1st sess., Senate Doc., No. 13, 34–48. For discussions of possible undercounts of Mexicans in early census data, see Albert Camarillo, *Chicanos in a Changing Society*, 233–40; and Richard Griswold del Castillo, "Tucsonenses and Angeleños," 59.

64. *Resources of Arizona with a Description of the Indian Tribes*, 17; Benjamin Butler Harris, "Journal: Crumbs of 49," 17. HM 17477, Huntington Library.

65. Altshuler, ed., *Latest from Arizona!* 69–70; James H. Tevis, *Arizona in the '50s*, 69; G. W. Barter, *Directory of the City of Tucson for the Year 1881*, 18, 30, 35. A thorough description of Tucson's appearance in the nineteenth century is given in Ray Brandes, "Guide to the Historic Landmarks

of Tucson." For more on plazas as physical and cultural centers of Mexican village life, see George J. Sánchez, *Becoming Mexican American*, 25–26.

66. Altshuler, ed., *Latest from Arizona!* 102; Carmony, ed., *The Civil War in Apacheland*, 69; "La Fiesta de San Agustin," *Arizona Quarterly Illustrated* 1 (October 1880): 8–9; *Weekly Arizonian*, June 30, 1859; *Weekly Arizonan*, September 4, 1869; *Arizona Weekly Citizen*, August 31, 1872; and Patricia Preciado Martin, *Images and Conversations*, 63.

67. *Weekly Arizonan*, September 3, 1870; Carmony, ed., *The Civil War in Apacheland*, 69–70; and A. M. Gustafson, ed., *John Spring's Arizona*, 300.

68. *Resources of Arizona*, 17; Jacob Samuel Mansfield, "Literature in the Territory of Arizona in 1870," 5. FAC 310, Huntington Library; Gustafson, ed., *John Spring's Arizona*, 47, 175, 189; *Arizona Citizen*, December 3, 1870, April 19, 1873, June 16, 1879; *Weekly Arizonan*, June 5, 1869, October 15, 1870.

69. "Tucson," *Arizona Quarterly Illustrated* 1 (July 1880): 9; "Smuggling into Sonora," *Arizona Quarterly Illustrated* 1 (October 1880): 7; William Henry Bishop, *Old Mexico and Her Lost Provinces*, 506; *Weekly Arizonan*, February 25, 1871, September 25, 1869; and Miguel Tinker Salas, *In the Shadow of the Eagles*, 63.

70. *Weekly Arizonan*, February 25, 1871. See also Egbert L. Viele, "The East and West Boundary Line between the United States and Mexico," 275; *Message of Governor McCormick to the Fifth Legislative Assembly of the Territory of Arizona at Tucson, November 16, 1868* (Tucson: Office of the Arizonan, 1868), in State Department Territorial Papers, Arizona, 1864–1872, RG 59, M342; Browne, 133; and J. H. Marion, *Notes of Travel Through the Territory of Arizona*, 12.

71. Tucson Schedules, 4, 26, 31, 32, 33, 35, 37, 52. Records of the Bureau of the Census, Ninth Census of the United States, 1870, Arizona Territory, RG 29, M593A. Sheridan terms Carrillo "the wealthiest individual in Tucson" in 1870, but my reading of the census data suggests there were at least three Anglos with greater total holdings. See Sheridan, *Los Tucsonenses*, 50–51.

72. Sheridan, *Los Tucsonenses*, 42–44; Tully and Ochoa appear as "retail" merchants in the 1870 census, each with $30,000 in holdings. See Tucson Schedules, 32, 34. Records of the Bureau of the Census, Ninth Census of the United States, 1870, Arizona Territory, RG 29, M593A.

73. These statistics are compiled from *Federal Census—Territory of New Mexico and Territory of Arizona*. See also Sheridan, *Los Tucsonenses*, 37–38.

74. *Federal Census—Territory of New Mexico and Territory of Arizona*, 37–48, 162–98. There is a growing body of research on intermarriage in the borderlands, although little of it focuses on Arizona: María Raquél Casas, *Married to a Daughter of the Land*; Deena J. González, *Refusing the Favor*, 107–22; Darlis A. Miller, "Cross-Cultural Marriages in the Southwest," 95–119; Peggy Pascoe, "Race, Gender, and Intercultural Relations"; and Carlos G. Vélez-Ibáñez, *Border Visions*, 59–60.

75. *Federal Census—Territory of New Mexico and Territory of Arizona*, 162–98. The Glasscock and McKenna marriages are on pages 174 and 184.

76. C. L. Sonnichsen, *Tucson: The Life and Times of an American City*, 54; Frank Lockwood, *Life in Old Tucson, 1854–1864*, xix.

77. José Francisco Velasco, for example, uses "blancos" to refer to the Mexican inhabitants of Sonora. See *Noticias estadísticas del estado de Sonora*, 151. Ramón Eduardo Ruiz explores Sonoran notions of whiteness in *The People of Sonora and Yankee Capitalists*, 162–73.

78. Daniel Ellis Conner, *Joseph Reddeford Walker and the Arizona Adventure*, 17.

79. Altshuler, ed., *Latest from Arizona!* 34.

80. Returns for June 1868. Returns from U.S. Military Posts, Fort Grant, Arizona, 1865–1874, Microcopy 617, Roll 414. National Archives—Microfilm Publications. The diary of Henry M. Lazelle, a lieutenant on the 1857 campaign, is reprinted in Frank D. Reeve, ed., "Puritan and Apache: A Diary," *New Mexico Historical Review* 23 (October 1948): 269–301 and (January 1949): 12–50. Lazelle's description of the "Guides and Spies" can be found on page 47.

81. Robert A. Nye, "Western Masculinities in War and Peace," 417–38. For a discussion of more recent linkages between Mexican-American military service and citizenship, see Lorena Oropeza, "Making History: The Chicano Movement," 200–204.

82. John Baylor to H. E. McCulloch, November 10, 1861, and Report of Lt. Col. Edward Eyre, July 6, 1862, in *The War of the Rebellion*, L:123, 716.

83. Deposition of Juan Elías (January 1893), 81, 86. Case 7550. Indian Depredations, RG 123. National

Archives—Washington, D.C. John Butler to J. B. Magruder, December 29, 1862, and Report of Ben Cutler, February 24, 1863, in *The War of the Rebellion*, XV:230, 916. Although Cutler only refers to New Mexico in his report, he describes activities in what would today be considered both New Mexico and Arizona.

84. H. S. Washburn to J. W. Goodwin, August 15, 1865, in "Arizona Volunteers: Correspondence and Reports, 1864–66." MS Film 197, Huntington Library. "Arizona Territorial Volunteers," Manuscript 599, Southwest Museum.

85. H. S. Washburn to J. W. Goodwin, August 15, 1865, in "Arizona Volunteers," MS Film 197, Huntington Library; *Arizona Miner*, February 28, 1866, April 11, 1866; *Journals of the Third Legislative Assembly of the Territory of Arizona*, 253. See also "Arizona Volunteers Muster Rolls, 1865–1866," MS 599, Southwest Museum.

86. *Arizona Miner*, February 28, 1866, April 11, 1866. See also *Journals of the Third Legislative Assembly of the Territory of Arizona*, 253, 260.

87. Officer, *Hispanic Arizona*, 317–24; James E. Officer, "Historical Factors in Interethnic Relations in the Community of Tuscon," 13; and Armando Elías Chomina, *Compendio de datos históricos de la familia Elías*.

88. "Elias, Jesus Maria." Arizona State University Libraries: Hayden Arizona Pioneer Biographies Collection, http://www.asu.edu/lib/archives/azbio/index.html (accessed 7/28/07). "Depositions, January 1893," 82–83. *Juan Elías v. U.S.*, Indian Depredation Case 7550, RG 123, National Archives—Washington, D.C. *Acts, Resolutions and Memorials Adopted by the First Legislative Assembly of the Territory of Arizona*, xi.

89. "Depositions, 1893," 52, 88, 124–25; *Arizona Daily Citizen*, August 3, 1893.

90. This description is compiled from Elías's testimony in "Depositions, 1893," 123–26. For more on the community pressures supporting the pursuit of Apache raiders, see Daniel Nugent, *Spent Cartridges of Revolution*, 94, 125–26; and Alonso, *Thread of Blood*, 39–43.

91. "Depositions, 1893," 91, 136; "Elías, Juan," Biographical File, Arizona Historical Society. Wise's wound was not fatal.

92. "Depositions, 1893," 119–21.

93. *Arizona Daily Citizen*, August 3, 1893; "Reminiscences of Amelia Elías," Arizona Historical Society.

94. "Abstract of Evidence" and "Depositions, 1893," 93. RG 123, National Archives—Washington, D.C. There is some discrepancy in the records as to whether Cornelio was killed in this raid, or only severely wounded and killed in a later raid.

95. *The War of the Rebellion*, L:422–23, 431–32; "Depositions, 1893," 10. See also "Elias, Jesus Maria," Arizona State University Libraries: Hayden Arizona Pioneer Biographies Collection; and *Alta California*, September 11, 1863, in Andrew E. Masich, *The Civil War in Arizona*, 257–60.

96. "Elías, Juan," Biographical File and "Reminiscences of Amelia Elías," Arizona Historical Society; *War of the Rebellion*, L:423.

97. *Alta California*, May 27, 1863, in Masich, *The Civil War in Arizona*, 256; "Depositions, 1893," 47; "Elias, Jesus Maria," Arizona State University Libraries: Hayden Arizona Pioneer Biographies Collection; Gustafson, ed., *John Spring's Arizona*, 247.

98. "Depositions, 1893," 54–55.

99. Ibid., 52, 54–57.

100. "Reminiscences of Alvina Rosenda Contreras," Arizona Historical Society; *Arizona Weekly Enterprise*, October 29, 1887; F. Aragon to Secretary of State, November 26, 1888 (Folio 9880, Expediente 8, 1888); and F. Aragon to Secretary of State, December 9, 1888 (Folio 9882, Expediente 8, 1888). Fondo Ejecutivo, Ramo Apaches, Archivo General del Estado de Sonora.

101. Grenville Goodwin and Neil Goodwin, *The Apache Diaries*, 45–47; Helge Ingstad, *The Apache Indians*, 170–80; and Alonso, *Thread of Blood*, 44–46.

102. "Reminiscences of Alvina Rosenda Contreras," Arizona Historical Society.

103. "Depositions, 1893," 49–52. I have restored the spelling of Captain Chiquito's name to its Spanish rendition, Capitán Chiquito.

104. James Carleton to Joseph West, October 11, 1862, in *The War of the Rebellion*, XV:580; *Arizona Miner*, May 20, 1871.

105. "Report from Camp McDowell, Oct. 16, 1865," 1–2. Clarence Bennett Papers, MS 69, Arizona Historical Society. Emphasis appears in the original. See also *The War of the Rebellion*, L:372.

106. "Depositions, 1893," 71, 117–19. *Arizona Citizen*, April 15, 1871, offers a slightly different tally of the number of animals taken by the Apache.

107. "Depositions, 1893," 3–6, 117–19.

108. *U.S. v. Sidney R. DeLong et al.*, File 2, 42, 57. Records of District Courts of the United States, Arizona Territorial District Court, RG 21, National Archives—Laguna Niguel.

109. See Oury's descriptions of the massacre in *Arizona Daily Star*, June 29, 1879, July 1, 1879; and *Arizona Daily Citizen*, April 7, 1885.

110. Donald L. Horowitz, *The Deadly Ethnic Riot*, 2, 71–123, 124.

111. *Arizona Daily Star*, June 29, 1879, July 1, 1879; *Arizona Daily Citizen*, April 7, 1885; Scott O'Mack, Scott Thompson, and Eric Eugene Klucas, *Little River*, 171.

VIOLENCE: THE AMERICANS

1. Garber, *Gadsden Treaty*, 131; Frederic A. Coffey, "Some General Aspects of the Gadsden Treaty," 145–64.

2. Nathaniel Dwight, *A Short but Comprehensive System of the Geography of the World*, 207–8.

3. Quoted in Reginald Horsman, *Race and Manifest Destiny*, 219.

4. Benjamin D. Wilson, "Narrative," 372. For an early account of American trappers in the Tucson vicinity, see Juan Romero to Governor of Sonora, January 4, 1827 (Folio 74, Expediente 3, 1827). Fondo Ejecutivo, Ramo Apaches, Archivos Generales del Estado de Sonora.

5. Cooke, "Journal of the March of the Mormon Battalion, 1846–1847," 147, 153 n.189, 159–60.

6. Officer, *Hispanic Arizona*, 230–33; K. Beeching, "Diary, 1849." HM 17430, Huntington Library.

7. Edward E. Dunbar, *The Mexican Papers*, 46; *Daily Evening Bulletin*, August 9, 1856; D. W. Meinig, *The Shaping of America*, 152–53. For more on Gadsden's notions of "natural" borders, see Chauncey S. Boucher, "In Re That Aggressive Slavocracy," 37 n.37.

8. Agreement of William Emory and José Salazar Ylarregui; William Emory to José Salazar Ylarregui, January 22, 1855; Emory to Sec. of the Interior, December 27, 1855, in *Presidential Message Communicating Information on the Mexican Boundary Line* (34th Congress, 1st sess., Sen. Executive Doc., No. 57), 9, 56, 62; Emory, *Report on the United States and Mexican Boundary Survey*, I:39.

9. Benedict Anderson, *Imagined Communities*. The dragoons did not reach Tucson until November 1856. B. Sacks, "The Origins of Fort Buchanan."

10. Lockwood, *Life in Old Tucson*, 9; Browne, *Adventures in the Apache Country*, 22.

11. Odie B. Faulk, *Arizona: A Short History*, 80, 117–19; *Charter and By-Laws of the Sopori Land and Mining Company*, 20. For early descriptions of the Gadsden Purchase, see "The Mesilla Valley," *DeBow's Review* (August 1856): 164–65; and "The New Territory of Arizona," *DeBow's Review* (November 1857): 543–44.

12. Nicolson, ed., *The Arizona of Joseph Pratt Allyn*, 179.

13. William H. Emory, *Notes of a Military Reconnaissance from Fort Leavenworth*, 76.

14. Browne, *Adventures in the Apache Country*, 107.

15. Sylvester Mowry, *Arizona and Sonora*, 30. See also Ferdinand Andrews, "The Indians of New Mexico and Arizona," I:1, 113. HM 989, Huntington Library.

16. Wilson, "Narrative," 372; Calhoun to Brown, May 10, 1850, in Annie Heloise Abel, ed., *The Official Correspondence of James S. Calhoun*, 196.

17. Clarke, ed., *Original Journals of Henry Smith Turner*, 86, 105; John G. Parke, *Report of Explorations*, 13; and Ralph A. Smith, *Borderlander*.

18. A. A. Humphreys, *Preliminary Report Concerning Explorations and Surveys*, 28; Reid, *Reid's Tramp*, 184. See also Raphael Pumpelly, *Across America and Asia*, 13; Francis Paul Prucha, *The Great Father*, I:356, 371–72; Joseph F. Park, "The Apaches in Mexican-American Relations," 50–57.

19. *Arizonian*, July 21, 1859; Charles D. Poston, *Building a State in Apache Land*, 67; and J. Hall, *Travels and Adventures in Sonora*, 143–44. Poston's book is a reprint of several articles by the same name that he wrote for *Overland Monthly* in 1894.

20. Poston, *Building a State in Apache Land*, 93; Gustafson, ed., *John Spring's Arizona*, 52; Mowry, *Arizona and Sonora*, 32; Altshuler, ed., *Latest from Arizona!* 47, 49; Jay J. Wagoner, *Arizona Territory, 1863–1912*, 417; Samuel Woodworth Cozzens, *The Marvelous Country*, 84–85.

21. *Annual Report of the Commissioner of Indian Affairs, 1854*, 225.

22. Quoted in George P. Hammond, ed., *Campaigns in the West, 1856–1861*, viii, 13.

23. Ibid., 29–30, 32; *Annual Report of the Commissioner of Indian Affairs, 1857*, 563, 582–84.

24. *Arizonian*, March 31, 1859, April 28, 1859.

25. Conner, *Joseph Reddeford Walker and the Arizona Adventure*, 221.

26. Hall, *Travel and Adventures in Sonora*, 210; *Weekly Arizonian*, July 21, 1859.

27. Camillo C. C. Carr, "The Days of the Empire—Arizona, 1866–1869," *Journal of the United States Cavalry Association* 2:4 (March 1889): 3–22, in Cozzens, ed., *Eyewitnesses to the Indian Wars*, 19; Conner, *Joseph Reddeford Walker and the Arizona Adventure*, 70.

28. *Annual Report of the Board of Indian Commissioners, 1870*, 106; *Annual Report of the Commissioner of Indian Affairs, 1868*, 141.

29. Poston, *Building a State in Apache Land*, 97–99; Faulk, *Arizona*, 96.

30. *Annual Report of the Secretary of War, 1859*, 300–301.

31. Poston, *Building a State in Apache Land*, 97–99. The "Bascom Affair" has for obvious reasons emerged as one of the most famous incidents in Arizona history. There are multiple accounts of the event, of which one of the most complete can be found in Edwin R. Sweeney, *Cochise*, 142–65. I have largely followed here the details offered by Poston, as I find it more important to understand how Poston framed the event than trying to sift out "what really happened."

32. *Arizona Weekly Citizen*, February 10, 1872; Altshuler, ed., *Latest from Arizona!* 106.

33. *Weekly Arizona Miner*, July 29, 1871; *Message of Governor Richard C. McCormick to the Third Legislative Assembly of the Territory of Arizona, October 8, 1866*, and *Message of Governor McCormick to the Fourth Legislature of Arizona, Delivered September 9, 1867*, in State Department Territorial Papers, Arizona, 1864–1872, RG 59, M342, National Archives—Microfilm Publications.

34. *Weekly Arizona Miner*, October 26, 1864; Mowry, *Arizona and Sonora*, 68.

35. *The War of the Rebellion*, L:1247; William A. Bell, "On the Basin of Colorado and the Great Basin of North America," 104; Patrick Brantlinger, *Dark Vanishings*, 50–52.

36. Cremony, *Life Among the Apaches*, 197; Robert Lee Kerby, *The Confederate Invasion of New Mexico and Arizona*, 29, 36.

37. Poston, *Building a State in Apache Land*, 103–4; Kerby, *The Confederate Invasion*, 124; *The War of the Rebellion*, L:475, 626–30, 635–41.

38. *Acts, Resolutions and Memorials Adopted by the First Legislative Assembly of the Territory of Arizona*, 69–70, 78–79; Jerry Don Thompson, *Colonel John Robert Baylor*, 75; J. M. Chivington to E. R. S. Canby, June 11, 1862, in *The War of the Rebellion*, Series 1, Volume IX, 677.

39. Nicolson, ed., *The Arizona of Joseph Pratt Allyn*, 68. This surprise attack is known in Arizona folklore as the "Massacre at Bloody Tanks." See Dan L. Thrapp, *The Conquest of Apacheria*, 31.

40. Nicolson, ed., *The Arizona of Joseph Pratt Allyn*, 70, 76; *Arizona Miner*, November 30, 1866, January 26, 1867.

41. Conner, *Joseph Reddeford Walker and the Arizona Adventure*, 188; Wesley Merritt, "Incidents of Indian Campaigning in Arizona," *Harper's New Monthly Magazine* 80:459 (April 1890): 725–31, in Cozzens, ed., *Eyewitnesses to the Indian Wars*, 156. For more on "defensive conquest," see Richard White, "Frederick Jackson Turner and Buffalo Bill," 6–10; and Philip J. Deloria, *Indians in Unexpected Places*, 15–21. For more on Conner, see "Connor, Daniel Ellis," Arizona State University Libraries: Hayden Arizona Pioneer Biographies Collection, http://www.asu.edu/lib/archives/azbio/azbio.htm (accessed 6/29/05). The Hayden biography seems to misspell Conner's name.

42. Conner, *Joseph Reddeford Walker and the Arizona Adventure*, 227–28, 302–3.

43. *Acts, Resolutions and Memorials Adopted by the First Legislative Assembly of the Territory of Arizona*, 69–70, 78–79; Browne, *Adventures in the Apache Country*, 100.

44. Herman J. Viola, ed., *The Memoirs of Charles Henry Veil*, 96–97.

45. Conner, *Joseph Reddeford Walker and the Arizona Adventure*, 34–41; Edwin R. Sweeney, *Mangas Coloradas*, 448–62; Orson S. Fowler, *Human Science*, 1195–97.

46. Conner, *Joseph Reddeford Walker and the Arizona Adventure*, 189–90.

47. King Woolsey to Gen. Carleton, March 29, 1864. Plaintiff's Exhibit No. 95, Box 401. Western Apache, Docket 22, Records of the Indian Claims Commission, RG 279, National Archives—Washington, D.C. Emphasis appears in the original.

48. Conner, *Joseph Reddeford Walker and the Arizona Adventure*, 232.

49. Walter Scribner Schuyler to George Washington Schuyler, September 29, 1872. WS 79, Huntington Library; Conner, *Joseph Reddeford Walker and the Arizona Adventure*, 232.

50. Conner, *Joseph Reddeford Walker and the Arizona Adventure*, 232.

51. Ibid., 266–67.

52. Ibid., 266–68.

53. *Annual Report of the Commissioner of Indian Affairs, 1869*, 102–3, 223; *Weekly Arizonan*, December 3, 1870.

54. The global discourse on the extinction of indigenous peoples is explored in Brantlinger, *Dark Vanishings*, 1–16. Graves's report appears in the *Annual Report of the Commissioner of Indian Affairs, 1854*, 389.

55. *Weekly Arizonan*, March 11, 1871.

56. *Weekly Arizona Miner*, October 26, 1864.

57. *The War of the Rebellion*, Series I, Volume IV, 20–21; *The War of the Rebellion*, L:399, 942.

58. *The War of the Rebellion*, XV:857, 914, 917, 919.

59. *The War of the Rebellion*, L:929, 1147; *The War of the Rebellion*, XV: 579, 580.

60. Masich, *The Civil War in Arizona*, 63–64; *The War of the Rebellion*, L:367.

61. For the original text of Lieber's code, see *The War of the Rebellion*, III:148–64; and *The War of the Rebellion*, Series 3, Volume II, 301–9. For more on the contrast between the U.S. Army's treatment of Confederates and American Indians, see Mark Grimsley, "'Rebels' and 'Redskins,'" 137–61.

62. Altshuler, ed., *Latest from Arizona!* 24; *Annual Report of the Commissioner of Indian Affairs, 1853*, 438–39.

63. For images of reconciliation, see *The American Pioneer, An Oration Delivered at Prescott, Arizona, before the Arizona Pioneer Society by Governor McCormick*, 11. The tallies of Apache casualties come from George W. Webb, *Chronological List of Engagements Between the Regular Army of the United States and Various Tribes of Hostile Indians Which Occurred During the Years 1790 to 1898, Inclusive*, 21–51.

64. Alonzo E. Davis, *Pioneer Days in Arizona by One Who Was There*, 106–7. Huntington: MS Film 135. The settler King Woolsey also used strychnine against Indians. See Bourke, *On the Border with Crook*, 118.

65. Cremony, *Life Among the Apaches*, 188; Cozzens, *The Marvelous Country*, 83. See also Mowry, *Arizona and Sonora*, 68; *Weekly Arizonan*, March 11, 1871; and Sherry L. Smith, *The View from Officers' Row*, 157–58. For more on the extermination campaign against wolves in the nineteenth century, see Peter Coates, "'Unusually Cunning, Vicious, and Treacherous,'" 163–84; and Jon T. Coleman, *Vicious*.

66. "General Howard's Mission," *Army and Navy Journal*, April 27, 1872, in Cozzens, ed., *Eyewitnesses to the Indian Wars*, 113; Conner, *Joseph Reddeford Walker and the Arizona Adventure*, 207; *Resources of Arizona*, 23; William A. Bell, "Ten Days' Journey in Southern Arizona," 55; Charles D. Poston, "History of the Apaches" (unpublished manuscript, 1886), 53. AZ 169, Special Collections, University of Arizona. The mutilation "in a manner too shocking to relate" to which Conner referred likely involved cutting off the male genitals.

67. Cremony, *Life Among the Apaches*, 227; Martha Summerhayes, *Vanished Arizona*, 117. Emphasis appears in the original.

68. Richard Irving Dodge, *Our Wild Indians*, 639–40, 641; Robert W. Mardock, "Indian Rights Movement Until 1887," 303.

69. Prucha, *Great Father*, I:479–83, 501–33.

70. Lawrie Tatum, *Our Red Brothers*, xvii.

71. *Annual Report of the Commissioner of Indian Affairs, 1869*, 50; Robert M. Utley, *The Indian Frontier of the American West, 1846–1890*, 129–34.

72. Grant quoted in Utley, *The Indian Frontier of the American West*, 130; Parker quoted in Prucha, *Great Father*, I:534.

73. *Annual Report of the Commissioner of Indian Affairs, 1869*, 103; Camillo C. C. Carr, "The Days of the

Empire—Arizona, 1866–1869," *Journal of the United States Cavalry Association* 2:4 (March 1889): 3–22, in Cozzens, ed., *Eyewitnesses to the Indian Wars*, 31; *Executive Orders Relating to Indian Reservations, 1855–1922*, 3–37.

74. Nicolson, ed., *The Arizona of Joseph Pratt Allyn*, 177; *Weekly Arizonan*, November 27, 1869; Thrapp, *The Conquest of Apacheria*, 33.

75. *Weekly Arizonan*, April 15, 1871, September 10, 1870.

76. Ibid., July 23, 1870.

77. *Arizona Citizen*, March 11, 1871; *Revised Outline Descriptions of the Posts and Stations of Troops in the Military Division of the Pacific Commanded by Major-General John M. Schofield* (1872), 5; Byrd H. Granger, *Will C. Barnes' Arizona Place Names*, 295. The quote about the Apache trail appears in Smith, "Indians in American-Mexican Relations before the War of 1846," 40.

78. *Annual Report of the Commissioner of Indian Affairs, 1871*, 485, 491. For an alternative rendering of the chief's name, see *Third Annual Report of the Board of Indian Commissioners, 1871*, 45.

79. *Annual Report of the Commissioner of Indian Affairs, 1871*, 485. It is theorized that this return of Whitman's report was intended to deflect responsibility for any failure in the effort to gather the Apache at Camp Grant from Stoneman to Whitman. See James L. Haley, *Apaches*, 258–59.

80. *Annual Report of the Commissioner of Indian Affairs, 1871*, 486–88. For a vivid description of Camp Grant in the 1870s, see Bourke, *On the Border with Crook*, 2–5.

81. *Annual Report of the Commissioner of Indian Affairs, 1871*, 485–86.

82. *Weekly Arizonan*, March 11, 1871; *Arizona Citizen*, March 11, 1871.

83. Stoneman quoted in Constance Wynn Altshuler, *Chains of Command*, 185; *Report of Colonel George Stoneman*, 1–2. See also Robert Wooster, *The Military and United States Indian Policy, 1865–1903*, 147.

84. *Report of Colonel George Stoneman*, 5–6; *Weekly Arizonan*, January 28, 1871.

85. *Memorial and Affidavits Showing Outrages Perpetrated by the Apache Indians, in the Territory of Arizona during the Years 1869 and 1870*. For discussions of the meetings, see *Arizona Citizen*, January 21, 1871, January 28, 1871; and *Weekly Arizonan*, January 28, 1871.

86. *Memorial and Affidavits*, 4, 14, 15, 16, 17, 20, 21, 22.

87. *Arizona Citizen*, March 25, 1871, April 1, 1871.

88. Cornelius C. Smith Jr., *William Sanders Oury*. See also Texas State Historical Association: Handbook of Texas Online, "Oury, William Sanders," http://www.tsha.utexas.edu/handbook/online/articles/OO/fou1.html; "Mier Expedition," http://www.tsha.utexas.edu/handbook/online/articles/MM/qym2.html (accessed 9/2/05).

89. Smith, *William Sanders Oury*, 75–83.

90. Ibid., 147–48; Frank Lockwood, *Life in Old Tucson*, 93–98; Josephine Clifford, "Camp-Life in Arizona," 246. For evidence of Oury as a translator, see "Minute Records, District Court of the First Judicial District of Arizona, May 31, 1864–April 16, 1874," 193. Records of District Courts of the United States, Arizona Territorial District Court, RG 21, National Archives—Laguna Niguel.

91. *Weekly Arizonan*, April 22, 1871.

92. "A Paper on Eskiminzin and his band of Apache Indians, 1867–1871 by Pioneer F. H. Goodwin. Read March 1, 1887, before the Society of Arizona Pioneers." Folder 3, Francis Goodwin Papers, MS 297, Arizona Historical Society. For an intimate portrait of Wooster by one of his business partners, see Gustafson, ed., *John Spring's Arizona*, 82–95, 188–90, 205–10.

93. *Arizona Citizen*, March 25, 1871; *Weekly Arizonan*, March 25, 1871.

94. *Arizona Citizen*, March 25, 1871, April 1, 1871; *Weekly Arizonan*, March 25, 1871. There was considerable confusion in the newspaper coverage as to Aguirre's last name. It was rendered in various newspaper accounts as "Aggerra" and "Iguera." *Arizona Citizen*, March 25, 1871; *Arizona Weekly Citizen*, October 28, 1871. Wooster and Aguirre are shown sharing a house in the Tubac Schedules, 5. Records of the Bureau of the Census, Ninth Census of the United States, 1870, Arizona Territory, RG 29, M593A, National Archives—Microfilm Publications. In addition to the folklore surrounding Aguirre that suggests a romantic link between her and Wooster, it is revealing that the census enumerator listed Aguirre's occupation as "keeping house." This was the standard description for married women; female employees were instead listed as "domestic servant." See Susan Johnson, "Sharing Bed and Board," 77–91.

95. For retellings of Aguirre's story, see *Arizona Daily Citizen*, January 14, 1891; and Frank C. Lockwood, *Pioneer Days in Arizona*, 165. "A Paper on Eskiminzin and his band of Apache Indians, 1867–1871 by Pioneer F. H. Goodwin. Read March 1, 1887, before the Society of Arizona Pioneers," 5–6. Folder 3, Francis Goodwin Papers, MS 297, Arizona Historical Society.

96. *Arizona Citizen*, May 6, 1871. For contemporary coverage of Aguirre's brooch, see the *Territorial Enterprise*, May 14, 1871, and the *Alta California*, May 11, 1871. For the denial of seeing any jewelry, see testimony of Gertrude McWard in *U.S. v. Sidney R. DeLong et al.*, File 2, 123–24. Records of District Courts of the United States, Arizona Territorial District Court, RG 21, National Archives—Laguna Niguel.

97. *Alta California*, May 12, 1871.

98. Center for Desert Archaeology: Rio Nuevo Project, City of Tucson Property Records, 1862–1864, http://www.cdarc.org/pages/heritage/rio_nuevo/people/records/property_1862.php (accessed 2/11/08).

99. Technically, Captain Stanwood was the commander of Camp Grant at the time of the attack. But he was away on a scout, leaving Whitman in charge of the fort.

100. This information is drawn from Oury's recollections and from the transcript of the trial. For more on Stevens and Hughes, see the profile by Frank Lockwood in the *Arizona Daily Star*, December 1, 1940, and Hughes's obituary in the *Arizona Daily Star*, June 21, 1917.

101. The rifles furnished to Arizona's adjutant general are described in the *Arizona Daily Citizen*, November 26, 1870. The role of technology in facilitating the act of killing is discussed in Joanna Bourke, *An Intimate History of Killing*, xvii–xix.

VIOLENCE: THE Nₙēē

1. Ferguson and Colwell-Chanthaphonh, *History Is in the Land*, 225–26. For a thoughtful discussion of this question in relation to another Athapaskan community, the Navajo/Diné, see Jennifer Nez Denetdale, *Reclaiming Diné History*, 7.

2. Eva Tulene Watt, *Don't Let the Sun Step Over You*, xv–xvi. Edward Spicer observed in 1962 that "Apaches complain constantly that all the history which is in print misrepresents them." Spicer, *Cycles of Conquest*, 593.

3. Watt, *Don't Let the Sun Step Over You*, xxiv; Goodwin, *Social Organization*, xv, 521; Goodwin, "Experiences of an Indian Scout," 39.

4. Goodwin, *Social Organization*, 130–31; Charles R. Kaut, "Western Apache Clan and Phratry Organization," 140–41; Keith Basso, *Western Apache Witchcraft*, 21–23; Keith Basso, "Western Apache," 472–76; Willem de Reuse (personal communication, 8/3/06).

5. Grenville Goodwin, "The Social Divisions and Economic Life of the Western Apache," 55–57; Goodwin, *Social Organization*, 167–68; Keith Basso, ed., *Western Apache Raiding and Warfare*, 270–75; Basso, "Western Apache," 475–79.

6. Goodwin, *Social Organization*, 2, 8, 21, 83. For the San Carlos Apache rendering of Chiricahua Apache, see de Reuse, *A Practical Grammar of the San Carlos Apache Language*, 194.

7. Basso, "Western Apache," 470–74; Grenville Goodwin, "Clans of the Western Apache," 176–82. The precise number of clans is something of an open question. Goodwin identifies sixty-one, Basso sixty. See also Charles R. Kaut, *The Western Apache Clan System*.

8. Goodwin, *Social Organization*, 608–9.

9. J. Loring Haskell, *Southern Athapaskan Migration, A.D. 200–1750*, 9–11; Robert W. Young, "Apachean Languages," 393–400; Miles and Machula, eds., *History of the San Carlos Apache*, 6. It is important to note that for all the parallels between the origin tales and the linguistic evidence, most clan legends cannot be interpreted as describing a complete migration from the Arctic, the hypothesized source of the Apaches' ancestors, as the legends give origin sites within what would today be northern Arizona. Furthermore, some Apaches, while acknowledging the linguistic links to Athapaskan speakers elsewhere, argue that it is just as possible that the migration flow was south to north as north to south.

10. Goodwin, *Social Organization*, 106–10; Goodwin, "Clans of the Western Apache," 180–82;

Goodwin, "The Characteristics and Function of Clan in a Southern Athapascan Culture," 398–99; Ferguson and Colwell-Chanthaphonh, *History Is in the Land*, 192; Jack D. Forbes, "The Early Western Apache, 1300–1700." For the proper spellings of the Apache names for other groups, see de Reuse, *A Practical Grammar of the San Carlos Apache Language*, 196.

11. "A Ride with the Apaches," 341–45; Karns, trans., *Unknown Arizona and Sonora*, 46, 49, 50; Report of General Juan Fernández de la Fuente, 1695, in Naylor and Polzer, eds., *The Presidio and Militia on the Northern Frontier of New Spain*, I:585; Goodwin, "Social Divisions of the Western Apache," 61; Bruce E. Hilpert, "The Indé (Western Apaches)," 73–74. The opposing argument that the Janos, Jocomes, and others were in fact Apaches all along is made in Jack D. Forbes, "The Janos, Jocomes, Mansos and Sumas Indians."

12. Winfred Buskirk, *The Western Apache*, 169–73; Grenville Goodwin, *Myths and Tales of the White Mountain Apache*, 56–57; Watt, *Don't Let the Sun Step Over You*, 60–61; Wallace Johnson interview with Diana Hadley, Bureau of Land Management, Safford, Arizona.

13. Dorothy Bray, ed., *Western Apache–English Dictionary*, 369, 395; Carol J. Condie, ed., *Vocabulary of the Apache or Indé Language of Arizona and New Mexico*, 33–35.

14. For more on feral animals and the Apache eating of mule, horse, and burro meat, see Pfefferkorn, *Sonora*, 101, 144–45, 147.

15. My description of these activities leans heavily on Keith H. Basso's essential *Western Apache Raiding and Warfare*, 16–17, 254; the translation and spelling of Nṇaa ch'iidn was provided to me by Willem de Reuse (personal communication, 8/2/06).

16. Basso, *Western Apache Raiding and Warfare*, 50.

17. Eve Ball, *In the Days of Victorio*, 12. See also Juliana Barr, *Peace Came in the Form of a Woman*, 164–65.

18. Basso, *Western Apache Raiding and Warfare*, 16–18; Goodwin, *Social Organization*, 412.

19. Basso, *Western Apache Raiding and Warfare*, 77, 284–85; Pfefferkorn, *Sonora*, 149–50.

20. Basso, *Western Apache Raiding and Warfare*, 264–65.

21. Report of Juan Bautista de Anza, 1735, in Polzer and Sheridan, eds., *The Presidio and Militia on the Northern Frontier of New Spain*, II:303, 307; Bray, ed., *Western Apache–English Dictionary*, 150; Goodwin, *Social Organization of the Western Apache*, 94–95.

22. Basso, *Western Apache Raiding and Warfare*, 29; Goodwin, *Myths and Tales of the White Mountain Apache*, v–vii; Keith Basso, *Wisdom Sits in Places*, 48–51. Basso's work is of central import to understanding the role of storytelling among the Western Apache.

23. Goodwin, *Myths and Tales of the White Mountain Apache*, 9.

24. Pliny Earle Goddard, "Myths and Tales from the San Carlos Apache," 47–48.

25. Goodwin, *Social Organization*, 620.

26. Under these conditions, the People's mental map of their homeland came, not surprisingly, to be organized around a series of sacred mountain peaks. See, for example, Ferguson and Colwell-Chanthaphonh, *History Is in the Land*, 193.

27. I do not mean to suggest in this passage that the Apache were the only indigenous group in all of Spanish America to be targeted for extermination. But with the possible exception of the much smaller Seri population along the Sonora coast, no other group in Pimería Alta received as brutal treatment from the Spanish as did the Apache.

28. Karns, *Unknown Arizona and Sonora*, 35, 67, 172–73.

29. Report of General Juan Fernández de la Fuente, 1695, in Naylor and Polzer, eds., *The Presidio and Militia on the Northern Frontier of New Spain*, I:642, 648.

30. Carl Sauer, "A Spanish Expedition into the Arizona Apacheria," 8–11; Ferguson and Colwell-Chanthaphonh, *History Is in the Land*, 219; George P. Hammond, ed., "The Zuñiga Journal, Tucson to Santa Fe," 55, 62.

31. For Apachean beliefs about death, see Morris E. Opler, "The Apachean Culture Pattern and Its Origins," 376–80; Charles R. Kaut, "Notes on Western Apache Religious and Social Organization"; and Basso, *Western Apache Raiding and Warfare*, 313 n.99.

32. Griffen, *Apaches at War and Peace*, 24–25, 168. For an Apache perspective on the use of white flags, see Jason Betzinez with Wilbur Sturtevant Nye, *I Fought with Geronimo*, 137. The place of female imagery in Western Apache religion is discussed in Grenville Goodwin, "White Mountain Apache Religion."

33. Griffen, *Apaches at War and Peace*, 25; Report of Juan Bautista de Anza, in Polzer and Sheridan, eds., *The Presidio and Militia on the Northern Frontier of New Spain*, II:305–6; Kessell, *Friars, Soldiers, and Reformers*, 107. Cynthia Radding discusses an Apache-initiated peace effort at Fronteras in 1762 in *Landscapes of Power and Identity*, 185–88.

34. Dobyns, *Spanish Colonial Tucson*, 98–99; Officer, *Hispanic Arizona*, 346 n.41; Ferguson and Colwell-Chanthaphonh, *History Is in the Land*, 193, 201, 219; Bringas, *Friar Bringas Reports to the King*, 119; Miles and Machula, eds., *History of the San Carlos Apache*, 6, 10; de Reuse, *Practical Grammar of the San Carlos Apache Language*, 73. The possible translation of Nautilnilce was provided me by Willem de Reuse (personal communication, 8/4/06). For more on Nautilnilce, see Pedro de Nava, "Estado que manifiesta de Rancherías Apaches existents de Paz en varios Parajes de la Provincia de Sonora, Nueva Vizcaya, y Nuevo México, y el Número de Personas de ambos sexos de que se compone cada una," May 2, 1793. Audiencia de Guadalajara, Archivo General de Indias, Sevilla. I am indebted to Matt Babcock for sharing this last document with me.

35. John, ed., *Views from the Apache Frontier*, 29; Goodwin, *Social Organization*, 403–6. Pedro de Nava, "Extracto y Resumen de hostilidades ocurridas en las Provincias Ynternas de Nueva España y de las operaciones executadas contra los Enemigos," May 30, 1793, enclosed with Pedro de Nava to Conde del Campo de Alange, No. 21, Chihuahua, May 30, 1793. 7022, Guerra Moderna, Exp. 2, Archivo General de Simancas, Spain. This document also comes to me courtesy of Matt Babcock.

36. Goodwin, *Social Organization*, 177; Barr, *Peace Came in the Form of a Woman*, 5.

37. José Romero to Antonio Narbona, May 21, 1819, in Dobyns, *Spanish Colonial Tucson*, 103. The possible translation of Chilitipagé's name was provided by Willem de Reuse (personal communication, 8/4/06). See also Alexo García Conde to Conde del Venedito, July 19, 1819, Durango, certified copy by Patricio Numana, August 31, 1819, Estado 33 (México), No. 35, Doc. 5, Papeles de Estado, Archivo General de Indias, Sevilla, Spain. Document courtesy of Matt Babcock.

38. McCarty, ed. and trans., *A Frontier Documentary*, 2, 50. There is considerable evidence that the Aravaipa band descended from the Pinal band, probably sometime in the mid-eighteenth century. For an insightful discussion of the connections between the two, see Ian Wilson Record, "Aravaipa: Apache Peoples and the Legacy of Particular Geography and Historical Experience," Ph.D. dissertation, University of Arizona, 2004, 71–73. For unrest among Tucson's *apaches de paz*, see Ignacio Pacheco to Vice Governor of Sonora, March 10, 1826 (Folio 63, Expediente 3, 1826); Ignacio Pacheco to Chief of Police, July 4, 1826 (Folio 72, Expediente 3, 1826). Fondo Ejecutivo, Ramo Apaches, Archivo General del Estado de Sonora.

39. Goodwin, *Social Organization*, 616; José Grijalva, October 1, 1831, in McCarty, ed. and trans., *A Frontier Documentary*, 33.

40. Joaquín Vicente Elías to Governor of Sonora, June 21, 1832 (Folio 307, Expediente 7, 1832); Joaquín Vicente Elías to Governor of Sonora, May 21, 1832 (Folio 283, Expediente 7, 1832); "Triunfo sobre los apaches," July 6, 1832 (Folio 316, Expediente 7, 1832). Fondo Ejecutivo, Ramo Apaches, Archivo General del Estado de Sonora. See also José Grijalva, October 1, 1831, in McCarty, ed. and trans., *A Frontier Documentary*, 33; and Kessell, *Friars, Soldiers, and Reformers*, 284. The translation of *apaches mansos* was provided by Willem de Reuse (personal communication, 8/3/06).

41. See Treaty Agreement, March 5, 1836, and José María Martínez to José María Elías González, February 6, 1837, in McCarty, ed. and trans., *A Frontier Documentary*, 50–54; Sweeney, *Cochise*, 24–25. The possible translation for Tutijé was provided by Willem de Reuse (personal communication, 8/4/06).

42. Britton Davis, *The Truth About Geronimo*, 261; Griffen, *Apaches at War and Peace*, 186; Goodwin, *Social Organization*, 93, 685; Goodwin, "White Mountain Apache Religion," 28; Bartlett, *Personal Narrative*, I:329.

43. Betzinez, *I Fought with Geronimo*, 82; Joseph C. Jastrzembski, "Treacherous Towns in Mexico."

44. Timothy Flint, ed., *The Personal Narrative of James O. Pattie of Kentucky*, 114; Mangas Coloradas quoted in Thomas Edwin Farish, *History of Arizona*, II:151–52; Betzinez, *I Fought with Geronimo*, 1, 80. The possible translation of Mangas Coloradas's name was provided by Willem de Reuse (personal communication, 7/19/07).

45. Goodwin, *Social Organization of the Western Apache*, 25, 95; Wilson, "Narrative," 372–73.

46. Goodwin, *Social Organization*, 25, 95.

47. Emory, *Notes of a Military Reconnaissance from Fort Leavenworth*, 60; Basso, *Western Apache Raiding and Warfare*, 19; Charles P. Stone, "Notes on the State of Sonora," 167.

48. Bartlett, *Personal Narrative*, 300–301.

49. Basso, *Western Apache Raiding and Warfare*, 59; Richard Van Valkenburgh, "Apache Ghosts Guard the Aravaipa," 17.

50. *Journal of the Second Annual Conference of the Board of Indian Commissioners, 1873*, 39; Sweeney, *Cochise*, 144. The possible translations of Cochise's name were provided to me by Willem de Reuse (personal communication, 7/19/07).

51. Goodwin, *Social Organization*, 83–85; Sweeney, *Cochise*, 144. The term "talk carriers" comes from the Apache scout Peaches, who was later to play a dramatic role in Geronimo's final surrender. See Tom Horn, *Life of Tom Horn*, 138.

52. *Arizonian*, March 3, 1859; *Annual Report of the Secretary of War, 1859*, II:306.

53. *Arizonian*, March 31, 1859. This event is also described in Goodwin, *Social Organization*, 22; and Van Valkenburgh, "Apache Ghosts Guard the Aravaipa," 17.

54. *Annual Report of the Commissioner of Indian Affairs, 1859*, I:721.

55. *Annual Report of the Secretary of War, 1859*, II:309–10, 323–25; *Arizonian*, May 12, 1859, July 21, 1859; de Reuse, *A Practical Grammar of the San Carlos Apache Language*, 196.

56. *Arizonian*, May 12, 1859; *Annual Report of the Secretary of War, 1860*, II:199–200; Altshuler, ed., *Latest from Arizona!* 30–31, 40–41.

57. Altshuler, ed., *Latest from Arizona!* 47–48, 52, 69; Donald C. Pfanz, *Richard S. Ewell*, 118–19; Tevis, *Arizona in the '50s*, 73.

58. Altshuler, ed., *Latest from Arizona!* 84–85, 114. For the Apache term for Camp Grant, see Chip Colwell-Chanthaphonh, "Western Apache Oral Histories and Traditions of the Camp Grant Massacre," 654.

59. Goodwin, *Social Organization*, 409, 610. The updated spelling of Bìszáhé would be Biszáhé or Biszáhá. See de Reuse, *A Practical Grammar of the San Carlos Apache Language*, 191.

60. Goodwin, *Social Organization*, 409–10, 602. The updated spelling of T'é'nádòljàgé would be Ténádoljagé. See de Reuse, *A Practical Grammar of the San Carlos Apache Language*, 192.

61. Goodwin, *Social Organization*, 411–12.

62. Report of Lt. Col. Clarence E. Bennett, July 6, 1865, in *The War of the Rebellion*, L:415. Although the U.S. Army may have downplayed the role of *apaches mansos* in the 1864 attack on Aravaipa Canyon in an effort to give primacy to its own actions, American folklore has preserved a few references to the *apaches mansos*. See Bell, *New Tracks in North America*, 303, which states that the U.S. troops in 1863 were "guided by some tamed Apaches"; and Fred Contzen, "The Contzens of Tucson," 15–16. "Contzen, Fritz" Biographical File, Arizona Historical Society.

63. John Walker to James L. Collins, September 6, 1860, in *Annual Report of the Commissioner of Indian Affairs, 1860*, 393. Report of Ruggles, Special Agent, Arizona, 1869. Letters Received by the Office of Indian Affairs, Arizona, 1863–9, RG 75, M234, National Archives—Microfilm Publications. Roll 3, Frame 764. *Federal Census—Territory of New Mexico and Territory of Arizona*, 51. One of the few Anglo histories to mention the Bāáchii is Officer, *Hispanic Arizona*, 309, 328–30.

64. Basso, *Western Apache Raiding and Warfare*, 286–87. For Western Apache folklore that makes reference to the Bāáchii, see Goodwin, *Myths and Tales of the White Mountain Apache*, 131, 133, 134, 136, and Goodwin, *Social Organization*, 86. Although historical evidence would seem to suggest a continuity between the *apaches mansos* and the Western Apache bands who settled in Tucson during the Spanish period, many Nnēē described the *apaches mansos* as speaking more like Chiricahua Apaches than Western Apaches. Morris Edward Opler, "The Identity of the Apache Mansos," 725.

65. Carmony, ed., *The Civil War in Apacheland*, 73, 80; Basso, *Western Apache Witchcraft*, 29–39; Report from Fort McDowell, June 21, 1866, 4. Clarence Bennett Papers, MS 69, Arizona Historical Society. It is possible that the husband and wife were from related clans, which would have violated a central marriage taboo among the Western Apache.

66. Report of C. H. Lord, Deputy Indian Agent, Tucson, Arizona, 1866, in *Annual Report of the Commissioner of Indian Affairs, 1866*, 112. See also *Annual Report of the Commissioner of Indian Affairs, 1867*, 165; *Arizona Miner*, May 23, 1866; and *Arizona Citizen*, June 21, 1873. For examples of Apache

tension with the Bāāchii, see Gallego, "Reminiscences of an Arizona Pioneer," 75–76; *Weekly Arizonan*, July 24, 1869; and *Arizona Citizen*, June 21, 1873.

67. M. O. Davidson to D. W. Cooley, January 23, 1866. Letters Received by the Office of Indian Affairs, Arizona, 1863–9, RG 75, M234, National Archives—Microfilm Publications, Frames 241–42; Officer, *Hispanic Arizona*, 309. For references to the *apaches mansos'* connection to Sonoita, see E. A[?] to Congressional Deputies, July 13, 1835 (Folio 33316, Expediente 22, 1835), and Rafael Manjarés and Pablo Valencia to Governor of Sonora, September 3, 1839 (Folio 33318, Expediente 22, 1835). Fondo Ejecutivo, Ramo Apaches, Archivo General del Estado de Sonora.

68. For reference to early Apache visits to what was at the time Fort Stanford, see Carleton to Drum, June 18, 1862, in *The War of the Rebellion*, L:1147. For accounts describing the destruction of crops and food supplies, see returns for August 1869, February 1870, August 1870, and January 1871. Records of the Adjutant General's Office, Returns from U.S. Military Posts, Fort Grant, Arizona, 1865–1874, RG 94, M617C, Roll 414, National Archives—Microfilm Publications. See also William French, Report of a Scout, June 1864. Plaintiff's Exhibit No. 100, Box 401, Western Apache case, Docket 22d, RG 279, Records of the Indian Claims Commission, National Archives—Washington, D.C.

69. The U.S. Army reoccupied Camp Grant in October of 1865. See Return for October 1865, Records of the Adjutant General's Office, Returns from U.S. Military Posts, Fort Grant, Arizona, 1865–1874, RG 94, M617C, Roll 414, National Archives—Microfilm Publications. For more on the treaty, see Guido Ilges to Thomas Foley, December 20, 1866. Letters Received by the Office of Indian Affairs, Arizona, 1863–9, RG 75, M234, National Archives—Microfilm Publications. The possible translations of Askinenha's and Askevanche's names were provided by Willem de Reuse (personal communication, 8/4/06). Professor de Reuse notes that since Apache culture decries selfishness, Hashkeé baa nchį', or "Angry, He Is Selfish," would be an unusual name among the People.

70. Guido Ilges to Thomas Foley, December 20, 1866. Letters Received by the Office of Indian Affairs, Arizona, 1863–9, RG 75, M234, National Archives—Microfilm Publications.

71. Ibid.

72. Ibid.

73. *Annual Report of the Secretary of War, 1867*, 155. Irving McDowell to James B. Fry, February 8, 1867. Letters Received by the Office of Indian Affairs, Arizona, 1863–9, RG 75, M234, National Archives—Microfilm Publications. Guido Ilges's superior officers ruled that Ilges had exceeded his authority in agreeing to grant the Apache safe passage throughout the territory, leading them to label his "so called" treaty "irregular, injudicious, and embarrassing."

74. Report of Julius Shaw, July 14, 1864, in *The War of the Rebellion*, L:370–76; Report from Fort McDowell, June 21, 1866, 3. Clarence Bennett Papers, MS 69, Arizona Historical Society.

75. My thoughts on the meanings behind the stripping of *Innaa* dead can be traced to Palmer Valor's references to the infantlike characteristics of his Mexican opponents. Basso, *Western Apache Raiding and Warfare*, 67, 276, 303 n.19. See also Lepore, *The Name of War*, 79–83; Record, "Aravaipa: Apache Peoples and the Legacy of Particular Geography and Historical Experience," 123–24; Richard J. Perry, *Apache Reservation*, 103–5; David Roberts, *Once They Moved Like the Wind*, 43–49; and *Chicago Tribune*, June 12, 1871.

76. Rusling, *Across America*, 404; Pumpelly, *Across America and Asia*, 24, 47; see also *Daily Evening Bulletin*, November 11, 1859, for an instance of Apaches leaving "a cross surmounted by a white flag" following a raid on an Anglo dwelling.

77. Report from Fort McDowell, June 21, 1866, 3. Clarence Bennett Papers, MS 69, Arizona Historical Society.

78. Report of Royal E. Whitman, May 17, 1871, in *Annual Report of the Board of Indian Commissioners, 1871*, 60. For Apache peace delegations, see Returns for April 1868 and January 1869. Records of the Adjutant General's Office, Returns from U.S. Military Posts, Fort Grant, Arizona, 1865–1874, RG 94, M617C, Roll 414, National Archives—Microfilm Publications. For the modern spelling of Hashkeé bá nzį́n, see Willem J. de Reuse, "Apache Personal Names in Spanish and Early Mexican Documents, II:235–51. Goodwin notes that although commonly translated as "angry," the Apache term "haské" more properly implies "fierceness, bravery, and fighting ability." Goodwin, *Social Organization*, 522, 580.

79. Report of Royal E. Whitman, May 17, 1871, in *Annual Report of the Board of Indian Commissioners, 1871*, 60.

80. Quoted in Colwell-Chanthaphonh, "Western Apache Oral Histories and Traditions of the Camp Grant Massacre," 654–55. This article is invaluable in assembling, comparing, and annotating most of the known Western Apache narratives of the massacre. The possible translation of Bi ja gush kai ye was provided by Willem de Reuse (personal communication, 8/4/06).

81. *U.S. v. Sidney R. DeLong et al.*, File 2, 16–17. Records of District Courts of the United States, Arizona Territorial District Court, RG 21, National Archives—Laguna Niguel.

82. Ibid.

83. Chip Colwell-Chanthaphonh, "Western Apache Oral Histories and Traditions of the Camp Grant Massacre," 657. For more on the notion of haunted landscapes, see Judith Richardson, *Possessions*.

PART II
JUSTICE

1. Bench Warrant, *U.S. v. Sidney R. DeLong et al.*, File 1. Records of District Courts of the United States, Arizona Territorial District Court, RG 21, National Archives—Laguna Niguel.

2. Ibid. For more on the difficulties of bringing the case to trial, see Larry D. Ball, *The United States Marshals of New Mexico and Arizona Territory, 1846–1912*, 67–71; and William B. Blankenburg, "The Role of the Press in an Indian Massacre, 1871," 68. There is a lengthy interview with Stoneman in the *Chicago Tribune*, June 12, 1871.

3. Blankenburg, "The Role of the Press in an Indian Massacre, 1871," 68–69.

4. *Daily Evening Bulletin*, December 27, 1871. The courthouse and adjoining plaza are described in Gustafson, ed., *John Spring's Arizona*, 274.

5. *U.S. v. Sidney R. DeLong et al.*, File 2, 6–7. Records of District Courts of the United States, Arizona Territorial District Court, RG 21, National Archives—Laguna Niguel.

6. Ibid., 121–22.

7. Ibid., 42–46, 50–52, 56–57, 122–23, 126–27. For more on Contzen, see "Contzen, Frederick (Fritz)." Arizona State University Libraries: Hayden Arizona Pioneer Biographies Collection, http://www.asu.edu/lib/archives/azbio/index.html (accessed 12/7/07).

8. *U.S. v. Sidney R. DeLong et al.*, File 2, 50, 90, 133–35; File 3, 149. Records of District Courts of the United States, Arizona Territorial District Court, RG 21, National Archives—Laguna Niguel. See also *Weekly Arizonan*, January 28, 1871; Thrapp, *Conquest of Apacheria*, 92–93; and Blankenburg, "The Role of the Press in an Indian Massacre," 68–69.

9. Titus's charge to the jury is reprinted in the *Arizona Weekly Citizen*, December 16, 1871.

10. *Weekly Arizona Miner*, December 30, 1871.

PART III
MEMORY: THE O'ODHAM

1. Thomas, "Papago Land Use," 372.

2. Underhill, *A Papago Calendar Record*, 36–37.

3. Kilcrease, "Ninety-Five Years of History," 302.

4. Russell, "The Pima Indians," 53.

5. Wilbur to Bendell, October 17, 1871: 4–11. Letterbook of Rueben Augustine Wilbur, 1871–74, AZ 344. Special Collections, University of Arizona.

6. Wilbur to Bendell, December 7, 1871: 21–24, and December 31, 1871: 39–47. Letterbook of Rueben Augustine Wilbur, 1871–74, AZ 344. Special Collections, University of Arizona.

7. *Among the Pimas: Or, The Mission to the Pima and Maricopa Indians*, 73.

8. Transcripts of the truce negotiations can be found in "General Howard's Treaties," 620–27; *Arizona Miner*, June 8, 1872; and *Arizona Weekly Citizen*, May 25, 1872, June 8, 1872. For more on Galerita,

see his obituary in the *Arizona Sentinel*, December 20, 1879; for more on Antonio Azul, see Shaw, *A Pima Past*, 63–65, 124.

9. Kilcrease, "Ninety-Five Years of History," 302; Wilbur to Bendell, Oct. 4, 1872. See also "Statement made by Papago Indians Regarding Property Stolen From Them in August 1872," in "Conflicts, 1872–1873," Box 1, Subject Files of the Indian Agent, 1871–79, Papago Agency, Records of the Bureau of Indian Affairs, RG 75, National Archives—Laguna Niguel; and *Arizona Weekly Citizen*, September 14, 1872: 3.

10. Russell, "The Pima Indians," 54. According to John G. Bourke, who was among the U.S. forces at this attack, some seventy-six Apaches were killed in this encounter. Bourke, *On the Border with Crook*, 196–201.

11. Underhill, *A Papago Calendar Record*, 39. I have updated Underhill's translations of the terms for San Xavier del Bac and Tucson.

12. Russell, "The Pima Indians," 32–33, 54–56; Alfonso Ortiz, "The Gila River Piman Water Problem: An Ethnohistorical Account," 252; Paul H. Ezell, "History of the Pima," 158–59; and David H. DeJong, "Forced to Abandon Their Farms."

13. *Arizona Weekly Citizen*, May 10, 1873, October 26, 1872, July 5, 1873; *Weekly Arizonan*, March 11, 1871; *Arizona Daily Citizen*, December 23, 1879; *Arizona Weekly Miner*, April 1, 1871; Ortiz, "The Gila River Piman Water Problem," 248–50; George Andrews to Eli Parker, November 9, 1869, frame 798, in Letters Received by the Office of Indian Affairs, Arizona, 1863–9, M 234, National Archives—Microfilm Publications.

14. Underhill, "Autobiography of a Papago Woman," 51; Underhill, *A Papago Calendar Record*, 47. The American perspective on this conflict is given in *Arizona Daily Star*, May 17, 1885, May 27, 1885; and *Arizona Daily Citizen*, May 18, 1885, May 19, 1885, May 21, 1885. According to the *Daily Star*, the People's quarrel was with an American named E. W. Dobbs, not a Mexican. This confusion may suggest the O'odham's occasional difficulty at distinguishing between the two groups.

15. For accusations of Tohono O'odham smuggling, see *Arizona Republic*, September 1, 1897; and *Arizona Daily Star*, October 3, 1896. For more on the raid on El Plomo, consult *Phoenix Weekly Herald*, April 28, 1898; and Darrow Dolan, "The Plomo Papers."

16. *Among the Pimas*, 59; James McCarthy, *A Papago Traveler*, 9. See also *Trails to Tiburón*, 47; and Theodore Rios and Kathleen Mullen Sands, *Telling a Good One*, 95, 204–5.

17. The villages of Santa Rosa, Ak Chin, Anegam, and Sil Nagia (Ge Aji), for example, had their young men learn war ceremonies after battling straw men into the 1950s. See Underhill et al., *Rainhouse and Ocean*, 89–90.

18. Underhill, *A Papago Calendar Record*, 56. I have updated Underhill's translation of San Xavier del Bac.

19. Papago Chiefs to Commissioner Burke, March 16, 1929, in *Survey of Conditions of the Indians in the United States*, Part 17: 8458–59.

20. F. S. Herndon to Commissioner of Indian Affairs, [1915]. File 307.4 (1915). Central Classified File, San Xavier Agency, 1907–39, Records of the Bureau of Indian Affairs, RG 75, National Archives—Washington, D.C. Archival documentation of the growing tensions between the Tohono O'odham and Mexicans and Americans alike in the early twentieth century is abundant. See, for example, Madeleine Mathiot, ed., "The Reminiscences of Juan Dolores," 233–315; Henry McQuigg to R. M. Blatchford, January 15, 1915. File 175 (1914); Jewell Martin to Commissioner of Indian Affairs, July 23, 1917. File 175 (1917); John F. Truesdell, "Memorandum Concerning Encroachments of Whites Upon the Papago Indian Country in Arizona." File 308.2 (1915). Central Classified File, San Xavier Agency, 1907–39, Records of the Bureau of Indian Affairs, RG 75, National Archives—Washington, D.C. Carlos Rios, Pablo Rios, Nunca Siembra, and Little Chico to Commissioner of Indian Affairs, August 3, 1900. Correspondence Sent, 1900–1910, Box 3. Subject Files of Farmer-in-Charge, John M. Berger, 1898–1910, Papago Agency, Records of the Bureau of Indian Affairs, RG 75, National Archives—Laguna Niguel.

21. Underhill, *A Papago Calendar Record*, 38. This account resonates with an Akimel O'odham account on the origin of the Apache. See Anna Moore Shaw, *Pima Indian Legends*, 4–5.

22. Shaw, *A Pima Past*, 63–65. The present-day spelling of "house foundation" would be *ki: ṣoncud.* Colleen Fitzgerald (personal communication, 8/29/07).

23. Webb, *A Pima Remembers*, 48. For more on the Tohono O'odham and Akimel O'odham in the twentieth century, see Thomas E. Sheridan, "The O'odham (Pimas and Papagos)," 115–40; and Eric V. Meeks, "The Tohono O'odham, Wage Labor, and Resistant Adaptation, 1900–1930."

MEMORY: LOS VECINOS

1. *Arizona Miner,* June 8, 1872; *Arizona Citizen,* May 6, 1871.
2. Bench Warrant for S. R. DeLong, William Oury, D. A. Bennett, and Others, October 23, 1871. *U.S. v. S.R. DeLong et al.,* Records of District Courts of the United States, Arizona Territorial District Court, RG 21, National Archives—Laguna Niguel.
3. *Arizona Citizen,* June 10, 1871.
4. I base this judgment on the fact that in their depositions taken in 1893, Juan and Tomás Elías, as well as several of their neighbors, testified in Spanish rather than English. Juan also confirms that he can read and write in Spanish. "Depositions, 1893," 59, 92, 97.
5. "Elias, Juan." Arizona State University Libraries: Hayden Arizona Pioneer Biographies Collection, http://www.asu.edu/lib/archives/azbio/index.html (accessed 7/28/07).
6. "Reminiscences of Juan I. Téllez," 86.
7. "Reminiscences of Alvina Rosenda Contreras."
8. "Reminiscences of Juan I. Téllez," 86.
9. *Arizona Daily Citizen,* August 3, 1893. For Crook's posting to Arizona, see Martin F. Schmitt, ed., *General George Crook,* 160–65. For more on Crook's role in popularizing the use of Indian scouts, see Thomas W. Dunlay, *Wolves for the Blue Soldiers,* 44–51.
10. Sonnichsen, *Tucson,* 125; Gustafson, ed., *John Spring's Arizona,* 289; *Arizona Daily Star,* August 1, 1879, August 3, 1879.
11. Joy S. Kasson, *Buffalo Bill's Wild West,* 20; Louis Warren, *Buffalo Bill's America.*
12. C. L. Sonnichsen, *Pioneer Heritage,* 18. I based my computations as to membership on the "List of Original Members of Arizona Pioneer Historical Society" in Sidney R. DeLong, *The History of Arizona,* 195–98. Since the children of pioneers, many of whom had Mexican mothers, were included in this list, one could argue for an even greater Mexican presence in the society than a simple tally of surnames might suggest. See Deborah J. Baldwin, "A Successful Search for Security," 228. This Mexican membership presents a notable contrast with pioneer societies elsewhere in the southwestern United States. The first "pioneer society" founded in Los Angeles in 1896, for example, included no Mexican name on the membership list and the organization's bylaws declared that "persons born in this state are not eligible for membership." Carey McWilliams, *North from Mexico,* 39.
13. Nugent, *Spent Cartridges of Revolution,* 94, 125–26; Weber, *The Mexican Frontier,* 284–85; Alonso, *Thread of Blood,* 15–20. For a modern-day discussion of the distinction between Mexico's "white" north and its "Indian" south, see Pablo Vila, *Crossing Borders,* 24–49.
14. *El Fronterizo,* September 29, 1878, December 19, 1880, March 26, 1884. For more on Velasco, see Manuel G. Gonzales, "Carlos I. Velasco."
15. Sonnichsen, *Tucson,* 105; Thomas E. Sheridan, *Arizona: A History,* 118.
16. Quote from *Arizona Daily Star,* July 16, 1879. See also "La Fiesta de San Agustin," 8–9; and Sheridan, *Los Tucsonenses,* 163.
17. *Arizona Daily Citizen,* June 2, 1886, June 3, 1886. Although the "rangers" were a mixed unit of Anglos and Mexicans, their commander was a Mexican, M. G. Samaniego.
18. "Reminiscences of Alvina Rosenda Contreras."
19. "Depositions, 1893," 52.
20. Martin, *Images and Conversations,* 49; "Reminiscences of Alvina Rosenda Contreras."
21. *El Fronterizo,* February 3, 1882, January 6, 1882. For a record of the *vecinos* within the bounds of the new reservation and their property, see Levi Ruggles to R. A. Wilbur, August 27, 1873, "Correspondence, U.S. Land Office, Arizona Territory, 1873–74," Box 1. Subject Files of Indian Agent, 1871–79, Sells (Papago Agency), Bureau of Indian Affairs, RG 75, National Archives—Laguna Niguel.

22. Petition and Findings of Fact, U.S. Court of Claims, Indian Depredation Case #7550. See also "Depositions, 1893," 82, 87, 88, 92.

23. *Arizona Citizen*, January 10, 1896. See also *Arizona Republic*, January 14, 1896; and *Arizona Daily Star*, January 11, 1896.

24. *Arizona Daily Citizen*, November 3, 1896. See also *Arizona Daily Star*, November 4, 1896, November 5, 1896; and *El Fronterizo*, November 7, 1896.

25. *El Fronterizo*, November 7, 1896; Olivia Arrieta, *"La Alianza Hispano-Americana,"* 109–26; Kaye Lynn Briegel, "Alianza Hispano-Americana"; and Sheridan, *Los Tucsonenses*, 108–113.

26. There is a growing literature that examines how and why Mexican Americans created a "Spanish" identity for themselves in New Mexico at this time; similar work still remains to be done for Arizona. See John Nieto-Phillips, *The Language of Blood*, esp. 31–39, 80–82; and Charlie Montgomery, *The Spanish Redemption*, esp. 57–72. For a cogent analysis of questions of citizenship elsewhere in the borderlands at this time, see Benjamin Heber Johnson, *Revolution in Texas*. A discussion of the evolving meaning of the term *vecino* can be found in Ross Frank, *From Settler to Citizen*, 1, 180.

27. See, for example, F. T. Dávila, *Sonora: Histórico y Descriptivo*; this tendency is also manifested in more recent studies, such as Ignacio Almada, *Breve historia de Sonora*.

28. Patricia Preciado Martin, *Beloved Land*, 111, 137. See also the clipping from *Arizona Daily Star*, February 13, 1909, in the "Acuna, Juan" file, Arizona State University Libraries: Hayden Arizona Pioneer Biographies Collection, http://www.asu.edu/lib/archives/azbio/index.html (accessed 7/28/07); and John Alexander Carroll, ed., *Pioneering in Arizona*, 50.

29. Martin, *Images and Conversations*, 47. Many other accounts from this oral history collection also stress the loss of land to Americans in the late nineteenth and early twentieth centuries. See Martin, *Images and Conversations*, 14, 21, 29, 81–83, 105. For extended analyses of the theme of dispossession, see John R. Chávez, *The Lost Land*, and Vincent Pérez, *Remembering the Hacienda*, esp. 5–7.

30. Frank F. Latta, *Joaquín Murrieta and His Horse Gangs*, 146–47, 150; Jim Griffith, "Heroes and Horses."

31. I have followed here the version of the *corrido* recorded by Los Madrugadores (also known as Los Hermanos Sánchez y Linares) as presented in Luis Leal, "El Corrido de Joaquín Murrieta," 13, 18. The translation from the Spanish is mine, although based predominantly on the text provided by María Herrera-Sobek in *Northward Bound*, 16–18.

32. Griffith, "Heroes and Horses."

33. Herrera-Sobek, *Northward Bound*, 21.

34. Leal, "El Corrido de Joaquín Murrieta," 16. For more on the origins of the *corrido* from earlier Latin American vernacular music forms, see Américo Paredes, *With His Pistol in His Hand*, 129–35. "Cahiguas" as a Mexican term for certain Apache groups is discussed in Velasco, *Noticias estadísticas*, 236.

MEMORY: THE AMERICANS

1. See the recollections of A. S. Reynolds in "Bailey, William H." Biographical File, Arizona Historical Society. As I discuss below, there is good reason to doubt Bailey's actual participation in the attack. But as a resident of Tucson at the time, he was nevertheless familiar with key details of the massacre.

2. *Arizona Citizen*, May 6, 1871. For a thorough study of the Arizona press at the time of the massacre, see Blankenburg, "The Role of the Press in an Indian Massacre," 61–70.

3. *Alta California*, May 12, 1871. For initial coverage of the massacre, see *Alta California*, May 11, 1871; *New York Herald*, May 12, 1871; *San Francisco Chronicle*, May 12, 1871; *New York Times*, May 12, 1871; *Territorial Enterprise*, May 14, 1871; *Los Angeles Star*, May 14, 1871; and *Daily Evening Bulletin*, May 17, 1871. The *New Mexican*, May 23, 1871, and *Evening Post*, May 17, 1871, both excerpt later articles from the *Citizen*. There is some suggestion that the spread of the *Citizen* version was far from accidental: the editor of the *Citizen* may have in fact telegraphed a copy of his article to many other newspapers. See the *Arizona Citizen*, May 27, 1871.

4. Whitman to Lee, May 17, 1871, in *Annual Report of the Commissioner of Indian Affairs, 1871*, 486.

5. For Whitman's report, see *New York Times*, May 31, 1871, and *Chicago Tribune*, June 2, 1871. For a

similar, anonymous letter describing the attack, see *San Francisco Chronicle*, May 21, 1871; and *New York Tribune*, June 10, 1871.

6. *San Francisco Chronicle*, May 24, 1871. For heated refutations of Whitman's and the anonymous letter writer's account of the massacre, see *Arizona Citizen*, June 3, 1871.

7. "War Not Massacre," 611–12. For examples of early descriptions of the attack on the Apache at Camp Grant as a massacre, see *San Francisco Chronicle*, May 24, 1871; and *New York Herald*, June 1, 1871. For a selection of "massacres" by Indians, see Lorenzo D. Oatman and Olive A. Oatman, *The Captivity of the Oatman Girls Among the Apache and Mohave Indians*; John Frost, *Frost's Pictorial History of Indian Wars and Captivities*, I:iv, 301; and Adrian J. Ebell, "The Indian Massacres and War of 1862," 1–25.

8. *Every Saturday*, August 19, 1871: 171; *New York Tribune*, July 21, 1871.

9. *Arizona Citizen*, June 3, 1871. For uses of terms such as "affair" to describe the attack at Camp Grant, see *Weekly Arizona Miner*, July 8, 1871, July 22, 1871; and *Arizona Citizen*, June 10, 1871.

10. Gustafson, ed., *John Spring's Arizona*, 201, 245; Colorado newspaper quoted in the *Arizona Citizen*, May 27, 1871; and *Weekly Arizona Miner*, July 8, 1871.

11. *New York Herald*, June 8, 1871.

12. *Annual Report of the Board of Indian Commissioners, 1871*, 5, 68.

13. *Arizona Weekly Citizen*, December 2, 1871; *Weekly Arizona Miner*, December 9, 1871; Schmitt, ed., *General George Crook*, 167–68; Crook to Rutherford B. Hayes, October 14, 1871, in Charles M. Robinson III, *General Crook and the Western Frontier*, 114.

14. Bancroft, *History of Arizona and New Mexico*, 560, 562; *Annual Report of the Board of Indian Commissioners, 1871*, 57. For the claims that Colyer served the purposes of the "Indian Ring," see Schmitt, ed., *General George Crook*, 167; and *Army and Navy Journal*, October 22, 1871, in Peter Cozzens, ed., *Eyewitnesses to the Indian Wars, 1890*, 105.

15. *Annual Report of the Board of Indian Commissioners, 1871*, 5; Schmitt, ed., *General George Crook*, 170.

16. *Army and Navy Journal*, October 22, 1871, in Cozzens, ed., *Eyewitnesses to the Indian Wars*, 105. Colyer's previous history—he raised a regiment of African-American troops during the Civil War and served as the unit's colonel—makes it hard to support the view that he was a radical pacifist.

17. *Annual Report of the Board of Indian Commissioners, 1871*, 32, 34–35.

18. Ibid., 45–46. For information on the collection of Apache remains from Camp Grant, see George A. Otis, *Check List of Preparations and Objects*, 68–70. I am indebted to Ann Fabian for bringing this last citation to my attention.

19. *Annual Report of the Board of Indian Commissioners, 1871*, 47, 75; *Executive Orders Relating to Indian Reservations*, 3.

20. *Annual Report of the Board of Indian Commissioners, 1871*, 47; *Executive Orders Relating to Indian Reservations*, 9–10. For a suggestive discussion of the import of borders in Indian policy, see Alan Taylor, *The Divided Ground*, 7–10.

21. General Orders No. 14, April 9, 1873, in Thrapp, *Conquest of Apacheria*, 143; *Executive Orders Relating to Indian Reservations*, 34–35; Bourke, *On the Border with Crook*, 192–200, 219; *Annual Report of Brigadier General George Crook, U.S. Army, Commanding Department of Arizona, 1883*, 2–3. Crook's use of tags is a classic example of the "state simplification" discussed by James C. Scott in *Seeing Like a State*.

22. For more on DeLong, see *Weekly Arizonan*, December 25, 1869; *Arizona Citizen*, November 5, 1870, June 24, 1871; and Randy Kane, "'An Honorable and Upright Man.'" For more on Etchells, consult "Etchells, Charles Tanner," Biographical File, Arizona Historical Society; Barter, *Directory of the City of Tucson for the Year 1881*, 45; "C.T. Etchells," 20. For more on Lee, see "Lee, James," Biographical File, Arizona Historical Society; *Weekly Arizonan*, January 1, 1870, April 16, 1870, August 6, 1870. For census information on the participants, see *Federal Census—Territory of New Mexico and Territory of Arizona*, 165, 172, 178, 186.

23. For negative portrayals of the Camp Grant Massacre perpetrators, see Bourke, *On the Border with Crook*, 105; Tatum, *Our Red Brothers*, xvi; and *San Francisco Chronicle*, May 24, 1871.

24. Sonnichsen, *Tucson*, 91; Barter, *Directory of the City of Tucson for the Year 1881*, 10, 15, 16, 18, 21, 23; *Hand-Book of Tucson and Surroundings*, 41; Frank C. Lockwood, "Who Was Who in Arizona," *Arizona Daily Star*, December 1, 1940.

25. *Weekly Arizona Miner*, July 22, 1871; *Arizona Daily Citizen*, June 9, 1879; *Arizona Citizen*, June 24, 1871; *Arizona Weekly Citizen*, March 15, 1884; Gustafson, ed., *John Spring's Arizona*, 205. See also

Arizona Weekly Enterprise, April 2, 1887. Clipping in "Oury, William," Biographical File, Arizona Historical Society.

26. *Annual Report of the Board of Indian Commissioners, 1871*, 37 (emphasis in the original); and *Arizona Citizen*, September 9, 1871: 4. See also *Journal of the Second Annual Conference of the Board of Indian Commissioners, 1873*, 25–26.

27. Hiram Hodge, *Arizona as it is*; Richard J. Hinton, *The Hand-Book to Arizona*, 33; Patrick Hamilton, *The Resources of Arizona*, 27.

28. Hinton, *The Hand-Book to Arizona*, 170; *Hand-Book of Tucson and Surroundings*, 2; Hamilton, *The Resources of Arizona*, 290.

29. Hamilton, *The Resources of Arizona*, 27; *Arizona Daily Star*, March 21, 1880.

30. *Arizona Business Directory and Gazetteer*, 185; Sheridan, *Los Tucsonenses*, 146–50.

31. Arizona Pioneers' Historical Society, *Constitution and By-Laws Adopted April 16, 1897*, 12; Eleanor B. Sloan, "Seventy-Five Years of the Arizona Pioneers' Historical Society, 1884–1959." For a perceptive overview of the phenomena of pioneer societies in the western United States, see David Wrobel, *Promised Lands*.

32. Mansfield quoted in Odie B. Faulk, ed., *Arizona's State Historical Society*, 2. Oury quoted in Sonnichsen, *Pioneer Heritage*, 8. Arizona Pioneers' Historical Society, *Constitution and By-Laws*, 23; Society of Arizona Pioneers, "Board Minutes, 1884–1890," 2. Arizona Historical Society.

33. Sonnichsen, *Pioneer Heritage*, 17, 19; Baldwin, "A Successful Search for Security," 227.

34. "Board Minutes, 1884–1890," 10–11, 24, 34, 70, 71; and *Arizona Daily Citizen*, June 15, 1885. See also Arizona Pioneers' Historical Society, *In Order that There May be a Full and Free Expression of the People; To Benjamin Harrison, President of the United States*. Both reprinted on microfilm in "Western Americana: Frontier History of the Trans-Mississippi West, 1550–1900" (New Haven, Conn. Research Publications, 1975), No. 204, 205.

35. George W. Manypenny, *Our Indian Wards*, 192–93; Helen Hunt Jackson, *A Century of Dishonor*, 298ff., 337. For another early "revisionist" history, see J. P. Dunn, *Massacres of the Mountains*, 623–24.

36. *Arizona Daily Citizen*, April 7, 1885. An original of Oury's speech is on file at the Arizona Historical Society.

37. *Arizona Daily Citizen*, April 7, 1885.

38. Ibid.

39. Ibid.; *Arizona Daily Star*, April 8, 1885.

40. Ray Brandes, "An Image of History," 6.

41. Sonnichsen, *Pioneer Heritage*, 70–71; DeLong, *History of Arizona*, 23, 31–33. For obituaries of Oury, see *Arizona Daily Star*, April 1, 1887, April 5, 1887. For examples of early histories that quote Oury verbatim for several pages, see Farish, *History of Arizona*, II: 269–82; James McClintock, *Arizona*, I:207–9. Paraphrases of Oury can be found in *Treasure Land: A Story*, 33–34, 39; Estelle Buehman, *Old Tucson*, 40–42; and Will H. Robinson, *The Story of Arizona*, 193–94. For more on the fraught relationship between history and memory, see Richard White, *Remembering Ahanagran*, esp. 4–5.

42. *Arizona Daily Star*, June 19, 1910; John Cady, *Arizona's Yesterday* (1916), 94–95.

43. For DeLong's obituary, see *Arizona Daily Star*, November 25, 1914. George J. Roskruge Papers, 1872–1928, Folder 2, 2. MS 697, Arizona Historical Society. In addition to Jones, Cady, and Dunham, I would include William Bailey, whose participation in the massacre has been uncritically accepted by most scholars, as one of the pretenders. Unlike Cady, Bailey resided in Tucson at the time of the massacre. Like Cady, however, he does not appear as a defendant in the court case, as a member of the Society of Arizona Pioneers, or in any other participant's account of the massacre. "Bailey, William H." Biographical File, Arizona Historical Society.

44. Martin, *Images and Conversations*, 31; *Arizona Daily Star*, August 19, 2001.

45. Carroll, ed., *Pioneering in Arizona*, 155–56; Sybil Ellinwood, *The Arizona Historical Society Today*, 2. For more on the rise of history as a scientific discipline, see Peter Novick, *That Noble Dream*, 31–46.

46. Notably, for example, Lawrence Clark Powell's, *Arizona: A Bicentennial History*, includes no mention of the Camp Grant Massacre. For examples of works on Geronimo, consult G. D. Cummings, *The History of Geronimo's Summer Campaign in 1885*, M. P. Freeman, *The Dread Apache*; William Trowbridge Larned, "Effacing the Frontier"; *Geronimo's Story of His Life*.

47. Orick Jackson, *The White Conquest of Arizona*. For the predominance of the progress motif in turn-of-the-century histories, see Ellen Fitzgerald, *History's Memory*, 5.

48. Ida Flood Dodge, *Arizona Under Our Flag*, 93–94, 113; Ida Flood Dodge, *Our Arizona*, vii, 152.

49. Augustus Thomas, *Arizona: A Drama in Four Acts*, 3, 7–8. The popularity of Thomas's play was such that he would later rework it into a novel of the same name: Augustus Thomas, *Arizona: A Romance of the Great Southwest*. For a sense of the popular acclaim for *Arizona*, see *Washington Post*, April 7, 1901; *Atlanta Constitution*, March 14, 1908; and *Chicago Daily Tribune*, June 13, 1899. (Quote from the last of these three reviews.)

50. Clarence Budington Kelland, *Arizona*, 126; Sonnichsen, *Pioneer Heritage*, 102–4. For a detailed discussion of the effect the movie *Arizona* had on Tucson, see Gerry Lujan Cadava, "Tucson and the Arizona-Sonora Borderlands During World War II" (paper in possession of author).

51. My conclusion here echoes the point that Dipesh Chakrabarty makes in the close of *Provincializing Europe*—that, as problematic as it often is in its particulars, European historical thought is in the end "a gift to us all. We can talk of provincializing it only in an anticolonial spirit of gratitude." Dipesh Chakrabarty, *Provincializing Europe*, 255.

MEMORY: THE N<u>dee</u>

1. Report of Royal Whitman, May 17, 1871, in *Report of the Board of Indian Commissioners, 1871*, 61; Keith H. Basso, "'To Give Up on Words,'" 156–59; Goodwin, *Social Organization*, 518–21.

2. Quoted in Colwell-Chanthaphonh, "Western Apache Oral Histories and Traditions of the Camp Grant Massacre," 655–56.

3. Ibid., 647.

4. Ibid., 647–50. The term for "Big Sycamore Stands There" can be found on 649. The updated spelling for Gashdla'áchoh o'āā was provided by Willem de Reuse (personal communication, 11/22/06).

5. Report of Royal Whitman, May 17, 1871, in *Annual Report of the Board of Indian Commissioners, 1871*, 62. See also *New York Tribune*, June 10, 1871.

6. *Annual Report of the Board of Indian Commissioners, 1871*, 44, 46; John P. Clum, "Es-kim-in-zin, Part I," 403–5; Davis, *The Truth About Geronimo*, 92–93. The white man Hashkēē bá nzín killed was named either Alex McKinsey or Charles McKinney. See *Arizona Weekly Miner*, April 29, 1871; *Tucson Weekly Citizen*, October 14, 1871, December 2, 1871; and *Arizona Weekly Enterprise*, May 17, 1890.

7. *New York Times*, July 13, 1871; *Chicago Tribune*, June 12, 1871. See also the discussion of Chiricahua awareness of the Camp Grant Massacre in Eve Ball, *Indeh*, 38–39, 80. For the flight from Fort Apache, see John Green to John Schofield, May 24, 1871; John Green to W. R. Price, May 18, 1871; John Green to Assistant Adjunct General, May 16, 1871, Frames 371, 399. Letters Received by the Office of Indian Affairs, Arizona, 1863–9, RG 75, M234, National Archives—Microfilm Publications.

8. *Daily Evening Bulletin*, October 14, 1871; *Annual Report of the Board of Indian Commissioners, 1871*, 47; *Executive Orders Relating to Indian Reservations*, 32. According to Colonel Stoneman, "The Arizona newspapers are carried off, quick as they appear, by Indian runners and translated by Mexicans or others and I venture to say that everybody concerned in the Camp Grant Massacre is known individually to the Apaches." *Chicago Tribune*, June 12, 1871.

9. *Annual Report of the Board of Indian Commissioners, 1871*, 46; *Arizona Weekly Citizen*, August 3, 1872; Henry Winfred Splitter, ed., "Tour in Arizona," 80.

10. *Arizona Weekly Citizen*, August 3, 1872; O. O. Howard, *My Life and Experiences Among Our Hostile Indians*, 148.

11. *Arizona Weekly Citizen*, May 25, 1872; "General Howard's Treaties," 623.

12. *Arizona Weekly Citizen*, June 1, 1872; Howard, *My Life and Experiences*, 156–57.

13. *Arizona Weekly Citizen*, June 1, 1872; "General Howard's Mission to the Indians." According to Howard, the six children were ultimately returned, by decree of President Grant, to their relatives. Howard, *My Life and Experiences*, 160–62; *Journal of the Second Annual Conference of the Board of Indian Commissioners, 1873*, 38.

14. Wilbur to Bendell, October 17, 1871. Letterbook of Rueben Augustine Wilbur, 1871–74, AZ 344. Special Collections, University of Arizona. "Reminiscences of Alvina Rosenda Contreras," Arizona Historical Society.

15. Chiqui in *Arizona Citizen*, June 10, 1871. For documentation of Bāāchii employment as scouts, see Returns for March, 1869; and May, 1869. Records of the Adjutant General's Office, Returns from U.S. Military Posts, Fort Grant, Arizona, 1865–1874, RG 94, M617C, Roll 414, National Archives—Microfilm Publications. For more on Duran, see *Weekly Citizen*, June 1, 1872; Bourke, *On the Border with Crook*, 19; Gustafson, ed., *John Spring's Arizona*, 252; and Wilbur to Royal Whitman, October 28, 1871. Letterbook of Rueben Augustine Wilbur, 1871–74, AZ 344. Special Collections, University of Arizona.

16. John Walker to James Collins, September 6, 1860, in *Annual Report of the Commissioner of Indian Affairs, 1860*, I:393; Morris Opler, "The Identity of the Apache Mansos," 725.

17. Howard, *My Life and Experiences*, 163–64, 175–76; O. O. Howard, *Famous Indian Chiefs I Have Known*, 85–86.

18. *Annual Report of the Board of Indian Commissioners, 1871*, 45.

19. Ralph Hedrick Ogle, *Federal Control of the Western Apaches*, 139–43; John P. Clum, "Geronimo, Part II," 122. See also the concerns about disease discussed in John P. Clum, "Apache Misrule," 139–40.

20. *Daily Evening Bulletin*, February 10, 1874; Thrapp, *Conquest of Apacheria*, 150–61. For more on this tactic of beheading Apaches, see Geronimo in *Letter from the Secretary of War, Transmitting Correspondence Regarding the Apache Indians* (51st Congress, 1st sess., Sen. Executive Doc., No. 88), 12.

21. Clum, "Es-kin-in-zin, Part I," 413–14, and "Es-kin-in-zin, Part II," 4–5; *Weekly Citizen*, January 10, 1874; Diana Hadley, Peter Warshall, and Don Bufkin, *Environmental Change in Aravaipa, 1870–1970*, 48–49. Information on Clum's Apache nickname can be found in Dale Miles, "Spirits of Old San Carlos" (manuscript in possession of author). The spelling of Mount Graham comes from Willem de Reuse (personal communication, 8/3/06). For an insightful study of Mount Graham's importance to the Western Apache, see John R. Welch, "White Eyes' Lies and the Battle for *dzilnchaa si'an*."

22. Clum, "Es-kin-in-zin, Part II," 12–13.

23. Davis, *The Truth About Geronimo*, 94–98; Hadley, Warshall, and Bufkin, *Environmental Change in Aravaipa*, 49–50, 209–10; Ogle, *Federal Control of the Western Apaches*, 188; *Arizona Weekly Citizen*, March 14, 1879.

24. Wallace Johnson interview with Diana Hadley, 1990. Bureau of Land Management, Safford, Arizona. Testimony of James Noline, June 28, 1927. File 350, Box 79, Year 1926. Central Classified Files, 1907–39. San Carlos Apache Reservation, Records of the Bureau of Indian Affairs, RG 75, National Archives—Washington, D.C.

25. Captain Chiquito to Indian Agent, March 1901. San Carlos Agency Records, 1896–1930, Box 6, Folder 133, MS 707. Arizona Historical Society. I am indebted to Chip Colwell-Chanthaphonh for generously sharing this material with me. The reference to Captain Chiquito's children helping him write his letters can be found in Captain Chiquito to L. G. Powers, May 8, 1901. Apache settlements in and around Aravaipa are discussed in the *Arizona Daily Star*, January 15, 1886; *St. Louis Globe-Democrat*, September 16, 1881; Hadley, Warshall, and Bufkin, *Environmental Change in Aravaipa*, 81–82, 209–10; and Eleanor Claridge, *Klondyke and the Aravaipa Canyon*, 167–69, 181. For accounts of earlier Apache remains in Aravaipa Canyon, see Viola, ed., *The Memoirs of Charles Henry Veil*, 94; and Bell, *New Tracks in North America*, 302–3. For Western Apache concerns about gravesites, see the remarks of Jeanette Cassa in Ferguson and Colwell-Chanthaphonh, *History Is in the Land*, 252. The information about the use of yellow corn pollen to protect against spiritual harm comes from Dale Miles (personal communication, 10/15/07).

26. Hadley, Warshall, and Bufkin, *Environmental Change in Aravaipa*, 81–82.

27. "Reminiscences of Alvina Rosenda Contreras," Arizona Historical Society.

28. Hashkēē bá nzį́n quoted in Clum, "Es-kin-in-zin, Part II," 22. See also *Washington Evening Star*, August 11, 1894, in "Eskiminzin" Biographical File, Arizona Historical Society. Hashkēē bá nzį́n was not the only one aware of the possible parallels with the Camp Grant Massacre. The *Globe Silver*

Belt editorialized that the Apaches "should be painfully reminded of the treatment of the tribe, by outraged citizens, at old Camp Grant, in 1870, (at which time Es-kim-in-zin was war chief), w[h]ere 64 of their number were made 'good' Indians." Quoted in *Arizona Weekly Enterprise*, October 1, 1887. For accounts of Hashkee̅e̅ bá nzį́n's supposed illicit undertakings along the San Pedro, see *Arizona Weekly Enterprise*, September 17, 1887, September 24, 1887, October 1, 1887, October 8, 1887, October 29, 1887, November 5, 1887; *Arizona Weekly Citizen*, September 24, 1887, November 5, 1887, October 1, 1887, October 29, 1887; *Arizona Daily Star*, June 15, 1886, July 10, 1888; and *New York Times*, August 12, 1882.

29. For the Kid's probable Apache name, see Miles and Machula, *History of the San Carlos Apache*, 27. The most perceptive essay on the Apache Kid—and the only one to present him from an Apache perspective—is Dale Miles's "Spirits of Old San Carlos" (manuscript in possession of author). Other works on Hashkee̅e̅ biṉa̅a̅ nteel include Phyllis de la Garza, *The Apache Kid*; Douglas Meed, *They Never Surrendered*; H. B. Wharfield, "Apache Kid and the Record"; and *Rocky Mountain News*, November 27, 1893, September 27, 1893.

30. Miles, "Spirits of Old San Carlos"; Clum, "Es-kin-in-zin, Part II," 26–27; *Arizona Republic*, December 18, 1895; *Arizona Daily Star*, December 17, 1895; *Appropriation for Apache Indians*, 5–6. The unfamiliar conditions in Mount Vernon proved exceedingly unhealthy for the Apache. See *A Letter of the Secretary of War and Reports Touching the Apache Indians at Governor's Island*, 10–11; and H. Henrietta Stockel, *Survival of the Spirit*, 137–84.

31. For Captain Chiquito's birth and death in Aravaipa, see John Terrell to Commissioner of General Land Office, June 24, 1919. File 741638, Serial Patent Files, 1908–31, Box 26215. Records of the Bureau of Land Management, RG 49, National Archives—Washington, D.C.; and E. B. Meritt to Secretary of the Interior, July 18, 1927. Central Classified Files, San Carlos, Box 79, File 350. Records of the Bureau of Indian Affairs, RG 75, National Archives—Washington, D.C. Captain Chiquito's desire to die at Aravaipa appears in Captain Chiquito to agent, March 16, 1900. San Carlos Agency Records, 1896–1930, Box 6, Folder 133, MS 707. Arizona Historical Society.

32. Meed, *They Never Surrendered*; Goodwin, *The Apache Diaries*; Miles and Machula, *History of the San Carlos Apache*, 28; Louis Lejeune, *La guerra apache en Sonora*, 52; O. H. Howarth, "The Western Sierra Madre of Mexico," 430–31. For information on José María Elías, see *Arizona Weekly Enterprise*, October 29, 1887; *El Imparcial*, July 14, 1996; and F. Aragon to Secretary of State, November 26, 1888 (Folio 9880, Expediente 8, 1888); F. Aragon to Secretary of State, December 9, 1888 (Folio 9882, Expediente 8, 1888). Fondo Ejecutivo, Ramo Apaches, Archivo General del Estado de Sonora.

33. Miles, "Spirits of Old San Carlos"; David Samuels, *Putting a Song on Top of It*, 46.

34. Watt, *Don't Let the Sun Step Over You*, xvi. Similarly, the anthropologist David Samuels observes that San Carlos tribe member Britton Goode's anticipated history of San Carlos "would have been distinct from more familiar schoolbook histories of Apaches. There is almost nothing in his collected papers about Geronimo or Cochise or about Generals Crook and Miles and the years of armed conflict between the Apaches and the United States." David Samuels, "Indeterminacy and History in Britton Goode's Western Apache Place Names," 284.

35. Perry, *Apache Reservation*, 146–54; Irene Burlison, *Yesterday and Today in the Life of the Apaches*, 91; *Los Angeles Times*, August 4, 1899; *Agreement with White Mountain Apaches on San Carlos Reservation*. Contemporary Apaches claimed that the Coolidge Dam reservoir displaced some 650 tribe members. See "Statement of Charles Dustin interpreted by Ben Randall," in James B. Kitch to Commissioner of Indian Affairs, November 25, 1930. Central Classified Files, San Carlos, Box 56, File 313, Part 1, Year 1930. Records of the Bureau of Indian Affairs, RG 75, National Archives—Washington, D.C. For a model discussion of Native American thinking about the reservation, see Frederick E. Hoxie, "From Prison to Homeland."

36. "Statement of Gila Moses interpreted by Ben Randall," in James B. Kitch to Commissioner of Indian Affairs, November 25, 1930. Central Classified Files, San Carlos, Box 56, File 313, Part 1, Year 1930. Records of the Bureau of Indian Affairs, RG 75, National Archives—Washington, D.C. For a perceptive analysis of San Carlos Apaches' relationship to the past, see David Samuels, "The Whole and the Sum of the Parts." Samuels develops these themes at greater length in *Putting a Song on Top of It*, 37–66.

37. "Statement of Mike Nelson interpreted by Ben Randall," in James B. Kitch to Commissioner of Indian Affairs, November 25, 1930. Central Classified Files, San Carlos, Box 56, File 313, Part 1, Year 1930. Records of the Bureau of Indian Affairs, RG 75, National Archives—Washington, D.C.

38. Testimony of Manuel Victer, in *Survey of Conditions of the Indians in the United States*, Part 17: 8585, 8594. I have been unable to locate the exact text Victer read to the assembled senators, although it echoes many of the themes in Clum's *The Truth About the Apaches*.

39. "Statement of Charles Naltway interpreted by Henry Chinn" and "Statement of John Rope interpreted by Ben Randall," in James B. Kitch to Commissioner of Indian Affairs, November 25, 1930. Central Classified Files, San Carlos, Box 56, File 313, Part 1, Year 1930. Records of the Bureau of Indian Affairs, RG 75, National Archives—Washington, D.C. For contemporary Nṉeē critiques of stereotypes of Apache peoples, see Dale Curtis Miles, "Western Apache: Resistance and Renewal," 73; John R. Welch, Nancy Mahaney, and Ramon Riley, "The Reconquest of Fort Apache"; and Chesley Goseyun Wilson et al., *When the Earth Was Like New*, 21–23.

40. For a number of recent works from San Carlos linking language, traditional foods, ceremonies, the environment, and history, see Seth Pilsk and Jeanette C. Cassa, "The Western Apache Home: Landscape Management and Failing Ecosystems"; "Apache Independence Day Celebration" and Sandra Rambler, "Traditionally Speaking," *San Carlos Apache Moccasin*, June 14, 2006; "First Meeting of Language Preservation Group," *San Carlos and Bylas Apache Sunrise News*, June 8, 2006.

41. The changing meanings attached to Aravaipa are captured with great eloquence in the oral histories Ian Record has taken among the San Carlos Apache. Record, "Aravaipa: Apache Peoples and the Legacy of Particular Geography and Historical Experience," 39, 156–58, 200; also Ferguson and Colwell-Chanthaphonh, *History Is in the Land*, 226–27. The quote about "No Trespassing" signs comes from the interview of Wallace Johnson by Diana Hadley, 1990. Bureau of Land Management, Safford, Arizona. See also Pilsk and Cassa, "The Western Apache Home: Landscape Management and Failing Ecosystems," 282–86

42. Interview of Wallace Johnson by Diana Hadley, 1990. Bureau of Land Management, Safford, Arizona.

43. Quoted in Ferguson and Colwell-Chanthaphonh, *History Is in the Land*, 210.

44. Interview of Della Steele by Diana Hadley, 1990. Bureau of Land Management, Safford, Arizona.

45. Ric Volante, "Massacred Apaches Commemorated," *Arizona Daily Star*, May 1, 1982; Dennis Marquez, "Apache Massacre at Camp Grant Recalled with 'Peace and Brotherhood,'" *San Manuel Miner*, May 9, 1984; Charles Bowden, "Apaches Honor the Memory of Massacre Victims," *Tucson Citizen*, April 30, 1984. For reasons of consistency, I updated the spelling of Hashkeē bá nzín's name in Cassadore's quote.

46. "Camp Grant Massacre Site, National Register of Historic Places Evalution/Return Sheet," National Park Service, Reference No. 98000171 (in possession of author); Paul L. Allen, "Kin Want Death Site Marked," "Camp Grant Massacre Remembered," *Tucson Citizen*, April 3, 1999; and William S. Collins to author (personal communication, 6/24/02).

47. San Carlos Apache Cultural Center Brochure (in possession of author). See also Miles and Machula, *History of the San Carlos Apache*, 31. A similar and equally important effort on the part of the White Mountain Apache Tribe to create a tribal museum is discussed in John R. Welch and Ramon Riley, "Reclaiming Land and Spirit in the Western Apache Homeland."

48. San Carlos Apache Cultural Center Exhibit, 2003. Interview of Dale C. Miles by author, June 2006 (notes in possession of author).

Epilogue

1. Stephanie Innes, "Tribes to Join Forces for Tenth Sacred Run," *Arizona Daily Star*, July 30, 2003; Brenda Norrell, "Spirit in Motion," *Indian Country Today*, August 20, 2003.

2. *Wilderness Management Plan: Aravaipa Canyon Wilderness*, 2; *Wilderness Draft Environmental Statement: Aravaipa Canyon* 1, 7; Kurt Vonnegut Jr., *Slaughterhouse-Five*, 17.

3. *Wilderness Draft Environmental Statement*, 7; interview of Patrick O'Neill by author, June 2006 (notes in possession of author).

4. Officer, *Hispanic Arizona*, 114–15. Oury's presence has not been completely effaced: the pool and recreation center at the park still bear his name.

5. Stephanie Innes, "Tribes to Join Forces for Tenth Sacred Run," *Arizona Daily Star*, July 30, 2003; Brenda Norrell, "Spirit in Motion," *Indian Country Today*, August 20, 2003; and John Kamin, "Tribes Run for Religion," *Eastern Arizona Courier*, July 30, 2003.

6. In 1996, a proposal by Tucson resident Brad Rollings that the city apologize for the Camp Grant Massacre and remove Sam Hughes's name from a local school triggered a heated exchange in the local press. Brad Rollings, "It's Time for Us to Make Amends to Native Americans," *Tucson Citizen*, May 21, 1996; Stirling Russell Sanford and Ruth Corbett Cross, "Tucson Should be Grateful for Pioneer Hughes," *Tucson Citizen*, June 19, 1996; and Bonnie Henry, "Old Massacre, New Twists," *Arizona Daily Star*, June 23, 1996. For more on the rise of Anglo-American memories of a mythic West, see Richard White, *"It's Your Misfortune and None of My Own,"* 613–31.

7. My thoughts on this point owe a considerable debt to the work of Joan W. Scott. See "History-writing as Critique."

8. The links between agrarianism and genocide are detailed in Ben Kiernan, *Blood and Soil*. For a thoughtful consideration of the question of genocide and the Camp Grant Massacre, consult Colwell-Chanthaphonh, *Massacre at Camp Grant*, 14–18.

9. The full text of the United Nations Convention on the Prevention and Punishment of the Crime of Genocide can be found at www.unhchr.ch/html/menu3/b/p_genoci.htm (accessed 5/20/07).

10. For more on the historicity of history, see Richard White, "The Gold Rush: Consequences and Contingencies," 49; Marshall Sahlins, *Apologies to Thucydides*, 292; Donald R. Kelley, *Frontiers of History*, 237; and Julie Cruikshank, "History, Narrative Strategies, and Native American Historiography," 3–28.

Bibliography

Because this is a work that invites readers to make their own assessments of the past, I have taken the step of making a number of the sources essential to researching *Shadows at Dawn* available online. Please consult www.brown.edu/aravaipa to see transcripts of the December 1871 trial and the 1872 treaty negotiations, Oury's speech about the massacre, Juan Elías's Indian depredation claim, O'odham calendar sticks, and other materials.

ARCHIVAL SOURCES

Archivo General del Estado de Sonora, Hermosillo, Sonora, México
    Fondo Ejecutivo, Ramo Apaches

Archivo General de Indias, Sevilla, Spain
    Audiencia de Guadalajara
    Papeles de Estado

Archivo General de Simancas, Simancas, Spain
    Guerra Moderna

Arizona Historical Society, Tucson, Arizona
    Biographical Files
    Charles Morgan Wood Papers, MS 881
    Clarence Bennett Papers, MS 69
    Don Jesús José Aguiar Collection, MS 916
    Francis Goodwin Papers, MS 297
    George J. Roskruge Papers, MS 697
    "Reminiscences of Amelia Elías"
    "Reminiscences of Alvina Rosenda Contreras"
    San Carlos Agency Records, MS 707
    Society of Arizona Pioneers, "Board Minutes, 1884–1890"

Bancroft Library, University of California, Berkeley, California
    Oscar Fitch, "Reminiscences," BANC MSS P-D 100:8
    Alphonse Pinart, "Vocabulario de la lengua Papaga," BANC MSS M-M 487
    Pinart Prints

Beinecke Library, Yale University, New Haven, Connecticut
  Diego Ortiz Parrilla, "Correspondence with Officials, 1752," WA MSS s-834 P248
  Francisco Moyano, "Liber de statu animarum hujus populi Sancti Antonio de Oquitoa, 1796 Oct. 20," WA MSS s-1542 m8731

Huntington Library, San Marino, California
  Ferdinand Andrews, "The Indians of New Mexico and Arizona," HM 989
  "Arizona Volunteers: Correspondence and Reports, 1864–66," MS Film 197
  William Bausman, "Reminiscences of the United States and Mexican Boundary Survey," DA 5
  K. Beeching, "Diary, 1849," HM 17430
  Cave Couts, "Journal, 1846–1848," CT 2541
  Benjamin Butler Harris, "Journal: Crumbs of 49," HM 17477
  Alonzo E. Davis, *Pioneer Days in Arizona by One Who Was There*, MS Film 135
  Jacob Samuel Mansfield, "Literature in the Territory of Arizona in 1870," FAC 310
  Charles D. Poston, "Reminiscences," FAC 308
  Walter Scribner Schuyler, correspondence, WS 79

John Carter Brown Library, Brown University, Providence, Rhode Island
  José Antonio de Alzate y Ramírez, "Nuevo mapa geographico de la America Septentrional, perteneciente al Virreynato de México, 1768"

Southwest Museum, Los Angeles, California
  "Arizona Territorial Volunteers," Manuscript 599

Special Collections, University of Arizona, Tucson, Arizona
  Charles D. Poston, "History of the Apaches," AZ 169
  Letterbook of Rueben Augustine Wilbur, AZ 344

National Archives—Microfilm Publications
  Letters Received by the Office of Indian Affairs, Arizona, 1863–9, RG 75, M234
  Records of the Adjutant General's Office, Returns from U.S. Military Posts, Fort Grant, Arizona, 1865–1874, RG 94, M617C
  Records of the Bureau of the Census, Ninth Census of the United States, 1870, Arizona Territory, RG 29, M593A
  State Department Territorial Papers, Arizona, 1864–1872, RG 59, M342

National Archives—Laguna Niguel, California
  Records of the Bureau of Indian Affairs, Papago Agency, RG 75
  Records of District Courts of the United States, Arizona Territorial District Court, RG 21

National Archives—Washington, D.C.
  Records of the Bureau of Indian Affairs, San Xavier Agency, RG 75
  Records of the Bureau of Indian Affairs, San Carlos Agency, RG 75
  Records of the Bureau of Land Management, RG 49
  Records of the United States Court of Claims, Indian Depredation Case Records, RG 123
  Records of the Indian Claims Commission, RG 279

Oral Interviews

Wallace Johnson. Interview by Diana Hadley, 1990. Bureau of Land Management, Safford, Arizona.
Dale Miles. Interview by author, June 2006.
Patrick O'Neill. Interview by author, June 2006.
Della Steele. Interview by Diana Hadley, 1990. Bureau of Land Management, Safford, Arizona.

Unpublished Manuscripts

Briegel, Kaye Lynn. "Alianza Hispano-Americana, 1894–1965: A Mexican American Fraternal Insurance Society." Ph.D. dissertation, University of Southern California, 1974.

Cadava, Gerry Lujan. "Tucson and the Arizona-Sonora Borderlands During World War II." 2007.

"Camp Grant Massacre Site, National Register of Historic Places Evalution/Return Sheet," National Park Service, Reference No. 98000171.

Miles, Dale. "Spirits of Old San Carlos." 2006.

Ostler, Jeff. "The Question of Genocide in U.S. History." 2006.

Record, Ian Wilson. "Aravaipa: Apache Peoples and the Legacy of Particular Geography and Historical Experience." Ph.D. dissertation, University of Arizona, 2004.

San Carlos Apache Cultural Center Brochure. 2006.

Witgen, Michael. "The World Beyond the Atlantic: Writing Indigenous Narratives into the History of Early America." 2006.

Newspapers

Alta California (San Francisco)
Arizona Daily Citizen (Tucson)
Arizona Daily Star (Tucson)
Arizona Miner (Prescott)
Arizona Republic (Phoenix)
Arizona Sentinel (Arizona City—Yuma)
Arizona Weekly Enterprise (Florence)
Arizona Weekly Citizen (Tucson)
Arizonan (Tucson)
Arizonian (Tubac)
Atlanta Constitution
Chicago Daily Tribune
Daily Evening Bulletin (San Francisco)
DeBow's Review (New Orleans—Washington, D.C.)
Eastern Arizona Courier (Safford)
El Fronterizo (Tucson)
El Imparcial (Hermosillo)
Evening Post (New York)
Every Saturday (Boston)
Indian Country Today (Oneida, NY)
Los Angeles Star
Los Angeles Times
New Mexican (Santa Fe)
New York Herald
New York Times
New York Tribune
Phoenix Weekly Herald
Rocky Mountain News (Denver)
San Carlos Apache Moccasin (Globe, AZ)
San Carlos and Bylas Apache Sunrise News (San Carlos, AZ)
San Francisco Chronicle
San Manuel Miner (San Manuel, AZ)
St. Louis Globe-Democrat
Territorial Enterprise (Virginia City, NV)
Washington Evening Star (Washington, D.C.)
Washington Post (Washington, D.C.)

Weekly Arizonan (Tucson)
Weekly Arizonian (Tubac)
Weekly Arizona Miner (Prescott)

ONLINE SOURCES

Arizona State University Libraries: Hayden Arizona Pioneer Biographies Collection, http://www.asu.edu/
    lib/archives/azbio/index.html
Center for Desert Archaeology: Rio Nuevo Project, http://www.cdarc.org/pages/heritage/rio_nuevo/index
    .php
Office of the United Nations High Commissioner for Human Rights, http://www.ohchr.org/english/
Texas State Historical Association: Handbook of Texas Online, http://www.tsha.utexas.edu/handbook/
    online/
Tumacácori National Historical Park Mission 2000: Searchable Spanish Mission Records, http://home
    .nps.gov/applications/tuma/search.cfm

SOUND RECORDINGS

Griffith, Jim. "Heroes and Horses: Corridos from the Arizona-Sonora Borderlands," Smithsonian
    Folkways Recordings, Washington, D.C., 2002.

UNITED STATES FEDERAL AND TERRITORIAL REPORTS

Abel, Annie Heloise, ed. *The Official Correspondence of James S. Calhoun while Indian Agent at Santa Fé and
    Superintendent of Indian Affairs in New Mexico.* Washington, D.C.: GPO, 1915.
Agreement with White Mountain Apaches on San Carlos Reservation. [54th Congress, 1st sess., H. Doc., No. 320.]
Appropriation for Apache Indians. [51st Congress, 2nd sess., H. Executive Doc., No. 41.]
Arizona Territory. *Acts, Resolutions and Memorials Adopted by the First Legislative Assembly of the Territory of
    Arizona.* Prescott: Arizona Miner, 1865.
————. *The American Pioneer: An Oration Delivered at Prescott, Arizona, before the Arizona Pioneer Society by
    Governor McCormick.* Prescott, 1866.
————. *Journals of the Third Legislative Assembly of the Territory of Arizona.* Prescott: Arizona Miner, 1867.
————. *Memorial and Affidavits Showing Outrages Perpetrated by the Apache Indians, in the Territory of
    Arizona during the Years 1869 and 1870.* San Francisco: Francis and Valentine, 1871.
————. *Message of Governor Richard C. McCormick to the Third Legislative Assembly of the Territory of Arizona,
    October 8, 1866.* Prescott: Arizona Miner, 1866.
————. *Message of Governor McCormick to the Fourth Legislature of Arizona, Delivered September 9, 1867.*
    [1867?].
————. *Message of Governor McCormick to the Fifth Legislative Assembly of the Territory of Arizona at Tucson,
    November 16, 1868.* Tucson: Office of the Arizonian, 1868.
Densmore, Frances. *Papago Music.* Bureau of American Ethnology Bulletin 90. Washington, D.C.: GPO,
    1929.
Emory, William H. *Notes of a Military Reconnaissance from Fort Leavenworth, in Missouri, to San Diego, in
    California.* Washington, D.C.: Wendell and Van Benthuysen, 1848.
————. *Report on the United States and Mexican Boundary Survey.* 2 vols. Washington, D.C.: Cornelius
    Wendell, 1857.
Federal Census—Territory of New Mexico and Territory of Arizona. [89th Congress, 1st sess., Sen. Document,
    No. 13.]
Grossman, F. E. "The Pima Indians of Arizona." *Annual Report of the Board of Regents of the Smithsonian
    Institution, 1871.* Washington, D.C.: GPO, 1873.
Humphreys, A. A. *Preliminary Report Concerning Explorations and Surveys Principally in Nevada and Arizona.*
    Washington, D.C.: GPO, 1872.

Letter from the Secretary of War Transmitting Correspondence Regarding the Apache Indians. [51st Congress, 1st sess., Sen. Executive Doc., No. 88.]

Letter of the Secretary of War and Reports Touching the Apache Indians at Governor's Island. [51st Congress, 1st sess., Sen. Executive Doc., No. 35.]

Parke, John G. *Report of Explorations for that Portion of a Railway Route, near the Thirty-Second Parallel of Latitude, Lying Between Doña Ana, on the Rio Grande, and Pimas Villages, on the Pima.* [33rd Congress, 1st sess., H. Executive Doc., No. 129.]

Presidential Message Communicating Information on the Mexican Boundary Line. [34th Congress, 1st sess., Sen. Executive Doc., No. 57.]

Russell, Frank. "The Pima Indians." *Twenty-Sixth Annual Report of the Bureau of American Ethnology, 1904–1905.* Washington, D.C.: GPO, 1908.

Survey of Conditions of the Indians in the United States: Hearings Before a Subcommittee of the Committee on Indian Affairs, United States Senate. Part 17. Washington, D.C.: GPO, 1931.

U.S. Bureau of Indian Affairs. *Annual Report of the Board of Indian Commissioners, 1870.* Washington, D.C.: GPO, 1871.

———. *Annual Report of the Board of Indian Commissioners, 1871.* Washington, D.C.: GPO, 1872.

———. *Annual Report of the Commissioner of Indian Affairs, 1853.* In *Message from the President of the United States to the Two Houses of Congress at the Commencement of the First Session of the Thirty-Third Congress.* Washington, D.C.: Robert Armstrong, 1853. [33rd Congress, 1st sess., H. Executive Doc., No. 11.]

———. *Annual Report of the Commissioner of Indian Affairs, 1854.* In *Message from the President of the United States to the Two Houses of Congress at the Commencement of the Second Session of the Thirty-Third Congress.* Washington: Beverley Tucker, 1854.

———. *Annual Report of the Commissioner of Indian Affairs, 1857.* In *Message of the President of the United States to the Two Houses of Congress at the Commencement of the First Session of the Thirty-Fifth Congress.* Washington, D.C.: William A. Harris, 1858. [35th Congress, 1st sess., Sen. Executive Doc., No. 11.]

———. *Annual Report of the Commissioner of Indian Affairs, 1858.* In *Message from the President of the United States to the Two Houses of Congress at the Commencement of the Second Session of the Thirty-Fifth Congress.* Washington, D.C.: James B. Steedman, 1858. [35th Congress, 2nd sess., H. Executive Doc., No 2.]

———. *Annual Report of the Commissioner of Indian Affairs, 1859.* In *Message from the President of the United States to the Two Houses of Congress at the Commencement of the Thirty-Sixth Congress.* Washington, D.C.: George W. Bowman, 1860. [36th Congress, 1st sess., Senate Executive Doc., No. 2.]

———. *Annual Report of the Commissioner of Indian Affairs, 1860.* Washington, D.C.: George W. Bowman, 1860. [36th Congress, 2nd sess., Senate Executive Doc., No. 1.]

———. *Annual Report of the Commissioner of Indian Affairs, 1862.* Washington, D.C.: GPO, 1863.

———. *Annual Report of the Commissioner of Indian Affairs, 1866.* In *Message of the President of the United States, and Accompanying Documents, to the Two Houses of Congress at the Commencement of the Second Session of the Thirty-Ninth Congress.* Washington, D.C.: GPO, 1866. [39th Congress, 2nd sess., H. Executive Doc., No. 1.]

———. *Annual Report of the Commissioner of Indian Affairs, 1867.* Washington, D.C.: GPO, 1868.

———. *Annual Report of the Commissioner of Indian Affairs, 1868.* Washington, D.C.: GPO, 1868.

———. *Annual Report of the Commissioner of Indian Affairs, 1869.* Washington, D.C.: GPO, 1870.

———. *Annual Report of the Commissioner of Indian Affairs, 1871.* Washington, D.C.: GPO, 1871.

———. *Journal of the Second Annual Conference of the Board of Indian Commissioners, 1873.* Washington, D.C.: GPO, 1873.

U.S. Bureau of Land Management. *Wilderness Draft Environmental Statement: Aravaipa Canyon.* 1978.

———. *Wilderness Management Plan: Aravaipa Canyon Wilderness.* 1988.

U.S. War Department. *Annual Report of Brigadier General George Crook, U.S. Army, Commanding Department of Arizona, 1883.* [1883?].

———. *Annual Report of the Secretary of War, 1859.* Washington, D.C.: George W. Bowman, 1859. [36th Congress, 1st sess., Sen. Executive Doc., No. 2.]

———. *Annual Report of the Secretary of War, 1860.* [36th Congress, 2nd sess., Sen. Executive Doc., No. 1.]

————. *Annual Report of the Secretary of War, 1867*. Washington, D.C.: GPO, 1867. [40th Congress, 2nd sess., H. Executive Doc., No. 1.]

————. *Annual Report of the Secretary of War, 1869*. Washington, D.C.: GPO, 1869. [41st Congress, 2nd sess., H. Executive Doc., No. 1.]

————. *Report of Colonel George Stoneman*. [1871?].

————. *Revised Outline Descriptions of the Posts and Stations of Troops in the Military Division of the Pacific Commanded by Major-General John M. Schofield*. (1872).

The War of the Rebellion: A Compilation of the Official Records of the Union and Confederate Armies. Series 1, Volume IV. Washington, D.C.: GPO, 1902.

The War of the Rebellion: A Compilation of the Official Records of the Union and Confederate Armies. Series 1, Volume IX. Washington, D.C.: GPO, 1902.

The War of the Rebellion: A Compilation of the Official Records of the Union and Confederate Armies. Series 1, Volume XV. Washington, D.C.: GPO, 1886.

The War of the Rebellion: A Compilation of the Official Records of the Union and Confederate Armies. Series 1, Volume L, 2 Parts. Washington, D.C.: GPO, 1897.

The War of the Rebellion: A Compilation of the Official Records of the Union and Confederate Armies. Series 3, Volume II. Washington, D.C.: GPO, 1899.

The War of the Rebellion: A Compilation of the Official Records of the Union and Confederate Armies. Series 3, Volume III. Washington, D.C.: GPO, 1899.

MEXICAN GOVERNMENT REPORTS

Almonte, Juan Nepomuceno. *Memoria del ministerio de estado y del despacho de guerra y marina del gobierno supremo de la República Mexicana, leida al augusto congreso nacional el dia 9 de diciembre de 1846*. México: Imprenta de Torres, 1846.

————. *Memoria del ministerio de guerra y marina, presentada a las cámaras del congreso general Mexicano en enero de 1841*. México: Imprenta del Aguila, [1841?].

Arista, Mariano. *Memoria del secretario del estado y del despacho de guerra y marina, leida en la cámara de diputados el dia 9, y en la de senadores el 11 de enero de 1849*. México: Imprenta de Vicente García Torres, 1849.

————. *Memoria del secretario de estado y del despacho de guerra y marina, 1850*. México: Tipografia de Vicente G. Torres, 1850.

————. *Memoria del secretario de estado y del despacho de guerra y marina, leida en la cámara de diputados el dia 3, y en la de senadores el 4 de enero de 1851*. México: Imprenta de Calle de Medinas, 1851.

García Conde, Pedro. *Memoria del secretario de estado y del despacho de guerra y marina, leida en la cámara de senadores el dia 10 y en la de diputados el dia 11 de marzo de 1845*. México: Imprenta de Vicente García Torres, 1845.

Memoria del estado de la administración pública, leida en la legislatura de Sonora en la sesión del dia 14 de noviembre de 1870. Ures: Imprenta del Gobierno a cargo de Adolfo Felix Diaz, 1870.

Robles, Manuel. *Memoria del secretario del estado y del despacho de guerra y marina, leida en la cámara de diputados los dias 30 y 31 de enero, y en la de senadores en 13 de febrero de 1852*. México: Imprenta de Vicente G. Torres, 1852.

Tornel, José María. *Memoria del secretario de estado y del despacho de guerra y marina, leida á las cámaras del congreso nacional de la República Mexicana, en enero de 1844*. México: Imprenta de I. Cumplido, [1844?].

BOOKS AND ARTICLES

"A Ride with the Apaches," *Overland Monthly* 6 (April 1871): 341–45.

Aboites Aguilar, Luis. "Nómadas y sedentarios en el norte de México: Elementos para una periodización." In *Nómadas y sedentarios en el norte de México*. Edited by Marie-Areti Hers, José Luis Mirafuentes, María de los Dolores Soto, and Miguel Vallebueno. México: Universidad Nacional Autónoma de México, 2000.

Alexander, J. C. "Massacre at Camp Grant." In *The American West*. Edited by Raymond Friday Locke. Los Angeles: Mankind Publishing, 1988.

Almada, Ignacio. *Breve historia de Sonora*. México: El Colegio de México, 2000.

Alonso, Ana María. *Thread of Blood: Colonialism, Revolution, and Gender on Mexico's Northern Frontier*. Tucson: University of Arizona Press, 1995.

Altshuler, Constance Wynn, ed. *Latest from Arizona! The Hesperian Letters, 1859–1861*. Tucson: Arizona Pioneers' Historical Society, 1969.

———. *Chains of Command: Arizona and the Army, 1856–1875*. Tucson: Arizona Historical Society, 1981.

Alvarez, Albert, and Kenneth Hale. "Toward a Manual of Papago Grammar: Some Phonological Terms." *International Journal of American Linguistics* 36 (April 1970): 83–97.

Among the Pimas: Or, The Mission to the Pima and Maricopa Indians. Albany, NY: Ladies' Union Mission School Association, 1893.

Anderson, Benedict. *Imagined Communities: Reflections on the Origin and Spread of Nationalism*. Rev. ed. New York: Verso, 1991.

Apostólicos afanes de la Compañía de Jesús escritos por un padre de la misma sagrada religión de su provincia de México. 1754, Reprint, México: Editorial Layac, 1944.

Archer, Christon I. "The Deportation of Barbarian Indians from the Internal Provinces of New Spain, 1789–1810." *The Americas* 29 (January 1973): 376–85.

Arizona Business Directory and Gazetteer. San Francisco: W. C. Disturnell, 1881.

Arizona Pioneers' Historical Society. *In Order that There May be a Full and Free Expression of the People of the Territory Upon the All-Absorbing Question of Apache Indian Depredation*. Tucson, 1886.

———. *To Benjamin Harrison, President of the United States*. Tucson, 1890.

———. *Constitution and By-Laws Adopted April 16, 1897*. Los Angeles: Kingsley-Barnes and Neuner, 1897.

Arnold, Elliot. *Camp Grant Massacre*. New York: Simon and Schuster, 1976.

Arrieta, Olivia. "*La Alianza Hispano-Americana*, 1894–1965: An Analysis of Collective Action and Cultural Adaptation." In *Nuevomexicano Cultural Legacy: Forms, Agencies, and Discourse*. Edited by Francisco A. Lomelí, Víctor A. Sorell, and Genaro M. Padilla. Albuquerque: University of New Mexico Press, 2002.

Bahr, Donald. *Pima and Papago Ritual Oratory: A Study of Three Texts*. San Francisco: The Indian Historian Press, 1975.

———, ed. *O'odham Creation and Related Events: As Told to Ruth Benedict in 1927 in Prose, Oratory, and Song by the Pimas William Blackwater, Thomas Vanyiko, Clara Ahiel, William Stevens, Oliver Wellington, and Kisto*. Tucson: University of Arizona Press, 2001.

Bahr, Donald, Juan Gregorio, David I. Lopez, and Albert Alvarez. *Piman Shamanism and Staying Sickness*. Tucson: University of Arizona Press, 1974.

Bahr, Donald, Juan Smith, William Smith Allison, and Julian Hayden. *The Short Swift Time of Gods on Earth: The Hohokam Chronicles*. Berkeley: University of California Press, 1994.

Baldwin, Deborah J. "A Successful Search for Security: Arizona Pioneer Society Widows." In Arlene Scadron, *On Their Own: Widows and Widowhood in the American Southwest, 1848–1939*. Urbana: University of Illinois Press, 1988.

Ball, Eve. *In the Days of Victorio: Recollections of a Warm Spring Apache*. Narrated by James Kaywaykla. Tucson: University of Arizona Press, 1970.

———. *Indeh: An Apache Odyssey*. 1980. Reprint, Norman: University of Oklahoma Press, 1988.

Ball, Larry D. *The United States Marshals of New Mexico and Arizona Territory, 1846–1912*. Albuquerque: University of New Mexico Press, 1978.

Bancroft, Hubert Howe. *History of Arizona and New Mexico, 1530–1888*. San Francisco: History Company, 1889.

Barr, Juliana. *Peace Came in the Form of a Woman: Indians and Spaniards in the Texas Borderlands*. Chapel Hill: University of North Carolina Press, 2007.

Barter, G. W. *Directory of the City of Tucson for the Year 1881*. San Francisco: H. S. Crocker, 1881.

Bartlett, John Russell. *Personal Narrative of Explorations and Incidents in Texas, New Mexico, California, Sonora, and Chihuahua*. 2 vols. New York: D. Appleton, 1854.

Basso, Keith H. *Western Apache Witchcraft*. Anthropological Papers of the University of Arizona, No. 15. Tucson: University of Arizona Press, 1969.

———. "'To Give Up on Words': Silence in Western Apache Culture." In *Apachean Culture History and Ethnology*. Edited by Keith H. Basso and Morris E. Opler, Anthropological Papers of the University of Arizona No. 21. Tucson: University of Arizona Press, 1971.

———, ed. *Western Apache Raiding and Warfare*. Tucson: University of Arizona Press, 1971.

———. "Western Apache." In *Handbook of North American Indians*. Vol. 10, *Southwest*. Edited by Alfonso Ortiz. Washington, D.C.: Smithsonian Institution Press, 1983.

———. *Wisdom Sits in Places: Landscape and Language Among the Western Apache*. Albuquerque: University of New Mexico Press, 1996.

Before Rebellion: Letters and Reports of Jacobo Sedelmayr, S.J. Translated by Daniel S. Matson. Introduction by Bernard L. Fontana. Tucson: Arizona Historical Society, 1996.

Bell, William A. "On the Basin of Colorado and the Great Basin of North America." *Journal of the Royal Geographical Society of London* 39 (1869): 95–120.

———. *New Tracks in North America*. London: Chapman and Hall, 1870.

———. "Ten Days' Journey in Southern Arizona." In *Wonderful Adventures: A Series of Narratives of Personal Experiences Among the Native Tribes of America*. 2nd ed. Philadelphia: William B. Evans, [1874?].

Betzinez, Jason, with Wilbur Sturtevant Nye. *I Fought with Geronimo*. Harrisburg, PA: Stackpole, 1959.

Bishop, William Henry. *Old Mexico and Her Lost Provinces*. New York: Harper and Brothers, 1889.

Blackhawk, Ned. *Violence Over the Land: Indians and Empires in the Early American West*. Cambridge: Harvard University Press, 2006.

Blankenburg, William B. "The Role of the Press in an Indian Massacre, 1871." *Journalism Quarterly* 45 (Spring 1968): 61–70.

Bolton, Herbert Eugene. *The Rim of Christendom: A Biography of Eusebio Francisco Kino, Pacific Coast Pioneer*. New York: Macmillan, 1936.

Boucher, Chauncey S. "In Re That Aggressive Slavocracy." *Mississippi Valley Historical Review* 8 (June–September 1921): 13–79.

Bourke, Joanna. *An Intimate History of Killing: Face-to-Face Killing in Twentieth-Century Warfare*. New York: Basic Books, 1999.

Bourke, John G. "General Crook in the Indian Country." *The Century Magazine* 41 (March 1891): 643–60.

———. *On the Border with Crook*. 1891. Reprint, Lincoln: University of Nebraska Press, 1971.

Box, Michael James. *Adventures and Explorations in New and Old Mexico*. New York: James Miller, 1869.

Brackett, A. G. "Arizona Territory." *Western Monthly* 1 (March 1869): 167–72.

Brandes, Ray. *Frontier Military Posts of Arizona*. Globe, AZ; Dale Stuart King, 1960.

———. "Guide to the Historic Landmarks of Tucson." *Arizoniana* 3 (Summer 1962): 27–40.

———. "An Image of History." *Arizona Highways* 38 (June 1962): 6.

Brantlinger, Patrick. *Dark Vanishings: Discourse on the Extinction of Primitive Races, 1800–1930*. Ithaca: Cornell University Press, 2003.

Bray, Dorothy, ed. *Western Apache–English Dictionary: A Community-Generated Bilingual Dictionary*. Tempe, AZ: Bilingual Press/Editorial Bilingüe, 1998.

Bright, William. *Native American Placenames of the United States*. Norman: University of Oklahoma Press, 2004.

Bringas de Manzaneda y Encinas, Diego Miguel. *Father Bringas Reports to the King: Methods of Indoctrination on the Frontier of New Spain, 1796–97*. Translated and edited by Daniel S. Matson and Bernard L. Fontana. Tucson: University of Arizona Press, 1977.

Brooks, James. *Captives and Cousins: Slavery, Kinship, and Community in the Southwest Borderlands*. Chapel Hill: University of North Carolina Press, 2002.

Brown, Dee. *Bury My Heart at Wounded Knee: An Indian History of the American West*. New York: Holt, Rinehart and Winston, 1970.

Browne, J. Ross. *Adventures in the Apache Country: A Tour Through Arizona and Sonora*. New York: Harper and Brothers, 1869.

Browning, Christopher R. *Ordinary Men: Reserve Police Battalion 101 and the Final Solution in Poland*. New York: HarperCollins, 1992.

Browning, Sinclair. *Enju: The Life and Struggle of an Apache Chief from the Little Running Water.* Flagstaff, AZ: Northland Publishing, 1982.

Bryan, Kirk. "Flood Water Farming." In *Ethnology of Northwest Mexico: Sourcebook.* Edited by Randall H. McGuire. New York: Garland Publishing, 1991.

Buehman, Estelle. *Old Tucson.* Tucson: State Consolidated Publishing, 1911.

Burlison, Irene. *Yesterday and Today in the Life of the Apaches.* Philadelphia: Dorrance, 1973.

Buskirk, Winfred. *The Western Apache: Living with the Land Before 1950.* Norman: University of Oklahoma Press, 1986.

"C.T. Etchells." *Arizona Quarterly Illustrated* 1 (April 1881): 20.

Cady, John. *Arizona's Yesterday.* 1916.

Camarillo, Albert. *Chicanos in a Changing Society: From Mexican Pueblos to American Barrios in Santa Barbara and Southern California, 1848–1930.* Cambridge: Harvard University Press, 1979.

Carmony, Neil, ed. *The Civil War in Apacheland: Sergeant George Hand's Diary.* Silver City, NM: High-Lonesome Books, 1996.

Carroll, John Alexander, ed., *Pioneering in Arizona: The Reminiscences of Emerson Oliver Stratton and Edith Stratton Kitt.* Tucson: Arizona Pioneers' Historical Society, 1964.

Casas, María Raquél. *Married to a Daughter of the Land: Spanish-Mexican Women and Interethnic Marriage in California, 1820–1880.* Reno: University of Nevada Press, 2007.

Castetter, Edward F., and Willis H. Bell. *Pima and Papago Indian Agriculture.* Albuquerque: University of New Mexico Press, 1942.

Chakrabarty, Dipesh. *Provincializing Europe: Postcolonial Thought and Historical Difference.* Princeton: Princeton University Press, 2000.

Charter and By-Laws of the Sopori Land and Mining Company. Providence: Knowles, Anthony, 1859.

Chávez, John R. *The Lost Land: The Chicano Image of the Southwest.* Albuquerque: University of New Mexico Press, 1984.

Claridge, Eleanor. *Klondyke and the Aravaipa Canyon.* Safford, AZ, 1989.

Clarke, Dwight L., ed., *The Original Journals of Henry Smith Turner.* Norman: University of Oklahoma Press, 1966.

Clifford, Josephine. "Camp-Life in Arizona." *Overland Monthly* 4 (March 1870): 246–52.

Clum, John P. "Geronimo, Part II." *New Mexico Historical Review* 3 (April 1928): 122–44.

———. "Es-kim-in-zin, Part I." *New Mexico Historical Review* 3 (October 1928): 399–420.

———. "Es-kim-in-zin, Part II." *New Mexico Historical Review* 4 (January 1929): 1–27.

———. "Apache Misrule: A Bungling Agent Sets the Military Arm in Motion, Part I." *New Mexico Historical Review* 5 (April 1930): 138–55.

———. *The Truth About the Apaches.* Los Angeles: Adcraft, 1931.

Coates, Peter. "'Unusually Cunning, Vicious, and Treacherous': The Extermination of the Wolf in United States History." In *The Massacre in History.* Edited by Mark Levene and Penny Roberts. New York: Bergahn Books, 1999.

Coffey, Frederic A. "Some General Aspects of the Gadsden Treaty." *New Mexico Historical Review* 8 (July 1933): 145–64.

Coleman, Jon T. *Vicious: Wolves and Men in America.* New Haven: Yale University Press, 2004.

Colwell-Chanthaphonh, Chip. "Western Apache Oral Histories and Traditions of the Camp Grant Massacre." *American Indian Quarterly* 27 (Summer & Fall 2003): 639–66.

———. "The Camp Grant Massacre in the Historical Imagination." *Journal of the Southwest* 45 (Autumn 2003): 349–69.

———. *Massacre at Camp Grant: Forgetting and Remembering Apache History.* Tucson: University of Arizona Press, 2007.

Condie, Carol J., ed. *Vocabulary of the Apache or Indé Language of Arizona and New Mexico Collected by John Gregory Bourke in the 1870s and 1880s.* Greeley: Museum of Anthropology, University of Northern Colorado, 1980.

Conner, Daniel Ellis. *Joseph Reddeford Walker and the Arizona Adventure.* Edited by Donald J. Berthrong and Odessa Davenport. Norman: University of Oklahoma Press, 1956.

Cooke, Philip St. George. "Journal of the March of the Mormon Battalion, 1846–1847." In *Exploring Southwestern Trails, 1846–1854.* Edited by Ralph P. Bieber, Glendale, CA: Arthur H. Clark Co., 1938.

Correspondencia del P. Kino con los Generales de la Compañía de Jesús, 1682–1707. Edited by Ernest J. Burrus. México: Editorial Jus, 1961.

Cozzens, Peter, ed. *Eyewitnesses to the Indian Wars, 1865–1890.* Mechanicsburg, PA: Stackpole Books, 2001.

Cozzens, Samuel Woodworth. *The Marvelous Country; Or, Three Years in Arizona and New Mexico, the Apaches' Home.* Boston: Shepard and Gill, 1873.

Craib, Raymond B. *Cartographic Mexico: A History of State Fixations and Fugitive Landscapes.* Durham, NC: Duke University Press, 2004.

Cremony, John C. *Life Among the Apaches.* San Francisco: A. Roman, 1868.

Cronon, William. "A Place for Stories: Nature, History, and Narrative." *Journal of American History* 78 (March 1992): 1347–76.

Cruikshank, Julie. "History, Narrative Strategies, and Native American Historiography: Perspectives from the Yukon Territory, Canada." In *Clearing a Path: Theorizing the Past in Native American Studies.* Edited by Nancy Shoemaker. New York: Routledge, 2002.

Cummings, G. D. *The History of Geronimo's Summer Campaign in 1885: A Drama.* 1890.

Cutter, Donald C., ed. and trans. *The Defenses of Northern New Spain: Hugo O'Conor's Report to Teodoro de Croix, July 22, 1777.* Dallas: Southern Methodist University Press, 1994.

Dávila, F. T. *Sonora: Histórico y Descriptivo.* Nogales, AZ: Tipografía de R. Bernal, 1894.

Davis, Britton. *The Truth About Geronimo.* 1929. Reprint, Chicago: Lakeside Press, 1951.

DeJong, David H. "Forced to Abandon Their Farms: Water Deprivation and Starvation among the Gila River Pima, 1892–1904." *American Indian Culture and Research Journal* 28 (2004): 29–56.

de la Garza, Phyllis. *The Apache Kid.* Tucson: Westernlore Press, 1995.

Delay, Brian. "Independent Indians and the U.S.-Mexican War." *American Historical Review* 112 (February 2007): 35–68.

DeLong, Sidney R. *The History of Arizona: From the Earliest Times Known to the People of Europe to 1903.* San Francisco: Whitaker and Ray, 1905.

Deloria, Philip J. *Indians in Unexpected Places.* Lawrence: University Press of Kansas, 2004.

Demos, John. *The Unredeemed Captive: A Family Story from Early America.* New York: Alfred A. Knopf, 1994.

———. "Afterword: Notes From, and About, the History/Fiction Borderland." *Rethinking History* 9 (June/September 2005): 329–35.

Denetdale, Jennifer Nez. *Reclaiming Diné History: The Legacies of Navajo Chief Manuelito and Juanita.* Tucson: University of Arizona Press, 2007.

de Reuse, Willem J. "Apache Personal Names in Spanish and Early Mexican Documents: Their Linguistic and Dialectological Significance." *Memorias del VII Encuentro de Lingüística en el Noroeste.* Hermosillo: Universidad de Sonora, 2004.

———. *A Practical Grammar of the San Carlos Apache Language.* With the assistance of Phillip Goode. Munich, Germany: Lincom Europa, 2006.

Dobyns, Henry F. *The Papago People.* Phoenix: Indian Tribal Series, 1972.

———. "Military Transculturation of Northern Piman Indians, 1782–1821." *Ethnohistory* 19 (Autumn 1972): 323–43.

———. *Spanish Colonial Tucson: A Demographic History.* Tucson: University of Arizona Press, 1976.

Dobyns, Henry F., Paul H. Ezell, Alden W. Jones, and Greta S. Ezell. "What Were Nixoras?" *Southwestern Journal of Anthropology* 16 (Summer 1960): 230–58.

Dodge, Ida Flood. *Arizona Under Our Flag.* Tucson: Arizona Daily Star, 1928.

———. *Our Arizona.* New York: Charles Scribner's Sons, 1929.

Dodge, Irving. *Our Wild Indians: Thirty-Three Years' Personal Experience Among the Red Men of the Great West.* Hartford CT: A. D. Worthington, 1890.

Dolan, Darrow. "The Plomo Papers," *Ethnohistory* 19 (Autumn 1972): 305–22.

Doyel, David E. "The Transition to History in Northern Pimería Alta." In *Columbian Consequences.* Vol. 1, *Archaeological and Historical Perspectices on the Spanish Borderlands West.* Edited by David Hurst Thomas. Washington, D.C.: Smithsonian Institution Press, 1989.

Dunbar, Edward E. *The Mexican Papers: The Mexican Question, the Great American Question, with Personal Reminiscences.* New York: J. A. H. Hasbrouck, 1860.

Dunlay, Thomas W. *Wolves for the Blue Soldiers: Indian Scouts and Auxiliaries with the United States Army, 1860–90.* Lincoln: University of Nebraska Press, 1982.

Dunn, J. P. *Massacres of the Mountains: A History of the Indian Wars of the Far West, 1815–1875.* 1886. Reprint, New York: Archer House, 1958.

Durivage, John E. "Through Mexico to California." In *Southern Trails to California in 1849.* Edited by Ralph P. Bieber. Glendale, CA: Arthur H. Clark Co., 1937.

Dwight, Nathaniel. *A Short but Comprehensive System of the Geography of the World by Way of Question and Answer.* New York: Evert Duyckinck, 1801.

Ebell, Adrian J. "The Indian Massacres and War of 1862." *Harper's New Monthly Magazine* 27 (June 1863): 1–25.

Echo-Hawk, Roger C. "Ancient History in the New World: Integrating Oral Traditions and the Archaeological Record in Deep Time." *American Antiquity* 65 (April 2000): 267–90.

Elías Chomina, Armando. *Compendio de datos históricos de la familia Elías.* Hermosillo, 1986.

Ellinwood, Sybil. *The Arizona Historical Society Today.* Tucson: Arizona Historical Society, 1973.

Erickson, Winston P. *Sharing the Desert: The Tohono O'odham in History.* Tucson: University of Arizona Press, 1994.

Executive Orders Relating to Indian Reservations, 1855–1922. 1912, 1922. Reprint, Wilmington, DE: Scholarly Resources, 1975.

Ezell, Paul H. *The Hispanic Acculturation of the Gila River Pimas.* Memoir 90. Menasha, WI: American Anthropological Association, 1961.

———. "History of the Pima." In *Handbook of North American Indians.* Vol. 10, *Southwest.* Edited by Alfonso Ortiz. Washington, D.C.: Smithsonian Institution Press, 1983.

Farish, Thomas Edwin. *History of Arizona.* Phoenix, 1915.

Faulk, Odie B., ed. *Arizona's State Historical Society: Its History and Its Leaders, and Its Services to the Public.* Tucson: Arizona Pioneers' Historical Society, 1966.

———. *Arizona: A Short History.* Norman: University of Oklahoma Press, 1970.

———. "The Presidio: Fortress or Farce?" In *New Spain's Far Northern Frontier: Essays on Spain in the American West, 1540–1821.* Edited by David J. Weber. Albuquerque: University of New Mexico Press, 1979.

Ferguson, T. J., and Chip Colwell-Chanthaphonh. *History Is in the Land: Multivocal Tribal Traditions in Arizona's San Pedro Valley.* Tucson: University of Arizona Press, 2006.

Fitzgerald, Ellen. *History's Memory: Writing America's Past, 1880–1980.* Cambridge: Harvard University Press, 2002.

Fixico, Donald L. *The American Indian Mind in a Linear World: American Indian Studies and Traditional Knowledge.* New York: Routledge, 2003.

Fleisher, Kass. *The Bear River Massacre and the Making of History.* Albany: State University of New York Press, 2004.

Flint, Timothy, ed. *The Personal Narrative of James O. Pattie of Kentucky.* 1831. Reprint, Chicago: Lakeside Press, 1930.

Fontana, Bernard L., ed. "Jose Lewis Brennan's Account of Papago 'Customs and Other References.'" *Ethnohistory* 6 (Summer 1959): 226–37.

———. "Report of Bernard L. Fontana Before the Indian Claims Commission." In *Papago Indians III.* Edited by David Agee Horr. New York: Garland Publishing, 1974.

———. *Of Earth and Little Rain: The Papago Indians.* Flagstaff, AZ: Northland Press, 1981.

———. "History of the Papago." In *Handbook of North American Indians.* Vol. 10, *Southwest.* Edited by Alfonso Ortiz. Washington, D.C.: Smithsonian Institution Press, 1983.

———. "Pima and Papago: Introduction." In *Handbook of North American Indians.* Vol. 10, *Southwest.* Edited by Alfonso Ortiz. Washington, D.C.: Smithsonian Institution Press, 1983.

Forbes, Jack D. "The Janos, Jocomes, Mansos and Sumas Indians." *New Mexico Historical Review* 32 (October 1957): 319–34.

———. "The Early Western Apache, 1300–1700." *Journal of the West* 5 (July 1966): 336–54.

Fowler, Orson S. *Human Science: Or, Phrenology.* San Francisco: A. L. Bancroft Co., 1873.

Frank, Ross. *From Settler to Citizen: New Mexican Economic Development and the Creation of Vecino Society, 1750–1820.* Berkeley: University of California Press, 2000.

Freeman, M. P. *The Dread Apache—That Early-Day Scourge of the Southwest.* Tucson, 1915.

Friedlander, Saul, ed. *Probing the Limits of Representation: Nazism and the "Final Solution."* Cambridge: Harvard University Press, 1992.

Frost, John. *Frost's Pictorial History of Indian Wars and Captivities.* New York: Wells Publishing, 1873.

Gallego, Hilario. "Reminiscences of an Arizona Pioneer." *Arizona Historical Review* 6 (January 1935): 75–81.

Gálvez, Bernardo de. *Instructions for Governing the Interior Provinces of New Spain, 1786.* Edited and translated by Donald E. Worcester. Berkeley: Quivara Society, 1951.

Garber, Paul Neff. *The Gadsden Treaty.* Philadelphia: University of Pennsylvania Press, 1923.

Gehlbach, Frederick R. *Mountain Islands and Desert Seas: A Natural History of the U.S.-Mexican Borderlands.* 2nd ed. College Station: Texas A&M Press, 1993.

"General Howard's Mission to the Indians." *The Friend: A Religious and Literary Journal* 45 (July 27, 1872): 390–91.

"General Howard's Treaties." *Old and New* 6 (November 1872): 620–27.

Geronimo's Story of His Life. Edited by S. M. Barrett. New York: Duffield and Company, 1907.

Goddard, Pliny Earle. "Myths and Tales from the San Carlos Apache." *Anthropological Papers of the American Museum of Natural History* 24 (1918): 1–86.

Gonzales, Manuel G. "Carlos I. Velasco." *Journal of Arizona History* 25 (Autumn 1984): 265–84.

González, Deena J. *Refusing the Favor: The Spanish-Mexican Women of Santa Fe, 1820–1880.* New York: Oxford University Press, 1999.

González de la Vara, Martín. "The Return to Mexico: The Relocation of New Mexican Families to Chihuahua and the Confirmation of a Frontier Region, 1848–1854." In *The Contested Homeland: A Chicano History of New Mexico.* Edited by Erlinda Gonzales-Berry and David R. Maciel. Albuquerque: University of New Mexico Press, 2000.

Goodman, James. *Stories of Scottsboro.* New York: Pantheon, 1994.

Goodwin, Grenville. "Clans of the Western Apache." *New Mexico Historical Review* 8 (July 1933): 176–82.

———. "The Social Divisions and Economic Life of the Western Apache." *American Anthropologist,* New Series 37 (January–March 1935): 55–64.

———. "Experiences of an Indian Scout: Excerpts from the Life of John Rope, an 'Old Timer' of the White Mountain Apaches." *Arizona Historical Review* 7 (January 1936): 31–68.

———. "The Characteristics and Function of Clan in a Southern Athapascan Culture." *American Anthropologist,* New Series 39 (July–September 1937): 394–407.

———. "White Mountain Apache Religion." *American Anthropologist,* New Series 40 (January–March 1938): 24–37.

———. *Myths and Tales of the White Mountain Apache.* New York: American Folk-Lore Society, 1939.

———. *The Social Organization of the Western Apache.* Chicago: University of Chicago Press, 1942.

Goodwin, Grenville, and Neil Goodwin. *The Apache Diaries: A Father-Son Journey.* Lincoln: University of Nebraska Press, 2000.

Granger, Byrd H. *Will C. Barnes' Arizona Place Names.* Rev. ed. Tucson: University of Arizona Press, 1960.

Gregg, Josiah. *Commerce of the Prairies.* Edited by Max L. Moorhead. Norman: University of Oklahoma Press, 1954.

Griffen, William B. *Apaches at War and Peace: The Janos Presidio, 1750–1858.* Albuquerque: University of New Mexico Press, 1988.

———. *Utmost Good Faith: Patterns of Apache-Mexican Hostilities in Northern Chihuahua Border Warfare, 1821–1848.* Albuquerque: University of New Mexico Press, 1988.

Grimsley, Mark. "'Rebels' and 'Redskins': U.S. Military Conduct toward White Southerners and Native Americans in Comparative Perspective." In *Civilians in the Path of War.* Edited by Mark Grimsley and Clifford J. Rogers. Lincoln: University of Nebraska Press, 2002.

Griswold del Castillo, Richard. "Tucsonenses and Angeleños: A Socio-Economic Study of Two Mexican-American Barrios, 1860–1880." *Journal of the West* 18 (January 1979): 58–66.

———. *The Treaty of Guadalupe Hidalgo: A Legacy of Conflict.* Norman: University of Oklahoma Press, 1990.

Gustafson, A. M., ed. *John Spring's Arizona*. Tucson: University of Arizona Press, 1966.

Hadley, Diana, Peter Warshall, and Don Bufkin. *Environmental Change in Aravaipa, 1870–1970: An Ethnoecological Survey*. Cultural Resource Series Monograph No. 7. Phoenix: Bureau of Land Management, 1991.

Haley, James L. *Apaches: A History and Culture Portrait*. Garden City, NY: Doubleday, 1981.

Hall, J. *Travels and Adventures in Sonora*. Chicago: J. M. W. Jones, 1881.

Hamilton, Patrick. *The Resources of Arizona*. 3rd ed. San Francisco: A. L. Bancroft, 1884.

Hammond, George P. "The Camp Grant Massacre: A Chapter in Apache History." *Proceedings of the Pacific Coast Branch of the American Historical Association* (1929): 200–215.

———, ed. "The Zuñiga Journal, Tucson to Santa Fe." *New Mexico Historical Review* 6 (January 1931): 40–65.

———, ed. *Campaigns in the West, 1856–1861: The Journal and Letters of Colonel John Van Deusen Du Bois*. Tucson: Arizona Pioneers Historical Society, 1949.

Hammond, George P., and Agapito Rey, eds. *Obregón's History of Sixteenth Century Explorations in Western America*. Los Angeles: Wetzel Publishing, 1928.

Hand-Book of Tucson and Surroundings. Tucson: Citizen Printing, 1880.

Hardy, R. W. H. *Travels in the Interior of Mexico in 1825, 1826, 1827 & 1828*. London: Henry Colburn and Richard Bentley, 1829.

Harvey, David. *Justice, Nature and the Geography of Difference*. Malden, MA: Blackwell, 1996.

Haskell, J. Loring. *Southern Athapaskan Migration, A.D. 200–1750*. Tsaile, AZ: Navajo Community College Press, 1987.

Hastings, James R. "The Tragedy at Camp Grant in 1871." *Arizona and the West* 1 (Summer 1959): 146–60.

Hernández Silva, Héctor Cuauhtémoc. "Sonora y la guerra con Estados Unidos." In *México al tiempo de su guerra con Estados Unidos, 1846–1848*. Edited by Josefina Zoraida Vázquez. México: Fondo de Cultura Económica, 1997.

Herrera-Sobek, María. *Northward Bound: The Mexican Immigrant Experience in Ballad and Song*. Bloomington: Indiana University Press, 1993.

Hilpert, Bruce E. "The Indé (Western Apaches)." In *Paths of Life: American Indians of the Southwest and Northern Mexico*. Edited by Thomas E. Sheridan and Nancy J. Parezo. Tucson: University of Arizona Press, 1996.

Hinton, Richard J. *The Hand-Book to Arizona: Its Resources, History, Towns, Mines, Ruins and Scenery*. New York: American News Co., 1878.

Hobsbawm, Eric J. *The Age of Extremes: A History of the World, 1914–1991*. New York: Pantheon Books, 1994.

Hodge, Hiram. *Arizona as it is; Or, the Coming Country*. New York: Hurd and Houghton, 1877.

Horn, Tom. *Life of Tom Horn*. Denver: Louthan Book Co., 1904.

Horowitz, Donald L. *The Deadly Ethnic Riot*. Berkeley: University of California Press, 2001.

Horsman, Reginald. *Race and Manifest Destiny: The Origins of American Racial Anglo-Saxonism*. Cambridge: Harvard University Press, 1981.

Howard, O. O. "Our Indians of the Southwest." *United Service* 2 (May 1880): 525–52.

———. *My Life and Experiences Among Our Hostile Indians*. Hartford, CT: A. D. Worthington, 1907.

———. *Famous Indian Chiefs I Have Known*. New York: Century, 1908.

Howarth, O. H. "The Western Sierra Madre of Mexico." *Geographical Journal* 6 (November 1895): 422–37.

Hoxie, Frederick E. "From Prison to Homeland: The Cheyenne River Indian Reservation Before WWI." *South Dakota History* 10 (Winter 1979): 1–24.

Hoy, Bill. "War in Papaguería: Manuel Gándara's 1840–41 Papago Expedition." *Journal of Arizona History* 35 (Summer 1994): 141–62.

Ingstad, Helge. *The Apache Indians: In Search of the Missing Tribe*. Translated by Janine K. Stenehjem. Lincoln: University of Nebraska Press, 2004.

Jackson, Helen Hunt. *A Century of Dishonor: A Sketch of the United States Government's Dealings with Some of the Indian Tribes*. New York: Harper and Brothers, 1882.

Jackson, Orick. *The White Conquest of Arizona: History of the Pioneers*. Los Angeles: Grafton Co., 1908.

Jastrzembski, Joseph C. "Treacherous Towns in Mexico: Chiricahua Apache Personal Narratives of Horrors." *Western Folklore* 54 (July 1995): 169–96.

John, Elizabeth. *Storms Brewed in Other Men's Worlds: The Confrontation of Indians, Spanish, and French in the Southwest, 1540–1795.* Lincoln: University of Nebraska Press, 1975.

John, Elizabeth, ed., and John Wheat, trans. *View from the Apache Frontier: Report on the Northern Provinces of New Spain by José Cortés, Lieutenant in the Royal Corps of Engineers, 1799.* Norman: University of Oklahoma Press, 1989.

Johnson, Benjamin Heber. *Revolution in Texas: How a Forgotten Rebellion and Its Bloody Suppression Turned Mexicans into Americans.* New Haven: Yale University Press, 2004.

Johnson, Susan. "Sharing Bed and Board: Cohabitation and Cultural Difference in Central Arizona Mining Towns, 1863–1873." In *The Women's West.* Edited by Susan Armitage and Elizabeth Jameson. Norman: University of Oklahoma Press, 1987.

———. *Roaring Camp: The Social World of the California Gold Rush.* New York: W. W. Norton, 2000.

Johnson, Walter. "Time and Revolution in African America: Temporality and the History of Atlantic Slavery." In *Rethinking American History in a Global Age.* Edited by Thomas Bender. Berkeley: University of California Press, 2002.

Kane, Randy. "'An Honorable and Upright Man': Sidney R. DeLong as Post Trader at Fort Bowie." *Journal of Arizona History* 19 (Autumn 1978): 297–314.

Karns, Harry J., trans. *Unknown Arizona and Sonora, 1693–1721: From the Francisco Fernández del Castillo Version of Luz de Tierra Incógnita.* Tucson: Arizona Silhouettes, 1954.

Kasson, Joy S. *Buffalo Bill's Wild West: Celebrity, Memory, and Popular History.* New York: Hill and Wang, 2000.

Kaut, Charles R. "Western Apache Clan and Phratry Organization." *American Anthropologist*, New Series 58 (February 1956): 140–46.

———. *The Western Apache Clan System: Its Origins and Development.* Albuquerque: University of New Mexico Press, 1957.

———. "Notes on Western Apache Religious and Social Organization." *American Anthropologist* 61 (February 1959): 99–102.

Kelland, Clarence Budington. *Arizona.* New York: Harper and Brothers, 1939.

Kelley, Donald R. *Frontiers of History: Historical Inquiry in the Twentieth Century.* New Haven: Yale University Press, 2006.

Kerby, Robert Lee. *The Confederate Invasion of New Mexico and Arizona, 1861–1862.* Los Angeles: Westernlore Press, 1958.

Kessell, John L., ed. and trans. "San José de Tumacácori—1773: A Franciscan Reports from Arizona," *Arizona and the West* 6 (Winter 1964): 303–12.

———. *Friars, Soldiers, and Reformers: Hispanic Arizona and the Sonora Mission Frontier, 1767–1856.* Tucson: University of Arizona Press, 1976.

Kiernan, Ben. *Blood and Soil: A World History of Genocide and Extermination from Sparta to Darfur.* New Haven: Yale University Press, 2007.

Kilcrease, A. T. "Ninety-Five Years of History of the Papago Indians." *Southwestern Monuments Supplement* (April 1939): 297–310.

King, Thomas. *The Truth About Stories: A Native Narrative.* Minneapolis: University of Minnesota Press, 2003.

Kino's Historical Memoir of Pimería Alta: A Contemporary Account of the Beginnings of California, Sonora, and Arizona, by Father Eusebio Francisco Kino, S.J. Translated and edited by Herbert Eugene Bolton. Berkeley: University of California Press, 1948.

Kitzmiller, Chelley. *Embrace the Wind.* New York: Topaz, 1997.

Knight, Alan. *Mexico: The Colonial Era.* New York: Cambridge University Press, 2002.

"La Fiesta de San Agustin." *Arizona Quarterly Illustrated* 1 (October 1880): 8–9.

Langellier, J. Phillip. "Camp Grant Affair, 1871: Milestone in Federal Indian Policy?" *Military History of Texas and the Southwest* 15 (1979): 17–29.

Larned, William Trowbridge. "Effacing the Frontier." *Lippincott's* (May 1895): 647–57.

Latta, Frank F. *Joaquín Murrieta and His Horse Gangs.* Santa Cruz, CA: Bear State Books, 1980.

Leal, Luis. "El Corrido de Joaquín Murrieta: Origen y difusión." *Mexican Studies/Estudios Mexicanos* 11 (Winter 1995): 1–23.

Lejeune, Louis. *La guerra apache en Sonora*. Translated by Michel Antochiw. Hermosillo: Gobierno del estado de Sonora, 1984.

León García, Ricardo, and Carlos González Herrera. *Civilizar o exterminar: Tarahumaras y apaches en Chihuahua, siglo xix*. México: Centro de Investigaciones y Estudios Superiores en Antropología Social, 2000.

Lepore, Jill. *The Name of War: King Philip's War and the Origins of American Identity*. New York: Alfred A. Knopf, 1998.

Levi, Primo. *The Drowned and the Saved*. Translated by Raymond Rosenthal. New York: Vintage, 1989.

Lewis, David Rich. *Neither Wolf nor Dog: American Indians, Environment, and Agrarian Change*. New York: Oxford University Press, 1994.

Lockwood, Frank C. *Pioneer Days in Arizona: From the Spanish Occupation to Statehood*. New York: Macmillan, 1932.

———. *Life in Old Tucson, 1854–1864: As Remembered by the Little Maid Atanacia Santa Cruz*. Los Angeles: Ward Ritchie Press, 1943.

Logan, Michael F. *The Lessening Stream: An Environmental History of the Santa Cruz River*. Tucson: University of Arizona Press, 2002.

———. *Desert Cities: The Environmental History of Phoenix and Tucson*. Pittsburgh: University of Pittsburgh Press, 2006.

Madley, Benjamin. "Patterns of Frontier Genocide 1803–1910: The Aboriginal Tasmanians, the Yuki of California, and the Herero of Namibia." *Journal of Genocide Research* 6 (June 2004): 167–92.

Malkii, Liisa H. *Purity and Exile: Violence, Memory, and National Cosmology among Hutu Refugees in Tanzania*. Chicago: University of Chicago Press, 1995.

Manypenny, George W. *Our Indian Wards*. Cincinnati: Robert Clarke, 1880.

Mardock, Robert W. "Indian Rights Movement Until 1887." In *Handbook of North American Indians*. Vol. 4, *History of Indian-White Relations*. Edited by Wilcomb Washburn. Washington, D.C.: Smithsonian Institution, 1988.

Marion, J. H. *Notes of Travel Through the Territory of Arizona; Being an Account of the Trip Made by General George Stoneman and Others in the Autumn of 1870*. Prescott: Office of the Arizona Miner, 1870.

Martin, Patricia Preciado. *Images and Conversations: Mexican Americans Recall a Southwestern Past*. Tucson: University of Arizona Press, 1983.

———. *Beloved Land: An Oral History of Mexican Americans in Southern Arizona*. Tucson: University of Arizona Press, 2004.

Masich, Andrew E. *The Civil War in Arizona: The Story of the California Volunteers, 1861–1865*. Norman: University of Oklahoma Press, 2006.

Mathiot, Madeleine, ed. "The Reminiscences of Juan Dolores, an Early O'odham Linguist." *Anthropological Linguistics* 33 (Fall 1991): 233–315.

Matson, Daniel S., and Albert H. Schroeder, eds. "Cordero's Description of the Apache, 1796." *New Mexico Historical Review* 32 (October 1957): 335–56.

McCarthy, James. *A Papago Traveler: The Memories of James McCarthy*. Edited by John G. Westover. Tucson: Sun Tracks and University of Arizona Press, 1985.

McCarty, Kieran, ed. and trans. *Desert Documentary: The Spanish Years, 1767–1821*. Tucson: Arizona Historical Society, 1976.

———, ed. and trans. *A Frontier Documentary: Sonora and Tucson, 1821–1848*. Tucson: University of Arizona Press, 1997.

McClintock, James. *Arizona: The Nation's Youngest Commonwealth Within a Land of Ancient Culture*. Chicago, S. J. Clark, 1916.

McGuire, Randall H., ed. *Ethnology of Northwest Mexico: A Sourcebook*. New York: Garland Publishing, 1991.

McMurtry, Larry. *Oh What a Slaughter: Massacres in the American West, 1846–1890*. New York: Simon and Schuster, 2005.

McWilliams, Carey. *North from Mexico: The Spanish-Speaking People of the United States*. Philadelphia: J. B. Lippincott, 1948.

Meed, Douglas. *They Never Surrendered: Bronco Apaches of the Sierra Madres, 1890–1935*. Tucson: Westernlore Press, 1993.

Meeks, Eric V. "The Tohono O'odham, Wage Labor, and Resistant Adaptation, 1900–1930." *Western Historical Quarterly* 34 (Winter 2003): 469–89.

Meinig, D. W. *The Shaping of America: Continental America, 1800–1867.* New Haven: Yale University Press, 1993.

Merrell, James H. *The Indian's New World: Catawbas and Their Neighbors from European Contact Through the Era of Removal.* New York: W. W. Norton, 1989.

Mihesuah, Devon. *Natives and Academics: Researching and Writing about American Indians.* Lincoln: University of Nebraska Press, 1998.

Miles, Dale Curtis. "Western Apache: Resistance and Renewal." In *Stories of the People: Native American Voices.* Washington, D.C.: Smithsonian Institution, 1997.

Miles, Dale Curtis, and Paul R. Machula. *History of the San Carlos Apache.* Rev. ed. San Carlos, AZ: San Carlos Apache Historic and Cultural Preservation Office, 1998.

Miller, Darlis A. "Cross-Cultural Marriages in the Southwest: The New Mexico Experience, 1846–1900." In *New Mexico Women: Intercultural Perspectives.* Edited by Darlis A. Miller and Joan M. Jensen. Albuquerque: University of New Mexico Press, 1986.

Montgomery, Charlie. *The Spanish Redemption: Heritage, Power, and Loss on New Mexico's Upper Rio Grande.* Berkeley: University of California Press, 2002.

Moorhead, Max L. *The Apache Frontier: Jacobo Ugarte and Spanish-Indian Relations in Northern New Spain, 1769–1791.* Norman: University of Oklahoma Press, 1968.

———. "Spanish Deportation of Hostile Apaches: The Policy and the Practice." *Arizona and the West* 17 (Autumn 1975): 205–20.

Mowry, Sylvester. *Arizona and Sonora: The Geography, History, and Resources of the Silver Region of North America.* 3rd ed. New York: Harper and Brothers, 1864.

Moyano Pahissa, Angela. "The Mesilla Treaty, or Gadsden Purchase." In *U.S.-Mexico Borderlands: Historical and Contemporary Perspectives.* Edited by Oscar J. Martínez. Wilmington, DE: Scholarly Resources, 1996.

Nabakov, Peter. *A Forest of Time: American Indian Ways of History.* New York: Cambridge University Press, 2002.

Nabhan, Gary Paul. *The Desert Smells Like Rain: A Naturalist in Papago Indian Country.* San Francisco: North Point Press, 1987.

Naylor, Thomas H., and Charles W. Polzer, eds. *The Presidio and Militia on the Northern Frontier of New Spain.* Vol. 1, *1570–1700.* Tucson: University of Arizona Press, 1986.

Nentvig, Juan. *Rudo Ensayo: A Description of Sonora and Arizona in 1764.* Translated and annotated by Alberto Francisco Pradeau and Robert R. Rasmussen. Tucson: University of Arizona Press, 1980.

Nicolson, John, ed. *The Arizona of Joseph Pratt Allyn: Letters from a Pioneer Judge.* Tucson: University of Arizona Press, 1974.

Nieto-Phillips, John. *The Language of Blood: The Making of Spanish-American Identity in New Mexico, 1880s–1930s.* Albuquerque: University of New Mexico Press, 2004.

Novick, Peter. *That Noble Dream: The "Objectivity Question" and the American Historical Profession.* New York: Cambridge University Press, 1988.

Nugent, Daniel. *Spent Cartridges of Revolution: An Anthropological History of Namiquipa, Chihuahua.* Chicago: University of Chicago Press, 1993.

Nye, Robert A. "Western Masculinities in War and Peace." *American Historical Review* 112 (April 2007): 417–38.

Oatman, Lorenzo D., and Olive A. Oatman. *The Captivity of the Oatman Girls Among the Apache and Mohave Indians.* 1857. Reprint, New York: Dover Publications, 1994.

Officer, James E. "Historical Factors in Interethnic Relations in the Community of Tuscon." *Arizoniana* 1 (Fall 1960): 12–16.

———. *Hispanic Arizona, 1536–1856.* Tucson: University of Arizona Press, 1987.

Ogle, Ralph Hedrick. *Federal Control of the Western Apaches.* Albuquerque: University of New Mexico Press, 1940.

Olasagarre, Manuel. *Cuenta de la percepción, distribución e inversión de los diez millones de pesos que produjo el Tratado de la Mesilla.* México: Imprenta de Ignacio Cumplido, 1855.

O'Mack, Scott, and Eric Eugene Klucas. *San Xavier to San Agustín: An Overview of Cultural Resources for the Paseo de las Iglesias Feasibility Study, Pima County, Arizona.* Tucson: Statistical Research Inc., 2004.

O'Mack, Scott, Scott Thompson, and Eric Eugene Klucas. *Little River: An Overview of Cultural Resources for the Rio Antiguo Feasibility Study, Pima County, Arizona.* Tucson: Statistical Research Inc., 2004.

Opler, Morris. "The Identity of the Apache Mansos," *American Anthropologist* 44 (October–December 1942): 725.

———. "The Apachean Culture Pattern and Its Origins." In *Handbook of North American Indians.* Vol. 10, *Southwest.* Edited by Alfonso Ortiz. Washington, D.C.: Smithsonian Institution Press, 1983.

Oropeza, Lorena. "Making History: The Chicano Movement." In *Voices of a New Chicana/o History.* Edited by Refugio I. Richín and Dennis N. Valdés. East Lansing: Michigan State University Press, 2000.

Orozco, Victor. "El conflicto entre apaches, rarámuris y mestizos en Chihuahua durante el siglo xix." In *Nómadas y sedentarios en el norte de México.* Edited by Marie-Areti Hers, José Luis Mirafuentes, María de los Dolores Soto, and Miguel Vallebueno. México: Universidad Nacional Autónoma de México, 2000.

Ortega, José, ed. *Historia del Nayarit, Sonora, Sinaloa y ambas Californias.* México: Tipografía de E. Abadiano, 1887.

Ortega Soto, Martha. "La colonizacion española en la primera mitad del siglo XVII." In *Historia general de Sonora.* Vol. 1, *De la conquista al Estado libre y soberano de Sonora.* Edited by Sergio Ortega Noriega. Hermosillo: Gobierno del Estado de Sonora, 1996.

Ortelli, Sara. *Trama de una guerra conveniente: Nueva Vizcaya y la sombra de los apaches (1748–1790).* México: El Colegio de México, 2007.

Ortiz, Alfonso. "The Gila River Piman Water Problem: An Ethnohistorical Account." In *The Changing Ways of Southwestern Indians: A Historic Perspective.* Edited by Albert H. Schroeder. Glorieta, NM: Rio Grande Press, 1973.

Ostler, Jeff. *The Plains Sioux and U.S. Colonialism from Lewis and Clark to Wounded Knee.* New York: Cambridge University Press, 2004.

Otis, George A. *Check List of Preparations and Objects in the Section of Human Anatomy of the United States Army Medical Museum.* Washington, D.C.: Army Medical Museum, 1876.

Pailes, Richard A. "An Archeological Perspective on the Sonoran Entrada." In *The Coronado Expedition to Tierra Nueva: The 1540–1542 Route Across the Southwest.* Edited by Richard Flint and Shirley Cushing Flint. Niwot: The University Press of Colorado, 1997.

Paredes, Américo. *With His Pistol in His Hand: A Border Ballad and Its Hero.* Austin: University of Texas Press, 1958.

Park, Joseph F. "The Apaches in Mexican-American Relations." In *U.S.-Mexico Borderlands: Historical and Contemporary Perspectives.* Edited by Oscar Martínez. Wilmington, DE: Scholarly Resources, 1996.

Pascoe, Peggy. "Race, Gender, and Intercultural Relations: The Case of Interracial Marriage." *Frontiers* 12 (1991): 15–18.

Paz, Ireneo. *Life and Adventures of the Celebrated Bandit Joaquín Murrieta: His Exploits in the State of California.* Trans. Francis P. Belle. Houston: Arte Público Press, 2001.

Pérez, Vincent. *Remembering the Hacienda: History and Memory in the Mexican American Southwest.* College Station: Texas A&M University Press, 2006.

Perry, Richard J. *Apache Reservation: Indigenous Peoples and the American State.* Austin: University of Texas Press, 1993.

Pfanz, Donald C. *Richard S. Ewell: A Soldier's Life.* Chapel Hill: University of North Carolina Press, 1998.

Pfefferkorn, Ignaz. *Sonora: A Description of the Province.* Translated by Theodore E. Treutlein. Albuquerque: University of New Mexico Press, 1949.

Pilsk, Seth, and Jeanette C. Cassa. "The Western Apache Home: Landscape Management and Failing Ecosystems." *USDA Forest Service Proceedings RMRS-P-36* (2005): 282–86.

Pitt, Leonard. *The Decline of the Californios: A Social History of the Spanish-Speaking Californians, 1846–1890.* New Haven: Yale University Press, 1966.

Polzer, Charles W., and Thomas E. Sheridan, eds. *The Presidio and Militia on the Northern Frontier of New Spain.* Vol. 2, *The Californias and Sinaloa-Sonora, 1700–1765.* Tucson: University of Arizona Press, 1997.

Poston, Charles D. *Speech on Indian Affairs Delivered in the House of Representatives, Thursday, March 2, 1865.* New York: Edmund Jones, 1865.

————. *Building a State in Apache Land: The Story of Arizona's Founding Told by Arizona's Founder*. Tempe, AZ: Aztec Press, 1963.

Powell, Lawrence Clark. *Arizona: A Bicentennial History*. New York: W. W. Norton, 1976.

Prucha, Francis Paul. *The Great Father: The United States Government and the American Indians*. 2 vols. Lincoln: University of Nebraska Press, 1984.

Pumpelly, Raphael. *Across America and Asia: Notes of a Five Year's Journey Around the World and of Residence in Arizona, Japan and China*. New York: Leypoldt and Holt, 1870.

Radding, Cynthia. *Wandering Peoples: Colonialism, Ethnic Spaces, and Ecological Frontiers in Northwestern Mexico, 1700–1850*. Durham: Duke University Press, 1997.

————. *Landscapes of Power and Identity: Comparative Histories in the Sonoran Desert and the Forests of Amazonia from Colony to Republic*. Durham: Duke University Press, 2005.

Reeve, Frank D., ed. "Puritan and Apache: A Diary." *New Mexico Historical Review* 23 (October 1948): 269–301 and (January 1949): 12–50.

Reff, Daniel T. *Disease, Depopulation, and Culture Change in Northwestern New Spain, 1518–1764*. Salt Lake City: University of Utah Press, 1991.

————. "Contact Shock in Northwestern New Spain, 1518–1764." In *Disease and Demography in the Americas*. Edited by John W. Verano and Douglas H. Ubelaker. Washington, D.C.: Smithsonian Institution Press, 1992.

Reid, John C. *Reid's Tramp: Or a Journal of the Incidents of Ten Months' Travel Through Texas, New Mexico, Arizona, Sonora, and California*. Selma, AL: John Hardy, 1858.

"Reminiscences of Juan I. Téllez." *Arizona Historical Review* 7 (January 1936): 85–89.

"Reminiscences of William Fourr." *Arizona Historical Review* 6 (October 1935): 68–84.

Reséndez, Andrés. "An Expedition and Its Many Tales." In *Continental Crossroads: Remapping U.S.-Mexico Borderlands History*. Edited by Samuel Truett and Elliott Young. Durham: Duke University Press, 2004.

Resources of Arizona with a Description of the Indian Tribes; Ancient Ruins; Cochise, Apache Chief; Antonio, Pima Chief; Stage and Wagon Roads; Trade and Commerce, etc. San Francisco: Francis and Valentine, 1871.

Richards, Thomas. *The Imperial Archive: Knowledge and the Fantasy of Empire*. New York: Verso, 1993.

Richardson, Judith. *Possessions: The History and Uses of Haunting in the Hudson Valley*. Cambridge: Harvard University Press, 2003.

Richter, Daniel. "Whose Indian History?" *William and Mary Quarterly* 50 (April 1993): 379–93.

Rios, Theodore, and Kathleen Mullen Sands. *Telling a Good One: The Process of a Native American Collaborative Biography*. Lincoln: University of Nebraska Press, 2000.

Roberts, David. *Once They Moved Like the Wind: Cochise, Geronimo, and the Apache Wars*. New York: Simon and Schuster, 1993.

Robinson III, Charles M. *General Crook and the Western Frontier*. Norman: University of Oklahoma Press, 2001.

Robinson, Will H. *The Story of Arizona*. Phoenix: Berryhill, 1919.

Ruibal Corella, Juan Antonio. "La desmembración territorial de Sonora y sus consequencías." In *Historia general de Sonora*. Vol. 2, *Período México independiente, 1831–1883*. Edited by Juan Antonio Ruibal Corella. Hermosillo: Gobierno del Estado de Sonora, 1997.

Ruiz, Ramón Eduardo. *The People of Sonora and Yankee Capitalists*. Tucson: University of Arizona Press, 1988.

Rusling, James F. *Across America: Or, The Great West and Pacific Coast*. New York: Sheldon and Company, 1874.

Sacks, B. "The Origins of Fort Buchanan: Myth and Fact." *Arizona and the West* 7 (Autumn 1965): 207–26.

Sahlins, Marshall. *Apologies to Thucydides: Understanding History as Culture and Vice Versa*. Chicago: University of Chicago Press, 2004.

Salisbury, Neal. "The Indians' Old World: Native Americans and the Coming of Europeans." *William and Mary Quarterly* 53 (July 1996): 435–58.

Salmon, Roberto Mario. "A Marginal Man: Luis of Saric and the Pima Revolt of 1751." *The Americas* 45 (July 1988): 61–77.

————. *Indian Revolts in Northern New Spain: A Synthesis of Resistance, 1680–1786*. Lanham, MD: University Press of America, 1991.

Samuels, David. "The Whole and the Sum of the Parts, or, How Cookie and the Cupcakes Told the Story of Apache History in San Carlos." *Journal of American Folklore* 112 (Summer 1999): 464–74.

———. "Indeterminacy and History in Britton Goode's Western Apache Place Names: Ambiguous Identity on the San Carlos Reservation." *American Ethnologist* 28 (2001): 277–302.

———. *Putting a Song on Top of It: Expression and Identity on the San Carlos Apache Reservation.* Tucson: University of Arizona Press, 2004.

Sánchez, George J. *Becoming Mexican American: Ethnicity, Culture and Identity in Chicano Los Angeles, 1900–1945.* New York: Oxford University Press, 1993.

Sauer, Carl. "A Spanish Expedition into the Arizona Apacheria." *Arizona Historical Review* 6 (1935): 3–13.

Saxton, Dean, and Lucille Saxton. *O'othham Hoho'ok A'agitha: Legends and Lore of the Papago and Pima Indians.* Tucson: University of Arizona Press, 1973.

Saxton, Dean, Lucille Saxton, and Susie Enos. *Dictionary: Papago/Pima-English, O'othham-Mil-gahn.* Edited by R. L. Cherry. Rev. ed. Tucson: University of Arizona Press, 1983.

Scarry, Elaine. *The Body in Pain: The Making and Unmaking of the World.* New York: Oxford University Press, 1985.

Schellie, Don. *Vast Domain of Blood: The Story of the Camp Grant Massacre.* Los Angeles: Westernlore Press, 1968.

Schmitt, Martin F., ed. *General George Crook: His Autobiography.* Norman: University of Oklahoma Press, 1946.

Scott, James C. *Seeing Like a State: How Certain Schemes to Improve the Human Condition Have Failed.* New Haven: Yale University Press, 1998.

Scott, Joan W. "History-writing as Critique." In *Manifestos for History.* Edited by Keith Jenkins et al. London: Routledge, forthcoming.

Shaw, Anna Moore. *Pima Indian Legends.* Tucson: University of Arizona Press, 1968.

———. *A Pima Past.* Tucson: University of Arizona Press, 1974.

Sheridan, Thomas E. *Los Tucsonenses: The Mexican Community in Tucson, 1854–1941.* Tucson: University of Arizona Press, 1986.

———. *Arizona: A History.* Tucson: University of Arizona Press, 1995.

———. "The O'odham (Pimas and Papagos): The World Would Burn Without Rain." In *Paths of Life: American Indians of the Southwest and Northern Mexico.* Edited by Thomas E. Sheridan and Nancy J. Parezo. Tucson: University of Arizona Press, 1996.

———. "The Columbian Exchange." In *The Pimería Alta: Missions and More.* Edited by James E. Officer, Mardith Schuetz-Miller, and Bernard L. Fontana. Tucson: Southwestern Mission Research Center, 1996.

———. *Landscapes of Fraud: Mission Tumacácori, the Baca Float, and the Betrayal of the O'odham.* Tucson: University of Arizona Press, 2006.

Sloan, Eleanor B. "Seventy-Five Years of the Arizona Pioneers' Historical Society, 1884–1959." *Arizona and the West* 1 (Spring 1959): 66–70.

Smith, Cornelius C., Jr. *William Sanders Oury: History-Maker of the Southwest.* Tucson: University of Arizona Press, 1967.

Smith, Ralph A. "Mexican and Anglo-Saxon Traffic in Scalps, Slaves, and Livestock, 1835–1841." *West Texas Historical Association Year Book* 36 (October 1960): 98–115.

———. "Indians in American-Mexican Relations before the War of 1846." *Hispanic American Historical Review* 43 (February 1963): 34–64.

———. *Borderlander: The Life of James Kirker, 1793–1852.* Norman: University of Oklahoma Press, 1999.

Smith, Sherry L. *The View from Officers' Row: Army Perceptions of Western Indians.* Tucson: University of Arizona Press, 1990.

"Smuggling into Sonora." *Arizona Quarterly Illustrated* 1 (October 1880): 7.

Sonnichsen, C. L. *Pioneer Heritage: The First Century of the Arizona Historical Society.* Tucson: Arizona Historical Society, 1984.

———. *Tucson: The Life and Times of an American City.* Norman: University of Oklahoma Press, 1982.

Spicer, Edward H. *Cycles of Conquest: The Impact of Spain, Mexico, and the United States on the Indians of the Southwest, 1533–1960.* Tucson: University of Arizona Press, 1962.

Splitter, Henry Winfred, ed. "Tour in Arizona: Footprints of an Army Officer." *Journal of the West* 1 (July 1962): 74–97.

Stabel, Roberta J. "The Natural Setting." In *The Pimería Alta: Missions and More.* Edited by James E. Officer, Mardith Schuetz-Miller, and Bernard L. Fontana. Tucson: Southwestern Mission Research Center, 1996.

Stern, Peter, and Robert Jackson. "Vagabundaje and Settlement Patterns in Colonial Northern Sonora." *The Americas* 44 (April 1988): 461–81.

Stevens, Robert C. "The Apache Menace in Sonora, 1831–1849." *Arizona and the West* 6 (Autumn 1964): 211–22.

Stockel, H. Henrietta. *Survival of the Spirit: Chiricahua Apaches in Captivity.* Reno: University of Nevada Press, 1993.

Stodder, Ann L. W., and Debra Martin. "Health and Disease in the Southwest before and after Spanish Contact." In *Disease and Demography in the Americas.* Edited by John W. Verano and Douglas H. Ubelaker. Washington, D.C.: Smithsonian Institution Press, 1992.

Stone, Charles P. "Notes on the State of Sonora." *Historical Magazine* 5 (June 1861): 161–69.

Summerhayes, Martha. *Vanished Arizona: Recollections of My Army Life.* Philadelphia: J. B. Lippincott, 1908.

Sweeney, Edwin R. *Cochise: Chiricahua Apache Chief.* Norman: University of Oklahoma Press, 1991.

———. *Mangas Coloradas: Chief of the Chiricahua Apaches.* Norman: University of Oklahoma Press, 1998.

Tatom, William M., ed. *The Papago Indian Reservation and the Papago People.* Sells, AZ: The Papago Tribe of Arizona, 1975.

Tatum, Lawrie. *Our Red Brothers and the Peace Policy of President Ulysses S. Grant.* Philadelphia: John C. Winston, 1899.

Taylor, Alan. *The Divided Ground: Indians, Settlers, and the Northern Borderland of the American Revolution.* New York: Alfred A. Knopf, 2006.

Teague, Lynn S. "Prehistory and the Traditions of the O'odham and Hopi." *Kiva* 58 (1993): 435–44.

Tevis, James H. *Arizona in the '50s.* Albuquerque: University of New Mexico Press, 1954.

Thomas, Alfred Barnaby, ed. and trans. *Forgotten Frontiers: A Study of the Spanish Indian Policy of Don Juan Bautista de Anza, Governor of New Mexico, 1777–1787.* Norman: University of Oklahoma Press, 1932.

———, ed. and trans. *Teodoro de Croix and the Northern Frontier of New Spain, 1776–1783.* Norman: University of Oklahoma Press, 1941.

Thomas, Augustus. *Arizona: A Drama in Four Acts.* New York: R. H. Russell, 1899.

———. *Arizona: A Romance of the Great Southwest.* New York: Grosset and Dunlap, 1914.

Thomas, Robert K. "Papago Land Use West of the Papago Indian Reservation, South of the Gila River and the Problem of Sand Papago Identity." In *Ethnology of Northwest Mexico: Sourcebook.* Edited by Randall H. McGuire. New York: Garland Publishing, 1991.

Thompson, Jerry Don. *Colonel John Robert Baylor: Texas Indian Fighter and Confederate Soldier.* Hillsboro, TX: Hill Junior College Press, 1971.

Thrapp, Dan L. *The Conquest of Apacheria.* Norman: University of Oklahoma Press, 1967.

Tinker Salas, Miguel. *In the Shadow of the Eagles: Sonora and the Transformation of the Border during the Porfiriato.* Berkeley: University of California Press, 1997.

Trails to Tiburón: The 1894 and 1895 Field Diaries of W. J. McGee. Transcribed by Hazel McFeely Fontana. Introduction by Bernard L. Fontana. Tucson: University of Arizona Press, 2000.

Treasure Land: A Story. Tucson: Arizona Advancement Company, 1897.

The Treaties Between the United States and Mexico, Called the Guadalupe Hidalgo and Gadsden Treaties. New York: New York Printing Company, 1871.

Treutlein, Theodore, trans. *Missionary in Sonora: The Travel Reports of Joseph Och, S.J., 1755–1767.* San Francisco: California Historical Society, 1965.

Trouillot, Michel-Rolph. *Silencing the Past: Power and the Production of History.* Boston: Beacon Press, 1995.

Truett, Samuel. *Fugitive Landscapes: The Forgotten History of the U.S.-Mexico Borderlands.* New Haven: Yale University Press, 2006.

"Tucson." *Arizona Quarterly Illustrated* 1 (July 1880): 9.

Underhill, Ruth M. "The Autobiography of a Papago Woman." *Memoirs of the American Anthropological Association* 46 (1936): 1–64.

———. *A Papago Calendar Record.* The University of New Mexico Bulletin: Anthropological Series 2 Albuquerque: University of New Mexico Press, 1938.

———. *Social Organization of the Papago Indians.* New York: Columbia University Press, 1939.

———. *Papago Indian Religion.* New York: Columbia University Press, 1946.

———. *Singing for Power: The Song Magic of the Papago Indians of Southern Arizona.* Tucson: University of Arizona Press, 1993.

Underhill, Ruth M., Donald M. Bahr, Baptisto Lopez, Jose Pancho, and David Lopez. *Rainhouse and Ocean: Speeches for the Papago Year.* 1979. Reprint, Tucson: University of Arizona Press, 1997.

Utley, Robert M. *The Indian Frontier of the American West, 1846–1890.* Albuquerque: University of New Mexico Press, 1984.

Van Valkenburgh, Richard. "Apache Ghosts Guard the Aravaipa." *Desert Magazine* 11 (April 1948): 16–20.

Velasco, José Francisco. *Noticias estadísticas del estado de Sonora.* México: Imprenta de Ignacio Cumplido, 1850.

Vélez-Ibáñez, Carlos G. *Border Visions: Mexican Cultures of the Southwest United States.* Tucson: University of Arizona Press, 1996.

Viele, Egbert L. "The East and West Boundary Line between the United States and Mexico." *Journal of the American Geographical Society of New York* 14 (1882): 259–84.

Vila, Pablo. *Crossing Borders: Social Categories, Metaphors, and Narrative Identities on the U.S.-Mexico Frontier.* Austin: University of Texas Press, 2000.

Viola, Herman J., ed. *The Memoirs of Charles Henry Veil: A Soldier's Recollections of the Civil War and Arizona Territory.* New York: Orion Books, 1993.

Vonnegut, Kurt, Jr. *Slaughterhouse-Five or the Children's Crusade.* New York: Delta Books, 1969.

Voss, Stuart F. *On the Periphery of Nineteenth-Century Mexico: Sonora and Sinaloa, 1810–1877.* Tucson: University of Arizona Press, 1982.

Wagoner, Jay J. *Arizona Territory, 1863–1912: A Political History.* Tucson: University of Arizona Press, 1970.

"War Not Massacre." *Putnam's Magazine* 15 (May 1870): 611–12.

Warren, Fintan. "Jesuit Historians of Sinaloa-Sonora." *The Americas* 18 (April 1962): 329–39.

Warren, Louis. *Buffalo Bill's America: William Cody and the Wild West Show.* New York: Alfred A. Knopf, 2005.

Waterfall, Richard. "Vengeance at Sunrise: The Camp Grant Massacre, 30 April 1871." *Journal of the West* 31 (July 1992): 110–18.

Watt, Eva Tulene. *Don't Let the Sun Step Over You: A White Mountain Apache Family Life (1860–1975).* With assistance from Keith H. Basso. Tucson: University of Arizona Press, 2004.

Webb, George. *A Pima Remembers.* Tucson: University of Arizona Press, 1959.

Webb, George W. *Chronological List of Engagements Between the Regular Army of the United States and Various Tribes of Hostile Indians Which Occurred During the Years 1790 to 1898, Inclusive.* St. Joseph, MO: Wing Printing, 1939.

Weber, David J. *The Mexican Frontier, 1821–1846: The American Southwest Under Mexico.* Albuquerque: University of New Mexico Press, 1982.

———. *The Spanish Frontier in North America.* New Haven: Yale University Press, 1992.

Welch, John R. "White Eyes' Lies and the Battle for *dzilnchaa si'an.*" *American Indian Quarterly* 21 (Winter 1997): 75–109.

Welch, John R., and Ramon Riley. "Reclaiming Land and Spirit in the Western Apache Homeland." *American Indian Quarterly* 25 (Winter 2001): 5–12.

Welch, John R., Nancy Mahaney, and Ramon Riley. "The Reconquest of Fort Apache." *Cultural Resource Management* 23 (2000): 15–19.

Wharfield, H. B. "Apache Kid and the Record." *Journal of Arizona History* 6 (Spring 1965): 37–46.

White, Hayden. *The Content of the Form: Narrative Discourse and Historical Representation.* Baltimore: Johns Hopkins University Press, 1987.

White, Richard. *"It's Your Misfortune and None of My Own": A New History of the American West.* Norman: University of Oklahoma Press, 1991.

——. *The Middle Ground: Indians, Empires, and Republics in the Great Lakes Region, 1650–1815.* New York: Cambridge University Press, 1991.

——. "Frederick Jackson Turner and Buffalo Bill." In *The Frontier in American Culture.* Edited by James R. Grossman. Berkeley: University of California Press, 1994.

——. "The Gold Rush: Consequences and Contingencies." *California History* 77 (Spring 1998): 42–55.

——. *Remembering Ahanagran: Storytelling in a Family's Past.* New York: Hill and Wang, 1998.

Wilson, Angela Cavender. "Grandmother to Granddaughter: Generations of Oral History in a Dakota Family." *American Indian Quarterly* 20 (Winter 1996): 7–13.

Wilson, Benjamin D. "Narrative." In *Pathfinders.* Edited by Robert Glass Cleland. San Francisco: Powell Publishing Co., 1929.

Wilson, Chesley Goseyun, Ruth Longcor Harnisch Wilson, and Bryan Burton. *When the Earth Was Like New: Western Apache Songs and Stories.* Danbury, CT: World Music Press, 1994.

Winter, Joseph C. "Cultural Modifications of the Gila Pima: A.D. 1697–A.D. 1846." *Ethnohistory* 20 (Winter 1973): 67–77.

Wolf, Eric R. *Europe and the People Without History.* Berkeley: University of California Press, 1982.

Woodward, Arthur, ed. *Journal of Lt. Thomas W. Sweeny, 1849–1853.* Los Angeles: Westernlore Press, 1956.

Wooster, Robert. *The Military and United States Indian Policy, 1865–1903.* New Haven: Yale University Press, 1988.

Worcester, Donald E. "The Beginnings of the Apache Menace of the Southwest." *New Mexico Historical Review* 16, No. 1 (January 1941): 1–14.

Wrobel, David. *Promised Lands: Promotion, Memory, and the Creation of the American West.* Lawrence: University of Kansas Press, 2002.

Young, Robert W. "Apachean Languages." In *Handbook of North American Indians.* Vol. 10, *Southwest.* Edited by Alfonso Ortiz. Washington, D.C.: Smithsonian Institution Press, 1983.

Zuñiga, Ignacio. *Rapida Ojeada al Estado de Sonora.* México: Juan Ojeada, 1835.

Index

Page numbers in *italics* refer to illustrations.